Tell us what you think about Shojo Beat Manga!

‖‖‖‖‖‖‖‖‖‖‖‖‖‖‖‖‖‖‖‖‖‖‖
W9-CUA-849

Our survey is now available online. Go to:

shojobeat.com/mangasurvey

Help us make our product offerings better!

Hot Gimmick

If you think being a teenager is hard, be glad your name isn't Hatsumi Narita

With scandals that wo[uld] make any gossip girl bl[ush] and more triangles than [you] can throw a geometry b[ook] at, this girl may never fig[ure] out the game of love!

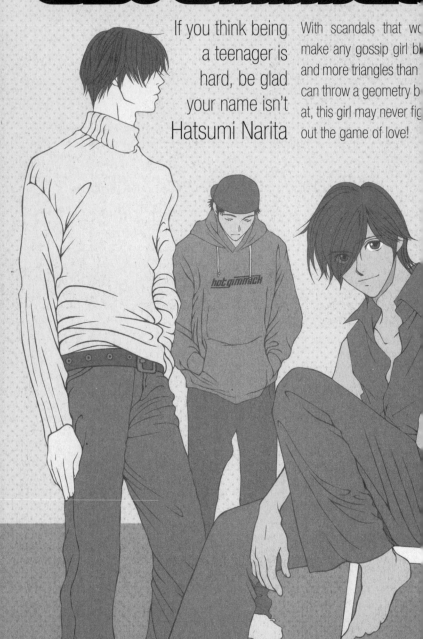

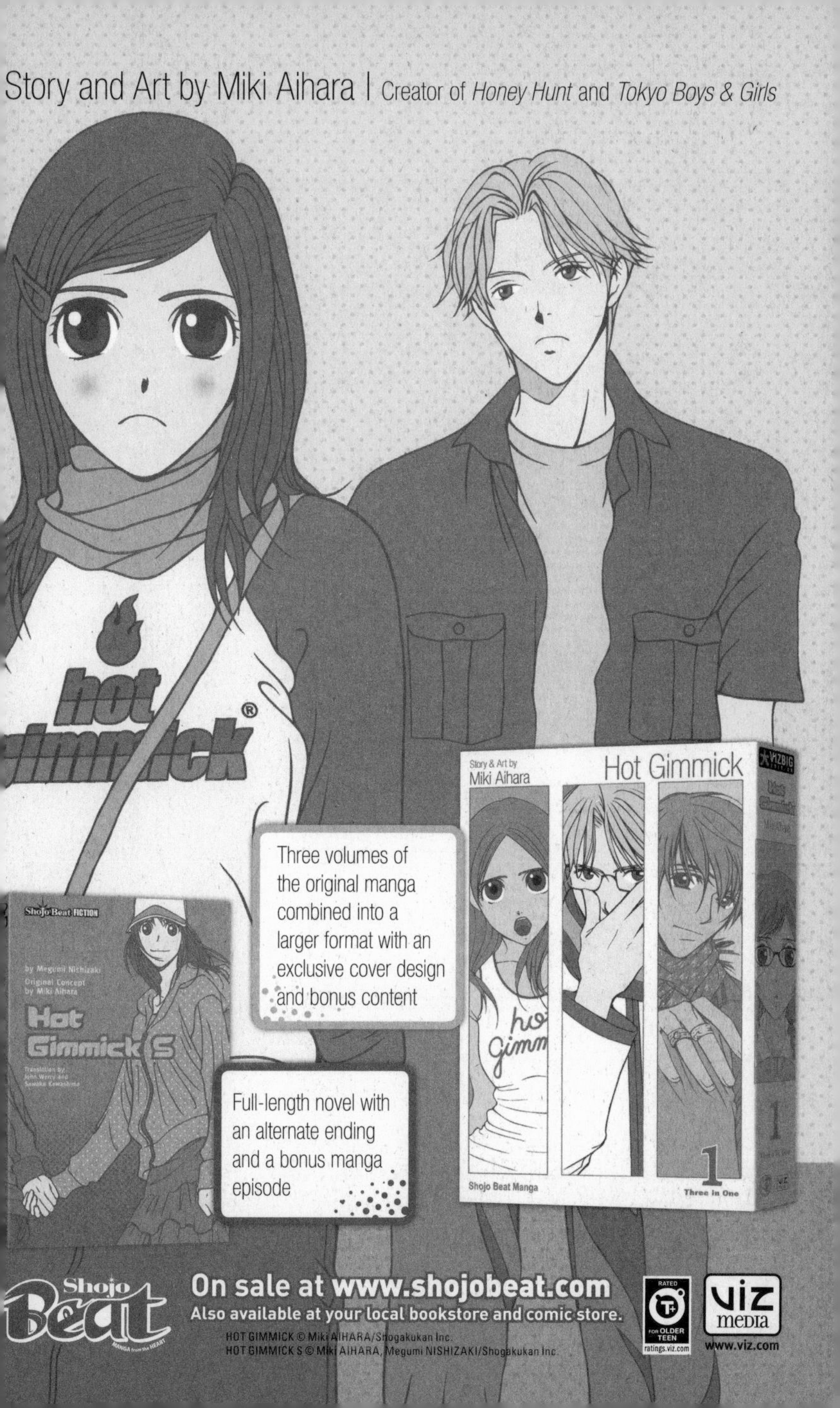

Story and Art by Miki Aihara | Creator of Honey Hunt and Tokyo Boys & Girls
hot gimmick
Shojo Beat FICTION
by Megumi Nishizaki
Original Concept by Miki Aihara
Hot Gimmick S
Three volumes of the original manga combined into a larger format with an exclusive cover design and bonus content
Story & Art by Miki Aihara
Hot Gimmick
VIZBIG
Shojo Beat Manga
1
Three in One
Full-length novel with an alternate ending and a bonus manga episode
Shojo Beat
On sale at www.shojobeat.com
Also available at your local bookstore and comic store.
HOT GIMMICK © Miki AIHARA/Shogakukan Inc.
HOT GIMMICK S © Miki AIHARA, Megumi NISHIZAKI/Shogakukan Inc.
RATED T+ FOR OLDER TEEN
ratings.viz.com
VIZ MEDIA
www.viz.com

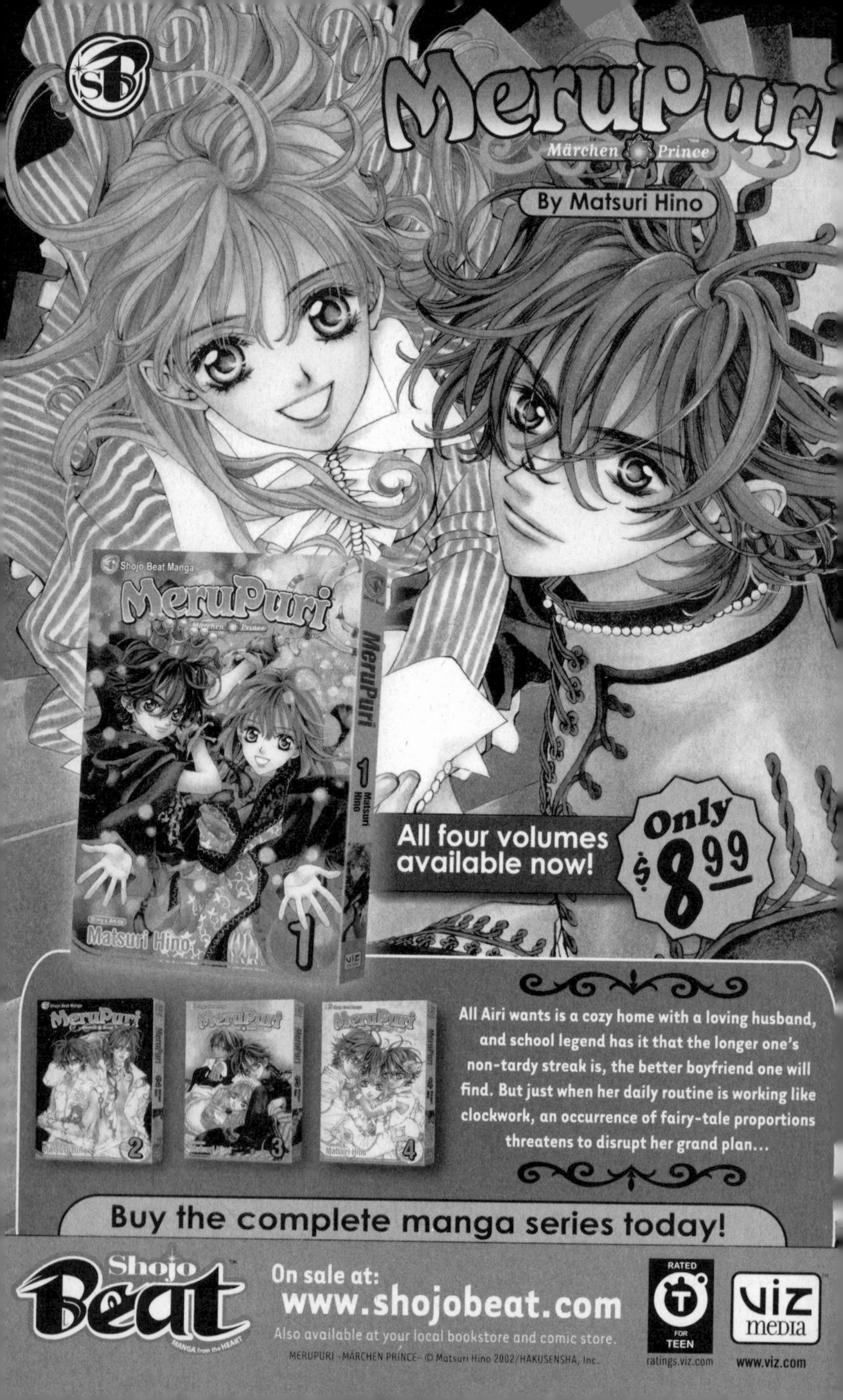

MeruPuri
Märchen Prince
By Matsuri Hino
Shojo Beat Manga
MeruPuri
Märchen Prince
MeruPuri
1
Matsuri Hino
Matsuri Hino
1
All four volumes available now!
Only $8.99
All Airi wants is a cozy home with a loving husband, and school legend has it that the longer one's non-tardy streak is, the better boyfriend one will find. But just when her daily routine is working like clockwork, an occurrence of fairy-tale proportions threatens to disrupt her grand plan...
Buy the complete manga series today!
Shojo Beat
MANGA from the HEART
On sale at:
www.shojobeat.com
Also available at your local bookstore and comic store.
MERUPURI -MÄRCHEN PRINCE- © Matsuri Hino 2002/HAKUSENSHA, Inc.
RATED T FOR TEEN
ratings.viz.com
VIZ MEDIA
www.viz.com

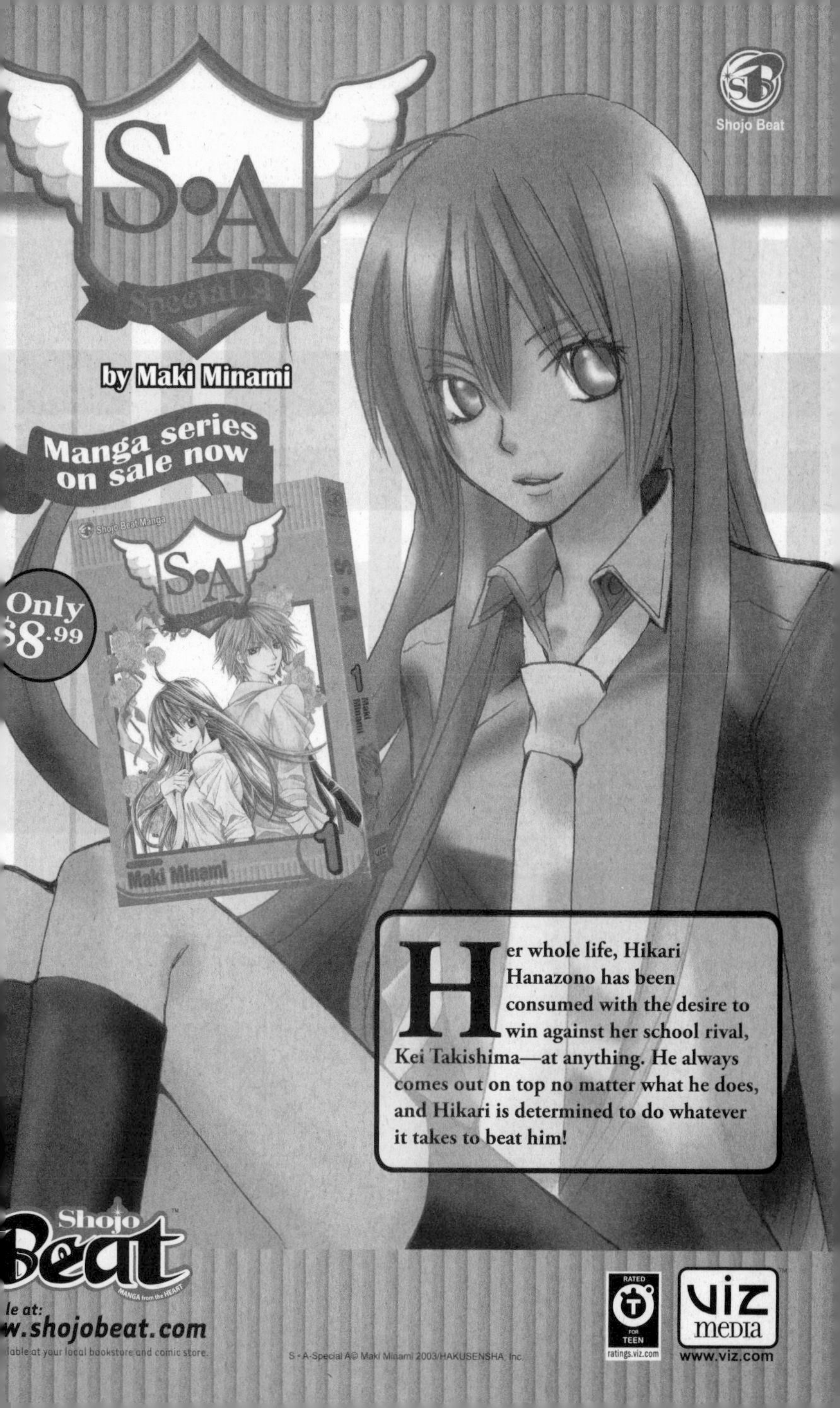
Shojo Beat
S·A
by Maki Minami
Manga series on sale now
Only $8.99
Shojo Beat Manga
S·A
1
Maki Minami
Her whole life, Hikari Hanazono has been consumed with the desire to win against her school rival, Kei Takishima—at anything. He always comes out on top no matter what he does, and Hikari is determined to do whatever it takes to beat him!
Shojo Beat
MANGA from the HEART
le at:
w.shojobeat.com
lable at your local bookstore and comic store.
S · A-Special A © Maki Minami 2003/HAKUSENSHA, Inc.
RATED T FOR TEEN
ratings.viz.com
VIZ media
www.viz.com

HIGH SCHOOL DEBUT
VOL. 12
Shojo Beat Manga Edition

STORY & ART BY
KAZUNE KAWAHARA

Translation & Adaptation/Gemma Collinge
Touch-up Art & Lettering/Rina Mapa
Cover Design/Courtney Utt
Interior Design/Amy Martin
Editor/Amy Yu

VP, Production/Alvin Lu
VP, Publishing Licensing/Rika Inouye
VP, Sales & Product Marketing/Gonzalo Ferreyra
VP, Creative/Linda Espinosa
Publisher/Hyoe Narita

KOKO DEBUT © 2003 by Kazune Kawahara
All rights reserved.
First published in Japan in 2003 by SHUEISHA Inc., Tokyo.
English translation rights arranged by SHUEISHA Inc.

The stories, characters and incidents mentioned in this publication are
entirely fictional.

Printed in the U.S.A.

Published by VIZ Media, LLC
P.O. Box 77010
San Francisco, CA 94107

10 9 8 7 6 5 4 3 2 1
First printing, November 2009

www.viz.com   www.shojobeat.com

I emailed Karuho Shiina [author of *Kimi ni Todoke*] saying that I like cool, standoffish characters that warm up to a heroine. She replied saying that she already knew this! Yesterday my editor emailed me saying that I was well known in the editorial department for liking uniforms, shaved heads and cool, standoffish characters. What?! Whaaaat?!

– Kazune Kawahara

Kazune Kawahara is from Hokkaido Prefecture and was born on March 11th (a Pisces!). She made her manga debut at age 18 with *Kare no Ichiban Sukina Hito* (His Most Favorite Person). Her other works include *Sensei!*, serialized in *Bessatsu Margaret* magazine. Her hobby is interior redecorating.

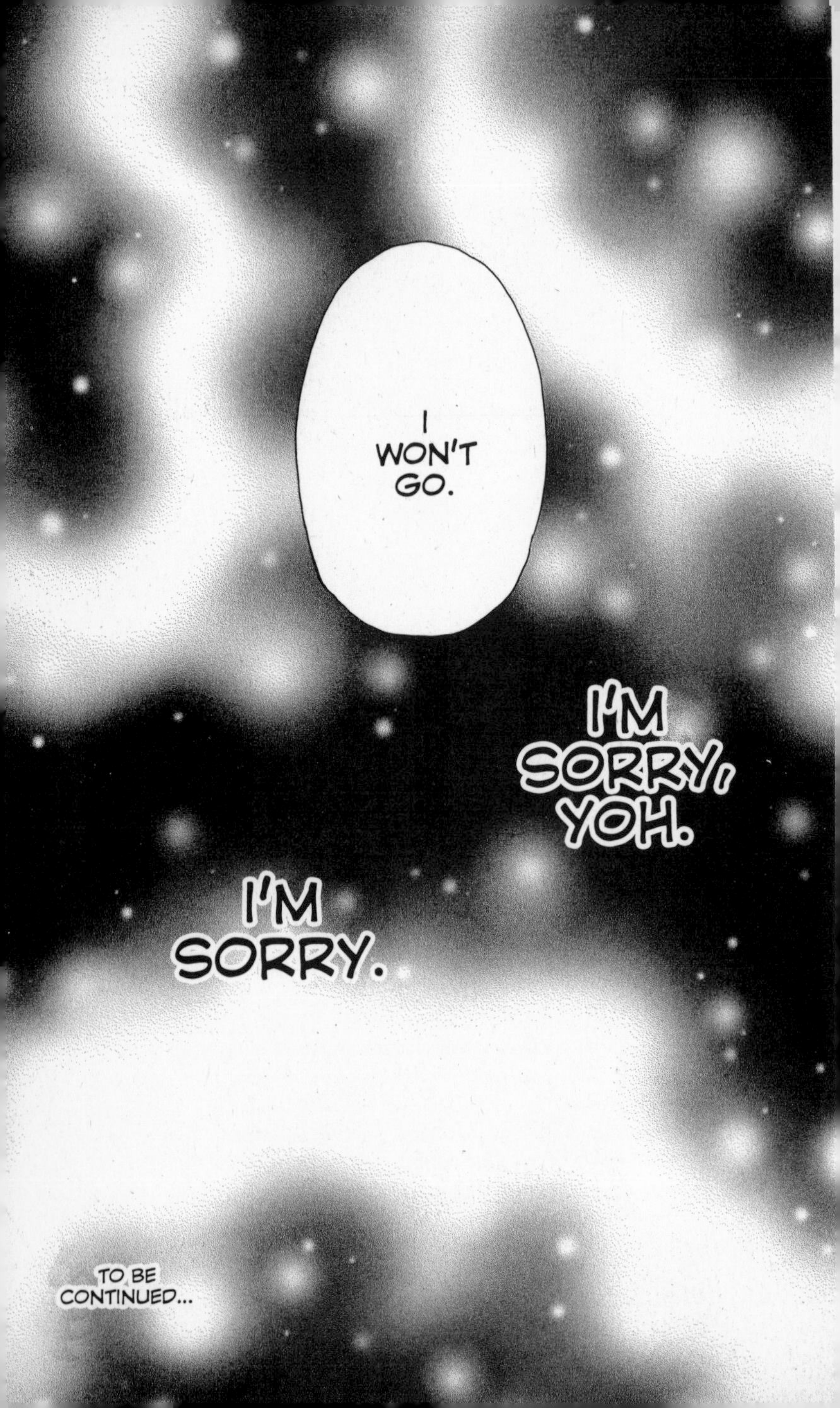
I WON'T GO.
I'M SORRY, YOH.
I'M SORRY.
TO BE CONTINUED...

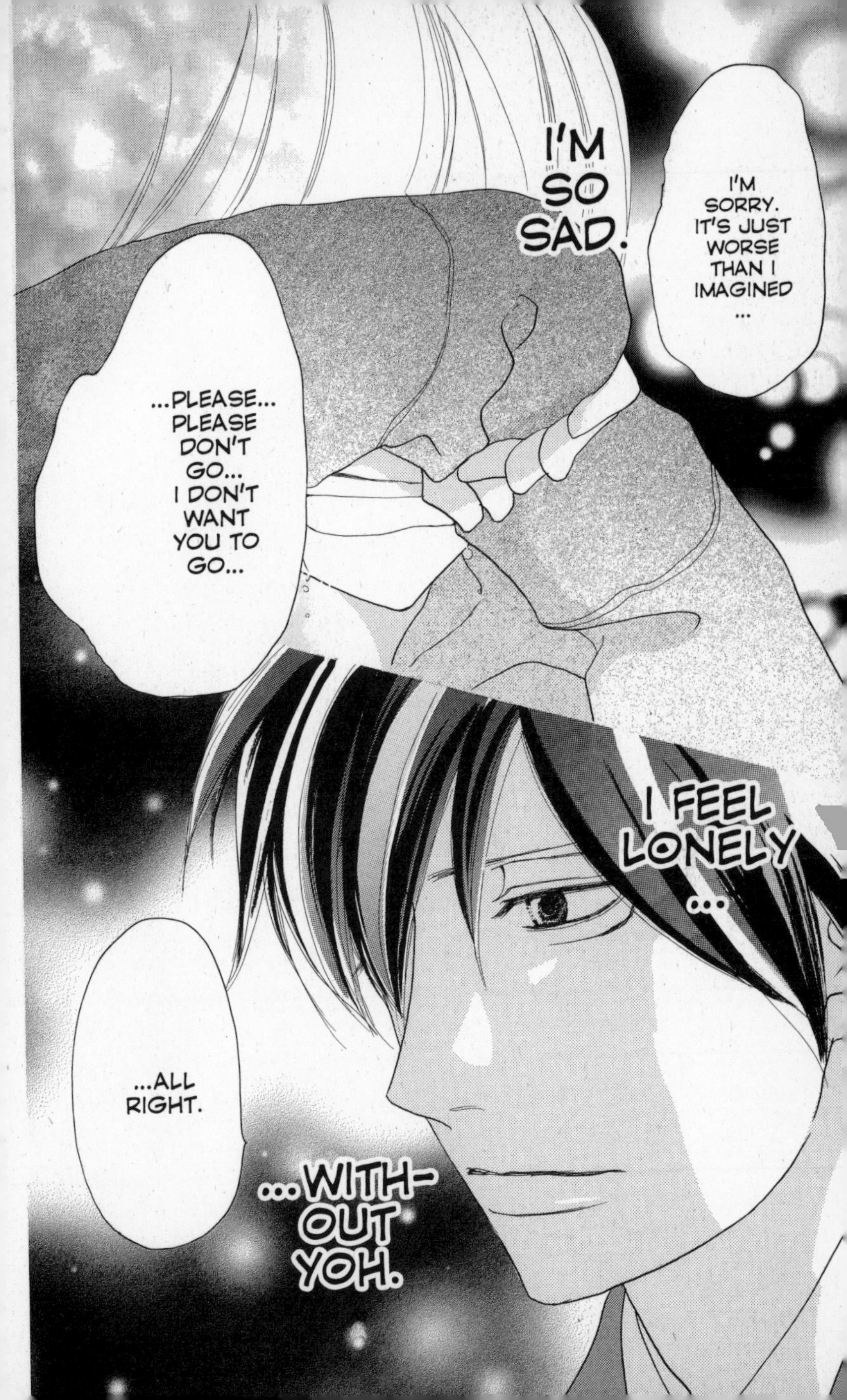
I'M SORRY. IT'S JUST WORSE THAN I IMAGINED ...
I'M SO SAD.
...PLEASE... PLEASE DON'T GO... I DON'T WANT YOU TO GO...
I FEEL LONELY ...
...WITH- OUT YOH.
...ALL RIGHT.

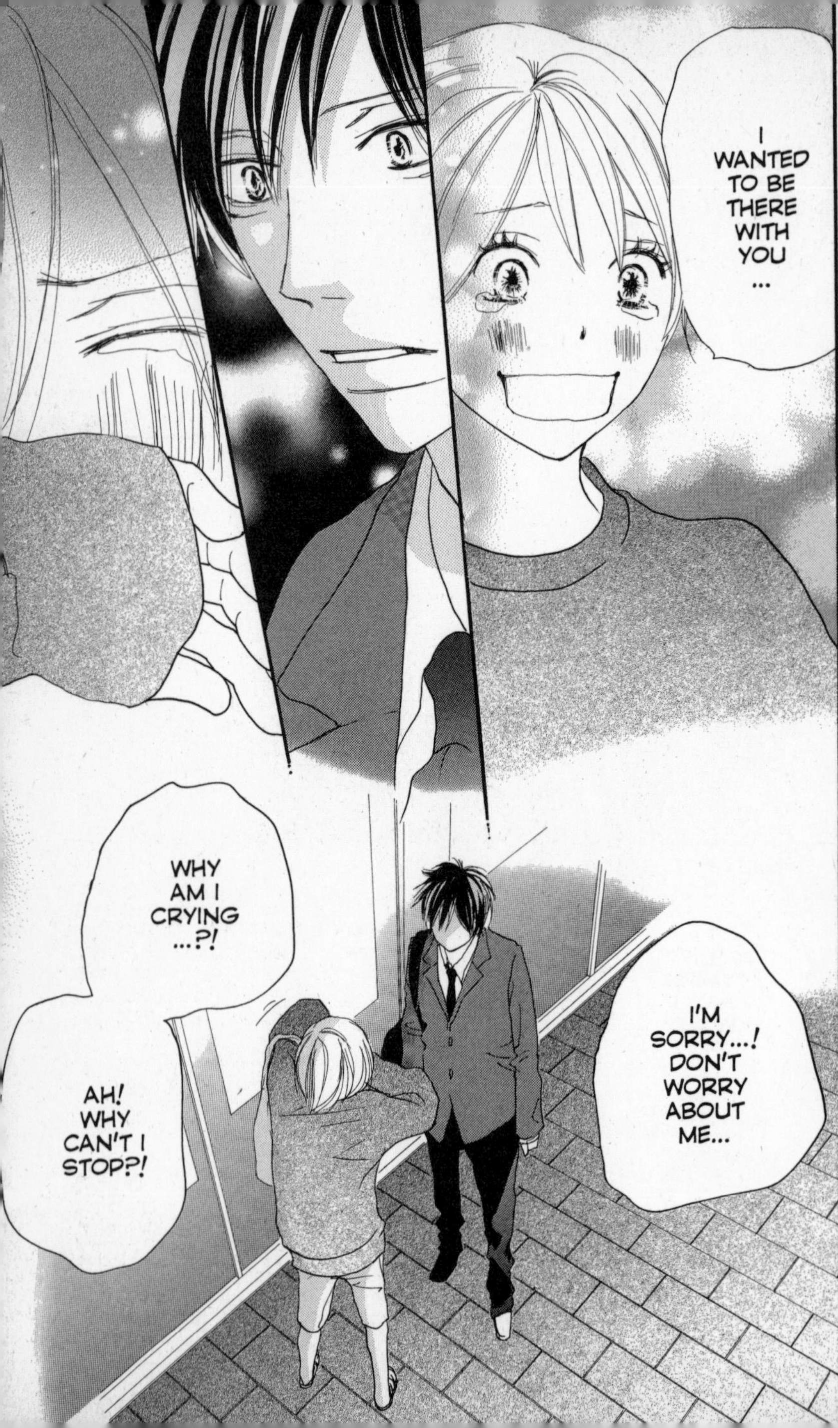
I WANTED TO BE THERE WITH YOU ...
I'M SORRY...! DON'T WORRY ABOUT ME...
WHY AM I CRYING ...?!
AH! WHY CAN'T I STOP?!

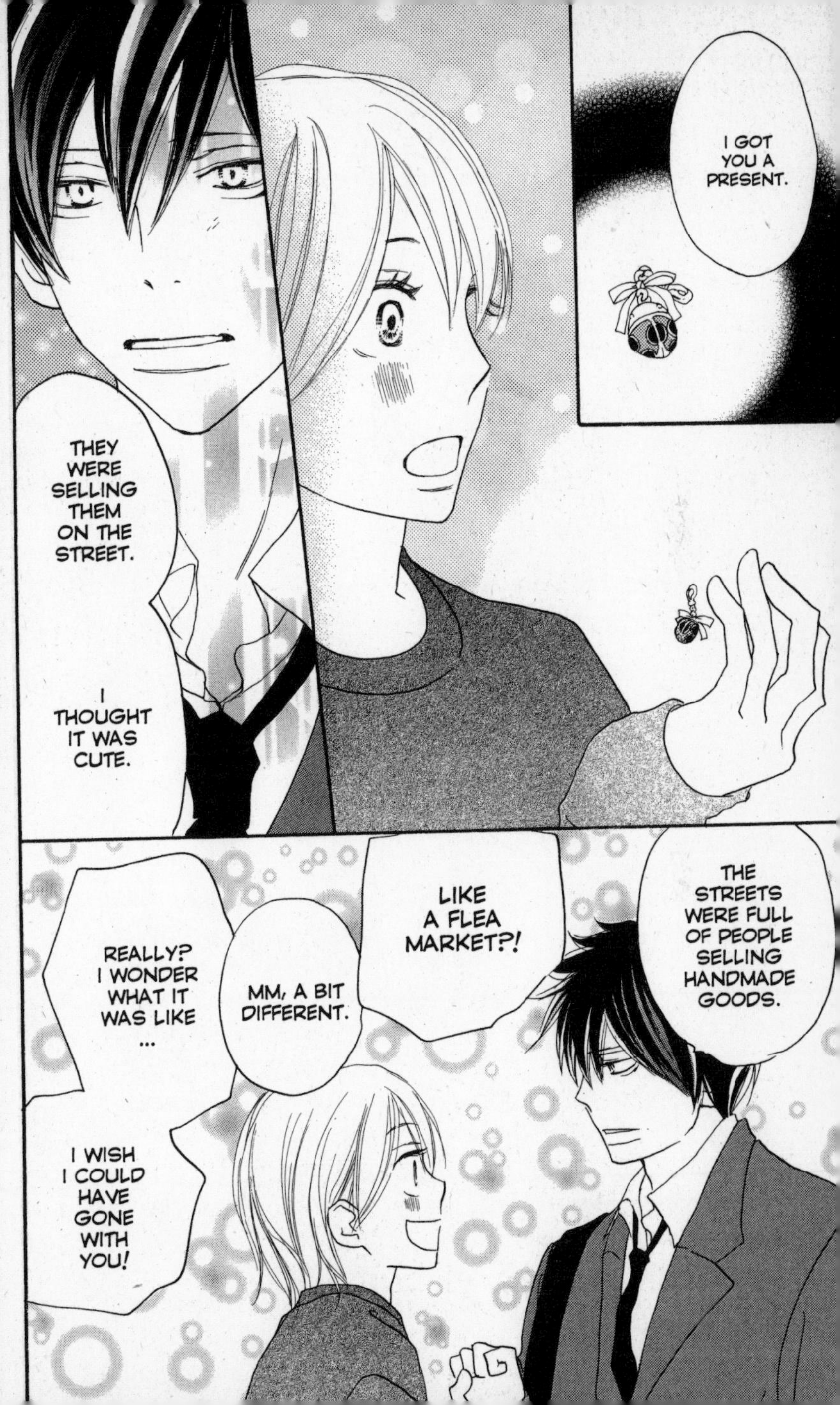
I GOT YOU A PRESENT.
THEY WERE SELLING THEM ON THE STREET.
I THOUGHT IT WAS CUTE.
THE STREETS WERE FULL OF PEOPLE SELLING HANDMADE GOODS.
LIKE A FLEA MARKET?!
MM, A BIT DIFFERENT.
REALLY? I WONDER WHAT IT WAS LIKE ...
I WISH I COULD HAVE GONE WITH YOU!

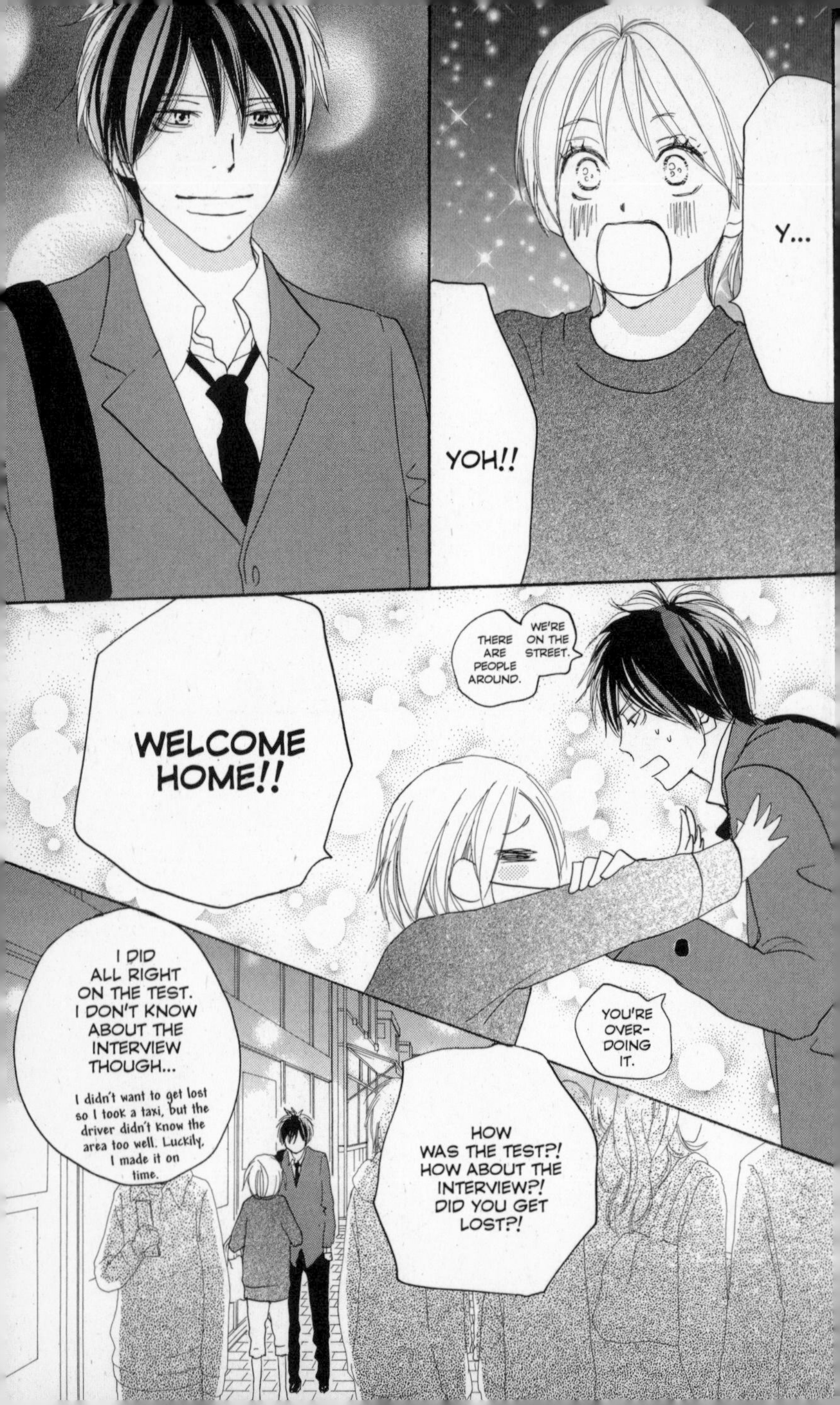

Y...
YOH!!
WELCOME HOME!!
THERE ARE PEOPLE AROUND. WE'RE ON THE STREET.
YOU'RE OVER-DOING IT.
HOW WAS THE TEST?! HOW ABOUT THE INTERVIEW?! DID YOU GET LOST?!
I DID ALL RIGHT ON THE TEST. I DON'T KNOW ABOUT THE INTERVIEW THOUGH...
I didn't want to get lost so I took a taxi, but the driver didn't know the area too well. Luckily, I made it on time.

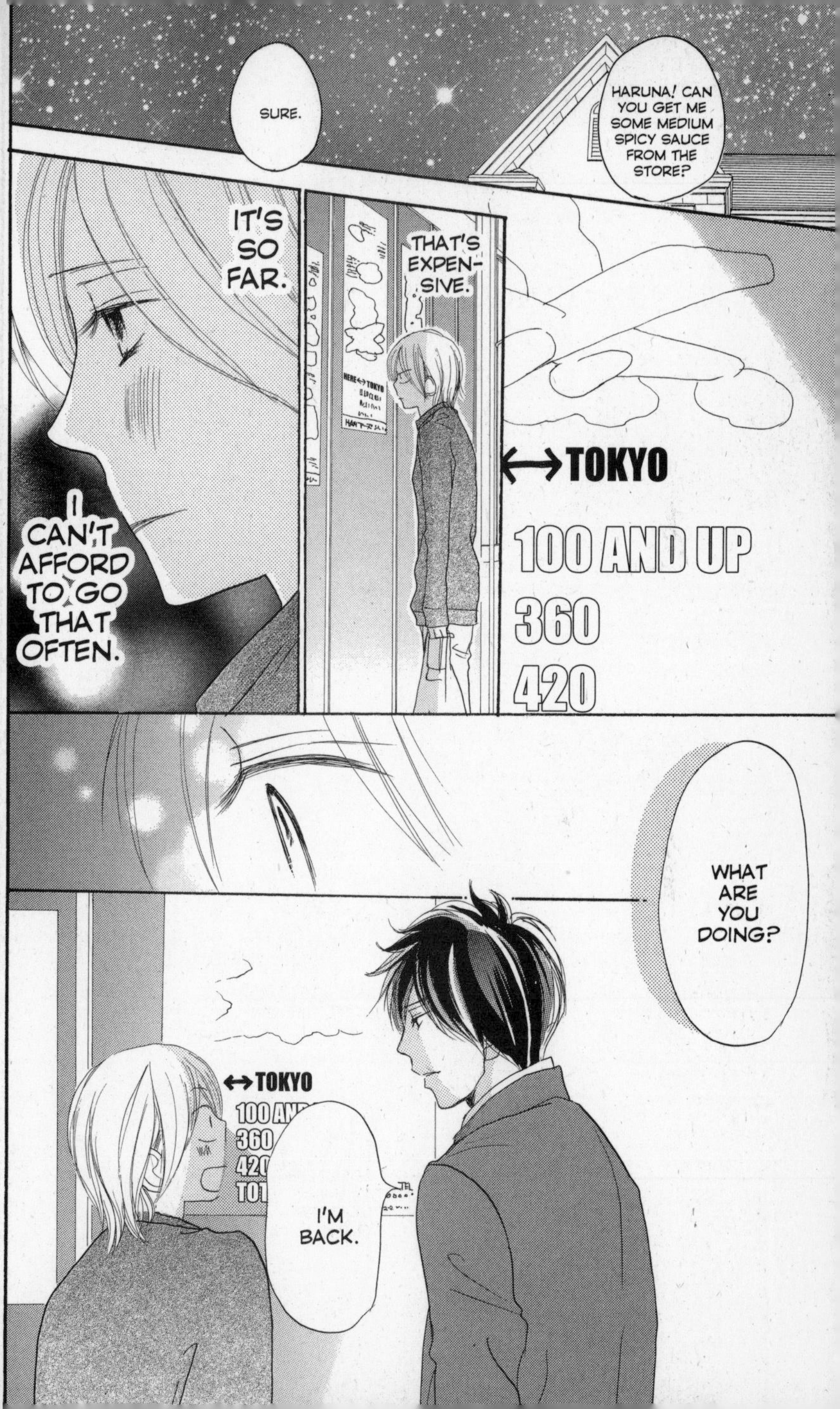
HARUNA! CAN YOU GET ME SOME MEDIUM SPICY SAUCE FROM THE STORE?
SURE.
↔TOKYO
100 AND UP
360
420
HERE↔TOKYO
THAT'S EXPEN-SIVE.
IT'S SO FAR.
I CAN'T AFFORD TO GO THAT OFTEN.
WHAT ARE YOU DOING?
I'M BACK.

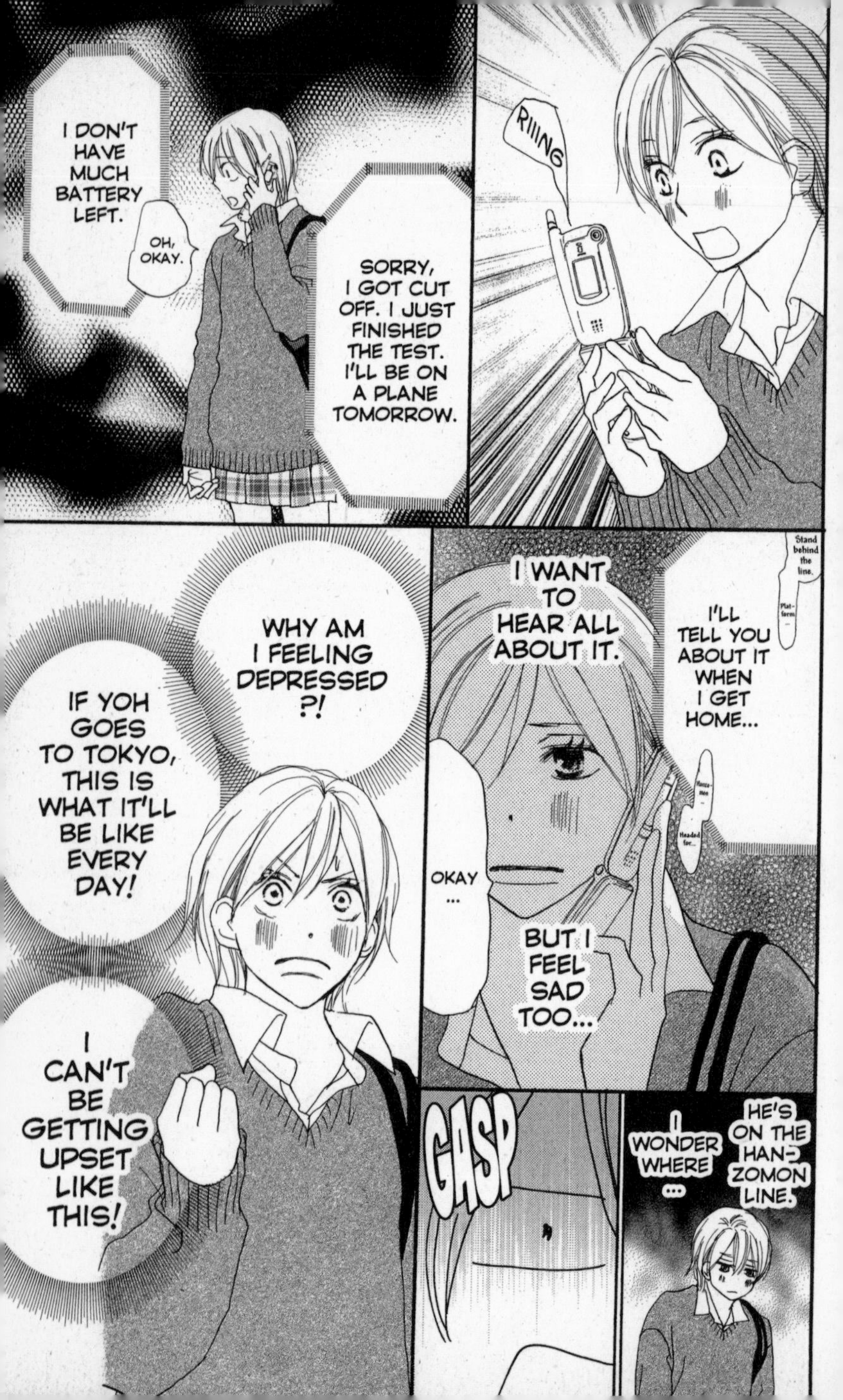
RIIING
SORRY, I GOT CUT OFF. I JUST FINISHED THE TEST. I'LL BE ON A PLANE TOMORROW.
OH, OKAY.
I DON'T HAVE MUCH BATTERY LEFT.
Stand behind the line.
Platform...
I'LL TELL YOU ABOUT IT WHEN I GET HOME...
I WANT TO HEAR ALL ABOUT IT.
Hanzomon...
Headed for...
OKAY...
BUT I FEEL SAD TOO...
HE'S ON THE HANZOMON LINE.
I WONDER WHERE...
GASP
WHY AM I FEELING DEPRESSED?!
IF YOH GOES TO TOKYO, THIS IS WHAT IT'LL BE LIKE EVERY DAY!
I CAN'T BE GETTING UPSET LIKE THIS!

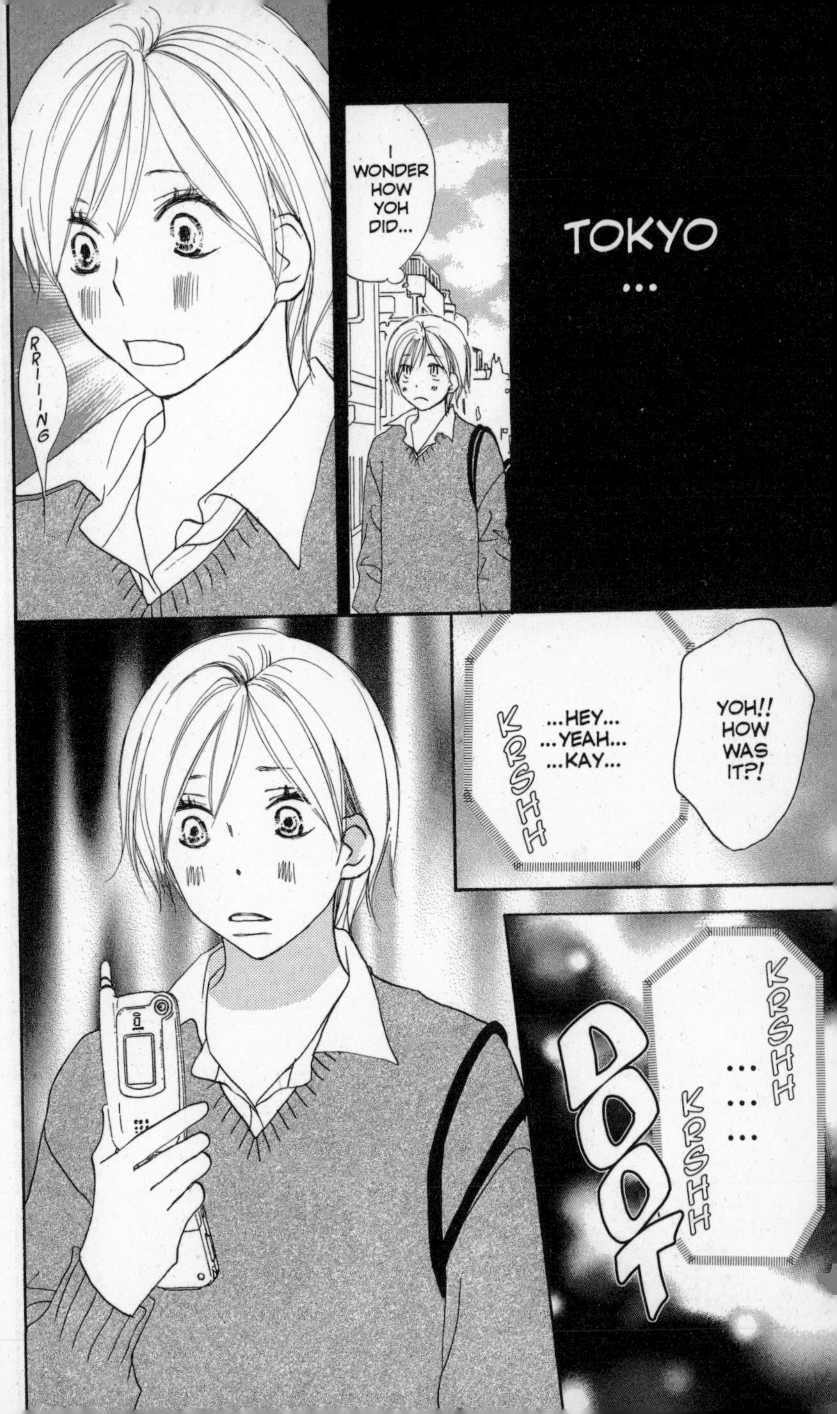
TOKYO
...
I WONDER HOW YOH DID...
RRIIING
YOH!! HOW WAS IT?!
...HEY... ...YEAH... ...KAY...
KRSHH
KRSHH
... ...
KRSHH
DOOT

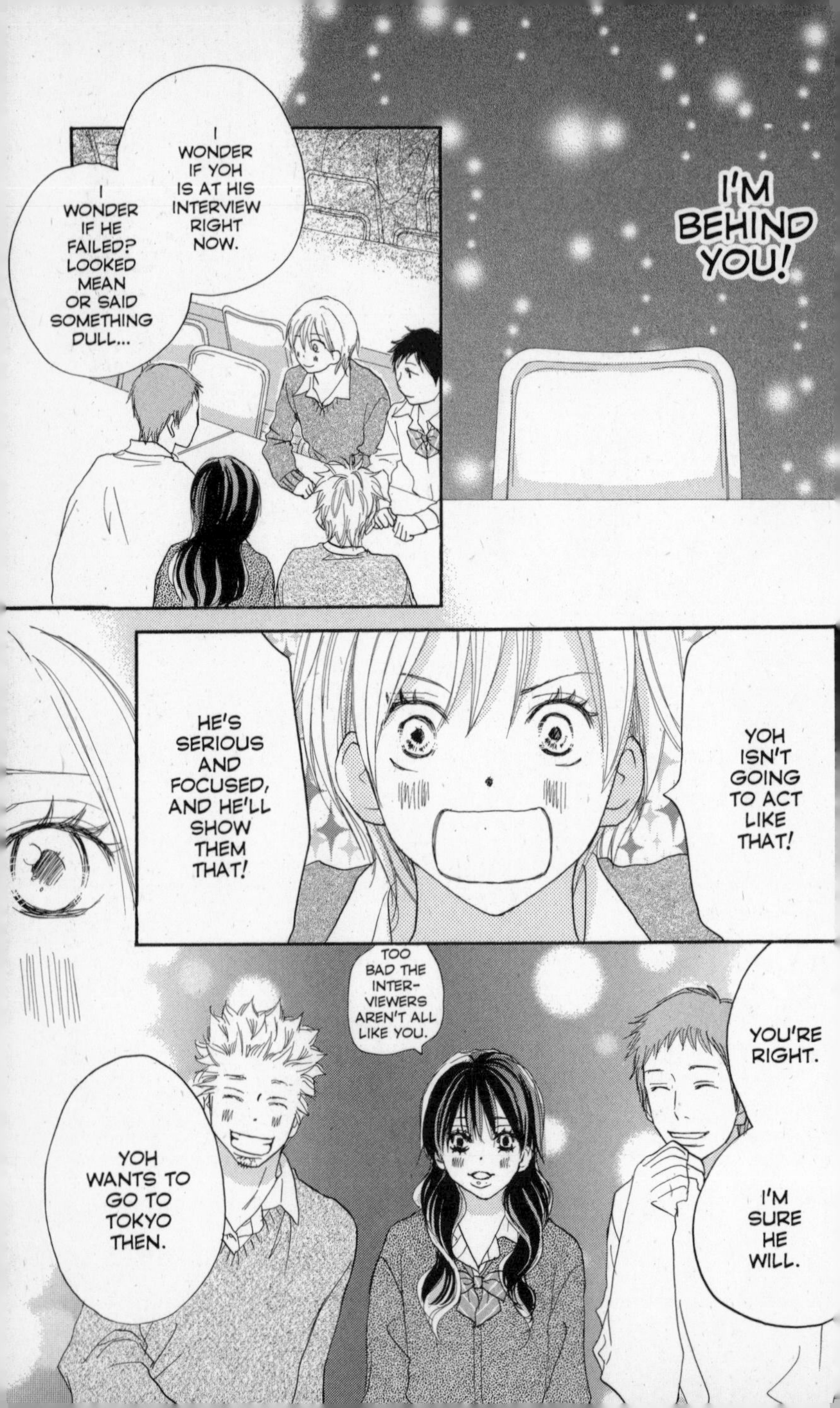
I'M BEHIND YOU!
I WONDER IF YOH IS AT HIS INTERVIEW RIGHT NOW.
I WONDER IF HE FAILED? LOOKED MEAN OR SAID SOMETHING DULL...
YOH ISN'T GOING TO ACT LIKE THAT!
HE'S SERIOUS AND FOCUSED, AND HE'LL SHOW THEM THAT!
YOU'RE RIGHT.
TOO BAD THE INTER-VIEWERS AREN'T ALL LIKE YOU.
I'M SURE HE WILL.
YOH WANTS TO GO TO TOKYO THEN.

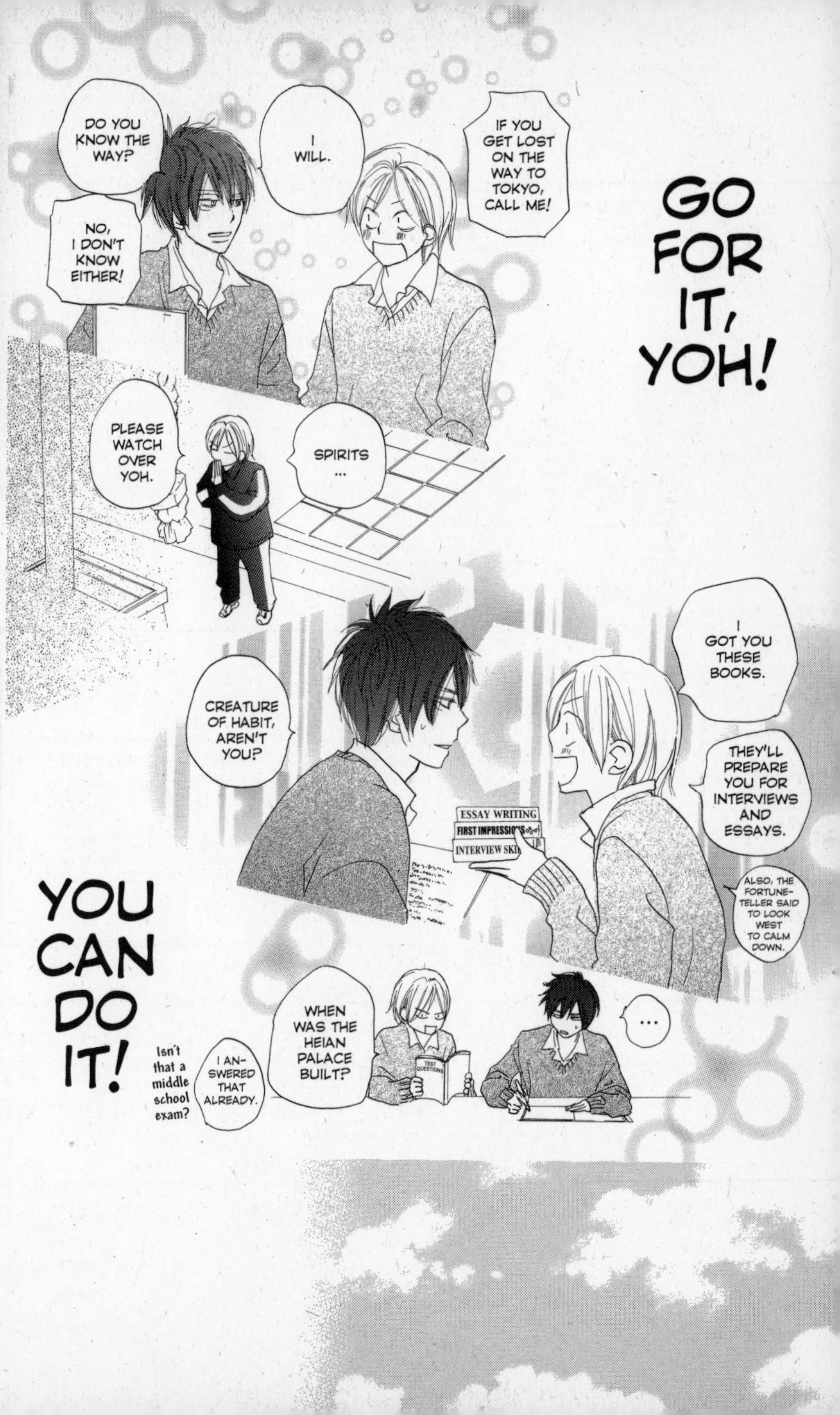
GO FOR IT, YOH!
IF YOU GET LOST ON THE WAY TO TOKYO, CALL ME!
I WILL.
DO YOU KNOW THE WAY?
NO, I DON'T KNOW EITHER!
SPIRITS ...
PLEASE WATCH OVER YOH.
I GOT YOU THESE BOOKS.
THEY'LL PREPARE YOU FOR INTERVIEWS AND ESSAYS.
ALSO, THE FORTUNE-TELLER SAID TO LOOK WEST TO CALM DOWN.
CREATURE OF HABIT, AREN'T YOU?
ESSAY WRITING
...
WHEN WAS THE HEIAN PALACE BUILT?
TEST QUESTIONS
I AN-SWERED THAT ALREADY.
Isn't that a middle school exam?
YOU CAN DO IT!

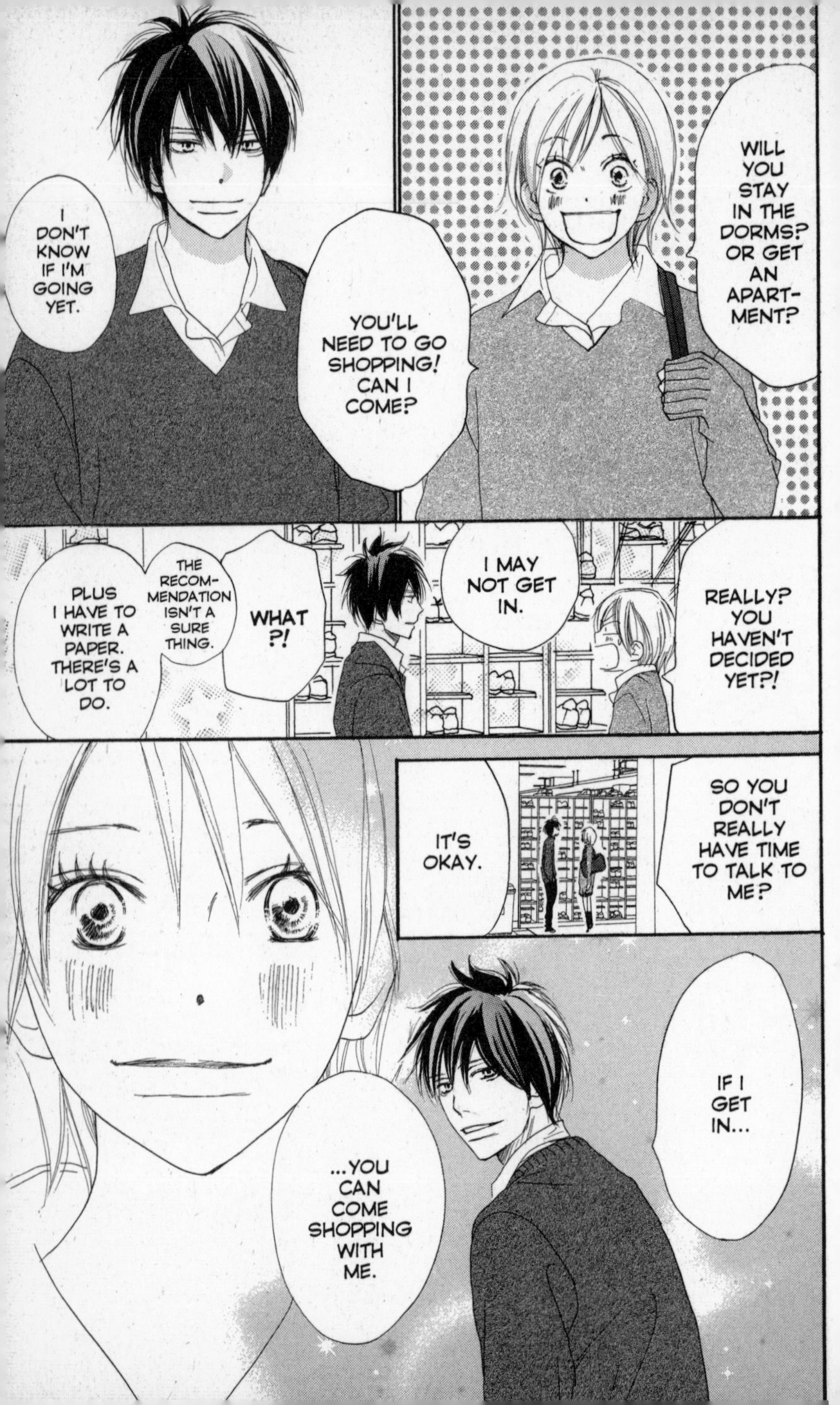
WILL YOU STAY IN THE DORMS? OR GET AN APARTMENT?
YOU'LL NEED TO GO SHOPPING! CAN I COME?
I DON'T KNOW IF I'M GOING YET.
REALLY? YOU HAVEN'T DECIDED YET?!
I MAY NOT GET IN.
WHAT?!
THE RECOMMENDATION ISN'T A SURE THING.
PLUS I HAVE TO WRITE A PAPER. THERE'S A LOT TO DO.
SO YOU DON'T REALLY HAVE TIME TO TALK TO ME?
IT'S OKAY.
IF I GET IN...
...YOU CAN COME SHOPPING WITH ME.

LONG DISTANCE

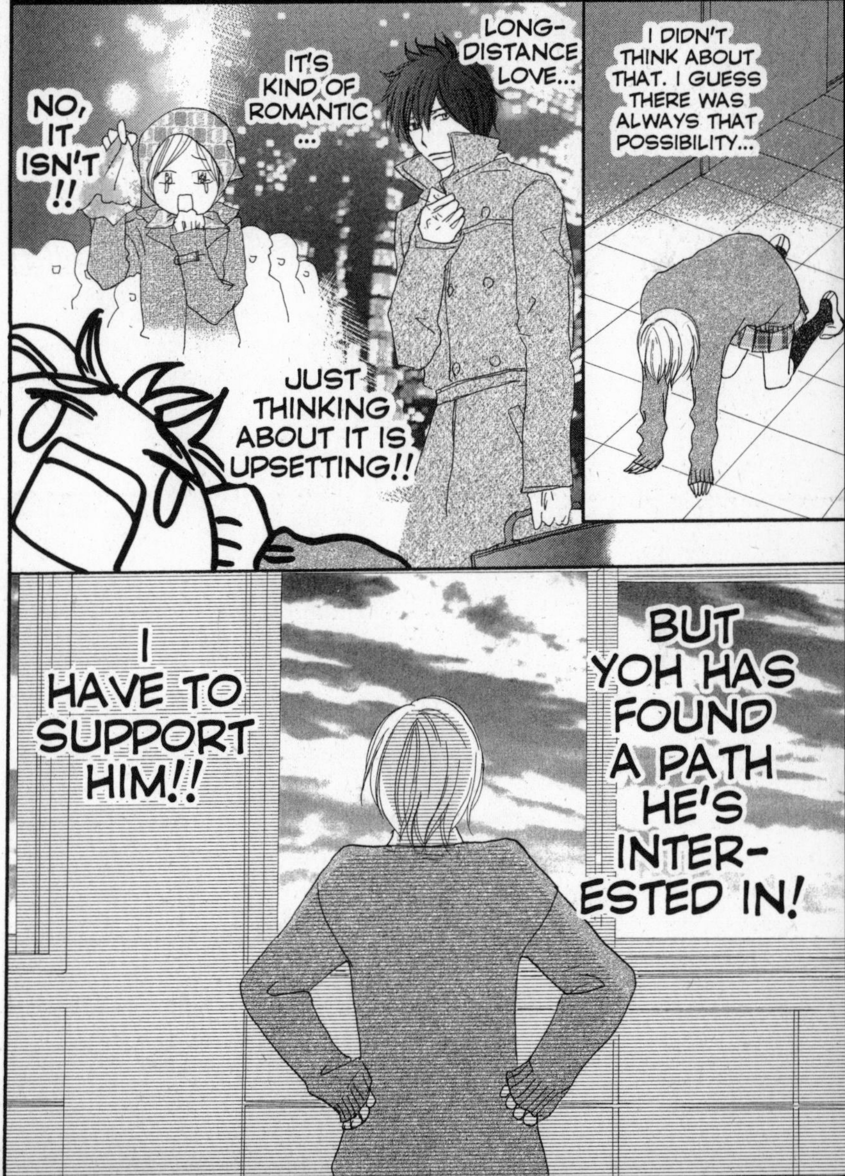
I DIDN'T THINK ABOUT THAT. I GUESS THERE WAS ALWAYS THAT POSSIBILITY...
LONG-DISTANCE LOVE...
IT'S KIND OF ROMANTIC...
NO, IT ISN'T!!
JUST THINKING ABOUT IT IS UPSETTING!!
BUT YOH HAS FOUND A PATH HE'S INTER-ESTED IN!
I HAVE TO SUPPORT HIM!!

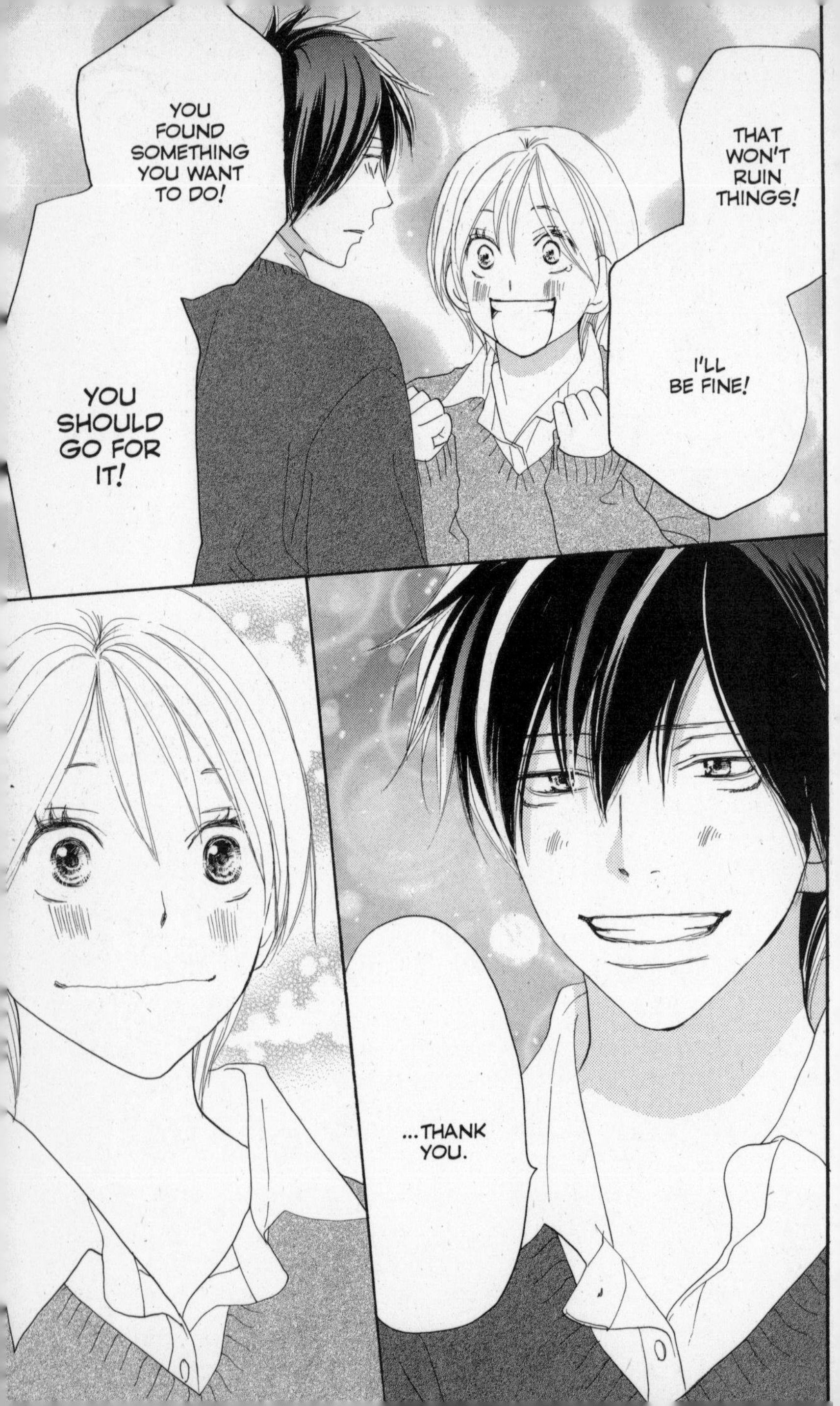
THAT WON'T RUIN THINGS!
I'LL BE FINE!
YOU FOUND SOMETHING YOU WANT TO DO!
YOU SHOULD GO FOR IT!
...THANK YOU.

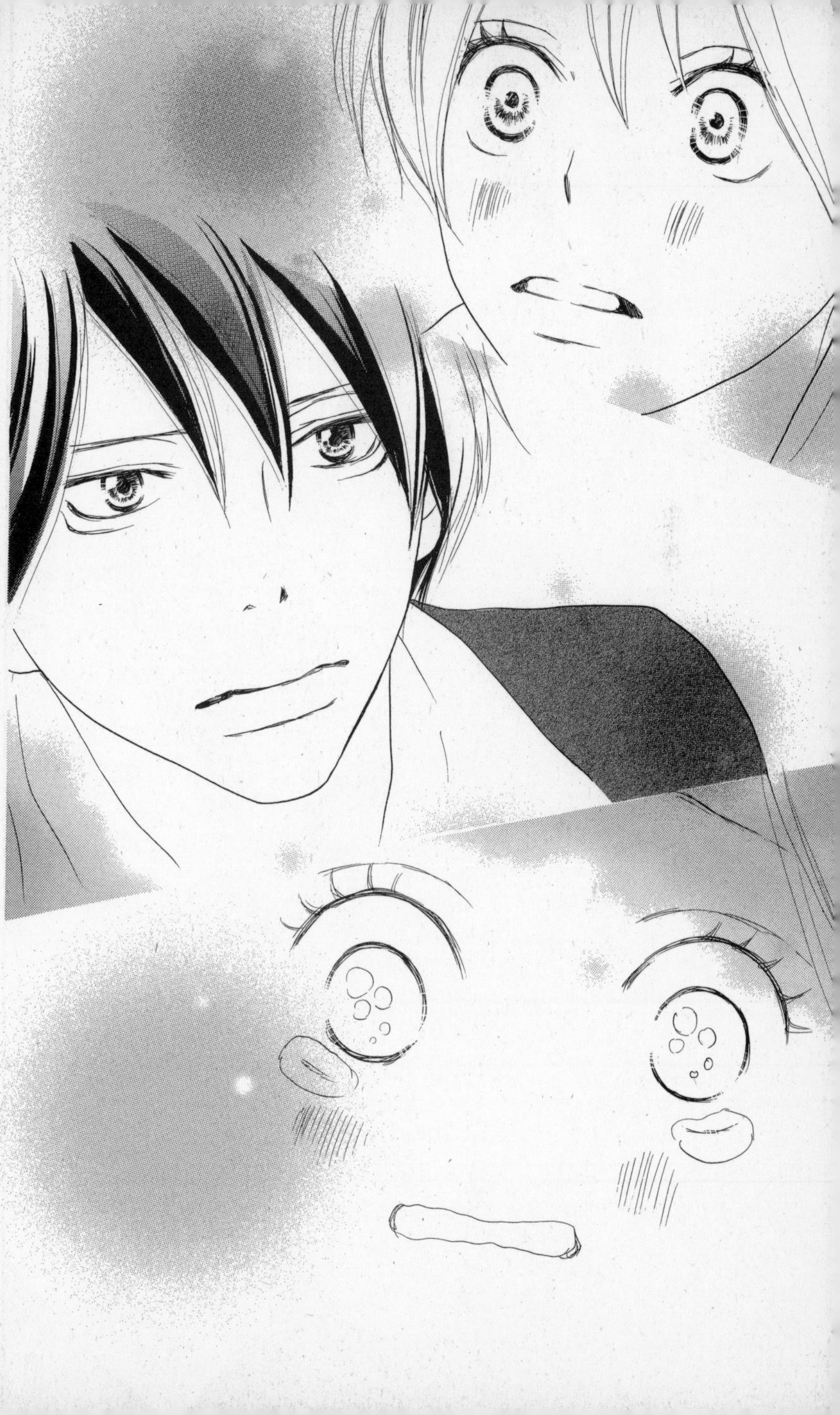

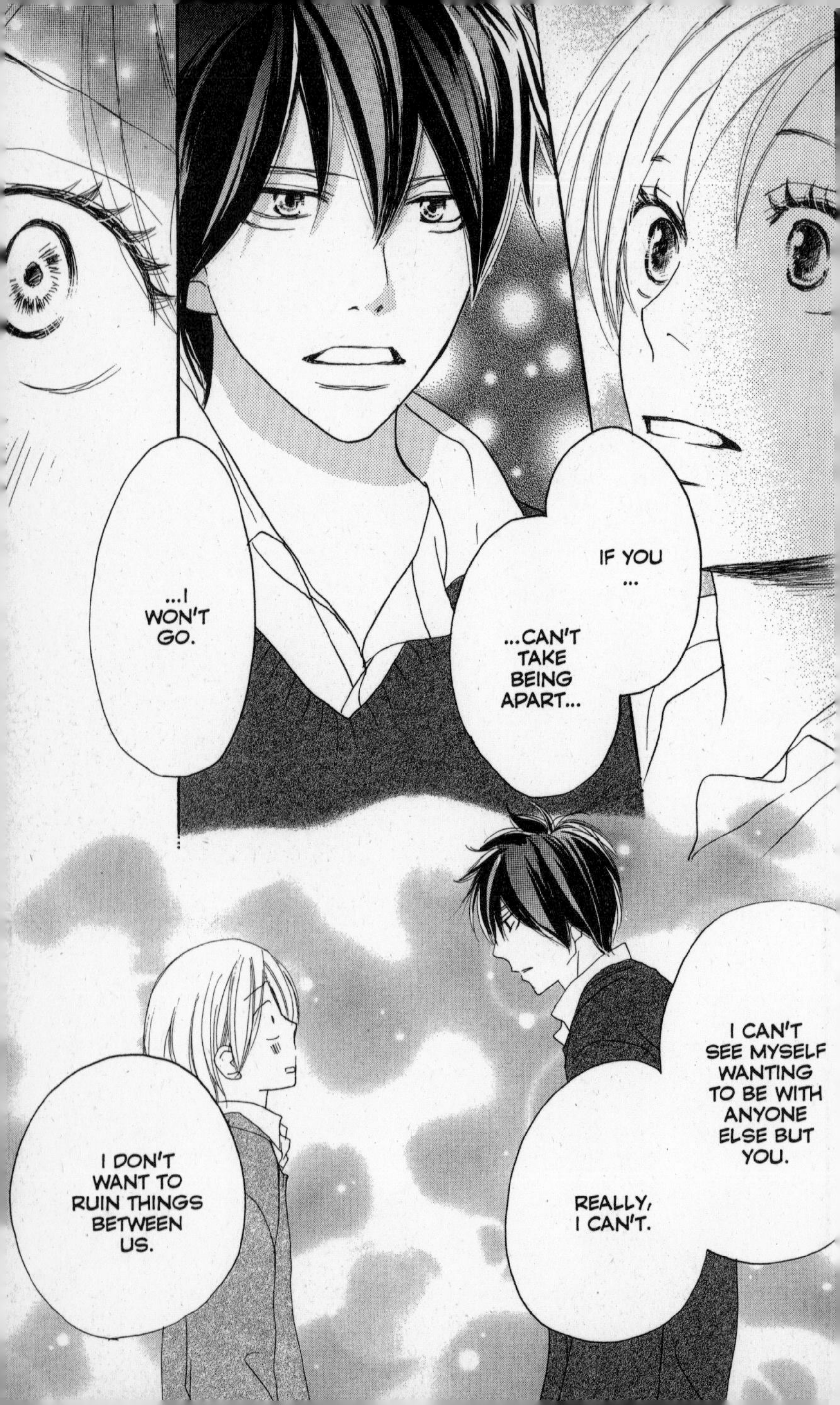
IF YOU ...
...CAN'T TAKE BEING APART...
...I WON'T GO.
I CAN'T SEE MYSELF WANTING TO BE WITH ANYONE ELSE BUT YOU.
REALLY, I CAN'T.
I DON'T WANT TO RUIN THINGS BETWEEN US.

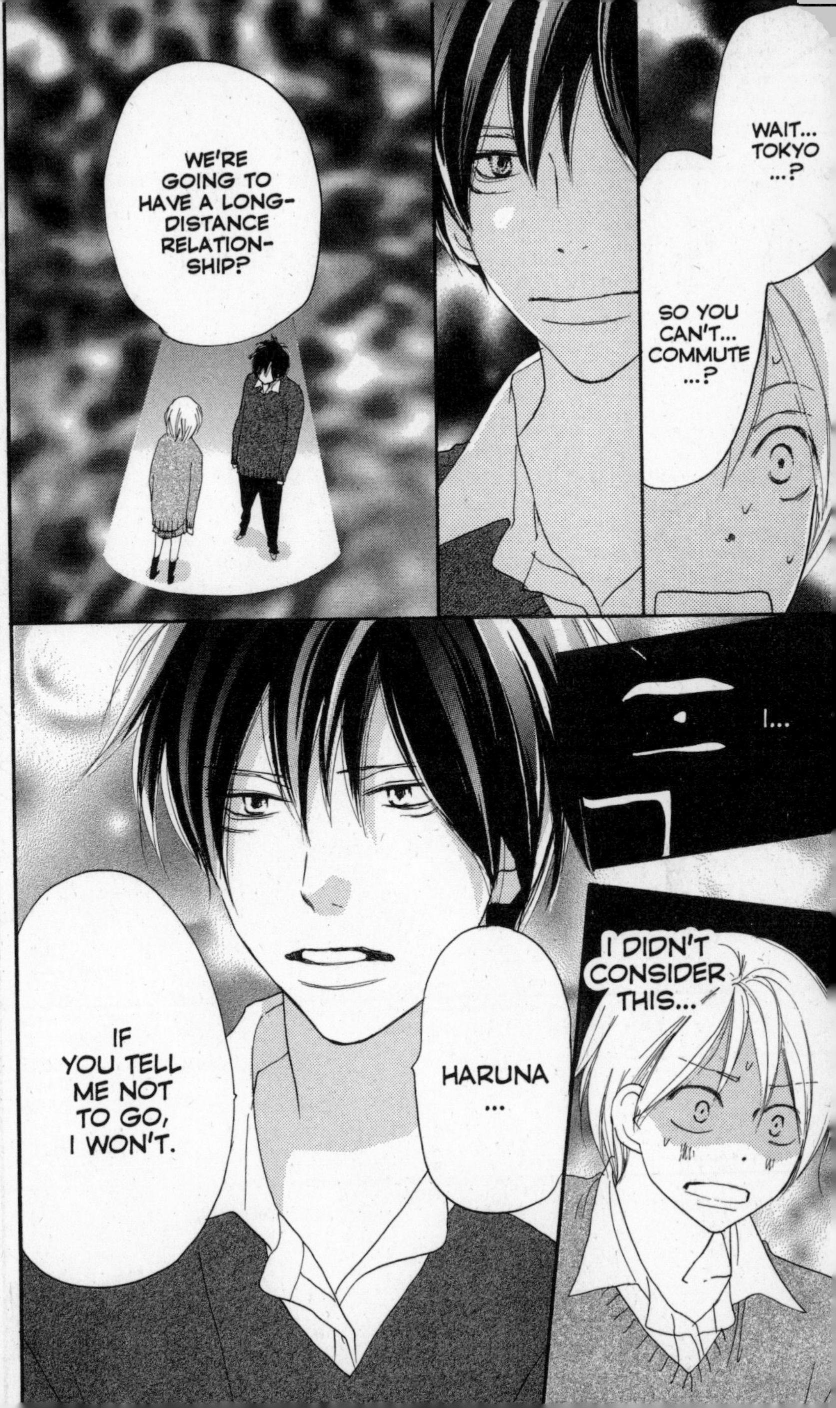
WAIT... TOKYO ...?
SO YOU CAN'T... COMMUTE ...?
WE'RE GOING TO HAVE A LONG-DISTANCE RELATION-SHIP?
I...
I DIDN'T CONSIDER THIS...
HARUNA ...
IF YOU TELL ME NOT TO GO, I WON'T.

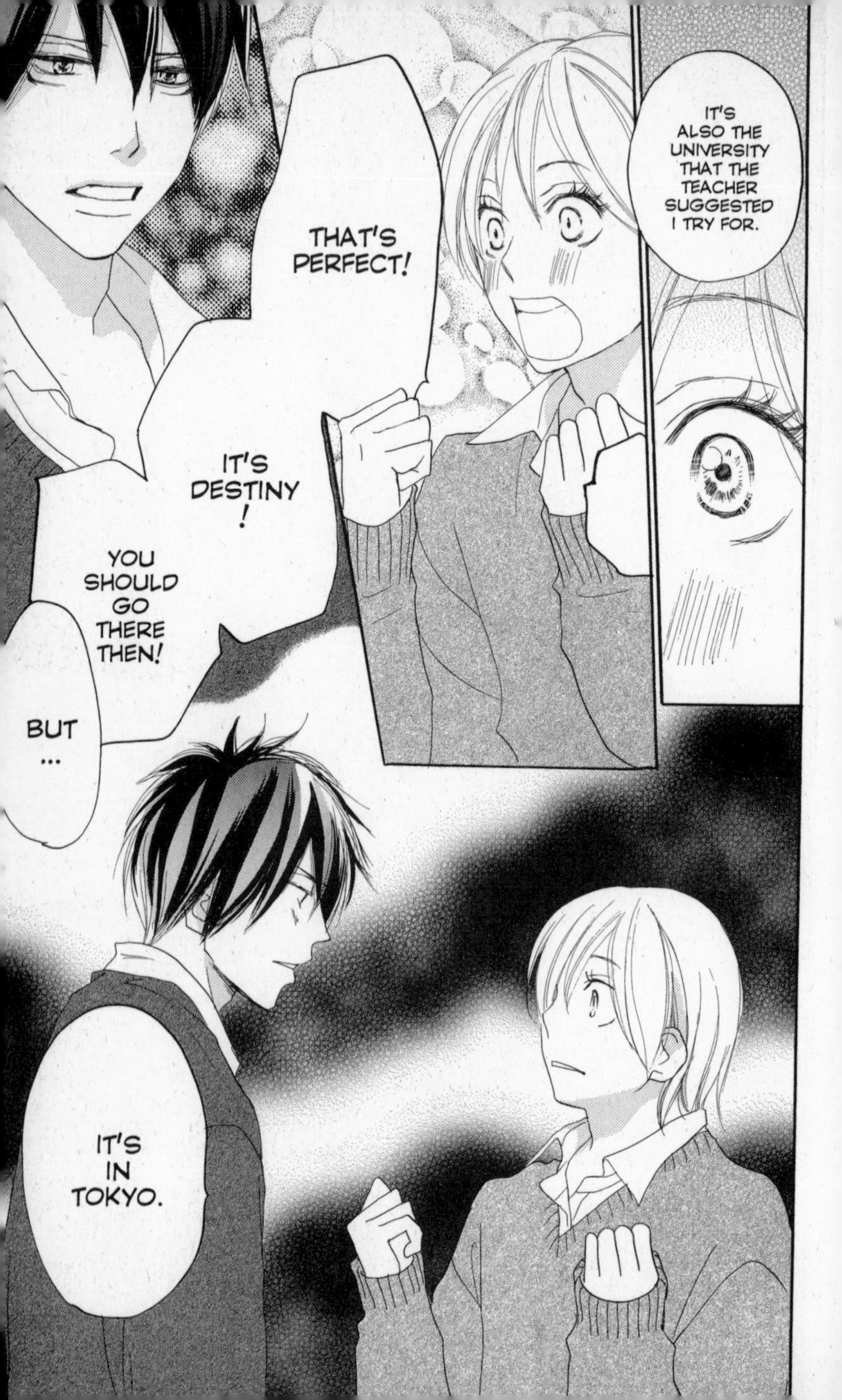
IT'S ALSO THE UNIVERSITY THAT THE TEACHER SUGGESTED I TRY FOR.
THAT'S PERFECT!
IT'S DESTINY!
YOU SHOULD GO THERE THEN!
BUT...
IT'S IN TOKYO.

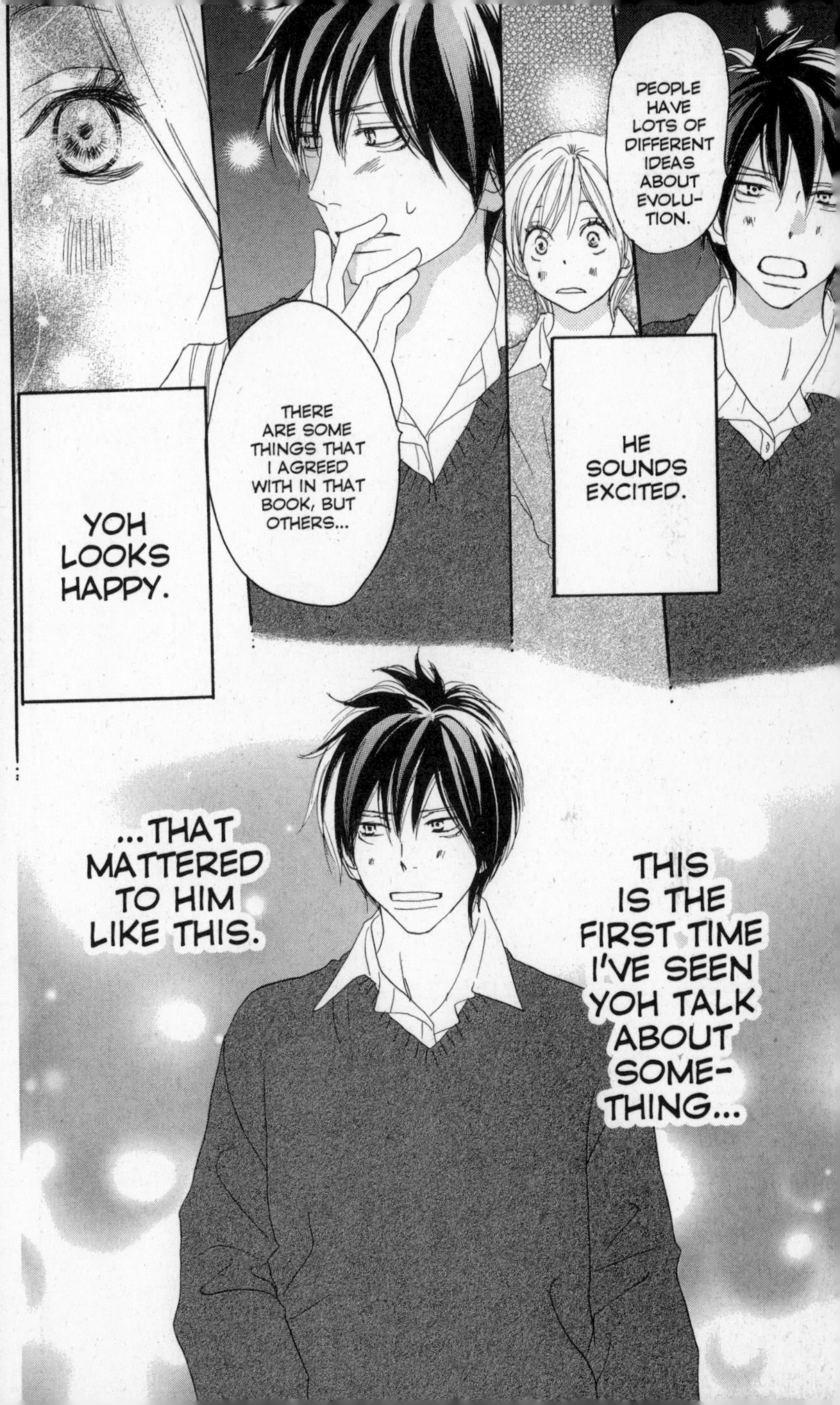
PEOPLE HAVE LOTS OF DIFFERENT IDEAS ABOUT EVOLU-TION.
HE SOUNDS EXCITED.
THERE ARE SOME THINGS THAT I AGREED WITH IN THAT BOOK, BUT OTHERS...
YOH LOOKS HAPPY.
THIS IS THE FIRST TIME I'VE SEEN YOH TALK ABOUT SOME-THING...
...THAT MATTERED TO HIM LIKE THIS.

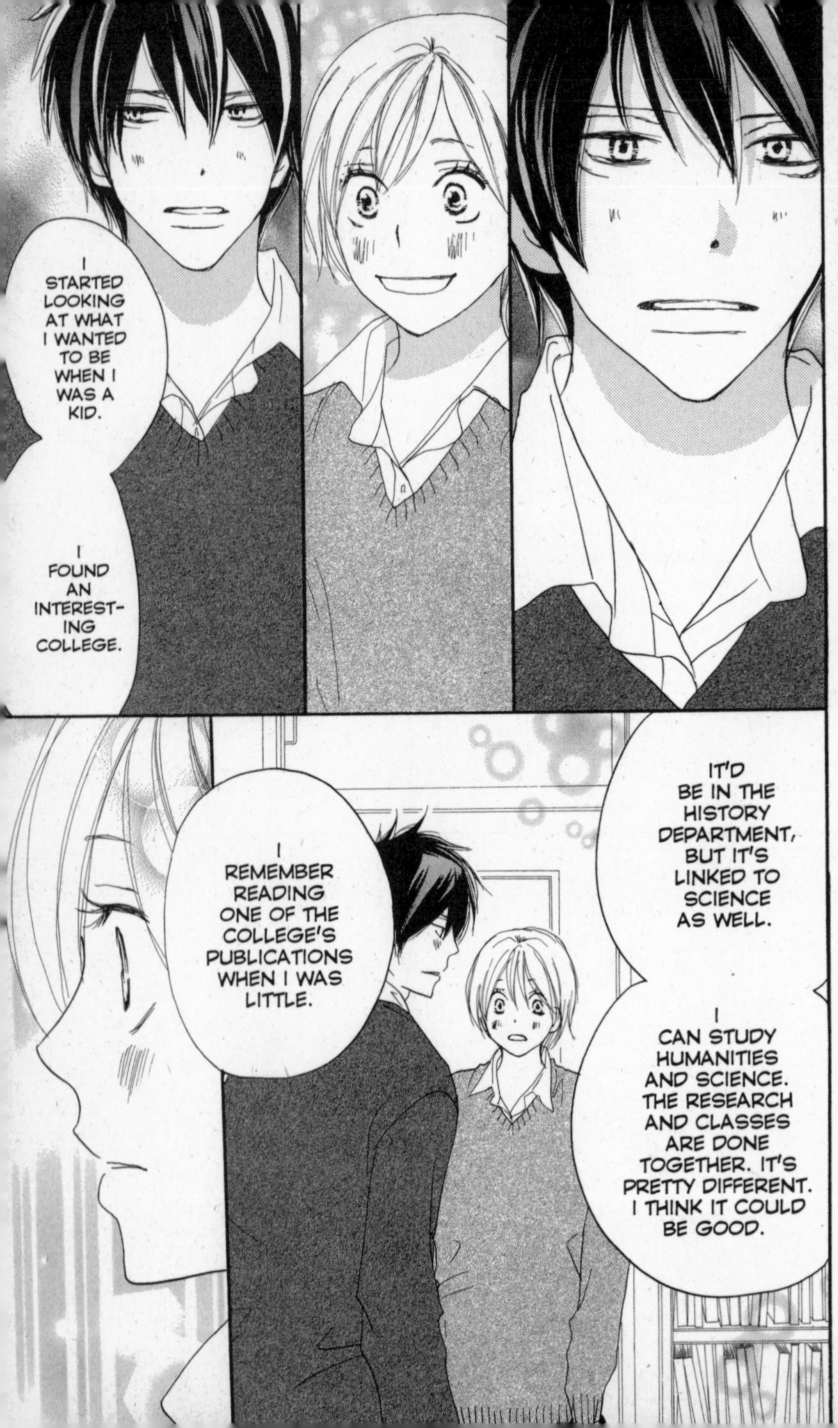
I STARTED LOOKING AT WHAT I WANTED TO BE WHEN I WAS A KID.
I FOUND AN INTERESTING COLLEGE.
IT'D BE IN THE HISTORY DEPARTMENT, BUT IT'S LINKED TO SCIENCE AS WELL.
I CAN STUDY HUMANITIES AND SCIENCE. THE RESEARCH AND CLASSES ARE DONE TOGETHER. IT'S PRETTY DIFFERENT. I THINK IT COULD BE GOOD.
I REMEMBER READING ONE OF THE COLLEGE'S PUBLICATIONS WHEN I WAS LITTLE.

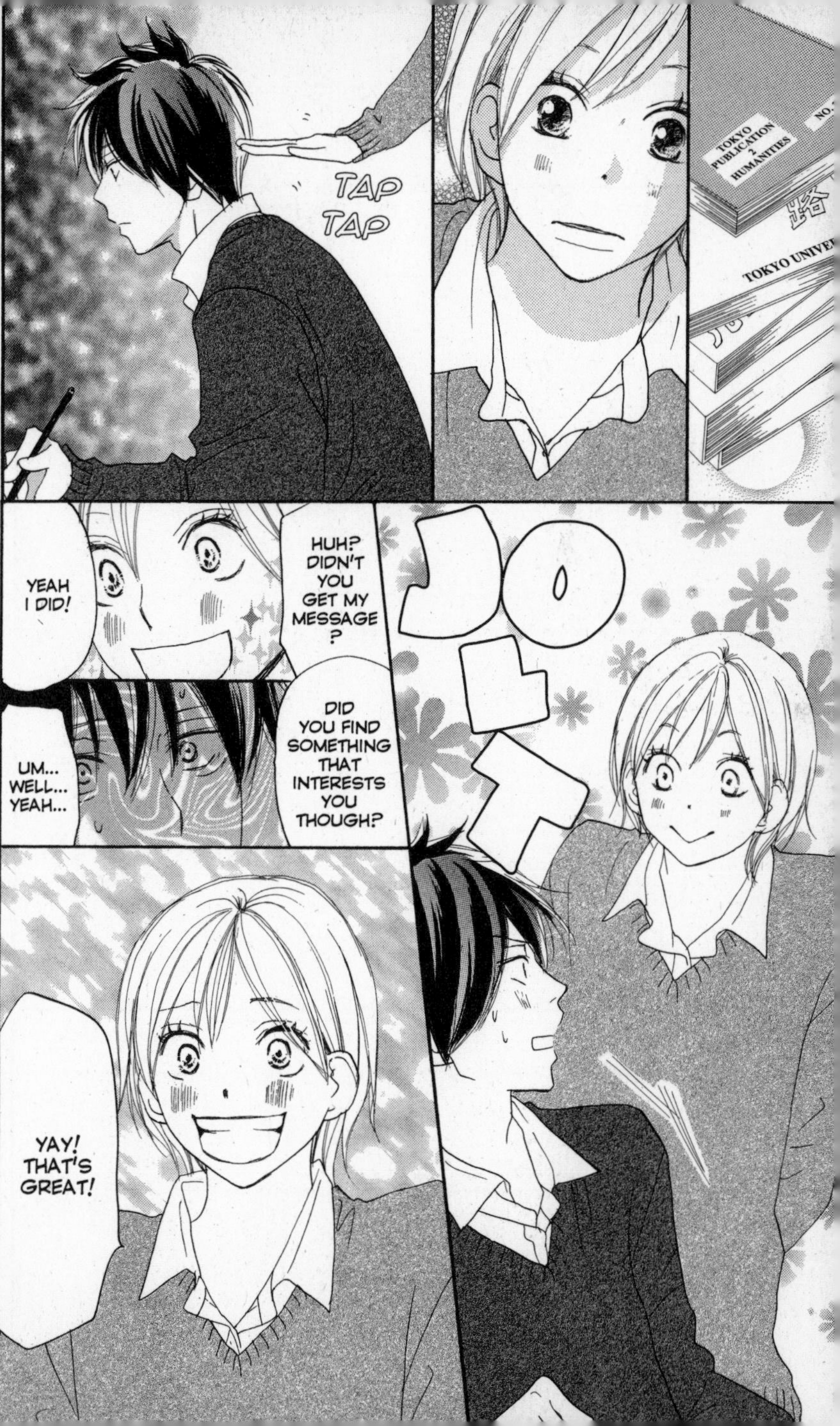
TOKYO PUBLICATION 2 HUMANITIES
TAP TAP
JOLT
HUH? DIDN'T YOU GET MY MESSAGE?
YEAH I DID!
DID YOU FIND SOMETHING THAT INTERESTS YOU THOUGH?
UM... WELL... YEAH...
YAY! THAT'S GREAT!

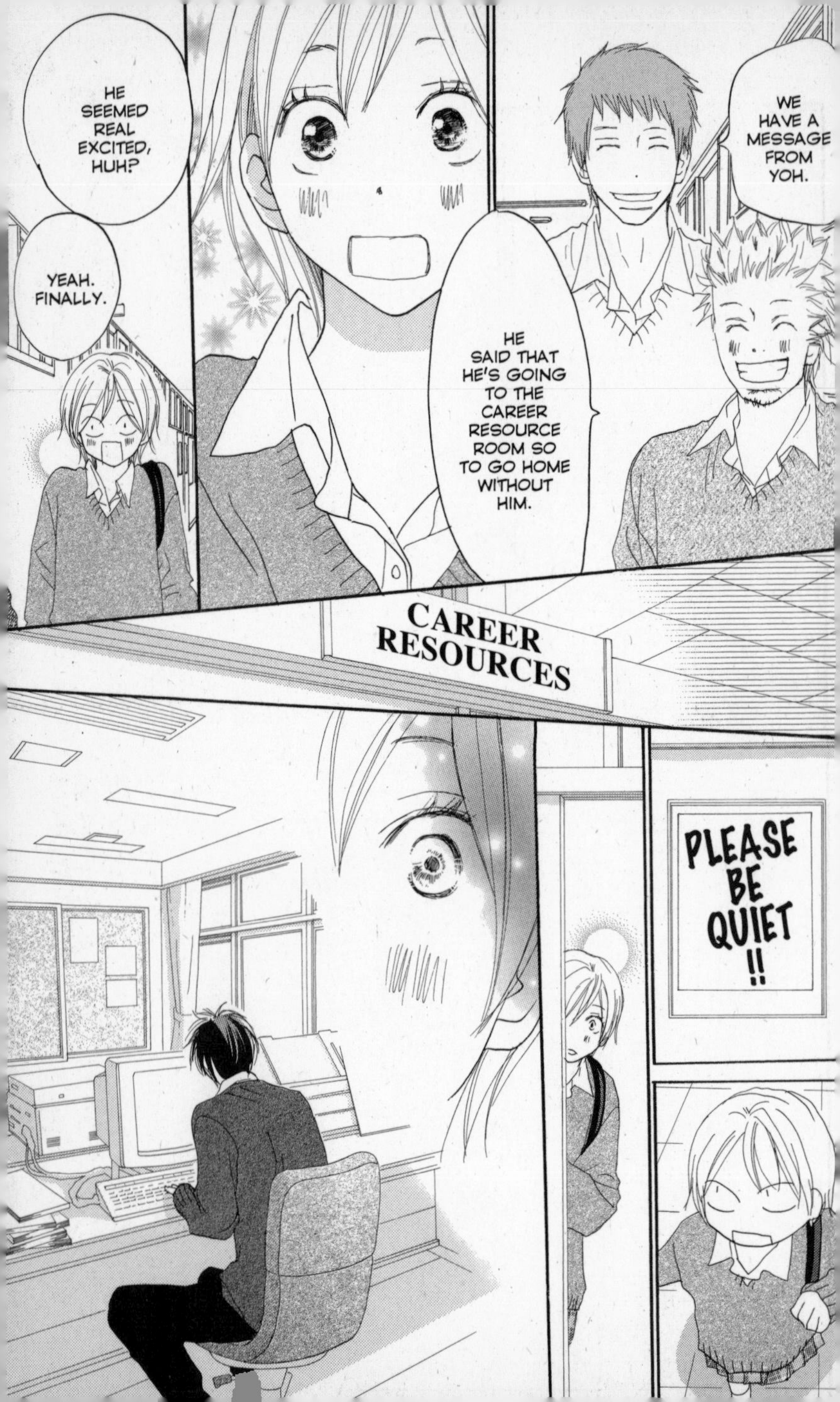
WE HAVE A MESSAGE FROM YOH.
HE SAID THAT HE'S GOING TO THE CAREER RESOURCE ROOM SO TO GO HOME WITHOUT HIM.
HE SEEMED REAL EXCITED, HUH?
YEAH. FINALLY.
CAREER RESOURCES
PLEASE BE QUIET !!

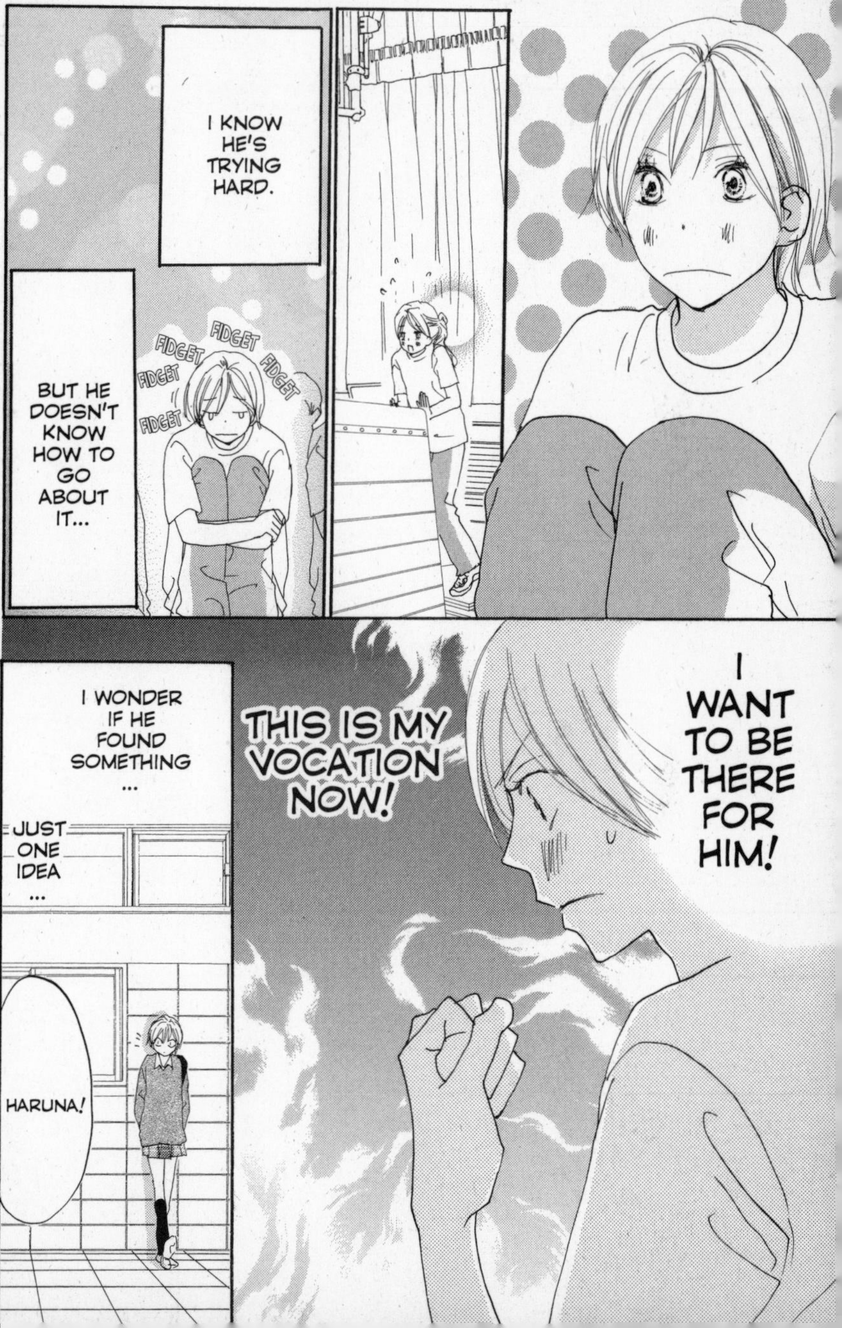
I KNOW HE'S TRYING HARD.
BUT HE DOESN'T KNOW HOW TO GO ABOUT IT...
FIDGET
FIDGET
FIDGET
FIDGET
FIDGET
I WANT TO BE THERE FOR HIM!
THIS IS MY VOCATION NOW!
I WONDER IF HE FOUND SOMETHING ...
JUST ONE IDEA ...
HARUNA!

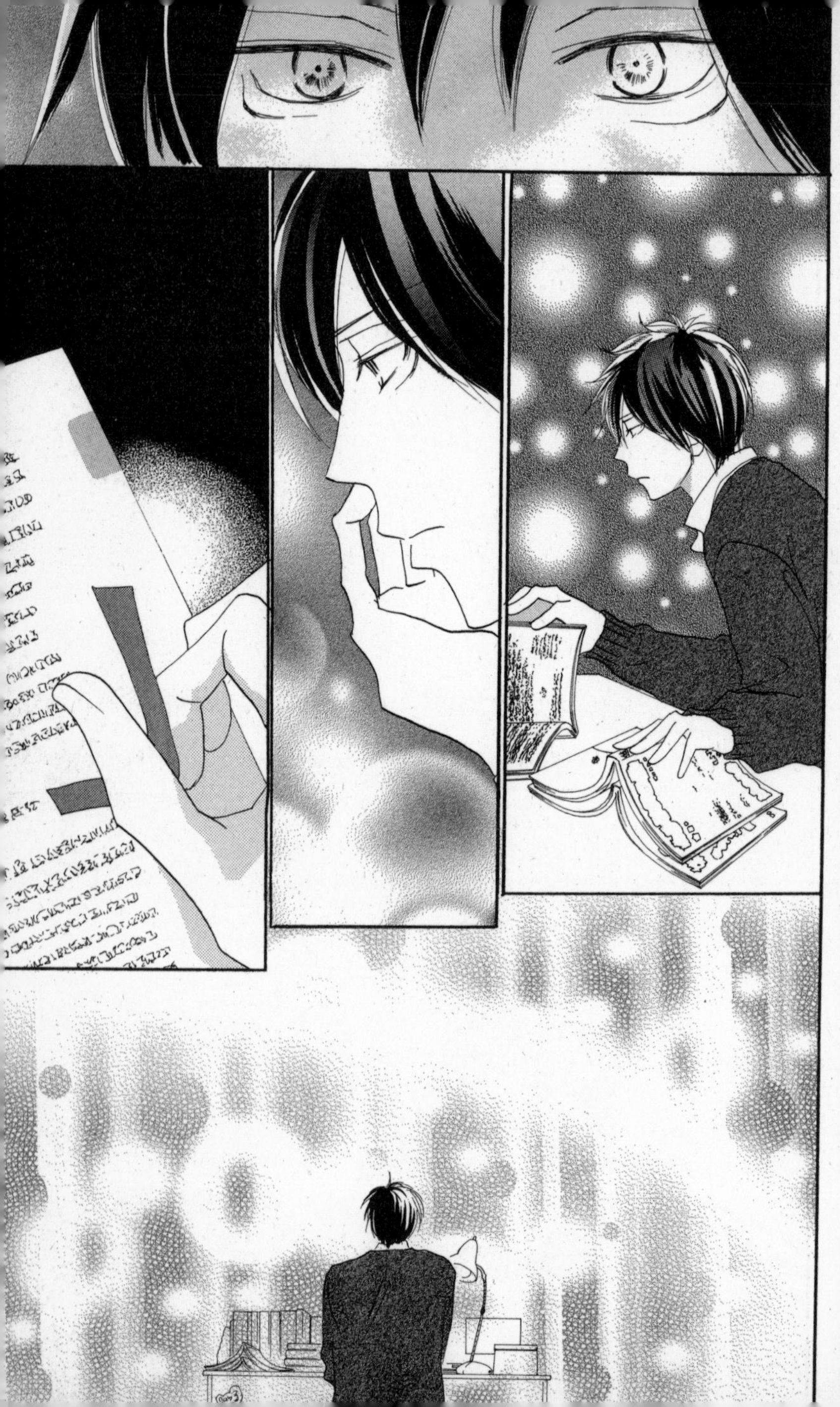

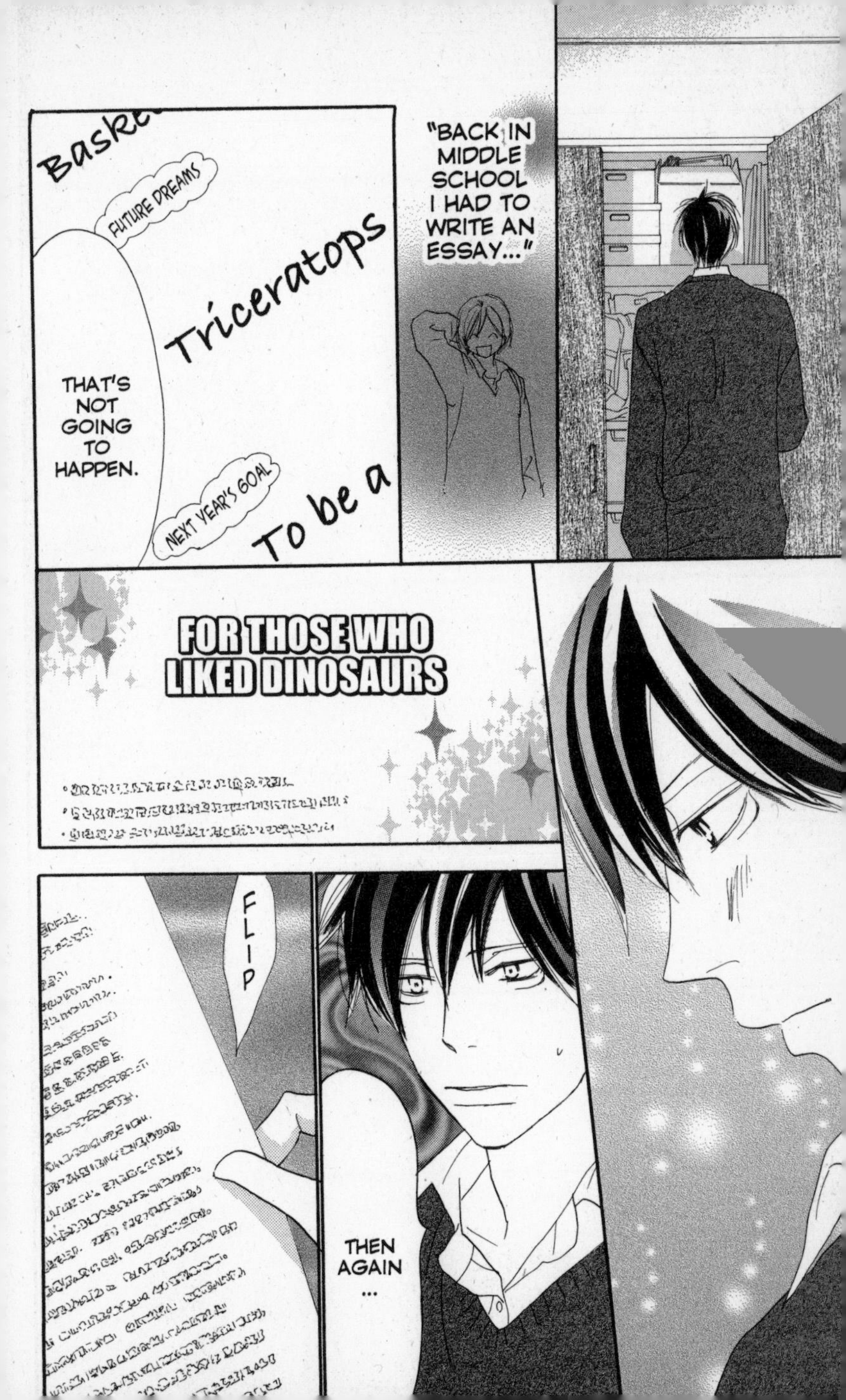
"BACK IN MIDDLE SCHOOL I HAD TO WRITE AN ESSAY..."
FUTURE DREAMS
Baske
Triceratops
To be a
NEXT YEAR'S GOAL
THAT'S NOT GOING TO HAPPEN.
FOR THOSE WHO LIKED DINOSAURS
FLIP
THEN AGAIN ...

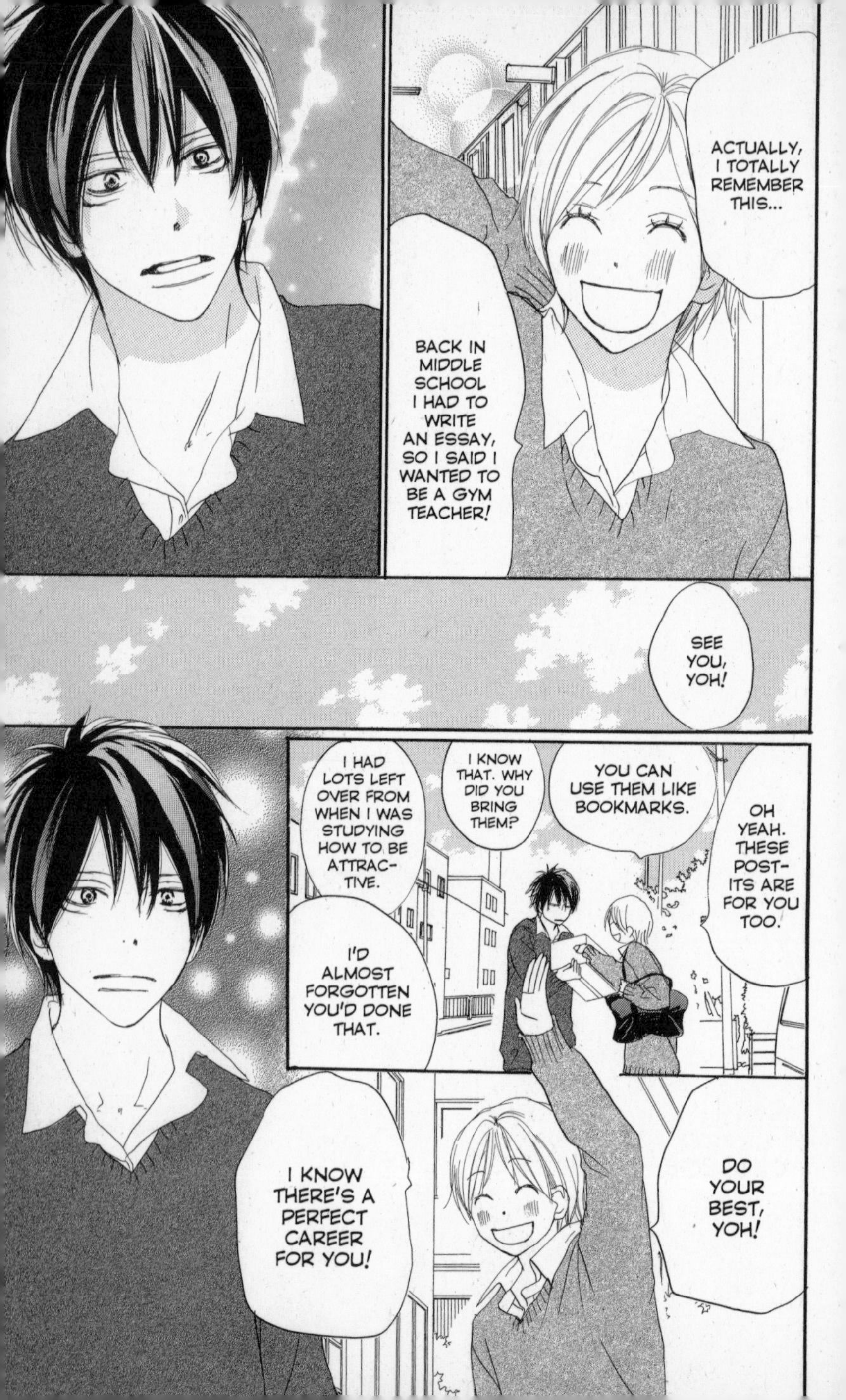
ACTUALLY, I TOTALLY REMEMBER THIS...
BACK IN MIDDLE SCHOOL I HAD TO WRITE AN ESSAY, SO I SAID I WANTED TO BE A GYM TEACHER!
SEE YOU, YOH!
OH YEAH. THESE POST-ITS ARE FOR YOU TOO.
YOU CAN USE THEM LIKE BOOKMARKS.
I KNOW THAT. WHY DID YOU BRING THEM?
I HAD LOTS LEFT OVER FROM WHEN I WAS STUDYING HOW TO BE ATTRACTIVE.
I'D ALMOST FORGOTTEN YOU'D DONE THAT.
DO YOUR BEST, YOH!
I KNOW THERE'S A PERFECT CAREER FOR YOU!

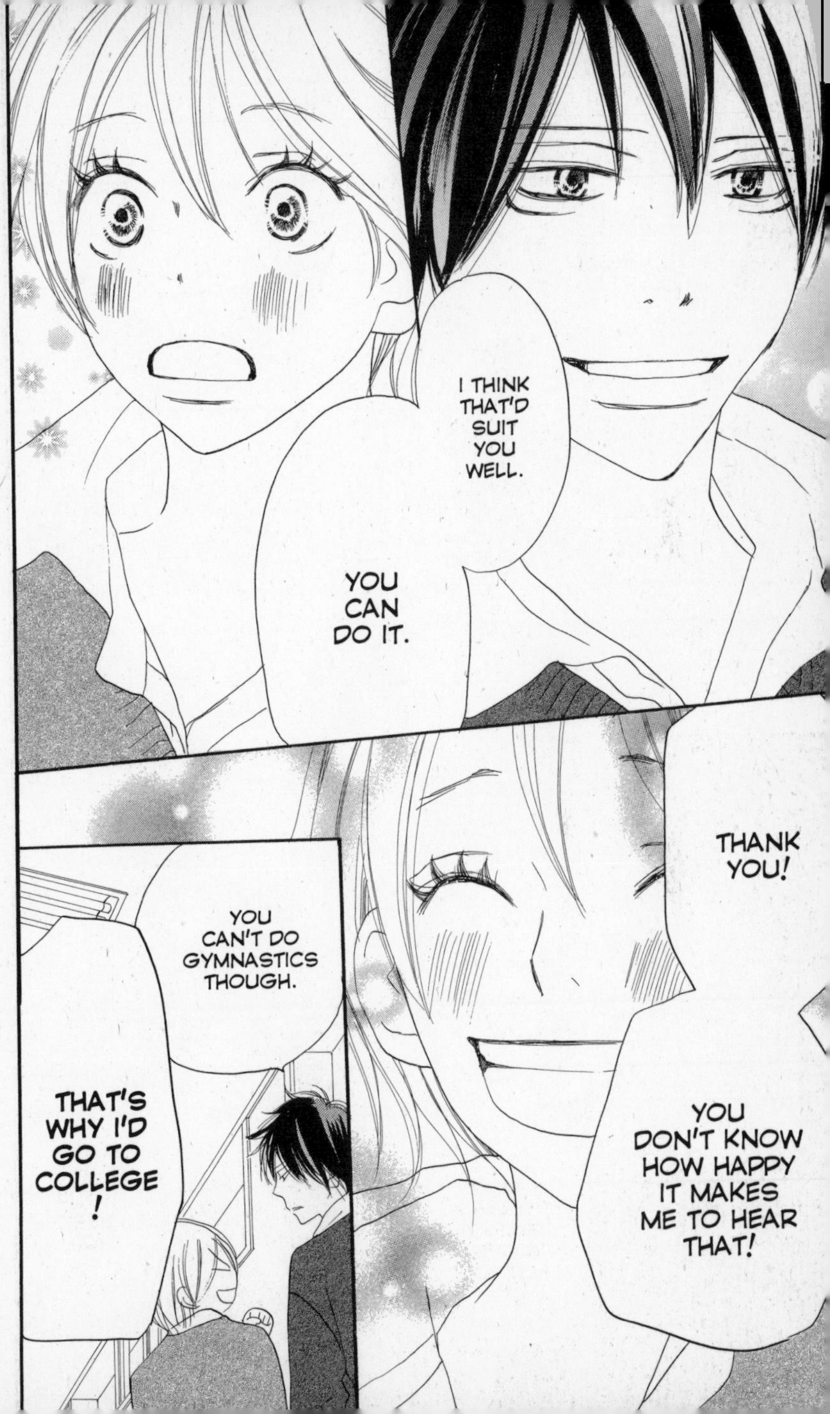
I THINK THAT'D SUIT YOU WELL.
YOU CAN DO IT.
THANK YOU!
YOU DON'T KNOW HOW HAPPY IT MAKES ME TO HEAR THAT!
YOU CAN'T DO GYMNASTICS THOUGH.
THAT'S WHY I'D GO TO COLLEGE!

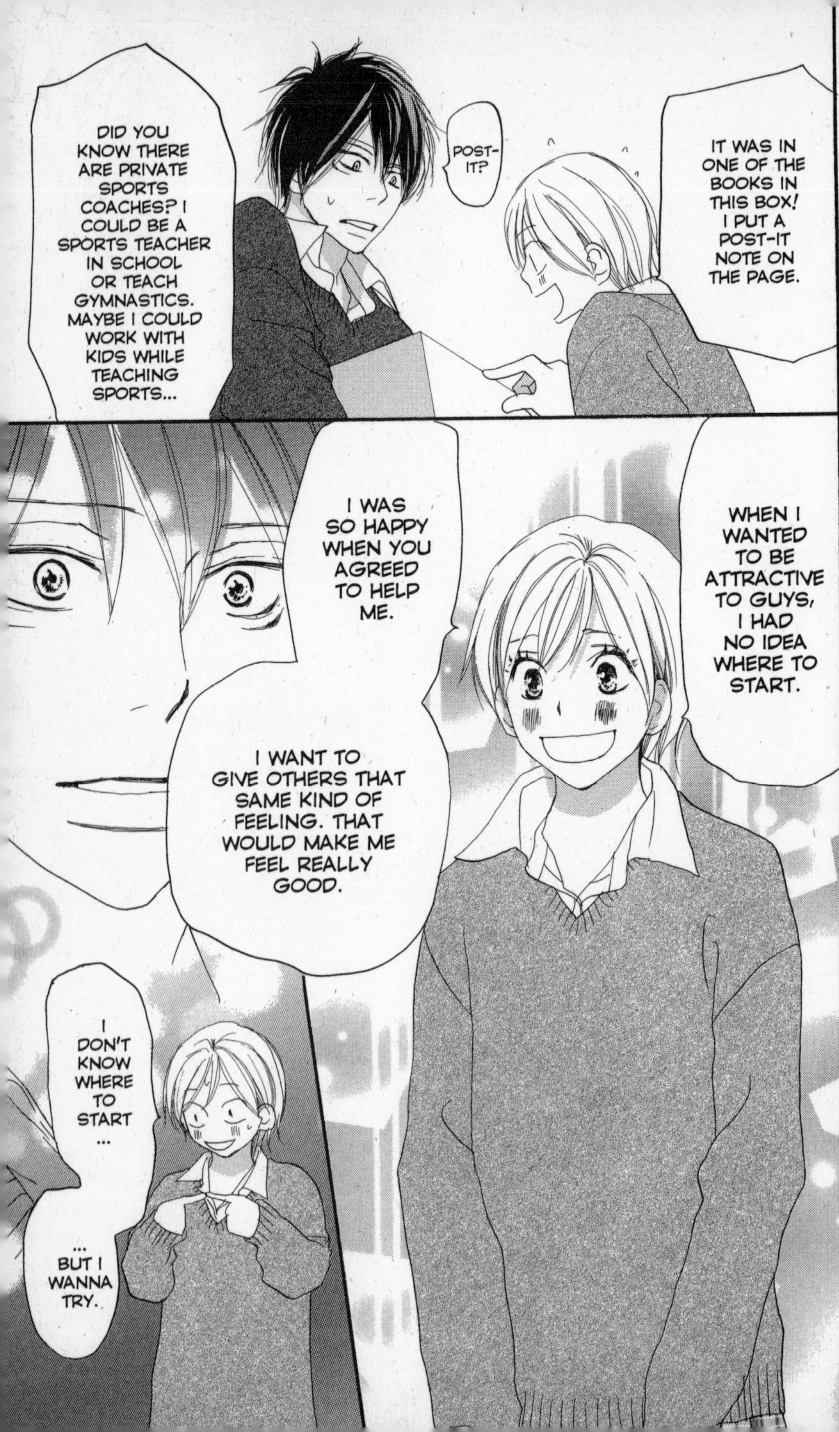
IT WAS IN ONE OF THE BOOKS IN THIS BOX! I PUT A POST-IT NOTE ON THE PAGE.
POST-IT?
DID YOU KNOW THERE ARE PRIVATE SPORTS COACHES? I COULD BE A SPORTS TEACHER IN SCHOOL OR TEACH GYMNASTICS. MAYBE I COULD WORK WITH KIDS WHILE TEACHING SPORTS...
WHEN I WANTED TO BE ATTRACTIVE TO GUYS, I HAD NO IDEA WHERE TO START.
I WAS SO HAPPY WHEN YOU AGREED TO HELP ME.
I WANT TO GIVE OTHERS THAT SAME KIND OF FEELING. THAT WOULD MAKE ME FEEL REALLY GOOD.
I DON'T KNOW WHERE TO START ...
... BUT I WANNA TRY.

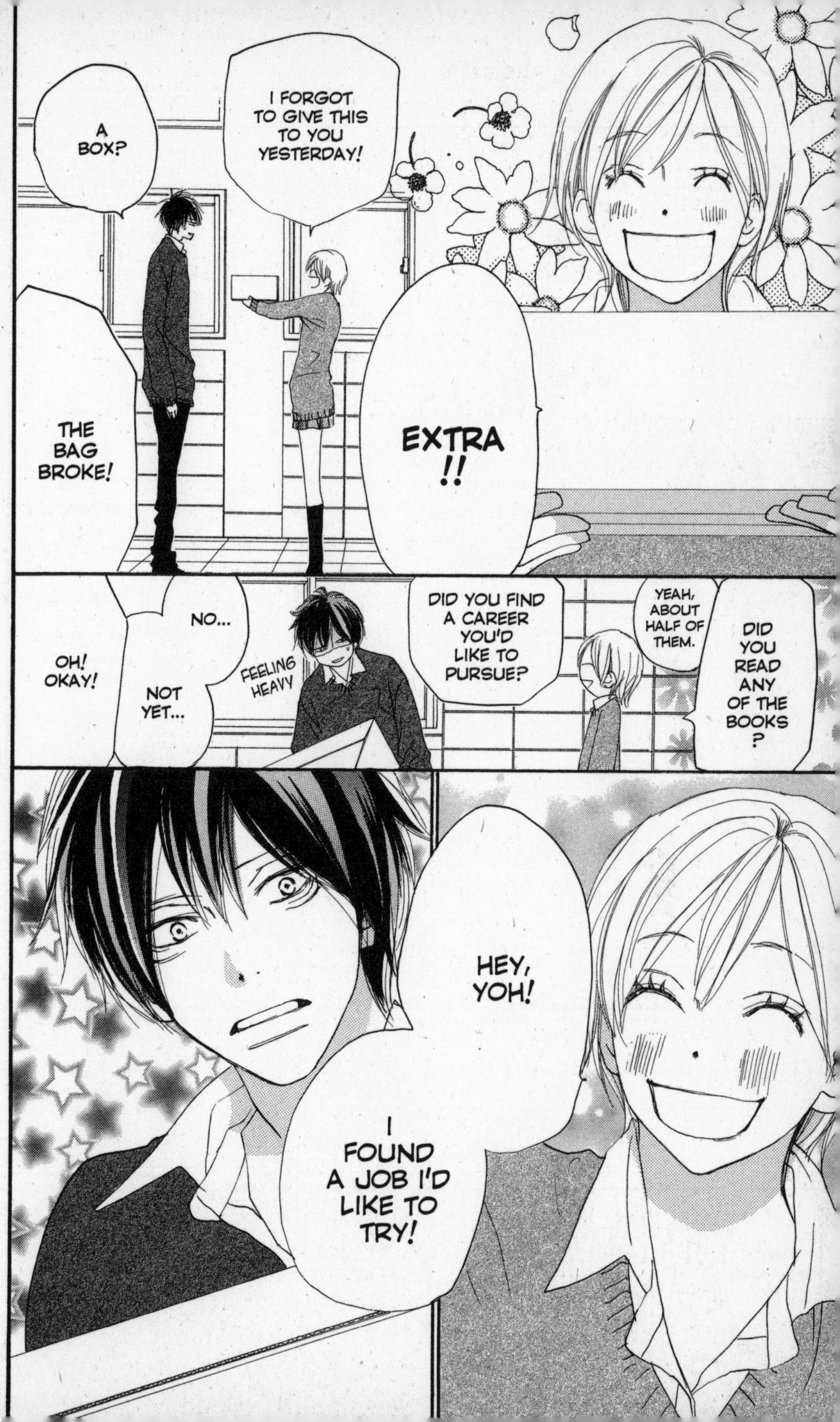
EXTRA !!
I FORGOT TO GIVE THIS TO YOU YESTERDAY!
A BOX?
THE BAG BROKE!
DID YOU READ ANY OF THE BOOKS?
YEAH, ABOUT HALF OF THEM.
DID YOU FIND A CAREER YOU'D LIKE TO PURSUE?
FEELING HEAVY
NO...
NOT YET...
OH! OKAY!
HEY, YOH!
I FOUND A JOB I'D LIKE TO TRY!

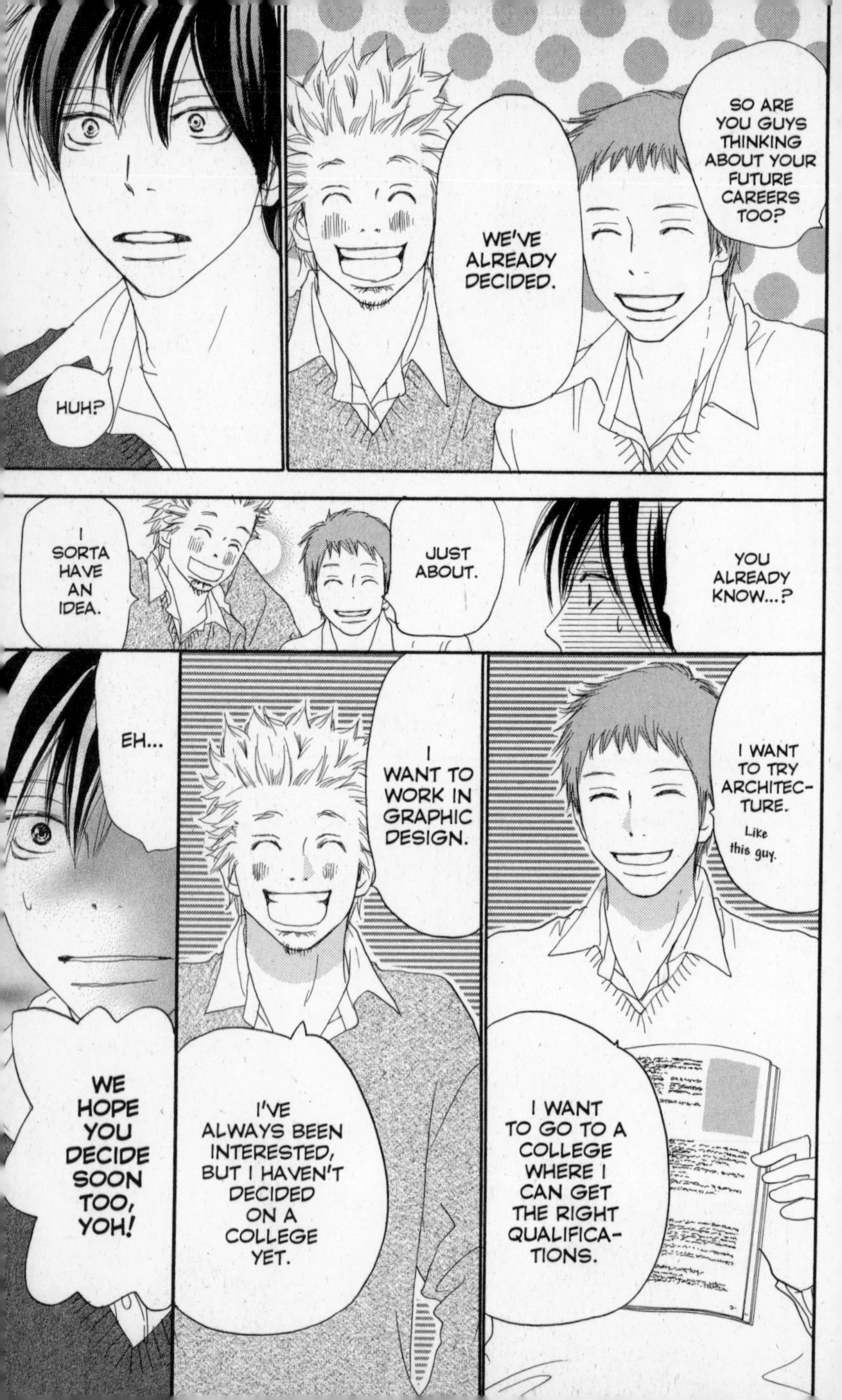
SO ARE YOU GUYS THINKING ABOUT YOUR FUTURE CAREERS TOO?
WE'VE ALREADY DECIDED.
HUH?
YOU ALREADY KNOW...?
JUST ABOUT.
I SORTA HAVE AN IDEA.
I WANT TO TRY ARCHITEC-TURE.
Like this guy.
I WANT TO GO TO A COLLEGE WHERE I CAN GET THE RIGHT QUALIFICA-TIONS.
I WANT TO WORK IN GRAPHIC DESIGN.
I'VE ALWAYS BEEN INTERESTED, BUT I HAVEN'T DECIDED ON A COLLEGE YET.
EH...
WE HOPE YOU DECIDE SOON TOO, YOH!

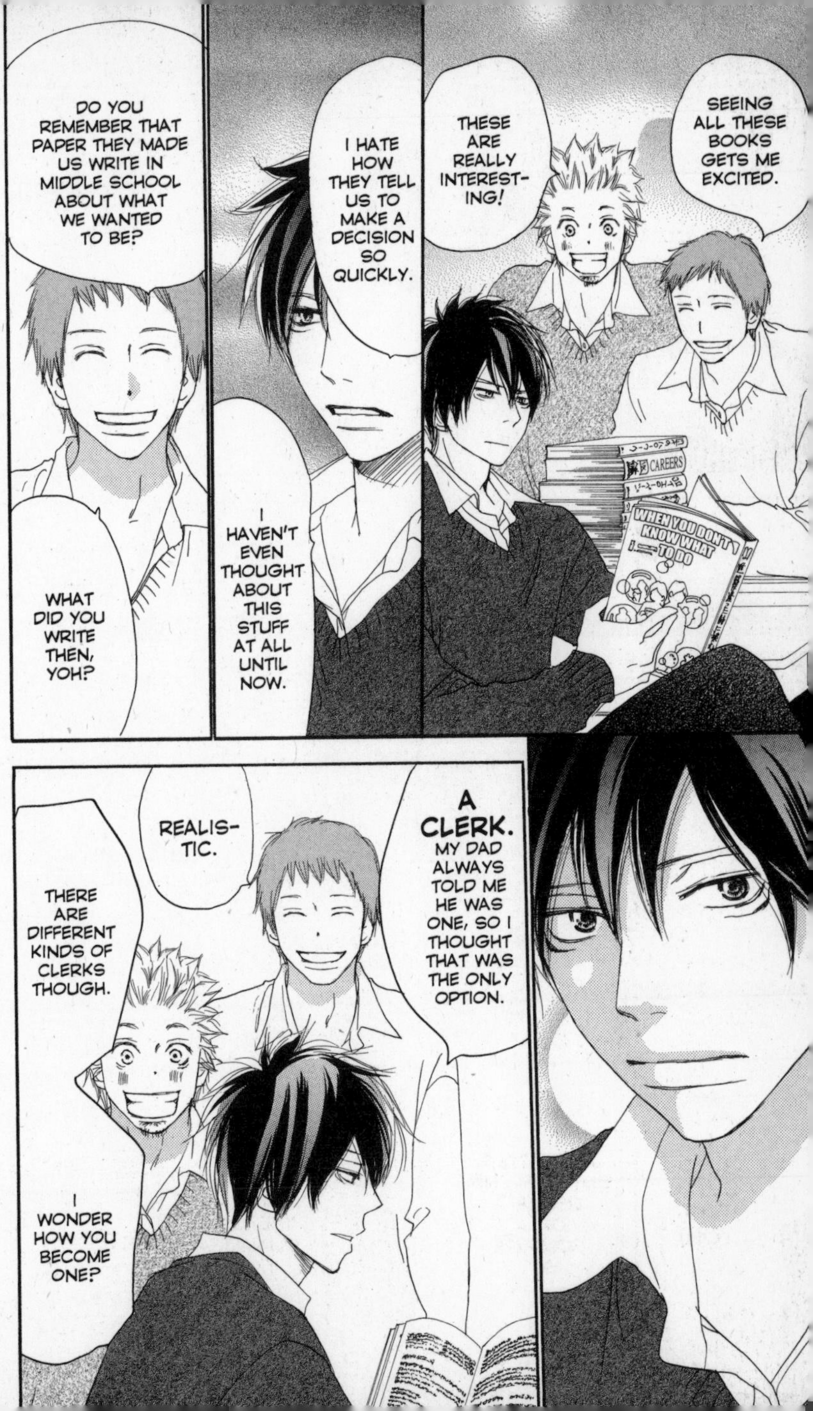
SEEING ALL THESE BOOKS GETS ME EXCITED.
THESE ARE REALLY INTEREST-ING!
CAREERS
WHEN YOU DON'T KNOW WHAT TO DO
I HATE HOW THEY TELL US TO MAKE A DECISION SO QUICKLY.
I HAVEN'T EVEN THOUGHT ABOUT THIS STUFF AT ALL UNTIL NOW.
DO YOU REMEMBER THAT PAPER THEY MADE US WRITE IN MIDDLE SCHOOL ABOUT WHAT WE WANTED TO BE?
WHAT DID YOU WRITE THEN, YOH?
A CLERK. MY DAD ALWAYS TOLD ME HE WAS ONE, SO I THOUGHT THAT WAS THE ONLY OPTION.
REALIS-TIC.
THERE ARE DIFFERENT KINDS OF CLERKS THOUGH.
I WONDER HOW YOU BECOME ONE?

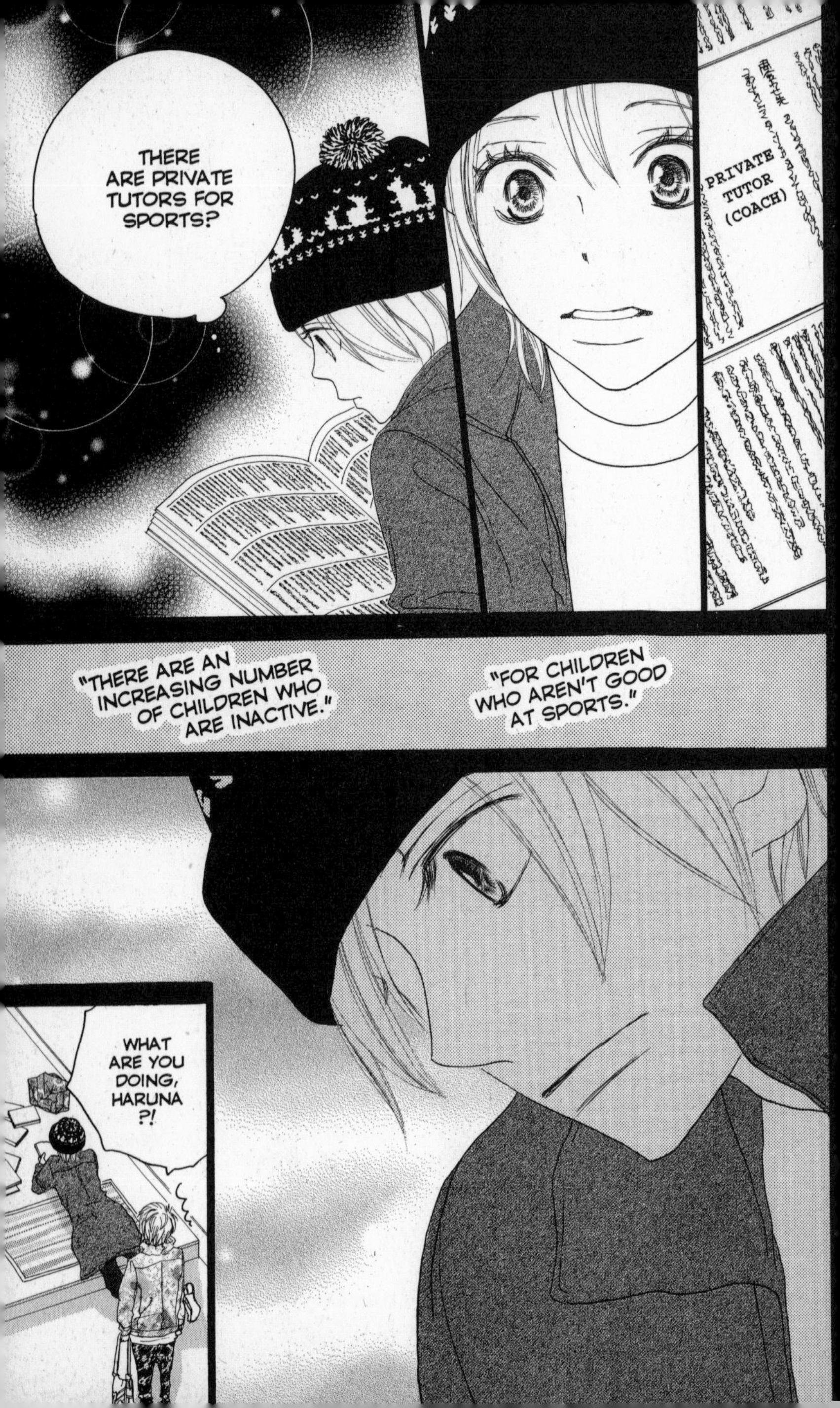
PRIVATE TUTOR (COACH)
THERE ARE PRIVATE TUTORS FOR SPORTS?
"FOR CHILDREN WHO AREN'T GOOD AT SPORTS."
"THERE ARE AN INCREASING NUMBER OF CHILDREN WHO ARE INACTIVE."
WHAT ARE YOU DOING, HARUNA ?!

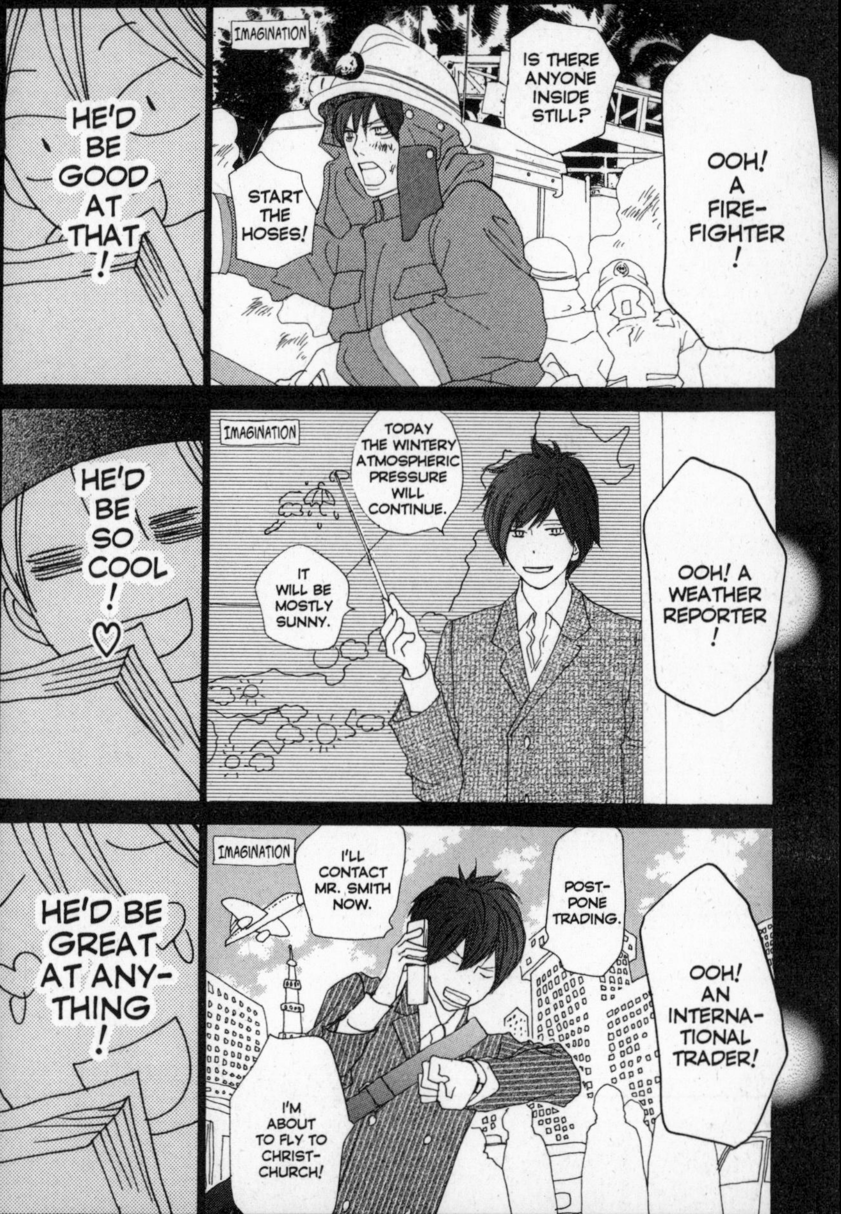
OOH! A FIREFIGHTER!
IS THERE ANYONE INSIDE STILL?
IMAGINATION
START THE HOSES!
HE'D BE GOOD AT THAT!
OOH! A WEATHER REPORTER!
TODAY THE WINTERY ATMOSPHERIC PRESSURE WILL CONTINUE.
IMAGINATION
IT WILL BE MOSTLY SUNNY.
HE'D BE SO COOL! ♡
OOH! AN INTERNATIONAL TRADER!
POSTPONE TRADING.
I'LL CONTACT MR. SMITH NOW.
IMAGINATION
I'M ABOUT TO FLY TO CHRISTCHURCH!
HE'D BE GREAT AT ANYTHING!

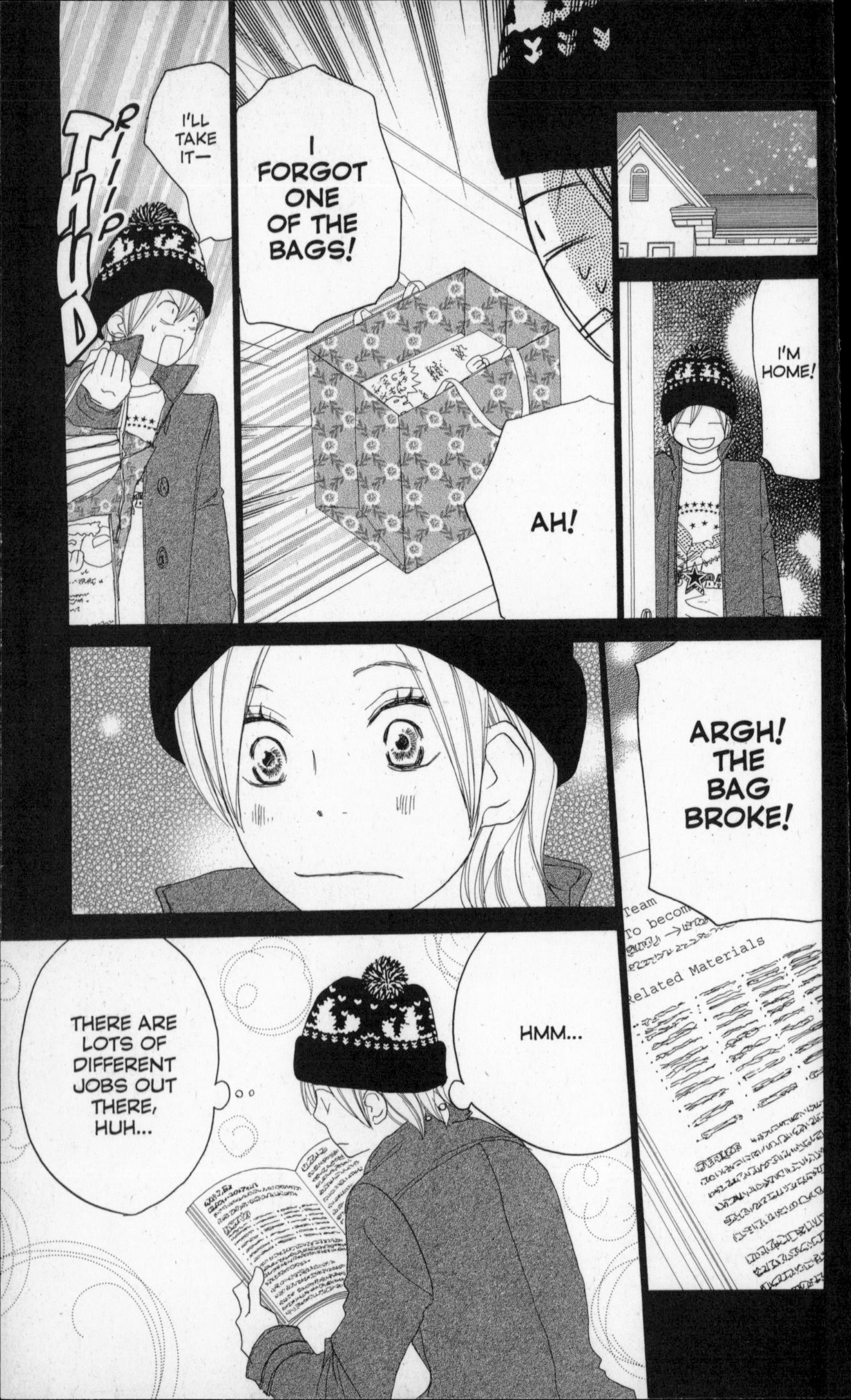
I'M HOME!
AH!
I FORGOT ONE OF THE BAGS!
I'LL TAKE IT—
RIIIP
THUD
ARGH! THE BAG BROKE!
Team
To becom
Related Materials
HMM...
THERE ARE LOTS OF DIFFERENT JOBS OUT THERE, HUH...

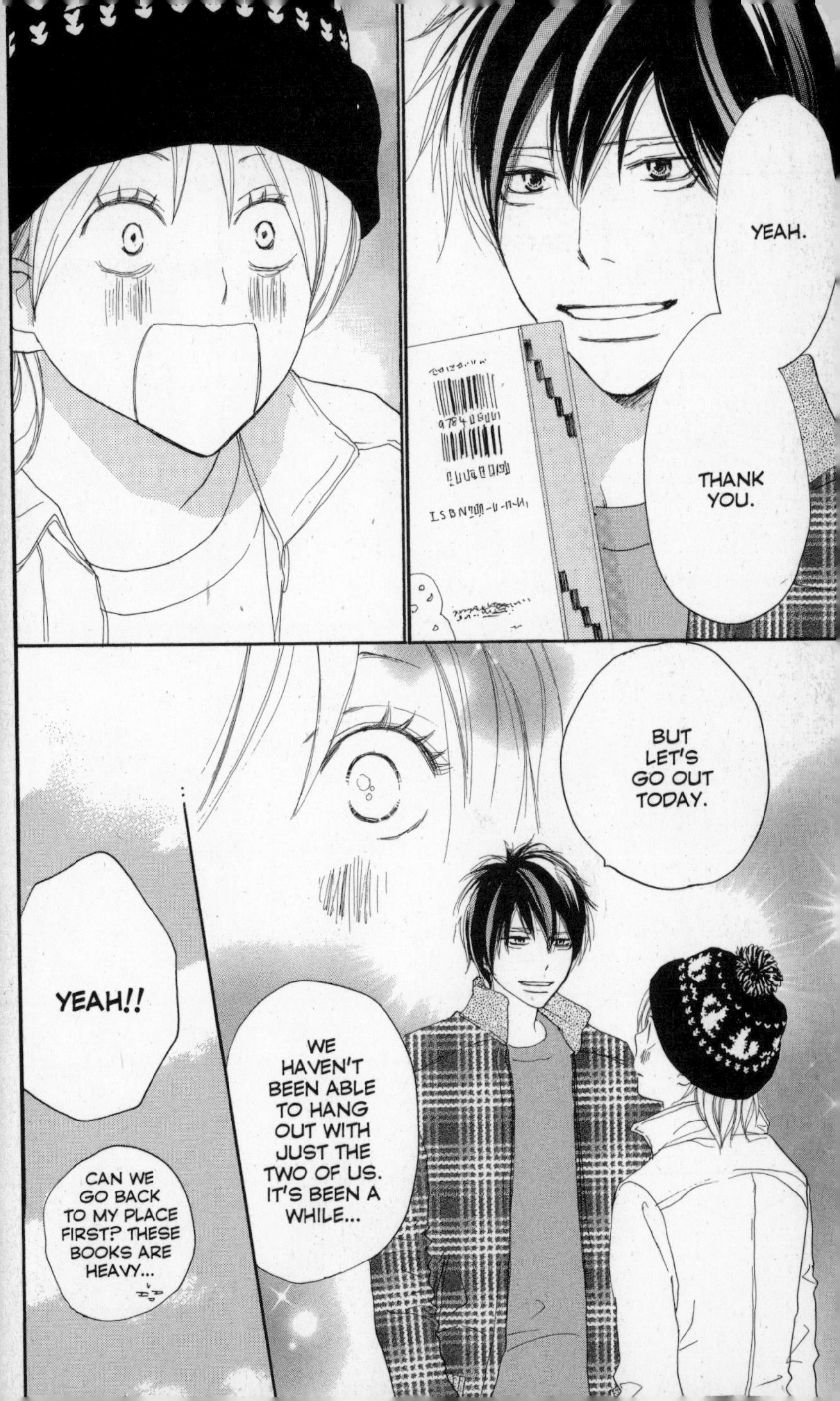
YEAH.
THANK YOU.
BUT LET'S GO OUT TODAY.
WE HAVEN'T BEEN ABLE TO HANG OUT WITH JUST THE TWO OF US. IT'S BEEN A WHILE...
YEAH!!
CAN WE GO BACK TO MY PLACE FIRST? THESE BOOKS ARE HEAVY...

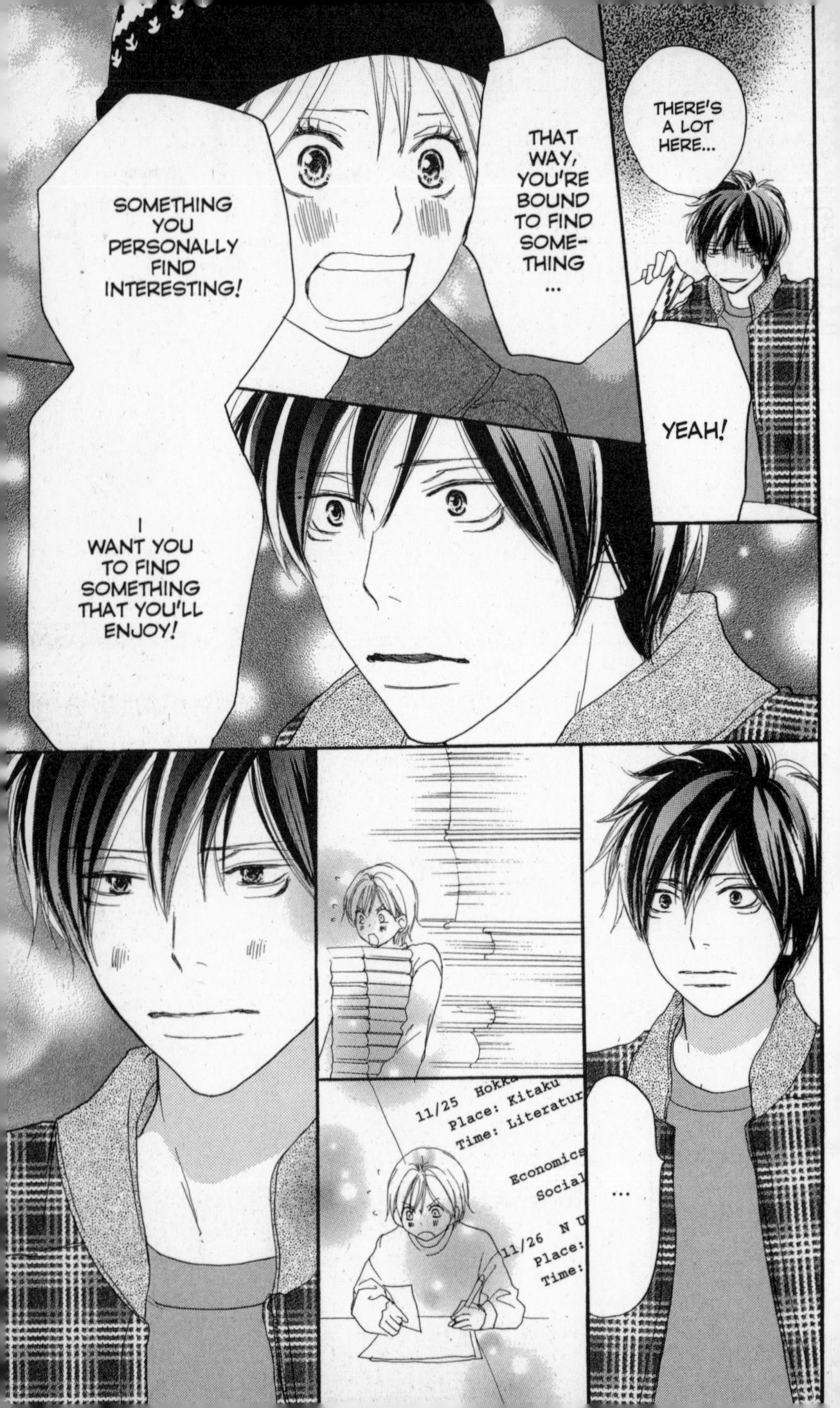
THERE'S A LOT HERE...
YEAH!
THAT WAY, YOU'RE BOUND TO FIND SOME-THING ...
SOMETHING YOU PERSONALLY FIND INTERESTING!
I WANT YOU TO FIND SOMETHING THAT YOU'LL ENJOY!
...
11/25 Hokka
Place: Kitaku
Time: Literatur
Economics
Social
11/26 N U
Place:
Time:

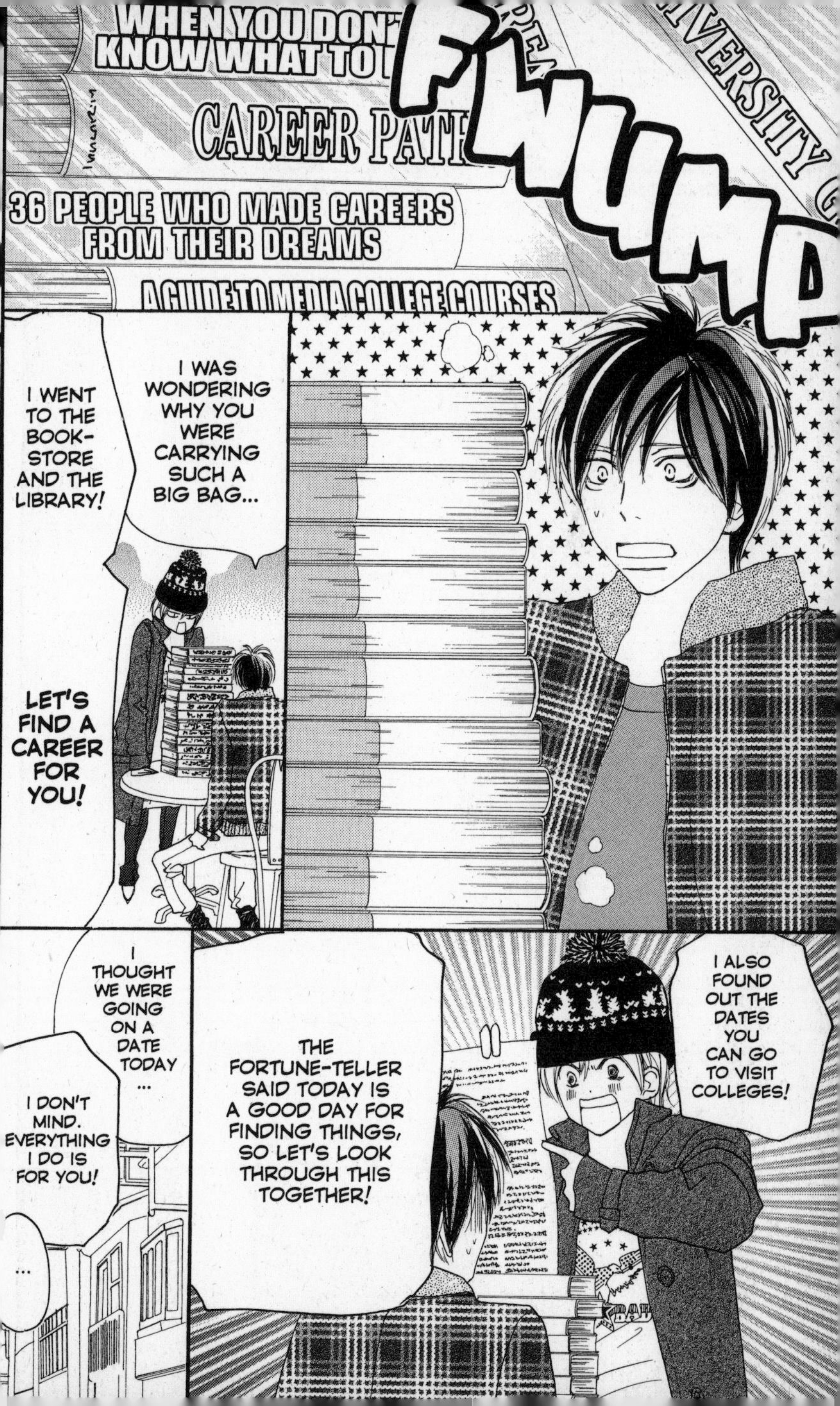

UNIVERSITY G
FWUMP
WHEN YOU DON'T KNOW WHAT TO
CAREER PATH
36 PEOPLE WHO MADE CAREERS FROM THEIR DREAMS
A GUIDE TO MEDIA COLLEGE COURSES
I WAS WONDERING WHY YOU WERE CARRYING SUCH A BIG BAG...
I WENT TO THE BOOK-STORE AND THE LIBRARY!
LET'S FIND A CAREER FOR YOU!
I ALSO FOUND OUT THE DATES YOU CAN GO TO VISIT COLLEGES!
THE FORTUNE-TELLER SAID TODAY IS A GOOD DAY FOR FINDING THINGS, SO LET'S LOOK THROUGH THIS TOGETHER!
I THOUGHT WE WERE GOING ON A DATE TODAY...
I DON'T MIND. EVERYTHING I DO IS FOR YOU!
...

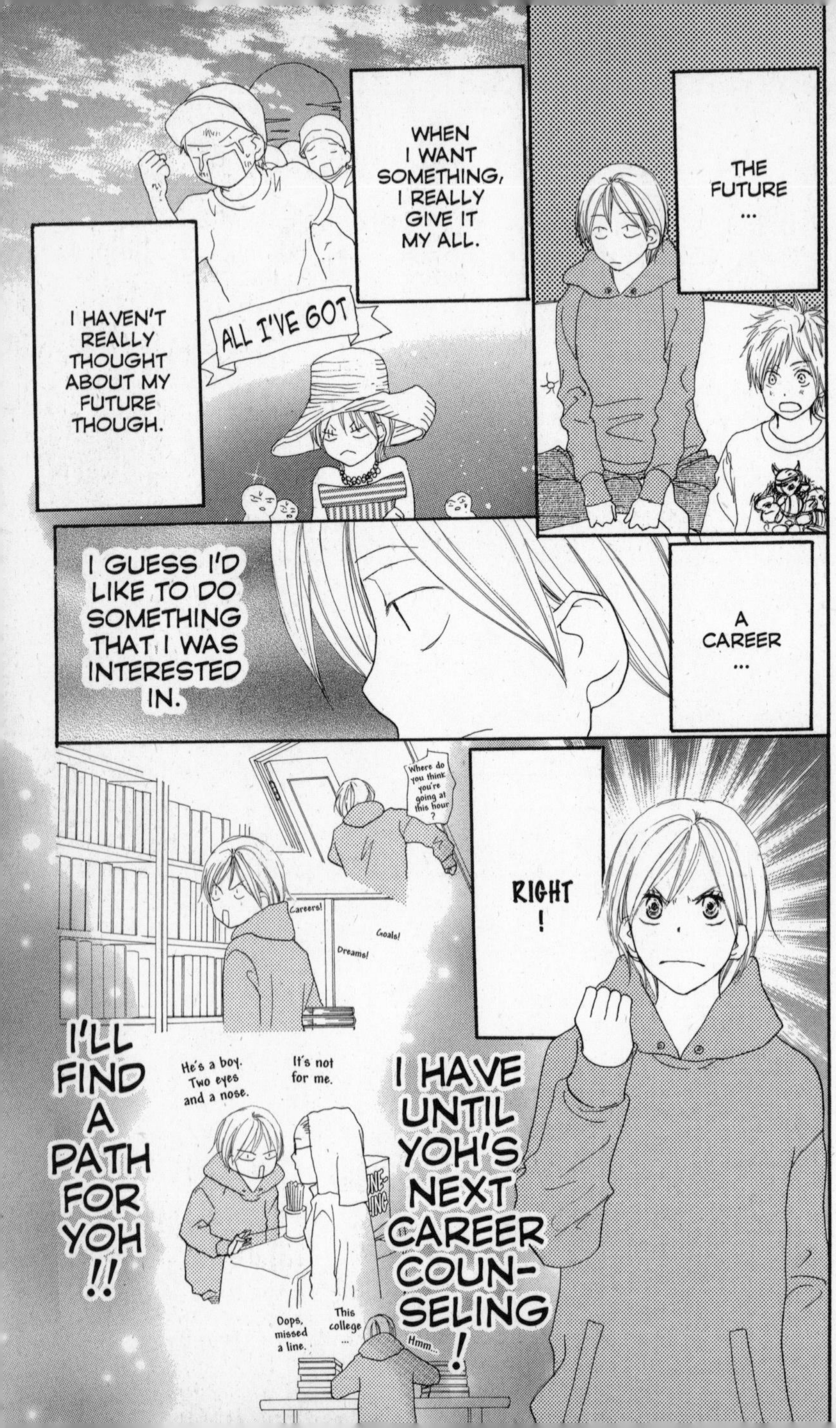

THE FUTURE ...
WHEN I WANT SOMETHING, I REALLY GIVE IT MY ALL.
ALL I'VE GOT
I HAVEN'T REALLY THOUGHT ABOUT MY FUTURE THOUGH.
A CAREER ...
I GUESS I'D LIKE TO DO SOMETHING THAT I WAS INTERESTED IN.
RIGHT !
I HAVE UNTIL YOH'S NEXT CAREER COUN-SELING !
Where do you think you're going at this hour ?
Careers!
Goals!
Dreams!
It's not for me.
He's a boy. Two eyes and a nose.
I'LL FIND A PATH FOR YOH !!
This college ...
Oops, missed a line.
Hmm...

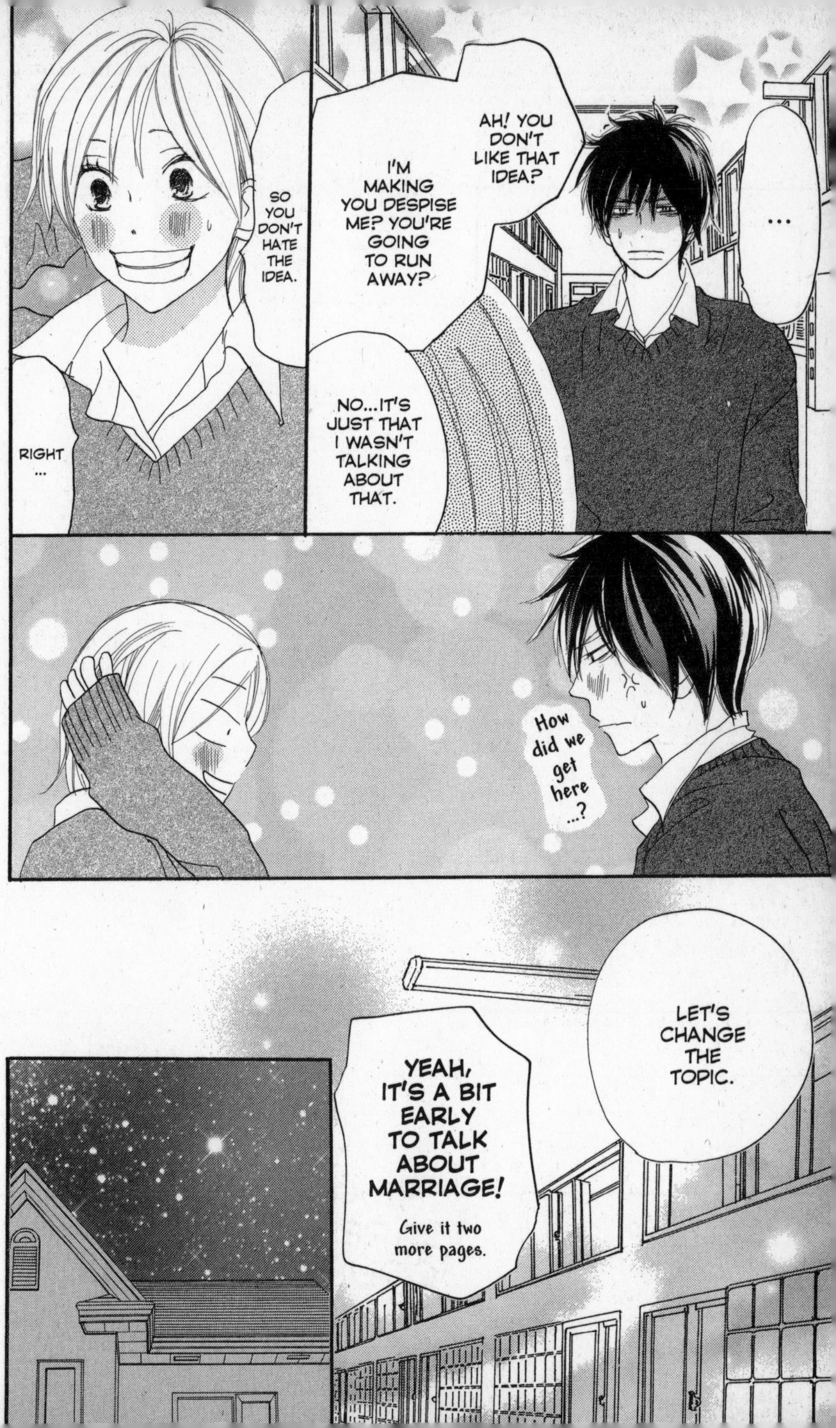
...
AH! YOU DON'T LIKE THAT IDEA?
I'M MAKING YOU DESPISE ME? YOU'RE GOING TO RUN AWAY?
NO...IT'S JUST THAT I WASN'T TALKING ABOUT THAT.
SO YOU DON'T HATE THE IDEA.
RIGHT ...
How did we get here ...?
LET'S CHANGE THE TOPIC.
YEAH, IT'S A BIT EARLY TO TALK ABOUT MARRIAGE!
Give it two more pages.

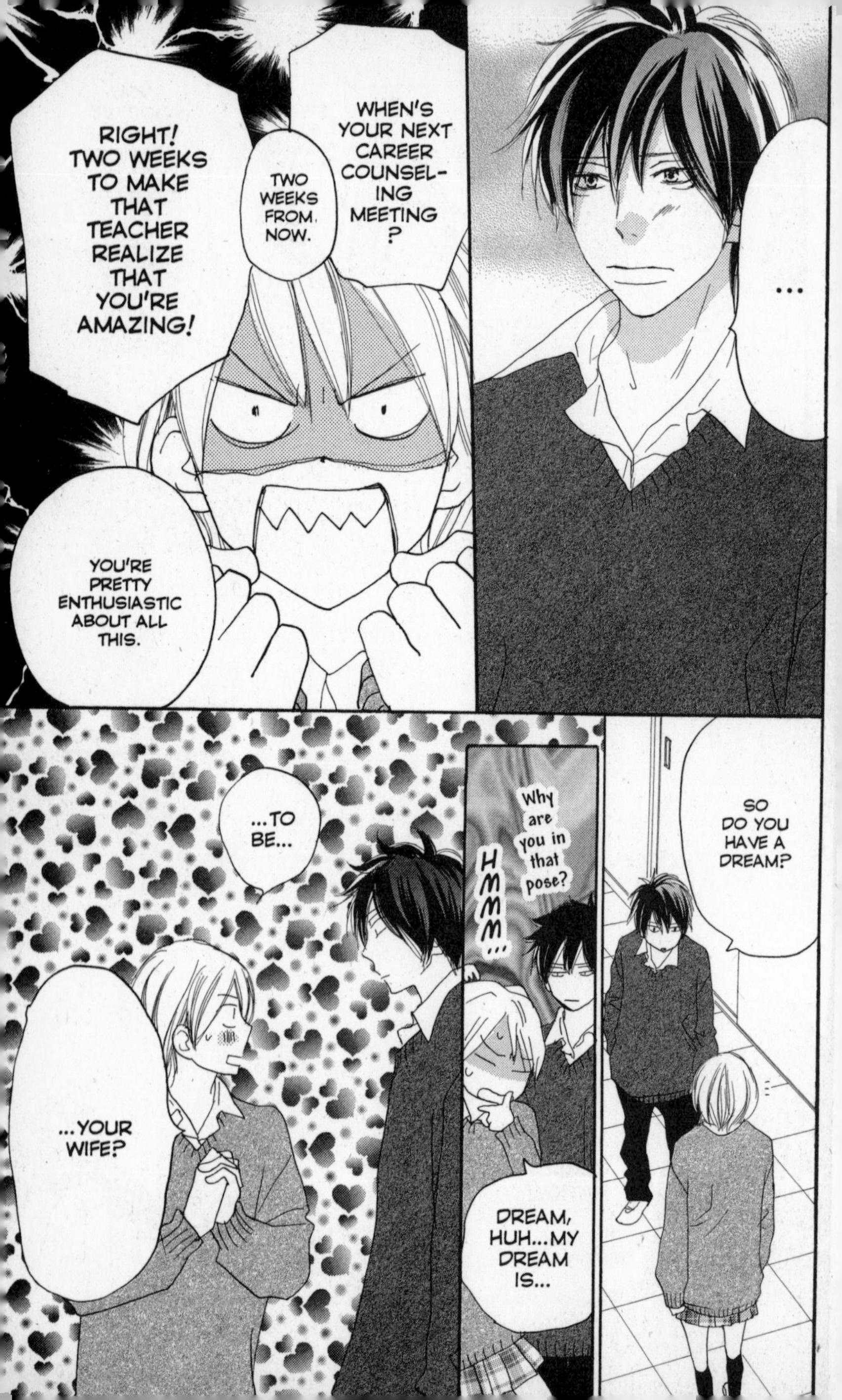

...
WHEN'S YOUR NEXT CAREER COUNSEL-ING MEETING?
TWO WEEKS FROM NOW.
RIGHT! TWO WEEKS TO MAKE THAT TEACHER REALIZE THAT YOU'RE AMAZING!
YOU'RE PRETTY ENTHUSIASTIC ABOUT ALL THIS.
SO DO YOU HAVE A DREAM?
Why are you in that pose?
HMMM...
DREAM, HUH...MY DREAM IS...
...TO BE...
...YOUR WIFE?

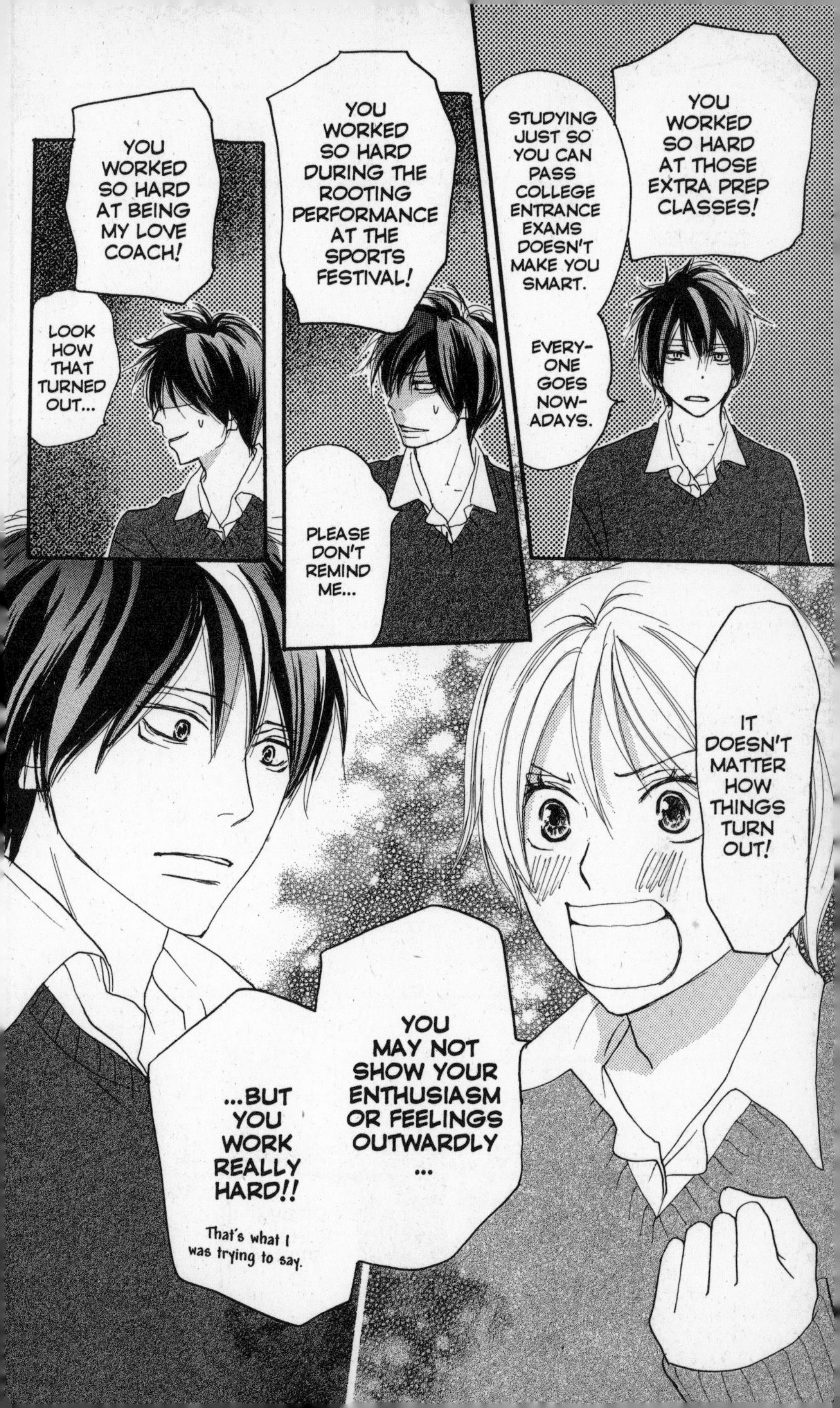
YOU WORKED SO HARD AT THOSE EXTRA PREP CLASSES!
STUDYING JUST SO YOU CAN PASS COLLEGE ENTRANCE EXAMS DOESN'T MAKE YOU SMART.
EVERY-ONE GOES NOW-ADAYS.
YOU WORKED SO HARD DURING THE ROOTING PERFORMANCE AT THE SPORTS FESTIVAL!
PLEASE DON'T REMIND ME...
YOU WORKED SO HARD AT BEING MY LOVE COACH!
LOOK HOW THAT TURNED OUT...
IT DOESN'T MATTER HOW THINGS TURN OUT!
YOU MAY NOT SHOW YOUR ENTHUSIASM OR FEELINGS OUTWARDLY ...
...BUT YOU WORK REALLY HARD!!
That's what I was trying to say.

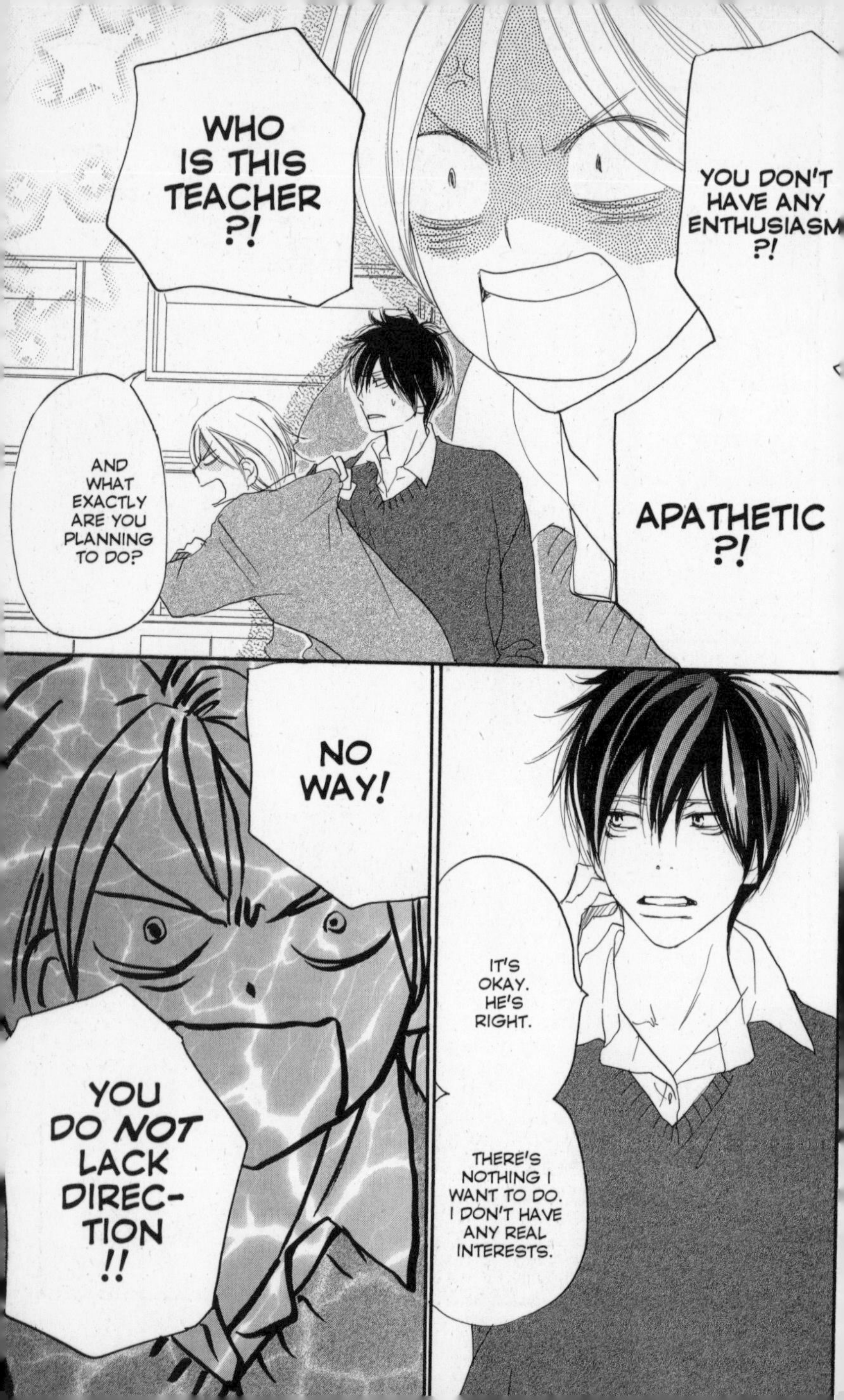
YOU DON'T HAVE ANY ENTHUSIASM?!
APATHETIC?!
WHO IS THIS TEACHER?!
AND WHAT EXACTLY ARE YOU PLANNING TO DO?
IT'S OKAY. HE'S RIGHT.
THERE'S NOTHING I WANT TO DO. I DON'T HAVE ANY REAL INTERESTS.
NO WAY!
YOU DO *NOT* LACK DIRECTION!!

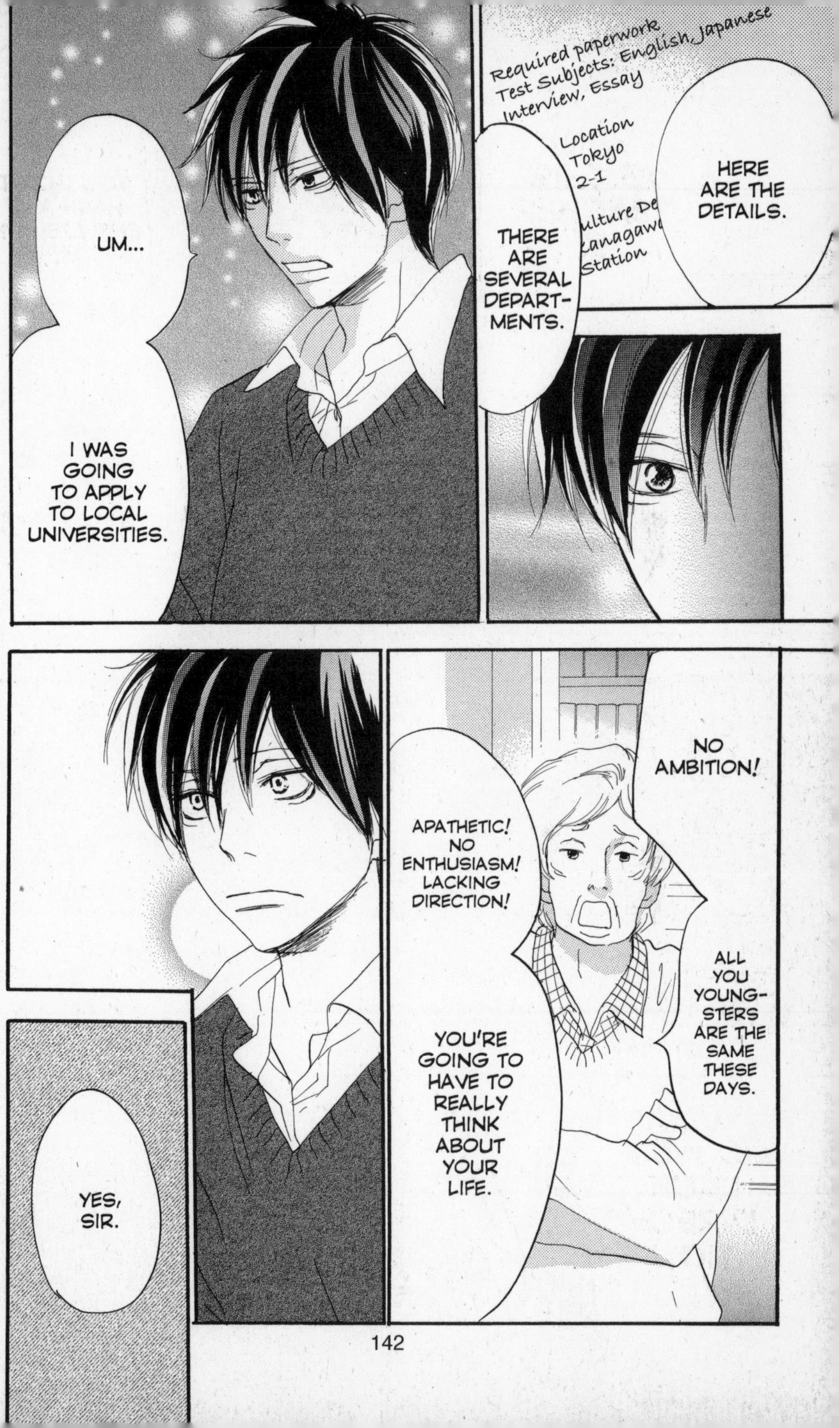

Required paperwork
Test Subjects: English, Japanese
Interview, Essay
Location
Tokyo
2-1
ulture De
anagaw
Station
HERE ARE THE DETAILS.
THERE ARE SEVERAL DEPART-MENTS.
UM...
I WAS GOING TO APPLY TO LOCAL UNIVERSITIES.
NO AMBITION!
APATHETIC! NO ENTHUSIASM! LACKING DIRECTION!
ALL YOU YOUNG-STERS ARE THE SAME THESE DAYS.
YOU'RE GOING TO HAVE TO REALLY THINK ABOUT YOUR LIFE.
YES, SIR.

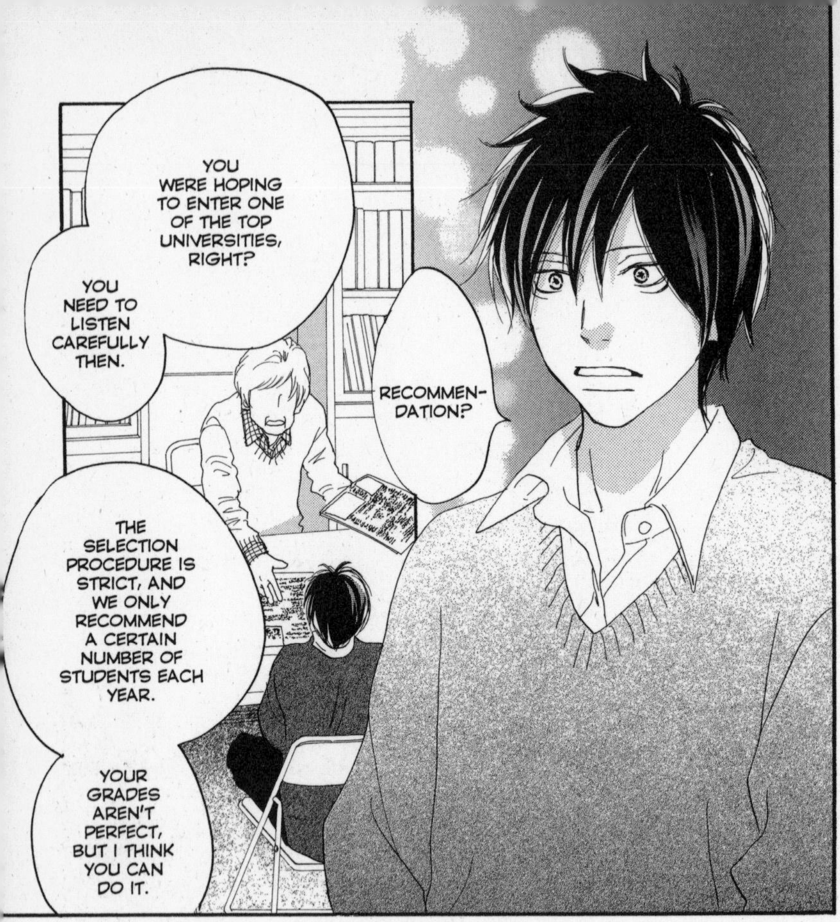
RECOMMEN-DATION?
YOU WERE HOPING TO ENTER ONE OF THE TOP UNIVERSITIES, RIGHT?
YOU NEED TO LISTEN CAREFULLY THEN.
THE SELECTION PROCEDURE IS STRICT, AND WE ONLY RECOMMEND A CERTAIN NUMBER OF STUDENTS EACH YEAR.
YOUR GRADES AREN'T PERFECT, BUT I THINK YOU CAN DO IT.
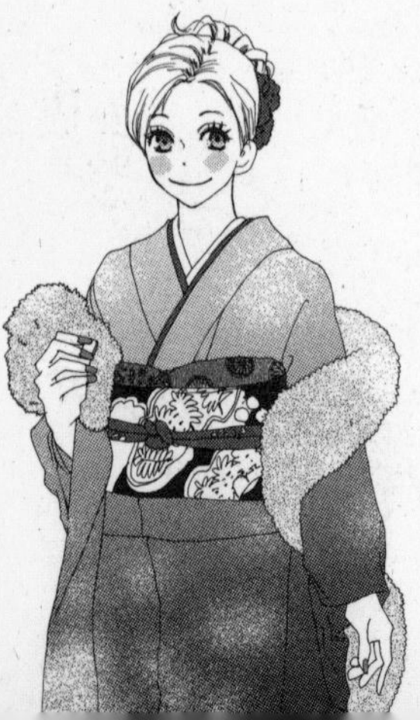

MEIRYOU
MEIRYOU
MEIRYOU
MEIRYOU
MEIRYOU
MEIRYOU
MEIRYOU
MEIRYOU
MEIRYOU
MEIRYOU

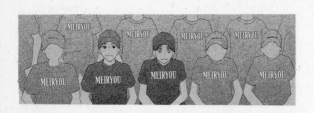

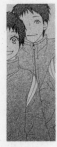

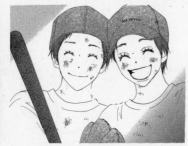

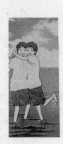

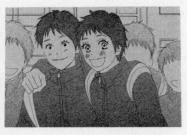

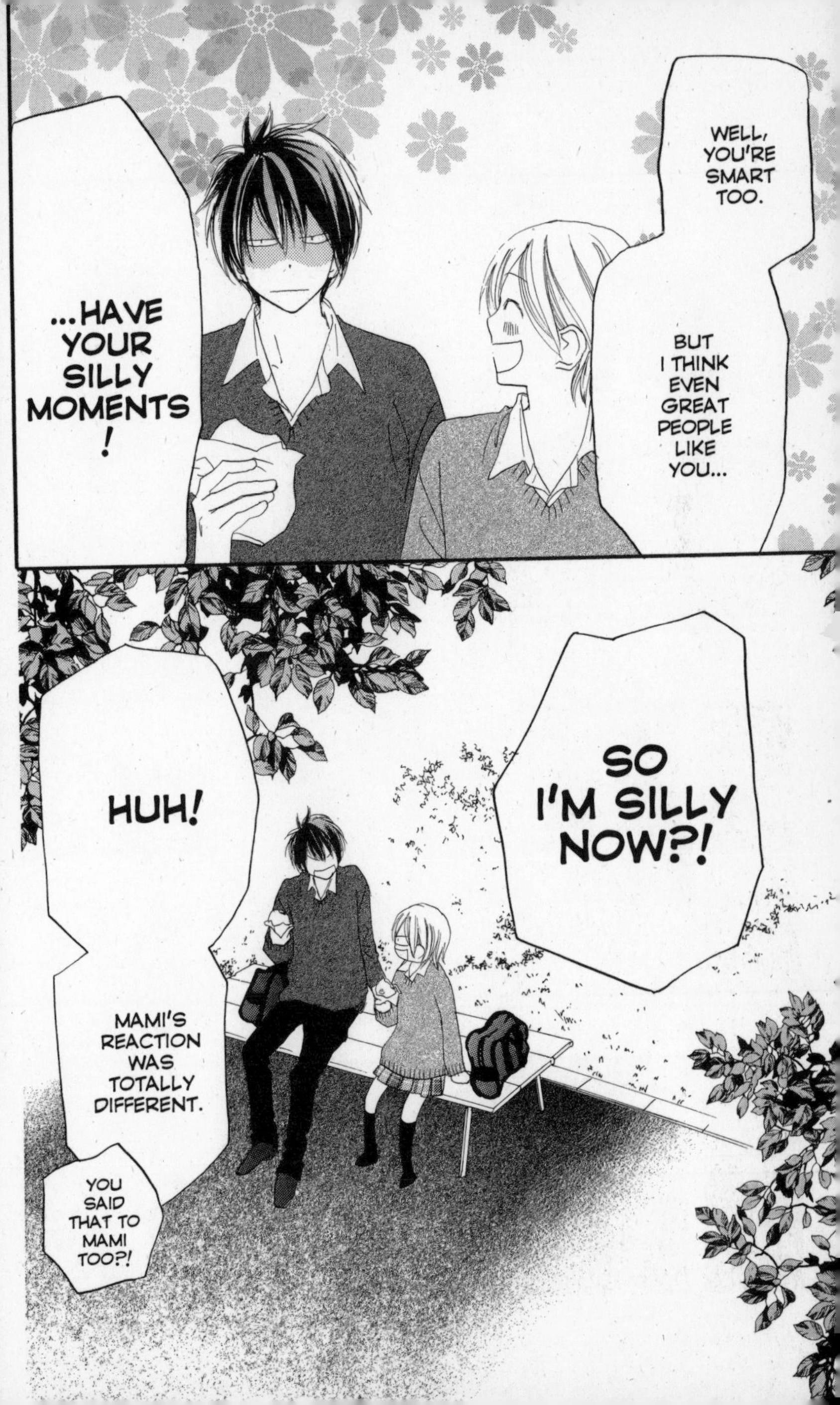
WELL, YOU'RE SMART TOO.
BUT I THINK EVEN GREAT PEOPLE LIKE YOU...
...HAVE YOUR SILLY MOMENTS!
SO I'M SILLY NOW?!
HUH!
MAMI'S REACTION WAS TOTALLY DIFFERENT.
YOU SAID THAT TO MAMI TOO?!

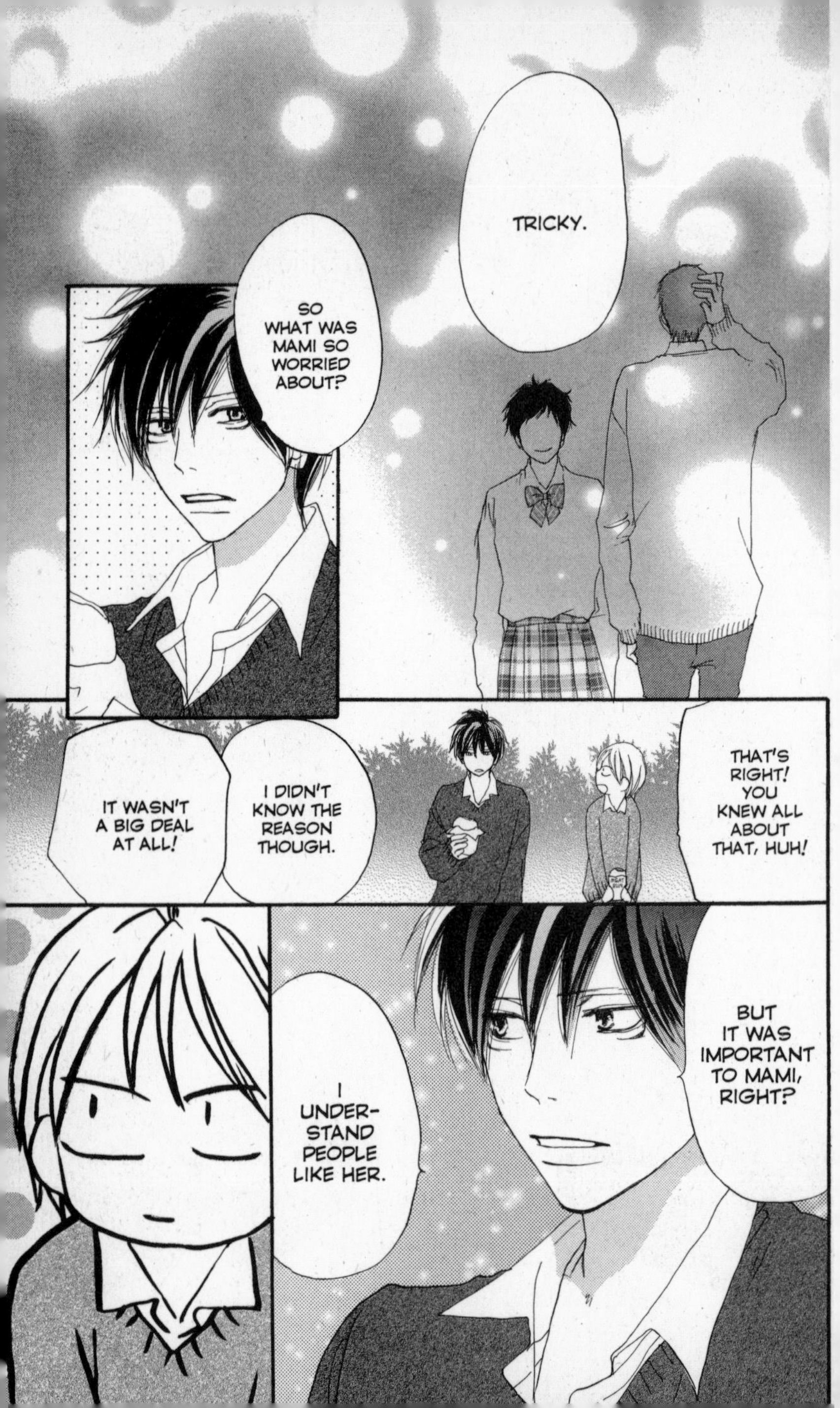
TRICKY.
SO WHAT WAS MAMI SO WORRIED ABOUT?
THAT'S RIGHT! YOU KNEW ALL ABOUT THAT, HUH!
I DIDN'T KNOW THE REASON THOUGH.
IT WASN'T A BIG DEAL AT ALL!
BUT IT WAS IMPORTANT TO MAMI, RIGHT?
I UNDER-STAND PEOPLE LIKE HER.

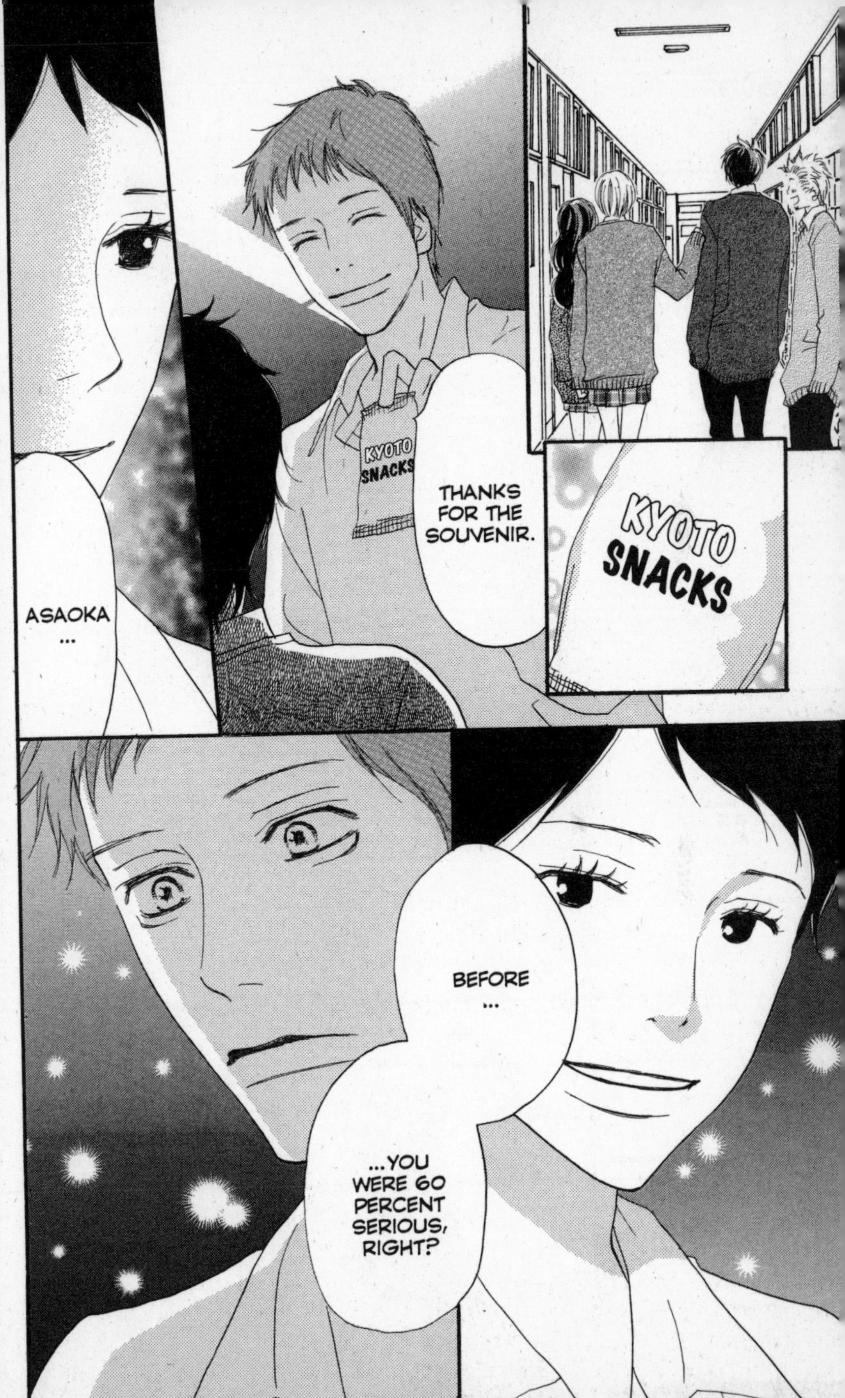
KYOTO SNACKS
KYOTO SNACKS
THANKS FOR THE SOUVENIR.
ASAOKA ...
BEFORE ...
...YOU WERE 60 PERCENT SERIOUS, RIGHT?

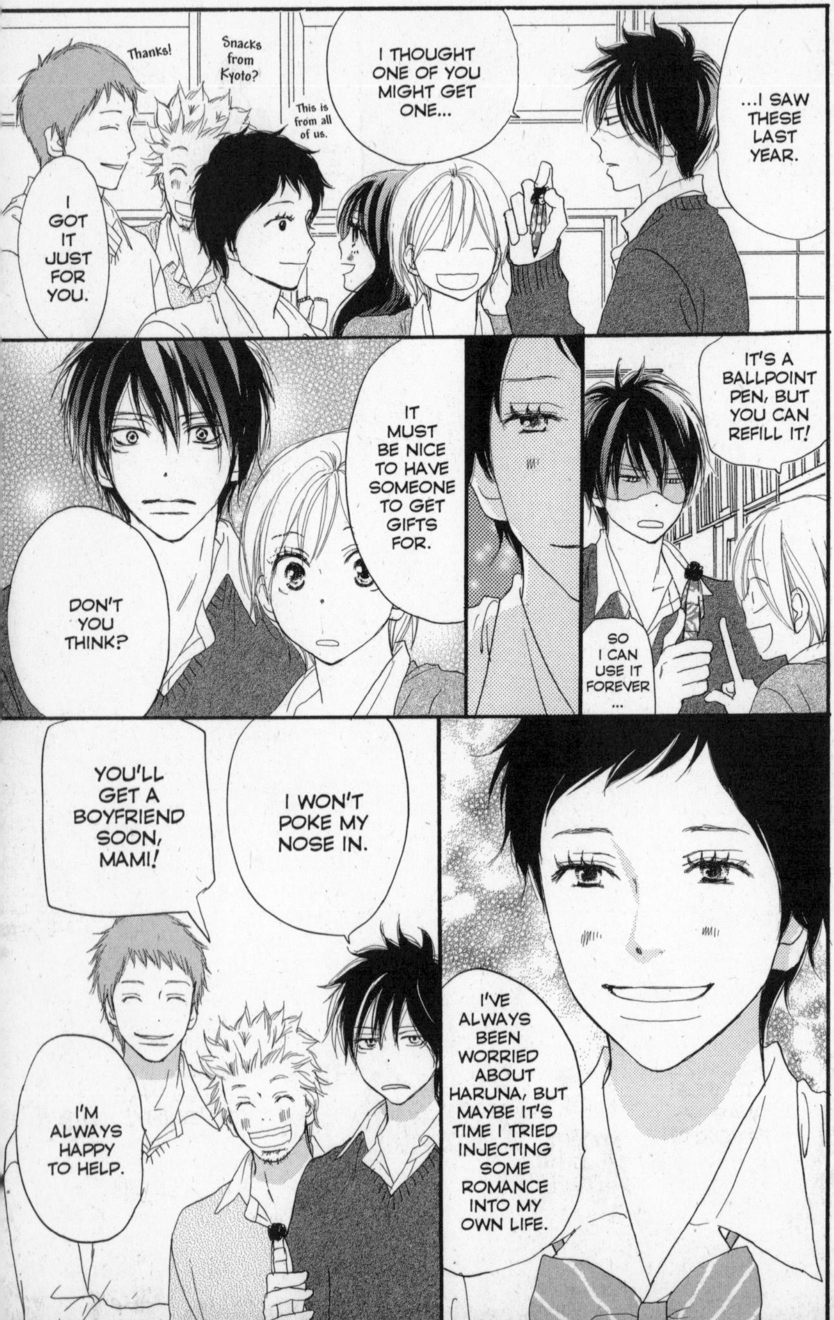
...I SAW THESE LAST YEAR.
I THOUGHT ONE OF YOU MIGHT GET ONE...
This is from all of us.
Snacks from Kyoto?
Thanks!
I GOT IT JUST FOR YOU.
IT'S A BALLPOINT PEN, BUT YOU CAN REFILL IT!
SO I CAN USE IT FOREVER ...
IT MUST BE NICE TO HAVE SOMEONE TO GET GIFTS FOR.
DON'T YOU THINK?
I'VE ALWAYS BEEN WORRIED ABOUT HARUNA, BUT MAYBE IT'S TIME I TRIED INJECTING SOME ROMANCE INTO MY OWN LIFE.
I WON'T POKE MY NOSE IN.
YOU'LL GET A BOYFRIEND SOON, MAMI!
I'M ALWAYS HAPPY TO HELP.

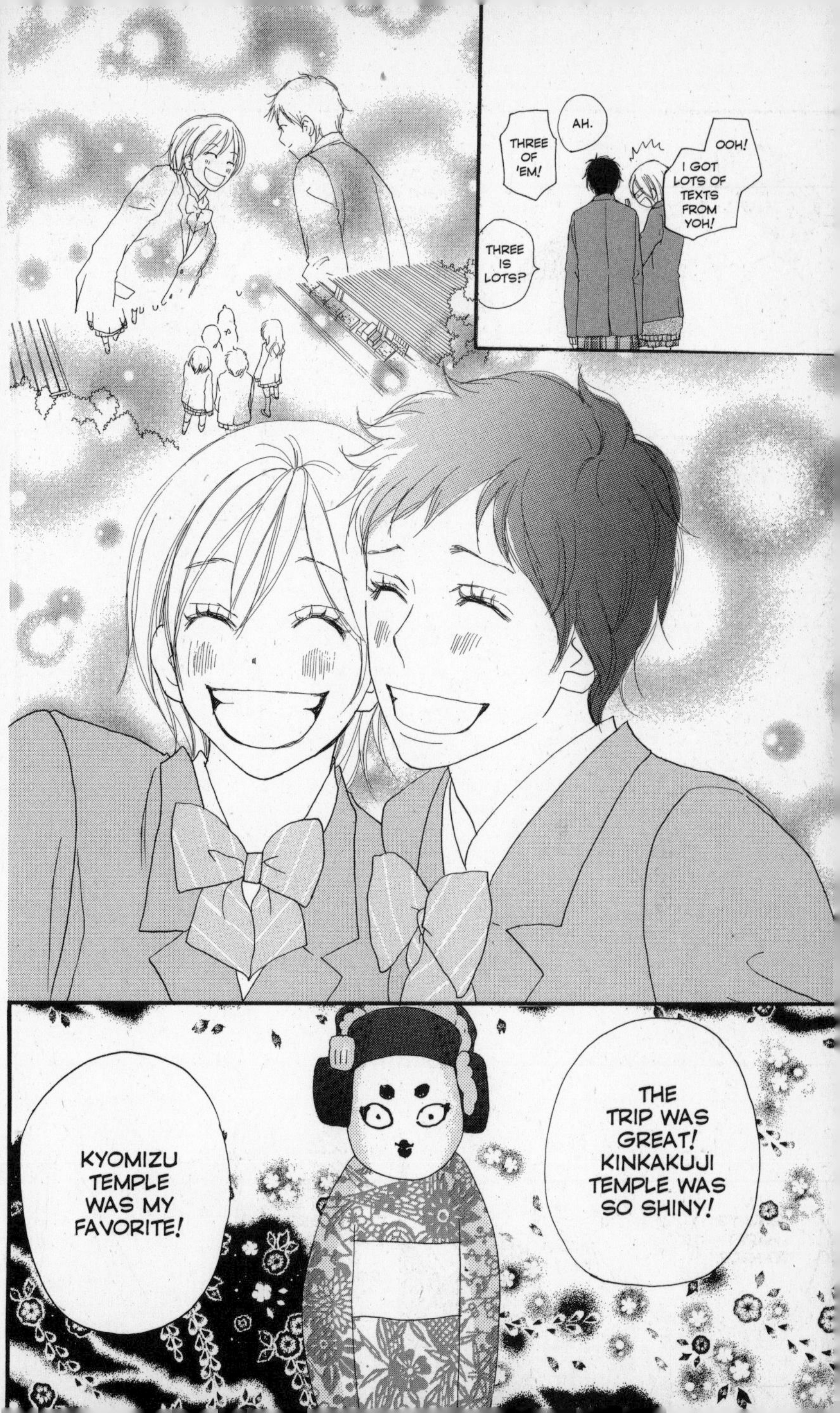
OOH! I GOT LOTS OF TEXTS FROM YOH!
AH.
THREE OF 'EM!
THREE IS LOTS?
THE TRIP WAS GREAT! KINKAKUJI TEMPLE WAS SO SHINY!
KYOMIZU TEMPLE WAS MY FAVORITE!

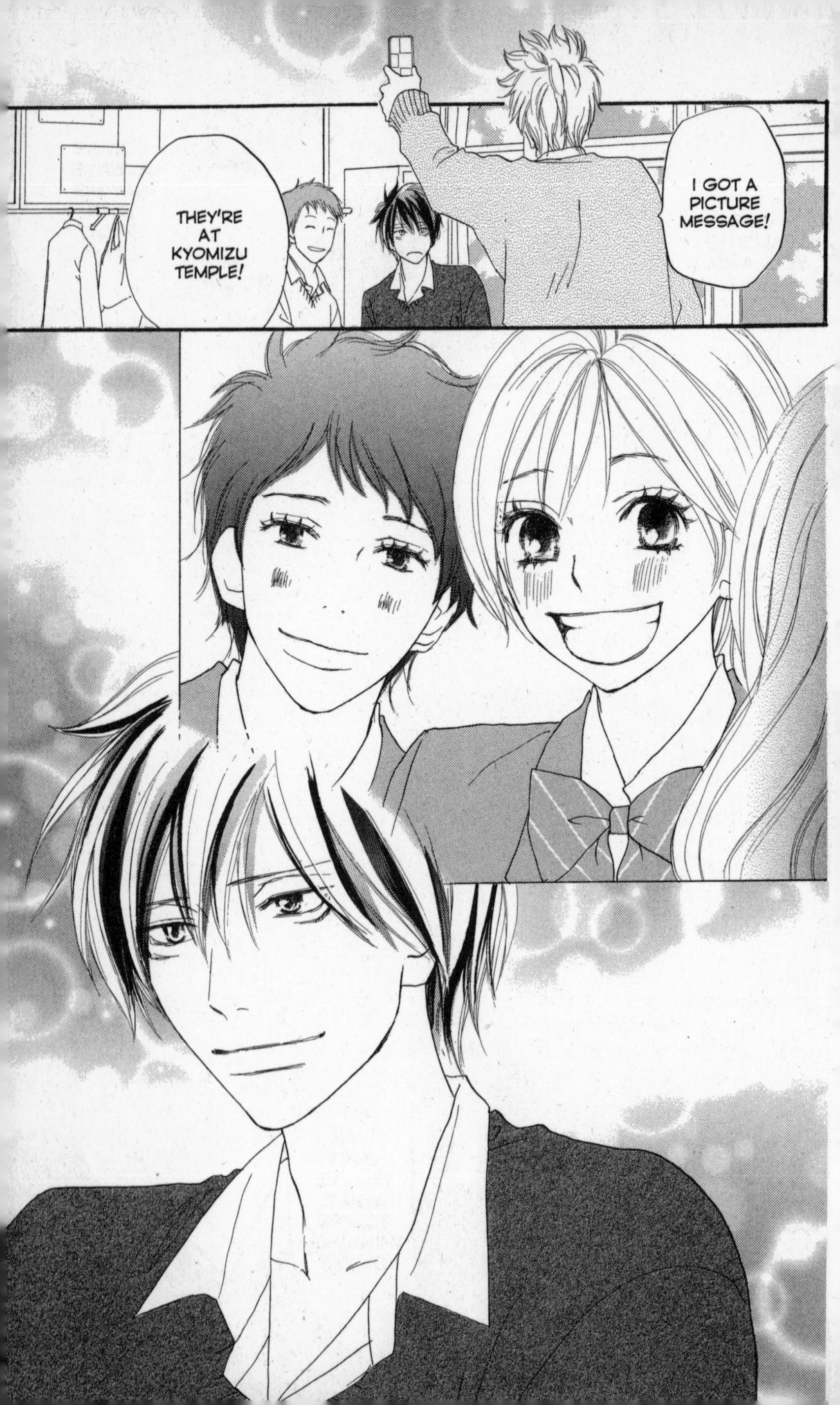
I GOT A PICTURE MESSAGE!
THEY'RE AT KYOMIZU TEMPLE!

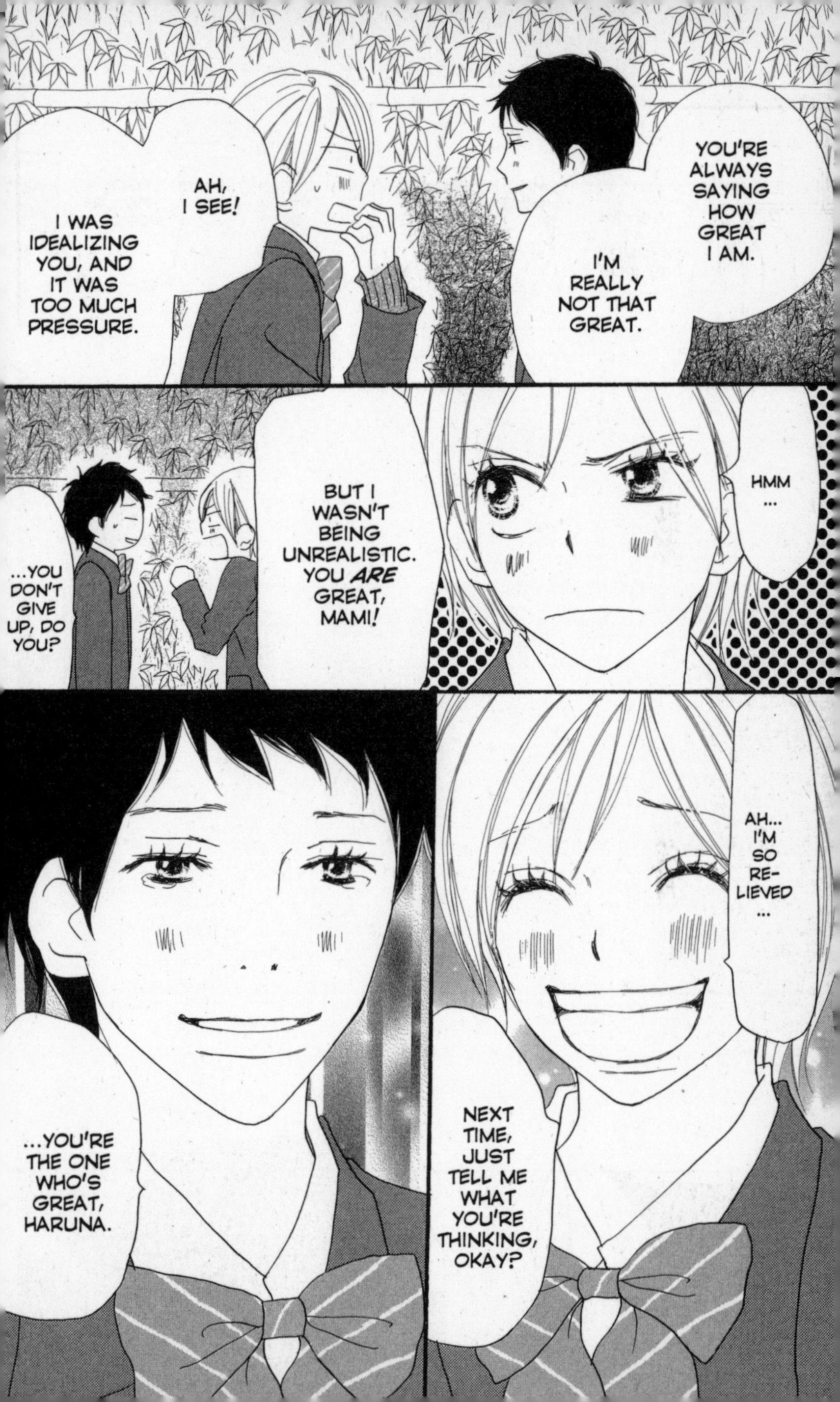
YOU'RE ALWAYS SAYING HOW GREAT I AM.
I'M REALLY NOT THAT GREAT.
AH, I SEE!
I WAS IDEALIZING YOU, AND IT WAS TOO MUCH PRESSURE.
HMM ...
BUT I WASN'T BEING UNREALISTIC. YOU *ARE* GREAT, MAMI!
...YOU DON'T GIVE UP, DO YOU?
AH... I'M SO RE-LIEVED ...
NEXT TIME, JUST TELL ME WHAT YOU'RE THINKING, OKAY?
...YOU'RE THE ONE WHO'S GREAT, HARUNA.

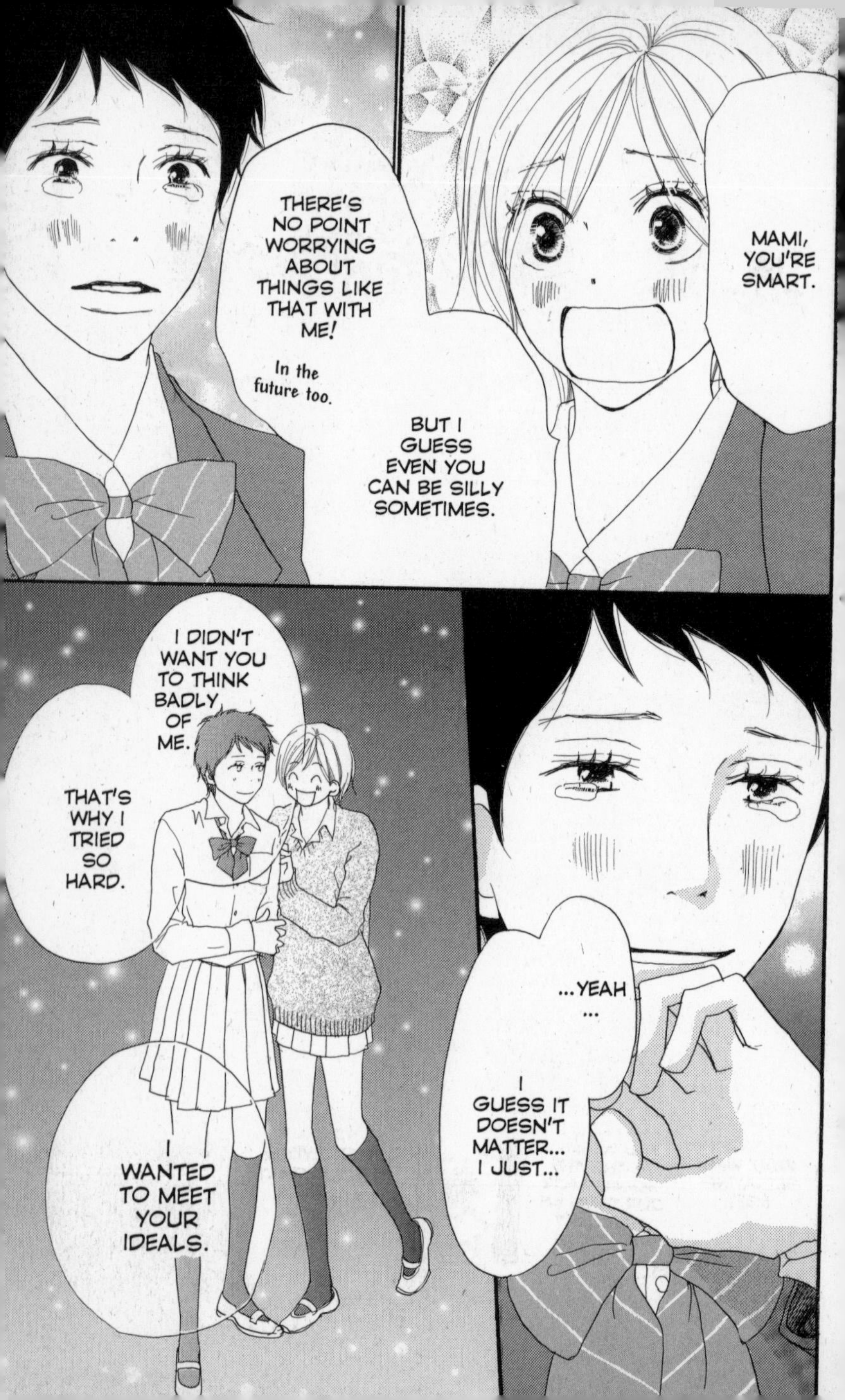
MAMI, YOU'RE SMART.
BUT I GUESS EVEN YOU CAN BE SILLY SOMETIMES.
THERE'S NO POINT WORRYING ABOUT THINGS LIKE THAT WITH ME!
In the future too.
...YEAH ...
I GUESS IT DOESN'T MATTER... I JUST...
I DIDN'T WANT YOU TO THINK BADLY OF ME.
THAT'S WHY I TRIED SO HARD.
I WANTED TO MEET YOUR IDEALS.

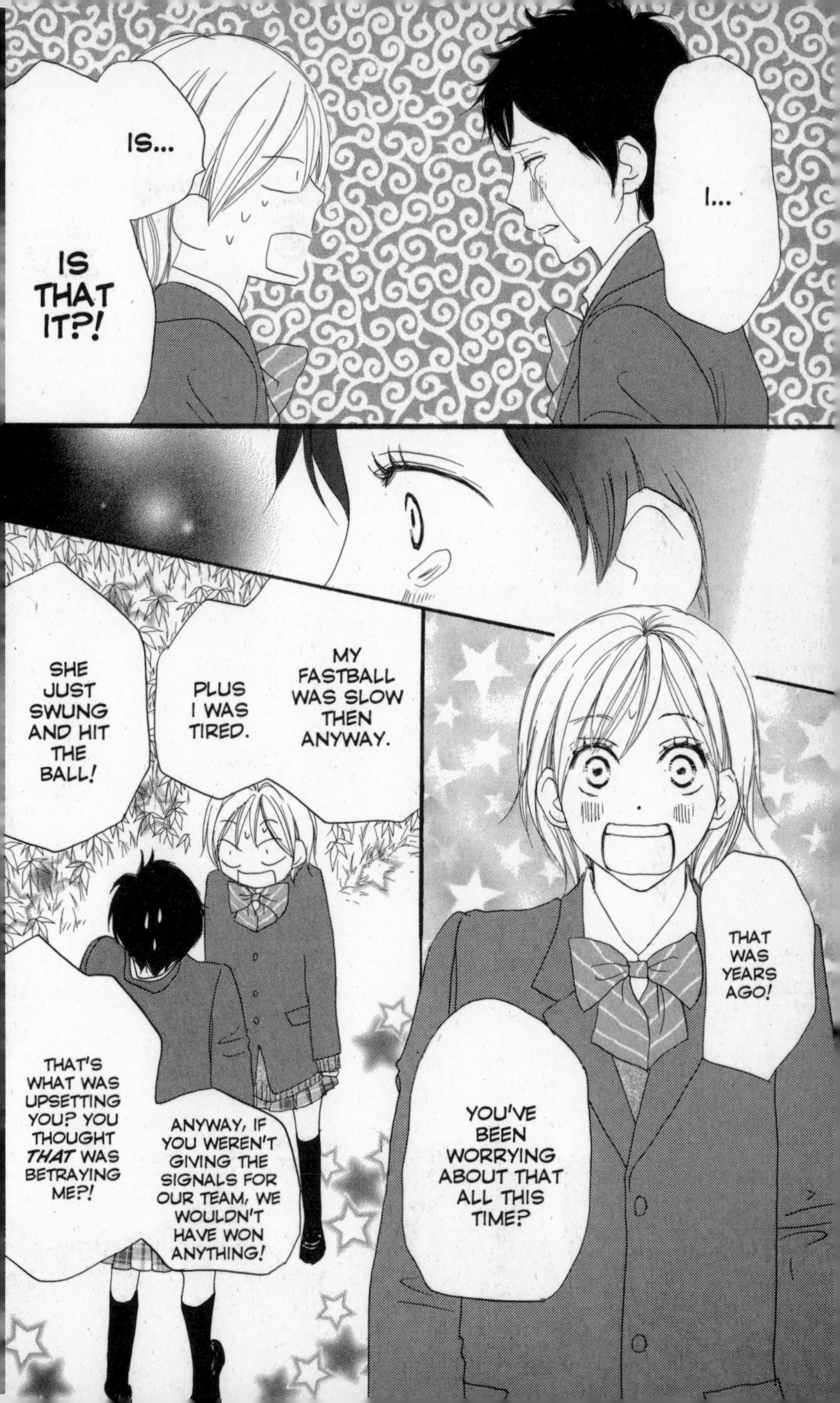
I...
IS...
IS THAT IT?!
THAT WAS YEARS AGO!
YOU'VE BEEN WORRYING ABOUT THAT ALL THIS TIME?
MY FASTBALL WAS SLOW THEN ANYWAY.
PLUS I WAS TIRED.
SHE JUST SWUNG AND HIT THE BALL!
ANYWAY, IF YOU WEREN'T GIVING THE SIGNALS FOR OUR TEAM, WE WOULDN'T HAVE WON ANYTHING!
THAT'S WHAT WAS UPSETTING YOU? YOU THOUGHT *THAT* WAS BETRAYING ME?!

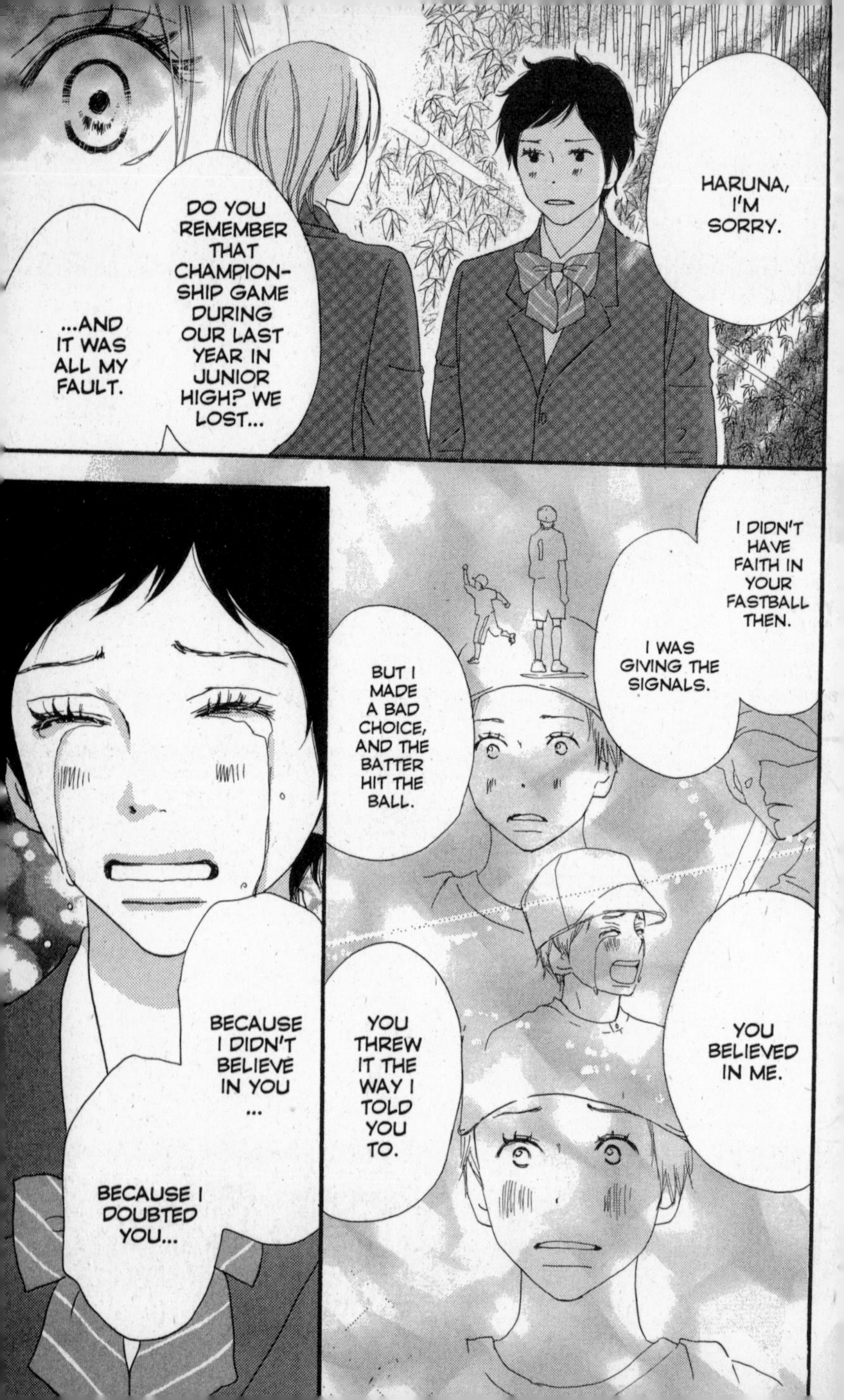
HARUNA, I'M SORRY.
DO YOU REMEMBER THAT CHAMPIONSHIP GAME DURING OUR LAST YEAR IN JUNIOR HIGH? WE LOST...
...AND IT WAS ALL MY FAULT.
I DIDN'T HAVE FAITH IN YOUR FASTBALL THEN.
I WAS GIVING THE SIGNALS.
BUT I MADE A BAD CHOICE, AND THE BATTER HIT THE BALL.
YOU BELIEVED IN ME.
YOU THREW IT THE WAY I TOLD YOU TO.
BECAUSE I DIDN'T BELIEVE IN YOU ...
BECAUSE I DOUBTED YOU...

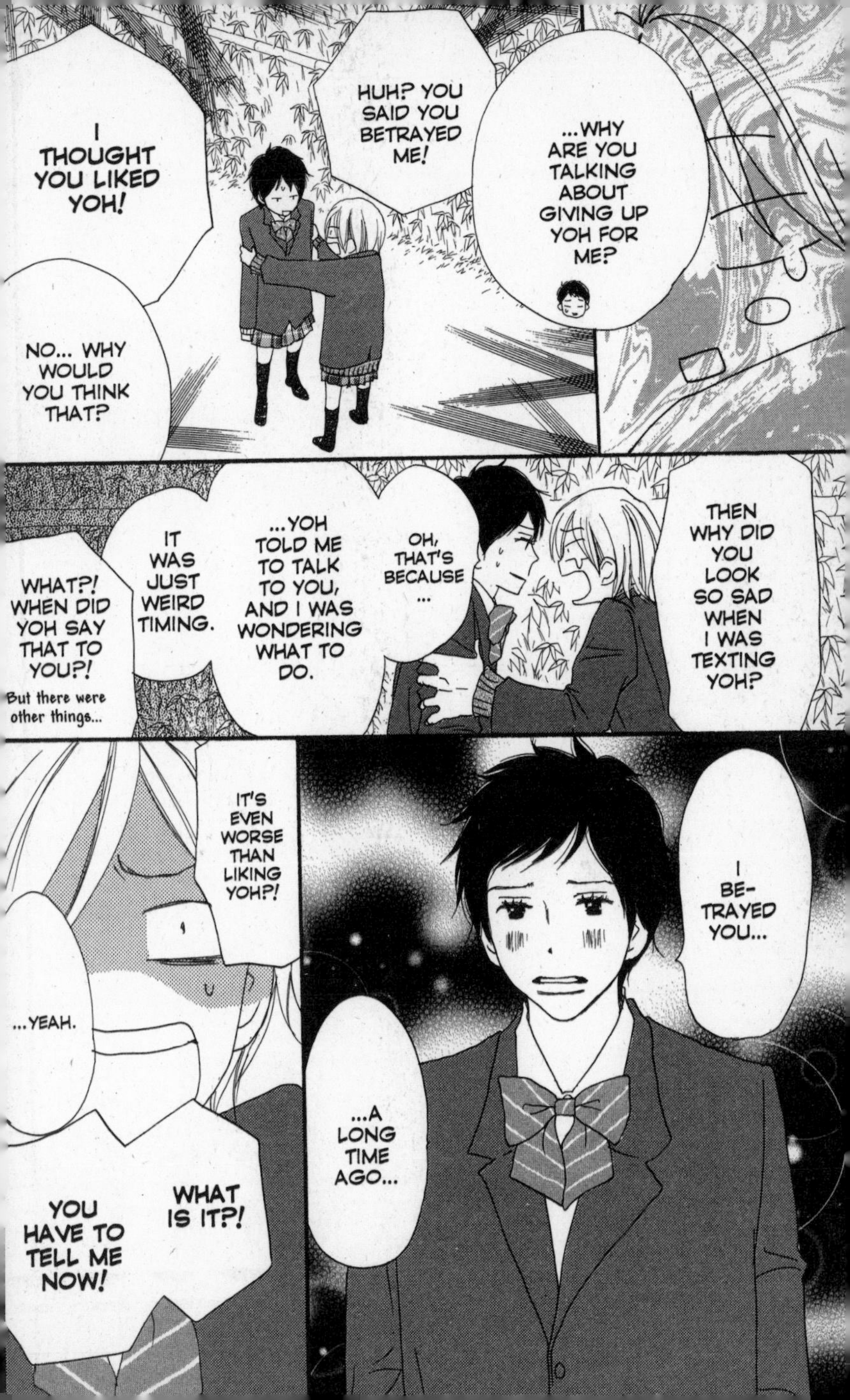
...WHY ARE YOU TALKING ABOUT GIVING UP YOH FOR ME?
HUH? YOU SAID YOU BETRAYED ME!
I THOUGHT YOU LIKED YOH!
NO... WHY WOULD YOU THINK THAT?
THEN WHY DID YOU LOOK SO SAD WHEN I WAS TEXTING YOH?
OH, THAT'S BECAUSE ...
...YOH TOLD ME TO TALK TO YOU, AND I WAS WONDERING WHAT TO DO.
IT WAS JUST WEIRD TIMING.
WHAT?! WHEN DID YOH SAY THAT TO YOU?!
But there were other things...
I BE-TRAYED YOU...
...A LONG TIME AGO...
IT'S EVEN WORSE THAN LIKING YOH?!
...YEAH.
WHAT IS IT?!
YOU HAVE TO TELL ME NOW!

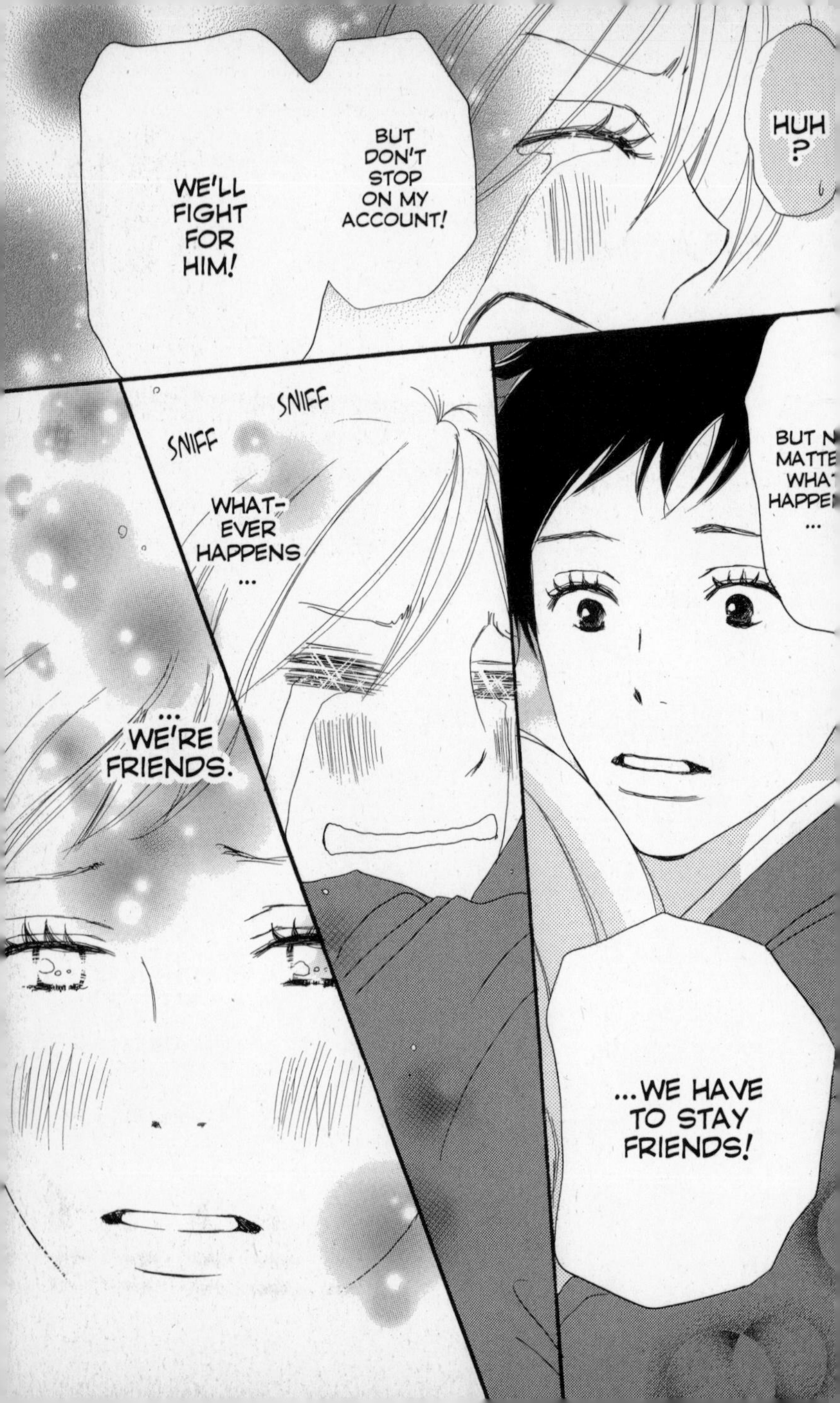
HUH?
BUT DON'T STOP ON MY ACCOUNT!
WE'LL FIGHT FOR HIM!
BUT N MATTE WHA HAPPE ...
...WE HAVE TO STAY FRIENDS!
SNIFF
SNIFF
WHAT-EVER HAPPENS ...
... WE'RE FRIENDS.

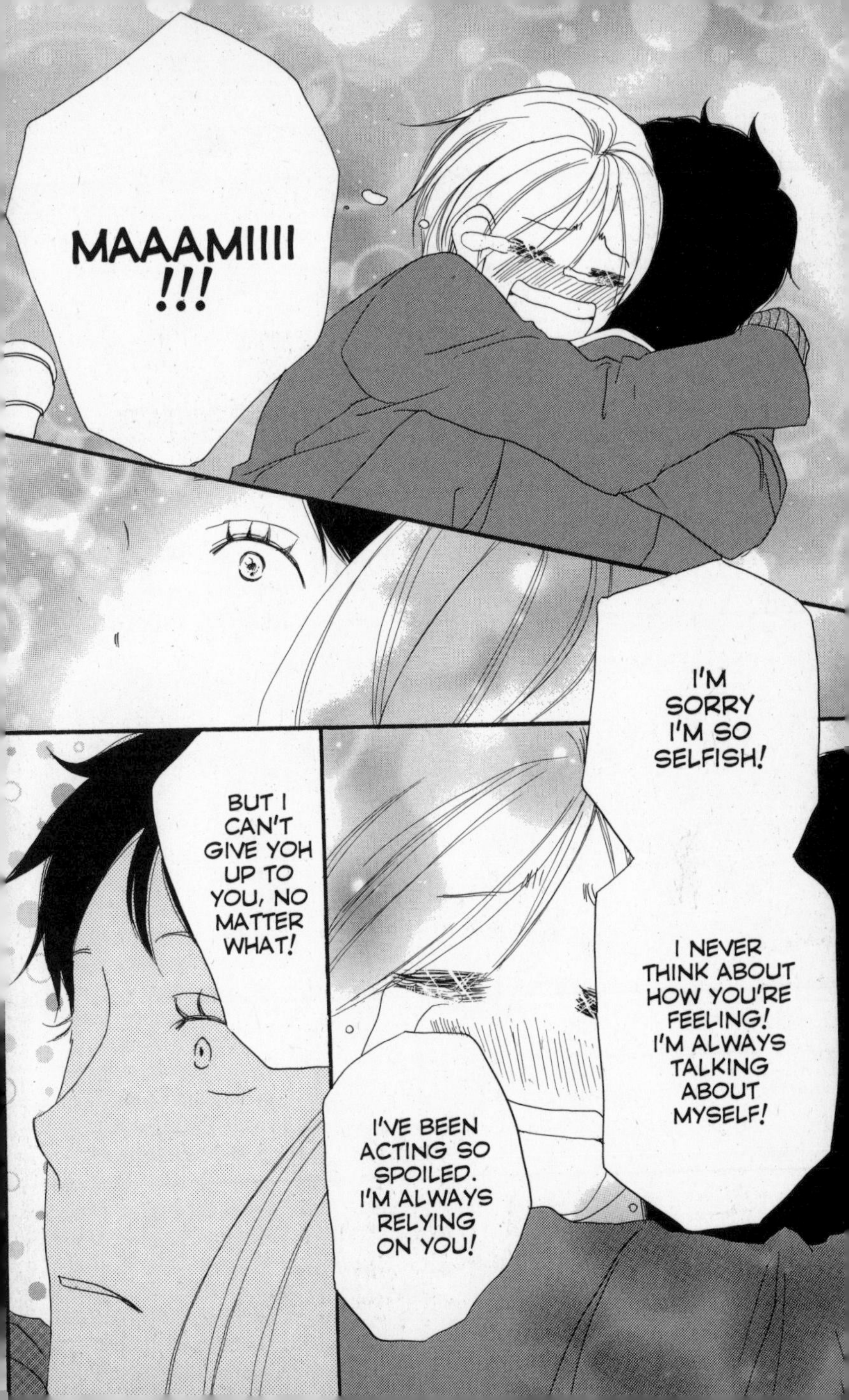
MAAAMIIII !!!
I'M SORRY I'M SO SELFISH!
I NEVER THINK ABOUT HOW YOU'RE FEELING! I'M ALWAYS TALKING ABOUT MYSELF!
I'VE BEEN ACTING SO SPOILED. I'M ALWAYS RELYING ON YOU!
BUT I CAN'T GIVE YOH UP TO YOU, NO MATTER WHAT!

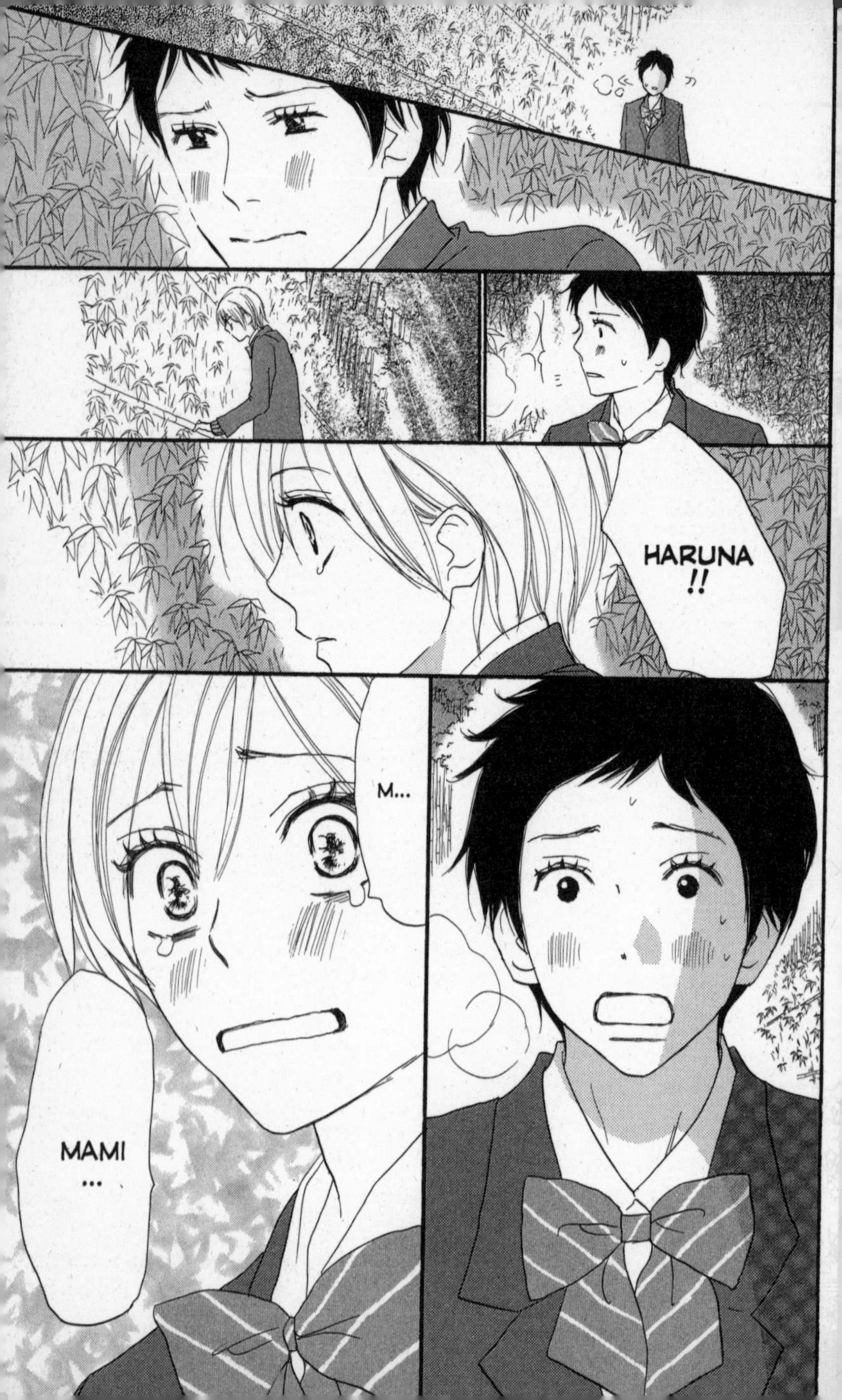
HARUNA !!
M...
MAMI ...

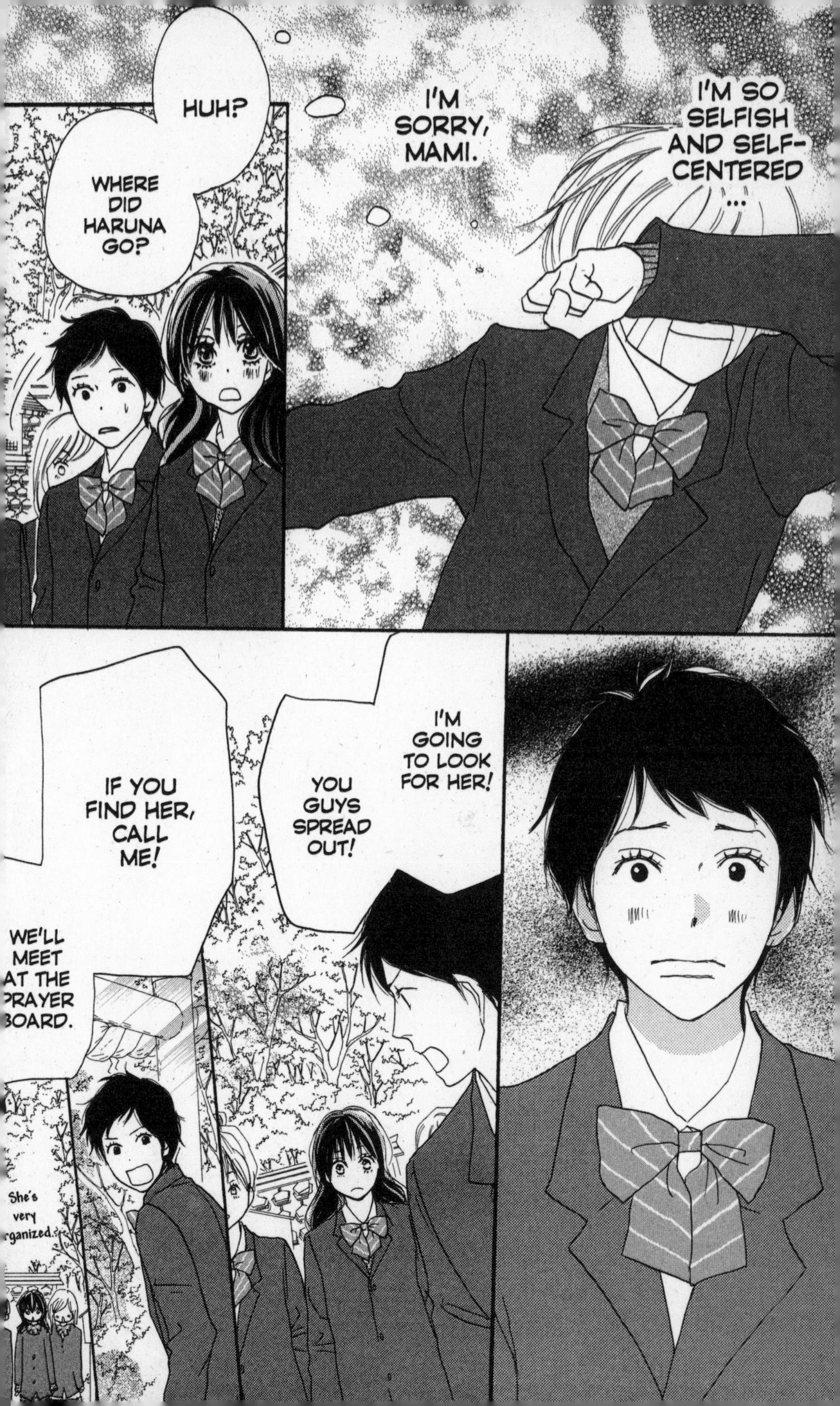

I'M SO SELFISH AND SELF-CENTERED ...
I'M SORRY, MAMI.
HUH?
WHERE DID HARUNA GO?
I'M GOING TO LOOK FOR HER!
YOU GUYS SPREAD OUT!
IF YOU FIND HER, CALL ME!
WE'LL MEET AT THE PRAYER BOARD.
She's very organized.

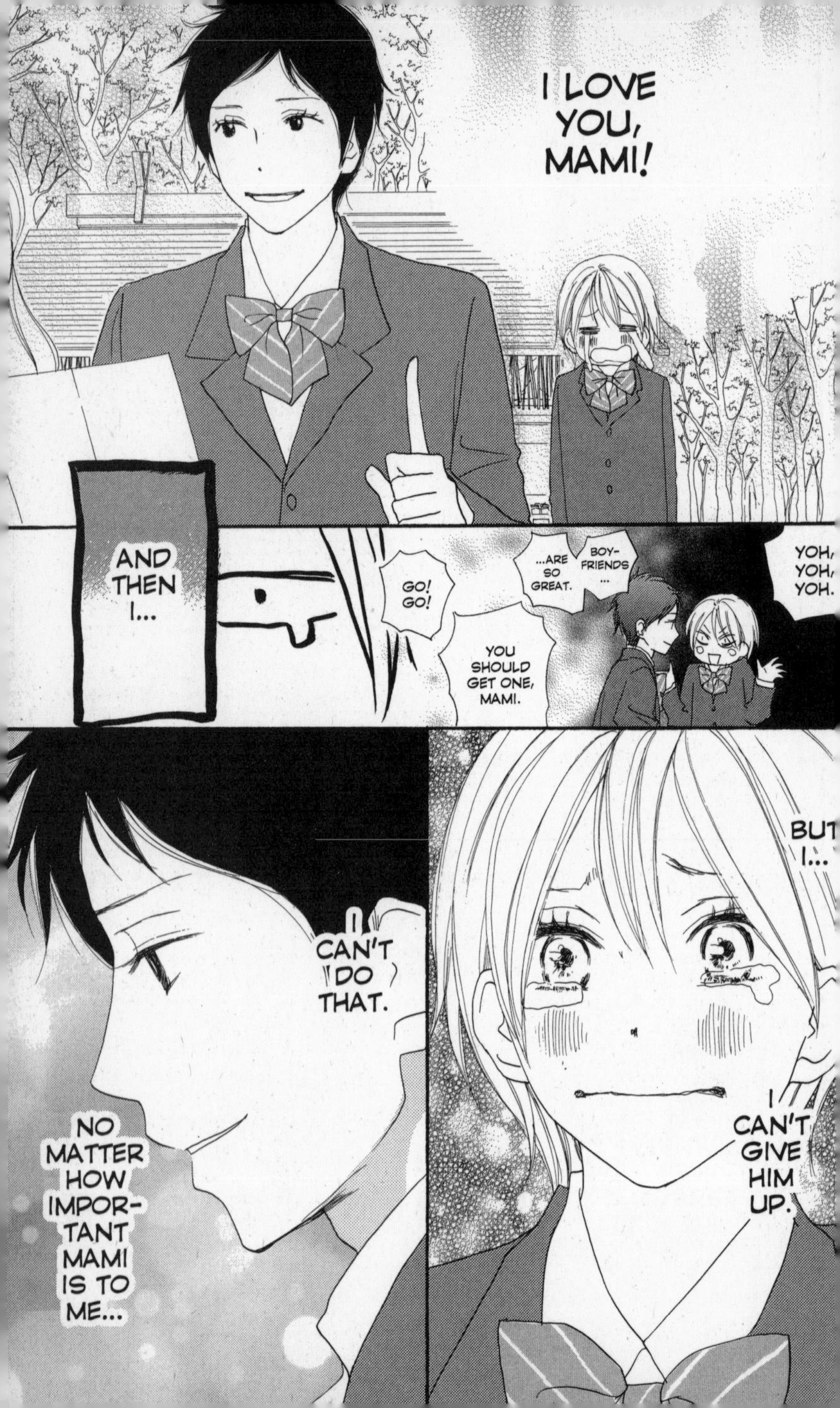
I LOVE YOU, MAMI!
YOH, YOH, YOH.
BOY-FRIENDS...
...ARE SO GREAT.
YOU SHOULD GET ONE, MAMI.
GO! GO!
AND THEN I...
BUT I...
I CAN'T GIVE HIM UP.
I CAN'T DO THAT.
NO MATTER HOW IMPOR-TANT MAMI IS TO ME...

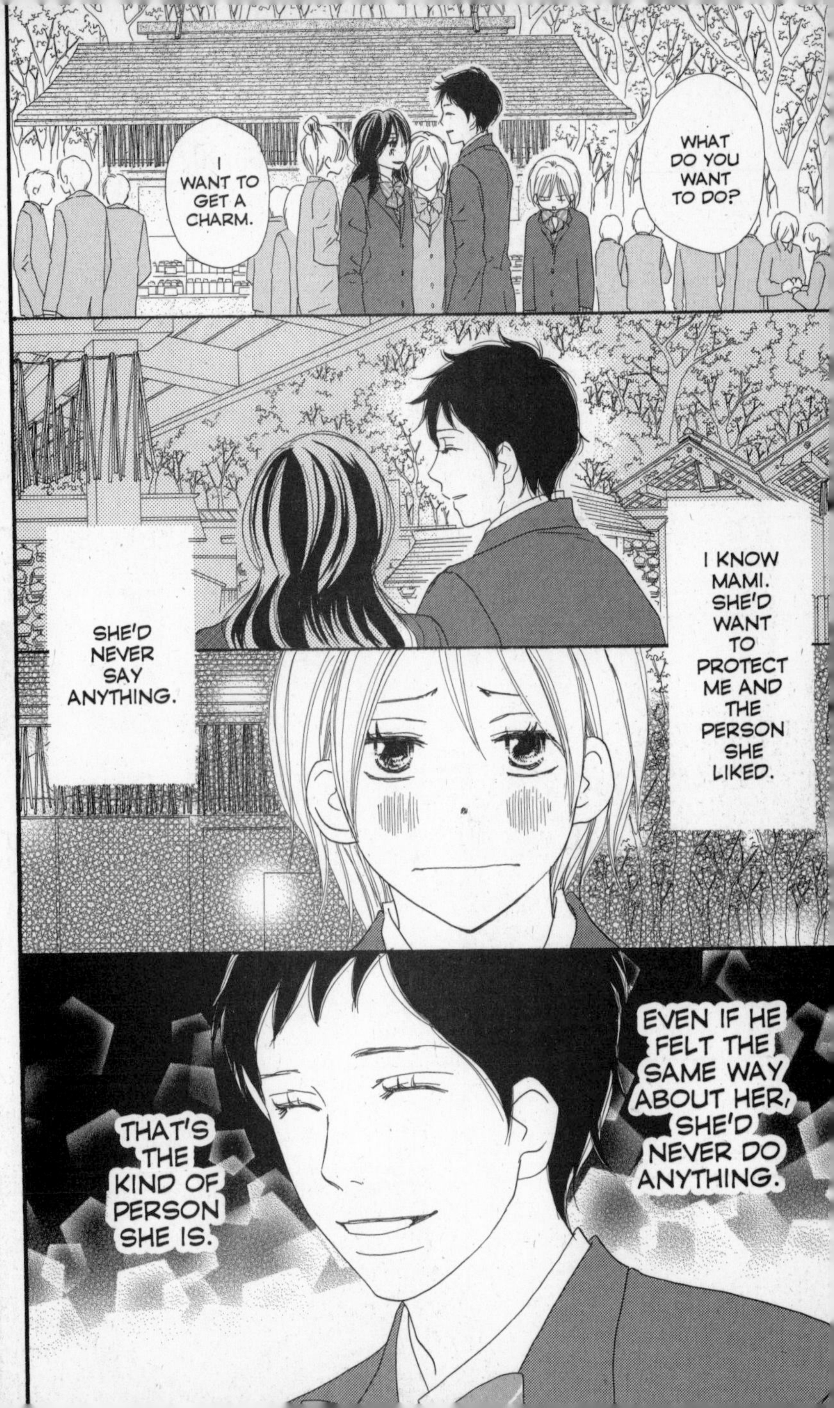
WHAT DO YOU WANT TO DO?
I WANT TO GET A CHARM.
I KNOW MAMI. SHE'D WANT TO PROTECT ME AND THE PERSON SHE LIKED.
SHE'D NEVER SAY ANYTHING.
EVEN IF HE FELT THE SAME WAY ABOUT HER, SHE'D NEVER DO ANYTHING.
THAT'S THE KIND OF PERSON SHE IS.

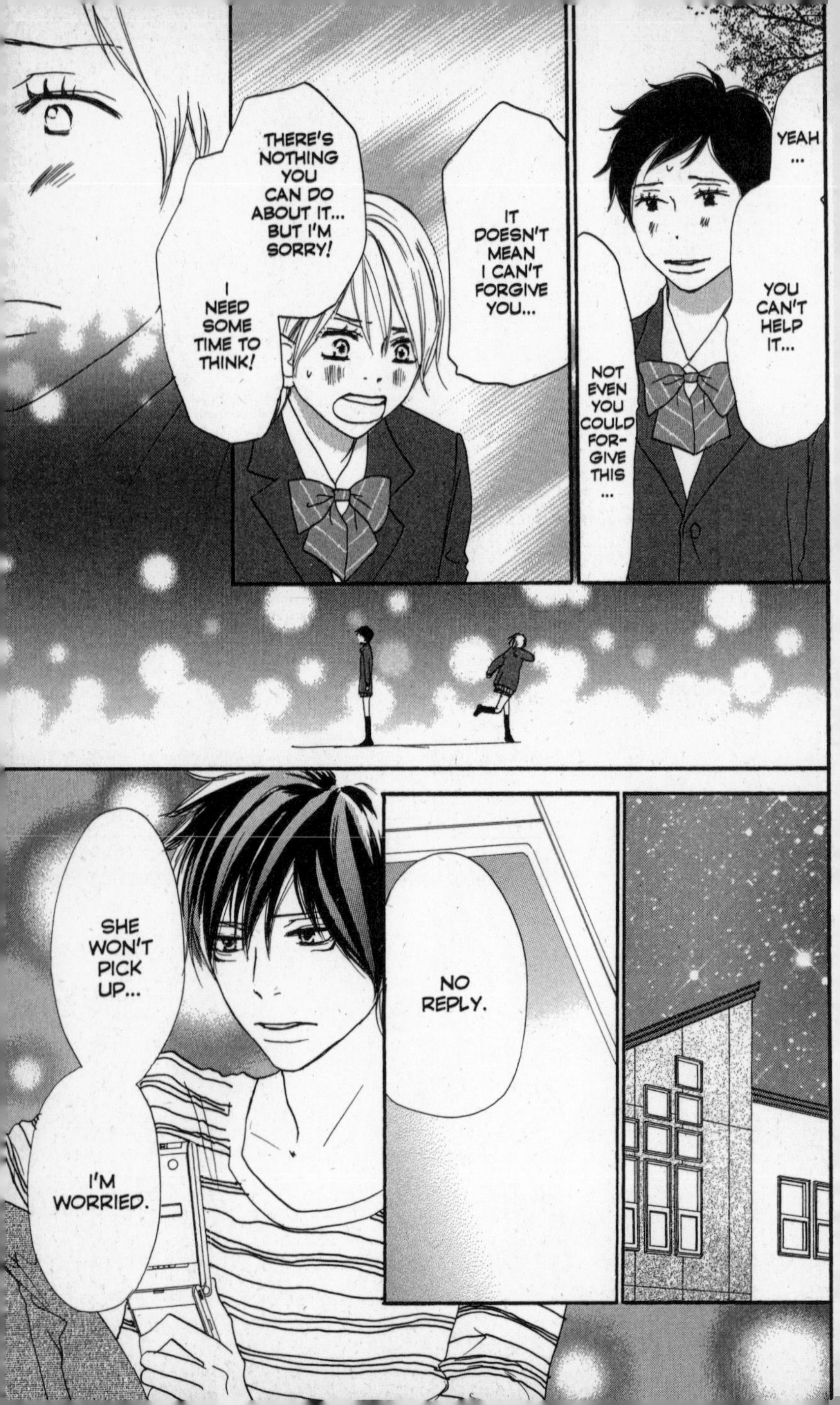
YEAH ...
YOU CAN'T HELP IT...
NOT EVEN YOU COULD FOR-GIVE THIS ...
IT DOESN'T MEAN I CAN'T FORGIVE YOU...
THERE'S NOTHING YOU CAN DO ABOUT IT... BUT I'M SORRY!
I NEED SOME TIME TO THINK!
NO REPLY.
SHE WON'T PICK UP...
I'M WORRIED.

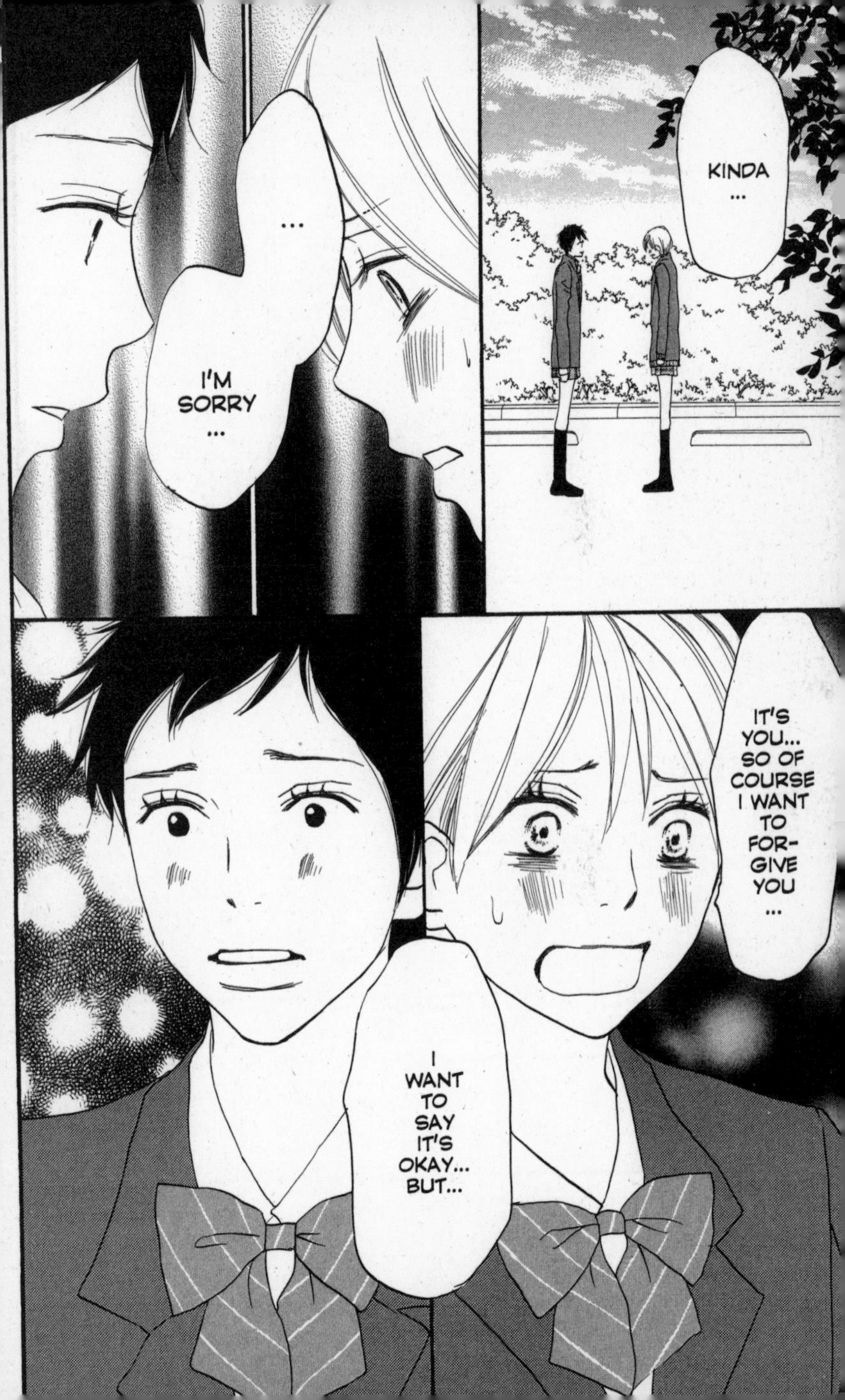
KINDA ...
...
I'M SORRY ...
IT'S YOU... SO OF COURSE I WANT TO FOR-GIVE YOU ...
I WANT TO SAY IT'S OKAY... BUT...

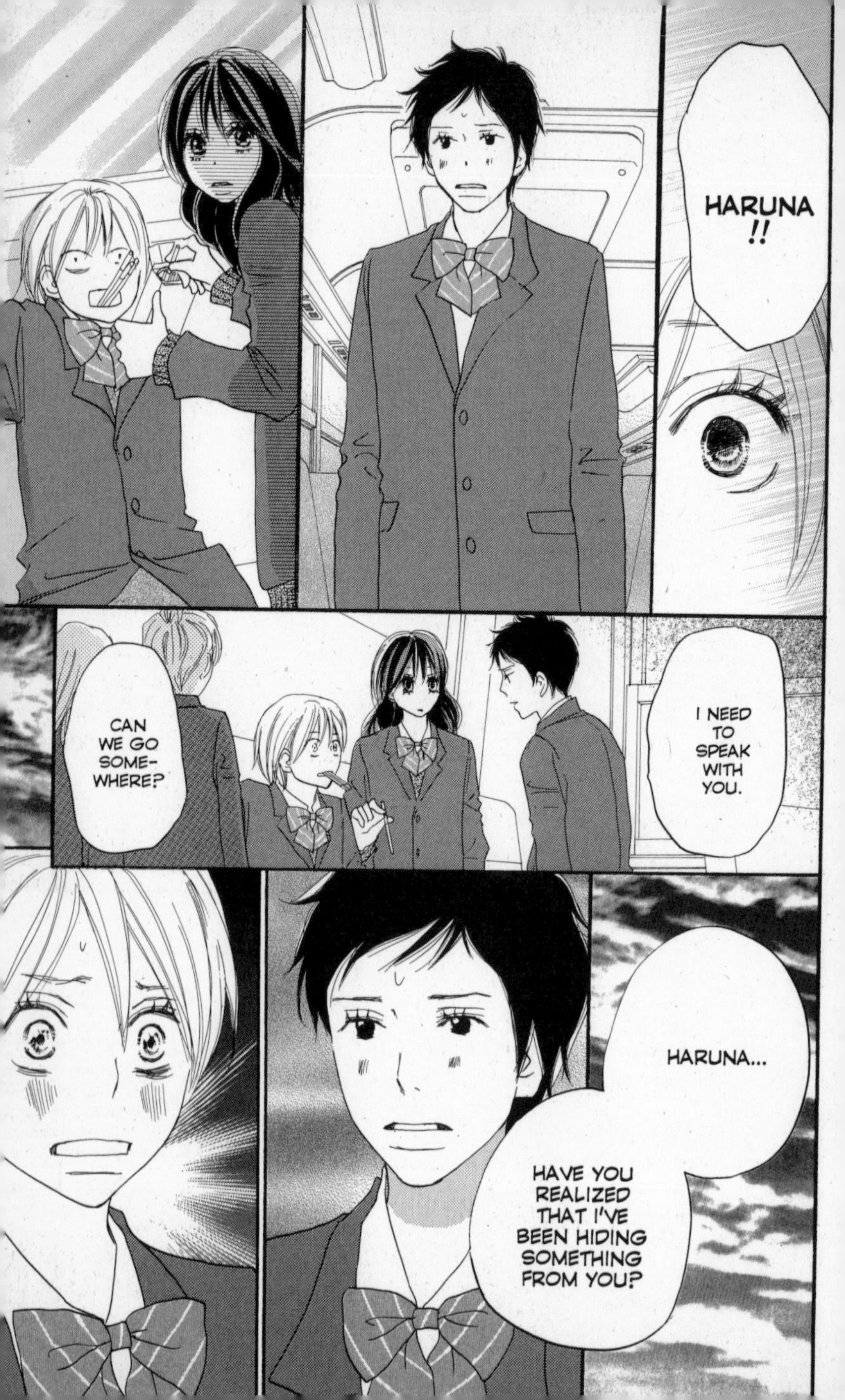
HARUNA !!
I NEED TO SPEAK WITH YOU.
CAN WE GO SOME-WHERE?
HARUNA...
HAVE YOU REALIZED THAT I'VE BEEN HIDING SOMETHING FROM YOU?

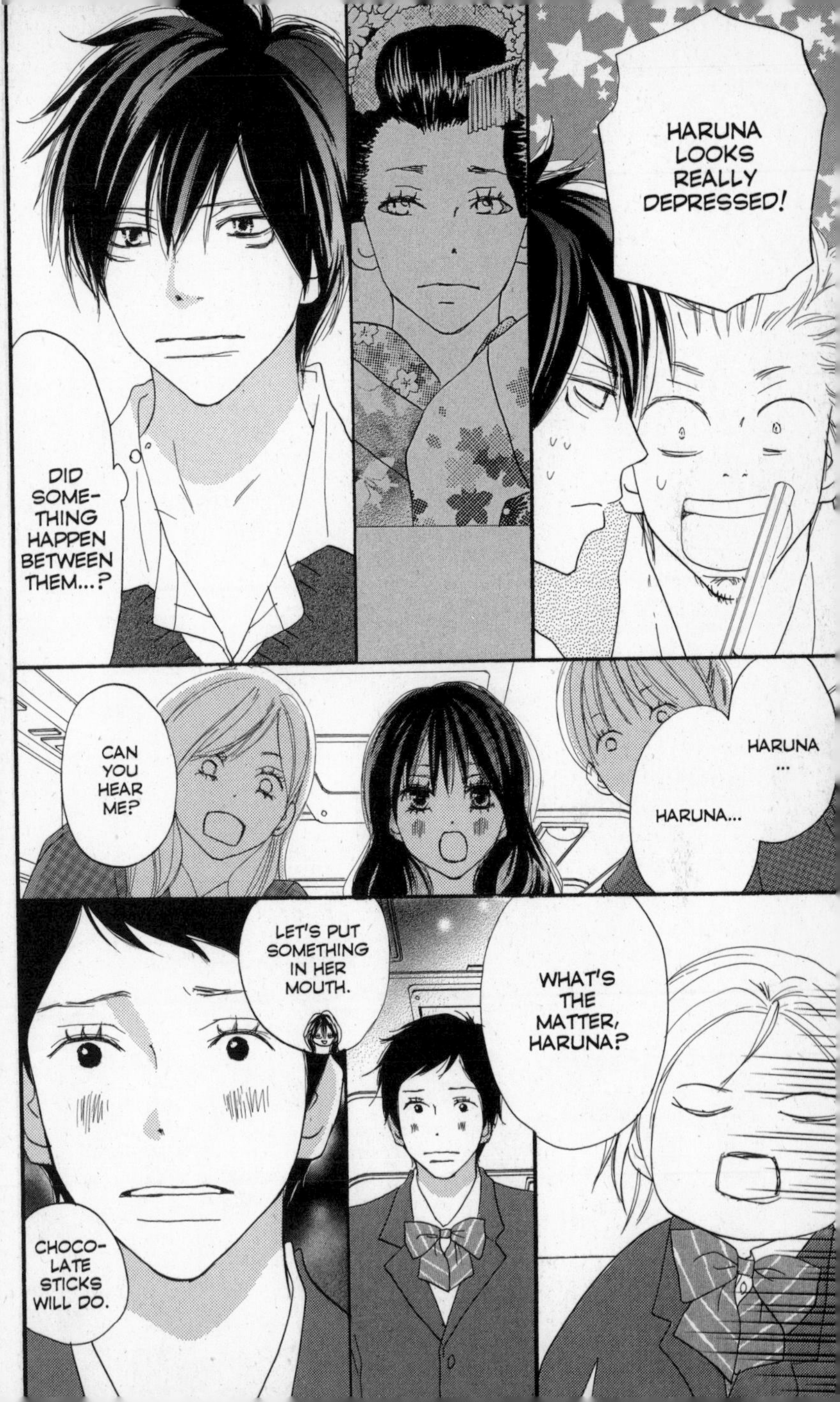
HARUNA LOOKS REALLY DEPRESSED!
DID SOME-THING HAPPEN BETWEEN THEM...?
HARUNA ...
HARUNA...
CAN YOU HEAR ME?
WHAT'S THE MATTER, HARUNA?
LET'S PUT SOMETHING IN HER MOUTH.
CHOCO-LATE STICKS WILL DO.

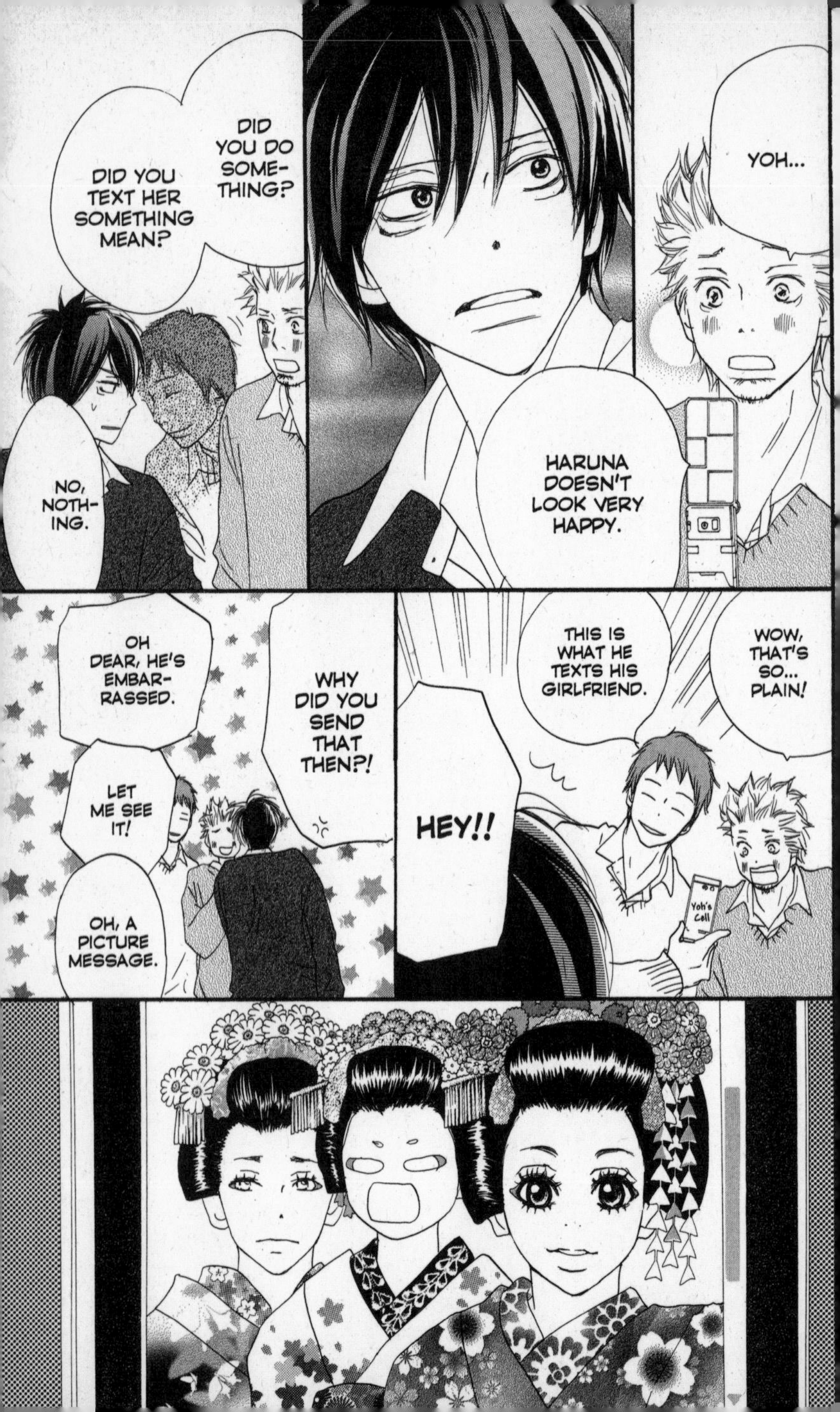
YOH...
HARUNA DOESN'T LOOK VERY HAPPY.
DID YOU DO SOME-THING?
DID YOU TEXT HER SOMETHING MEAN?
NO, NOTH-ING.
WOW, THAT'S SO... PLAIN!
THIS IS WHAT HE TEXTS HIS GIRLFRIEND.
Yoh's Cell
HEY!!
WHY DID YOU SEND THAT THEN?!
OH DEAR, HE'S EMBAR-RASSED.
LET ME SEE IT!
OH, A PICTURE MESSAGE.

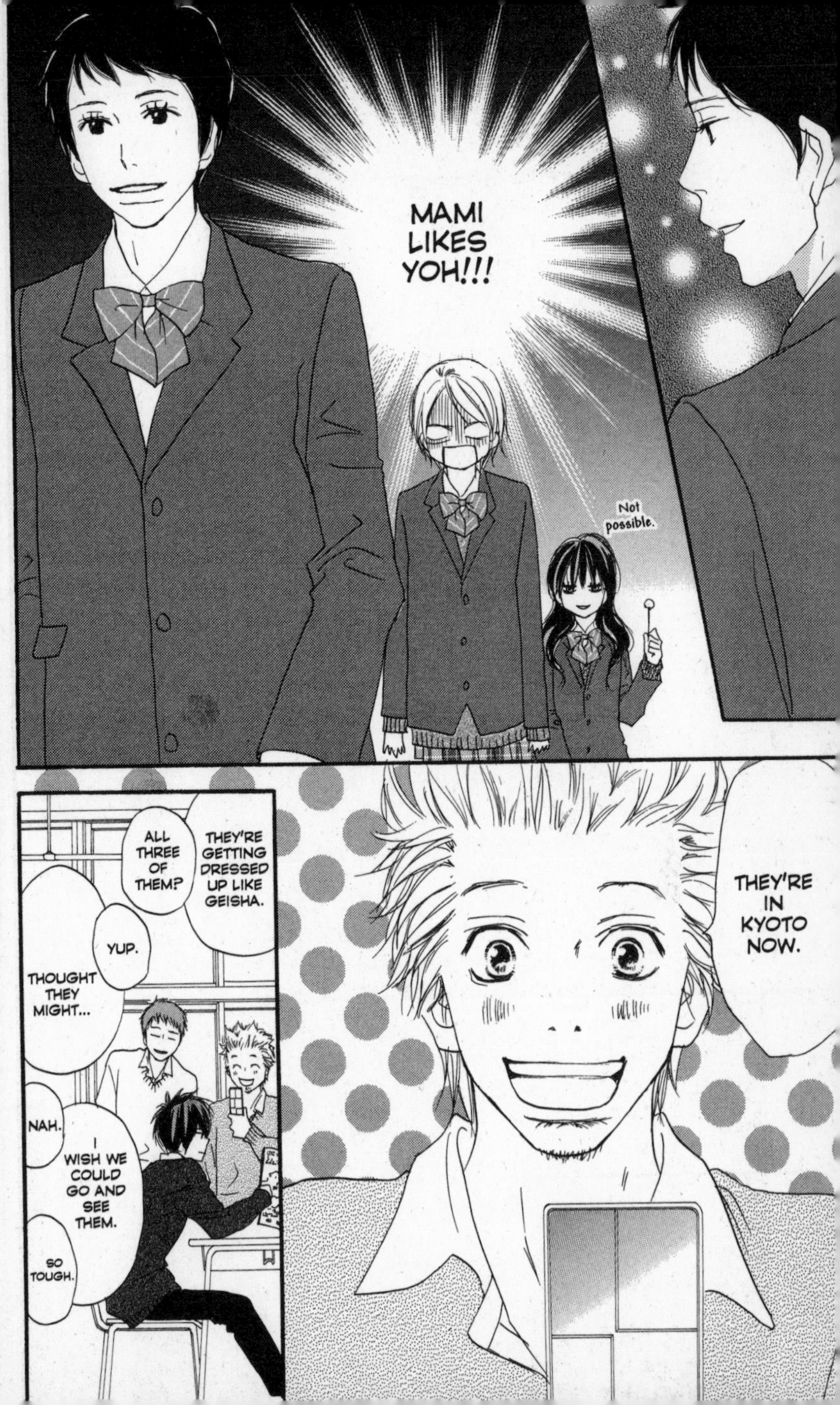
MAMI LIKES YOH!!!
Not possible.
THEY'RE IN KYOTO NOW.
THEY'RE GETTING DRESSED UP LIKE GEISHA.
ALL THREE OF THEM?
YUP.
THOUGHT THEY MIGHT...
NAH.
I WISH WE COULD GO AND SEE THEM.
SO TOUGH.

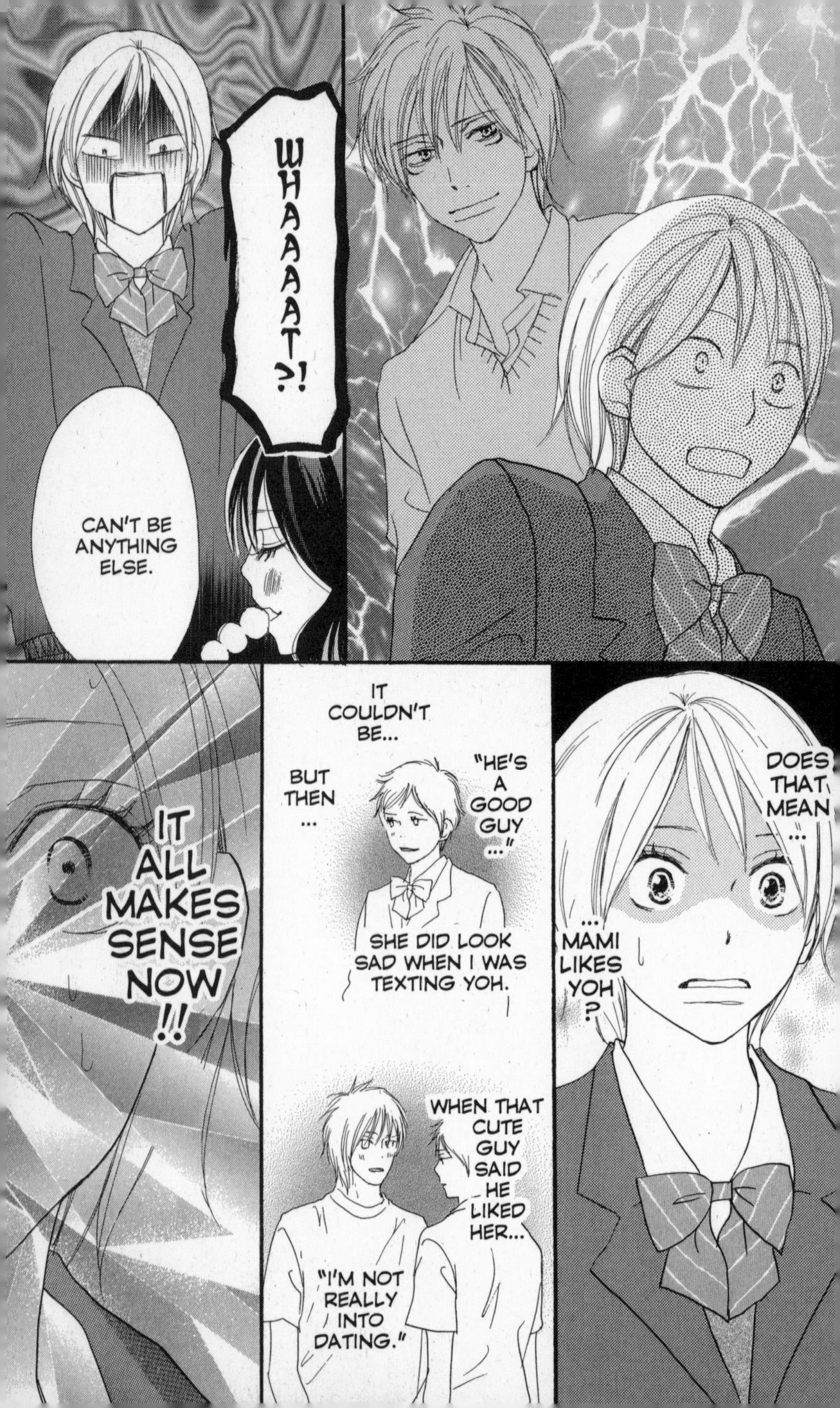
WHAAAAAT?!
CAN'T BE ANYTHING ELSE.
DOES THAT MEAN...
...MAMI LIKES YOH?
IT COULDN'T BE...
"HE'S A GOOD GUY..."
BUT THEN...
SHE DID LOOK SAD WHEN I WAS TEXTING YOH.
WHEN THAT CUTE GUY SAID HE LIKED HER...
"I'M NOT REALLY INTO DATING."
IT ALL MAKES SENSE NOW!!

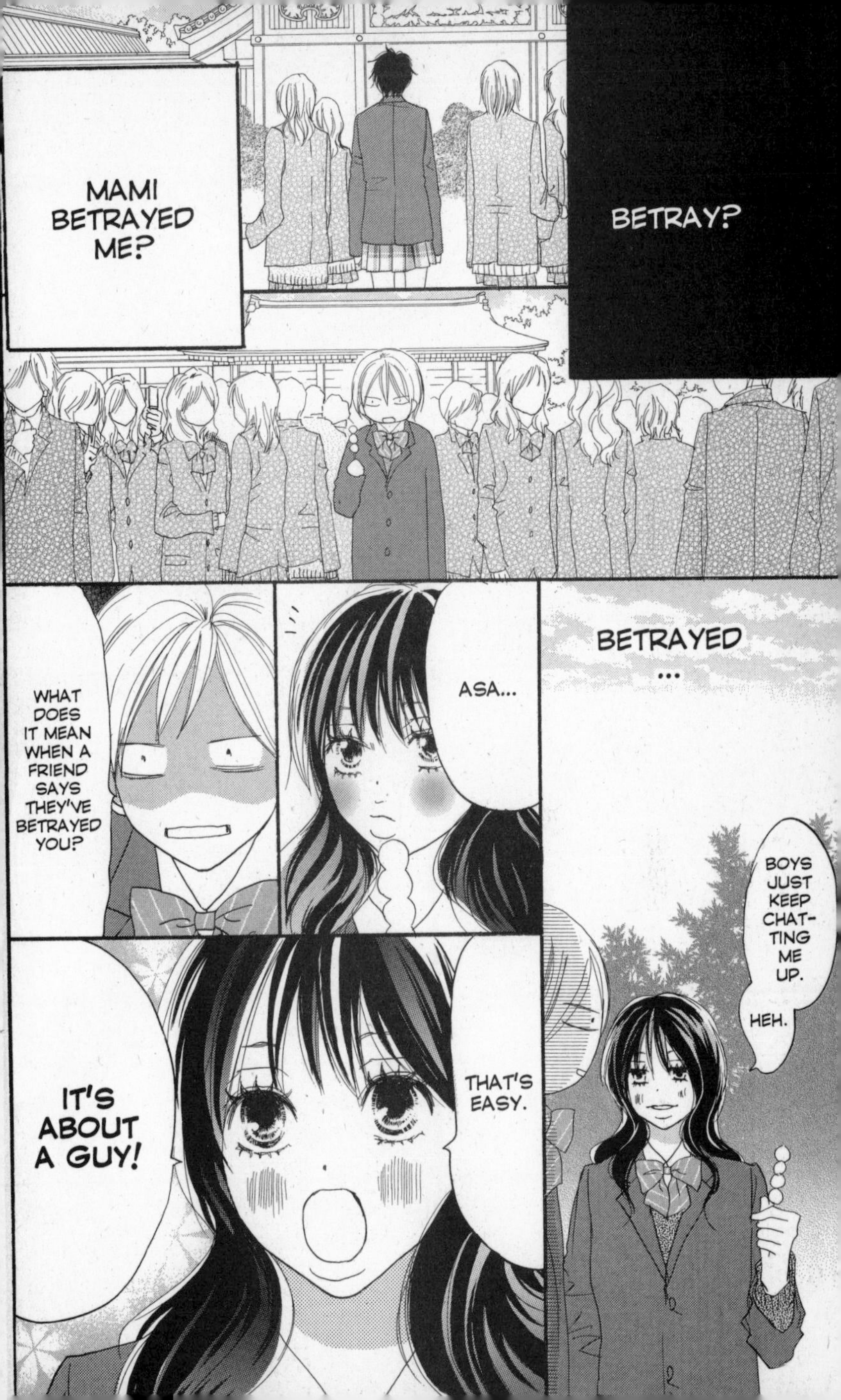
BETRAY?
MAMI BETRAYED ME?
BETRAYED...
BOYS JUST KEEP CHAT-TING ME UP.
HEH.
ASA...
WHAT DOES IT MEAN WHEN A FRIEND SAYS THEY'VE BETRAYED YOU?
THAT'S EASY.
IT'S ABOUT A GUY!

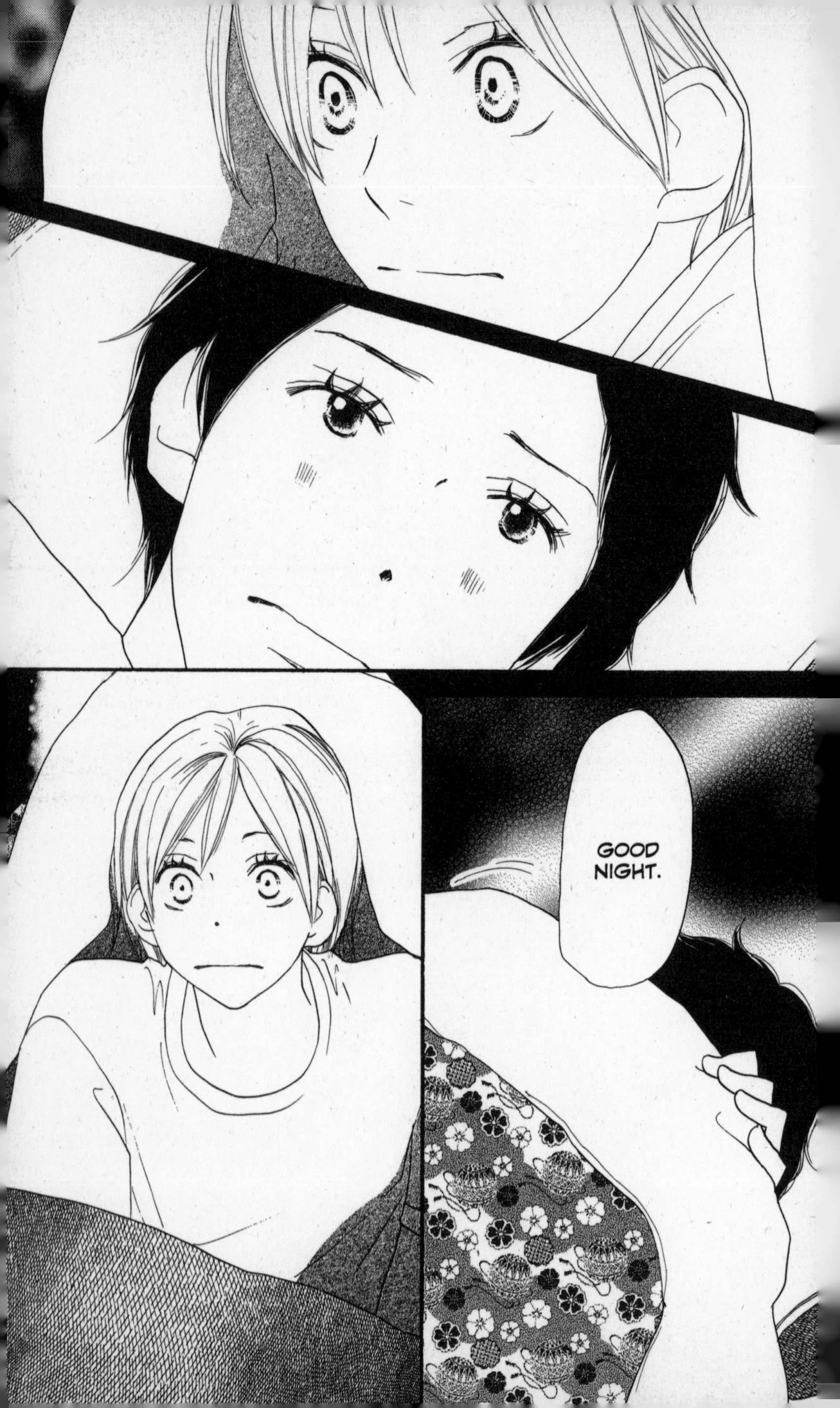
GOOD NIGHT.

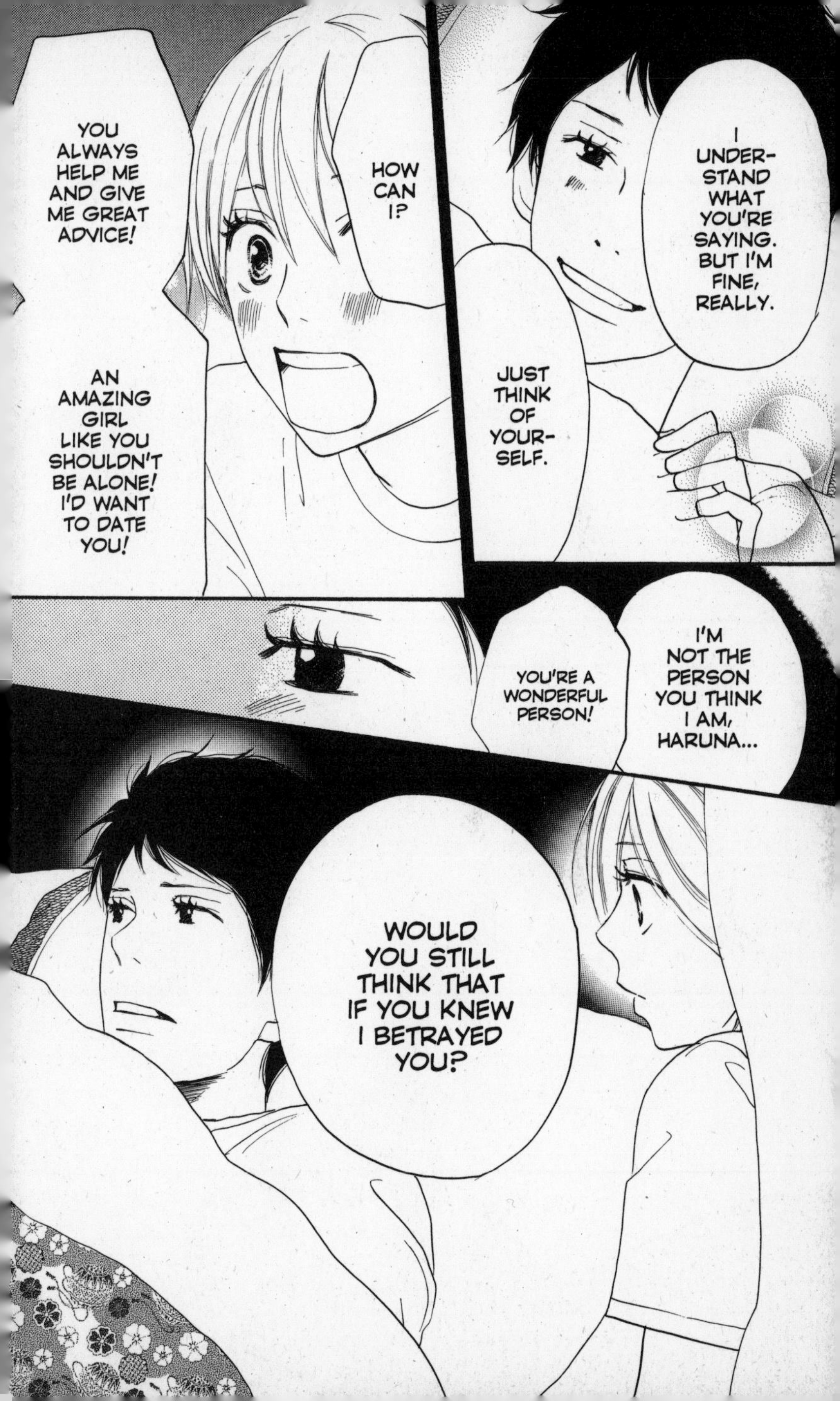

I UNDER-STAND WHAT YOU'RE SAYING. BUT I'M FINE, REALLY.
JUST THINK OF YOUR-SELF.
HOW CAN I?
YOU ALWAYS HELP ME AND GIVE ME GREAT ADVICE!
AN AMAZING GIRL LIKE YOU SHOULDN'T BE ALONE! I'D WANT TO DATE YOU!
I'M NOT THE PERSON YOU THINK I AM, HARUNA...
YOU'RE A WONDERFUL PERSON!
WOULD YOU STILL THINK THAT IF YOU KNEW I BETRAYED YOU?

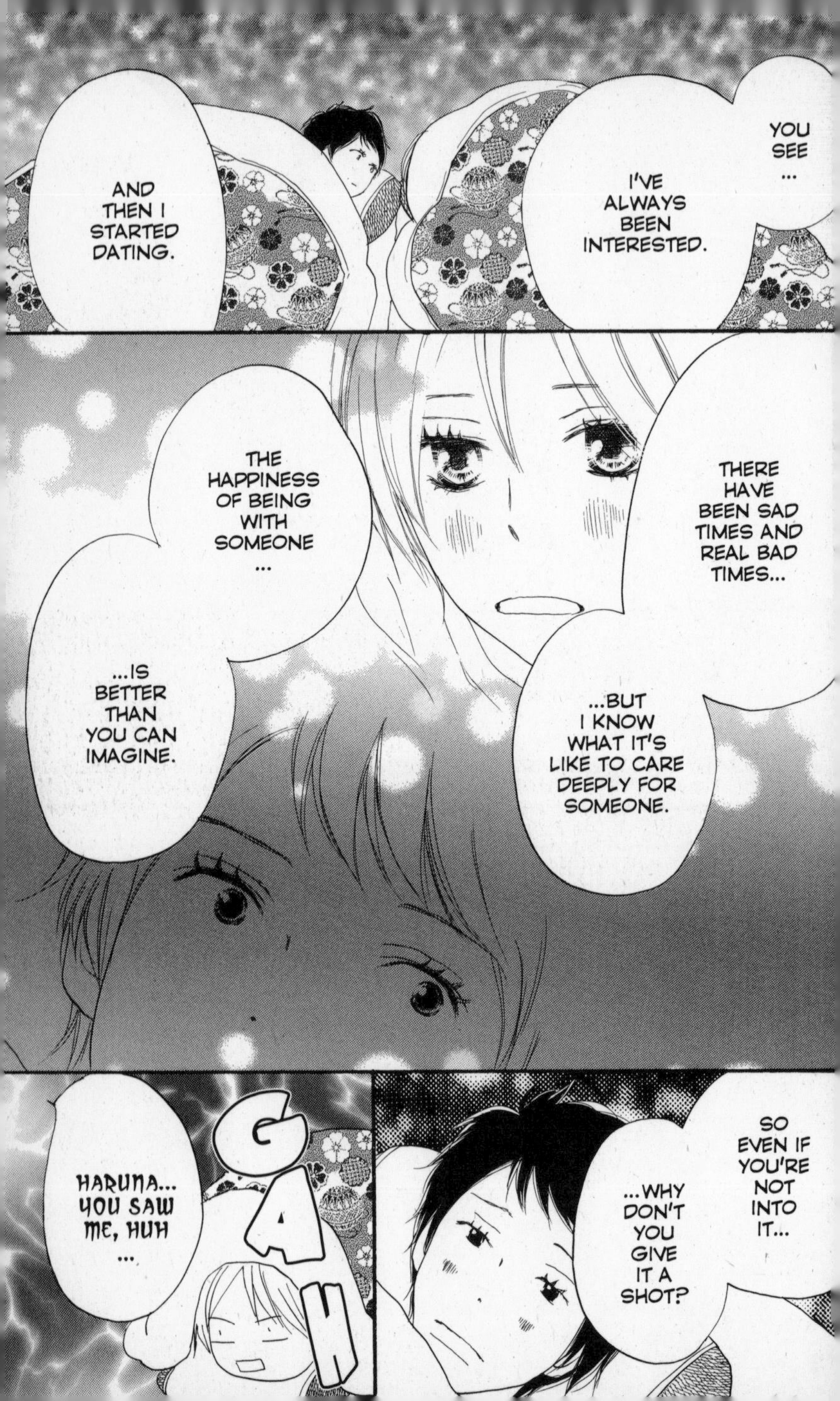
YOU SEE ...
I'VE ALWAYS BEEN INTERESTED.
AND THEN I STARTED DATING.
THERE HAVE BEEN SAD TIMES AND REAL BAD TIMES...
...BUT I KNOW WHAT IT'S LIKE TO CARE DEEPLY FOR SOMEONE.
THE HAPPINESS OF BEING WITH SOMEONE ...
...IS BETTER THAN YOU CAN IMAGINE.
SO EVEN IF YOU'RE NOT INTO IT...
...WHY DON'T YOU GIVE IT A SHOT?
GAH
HARUNA... YOU SAW ME, HUH ...

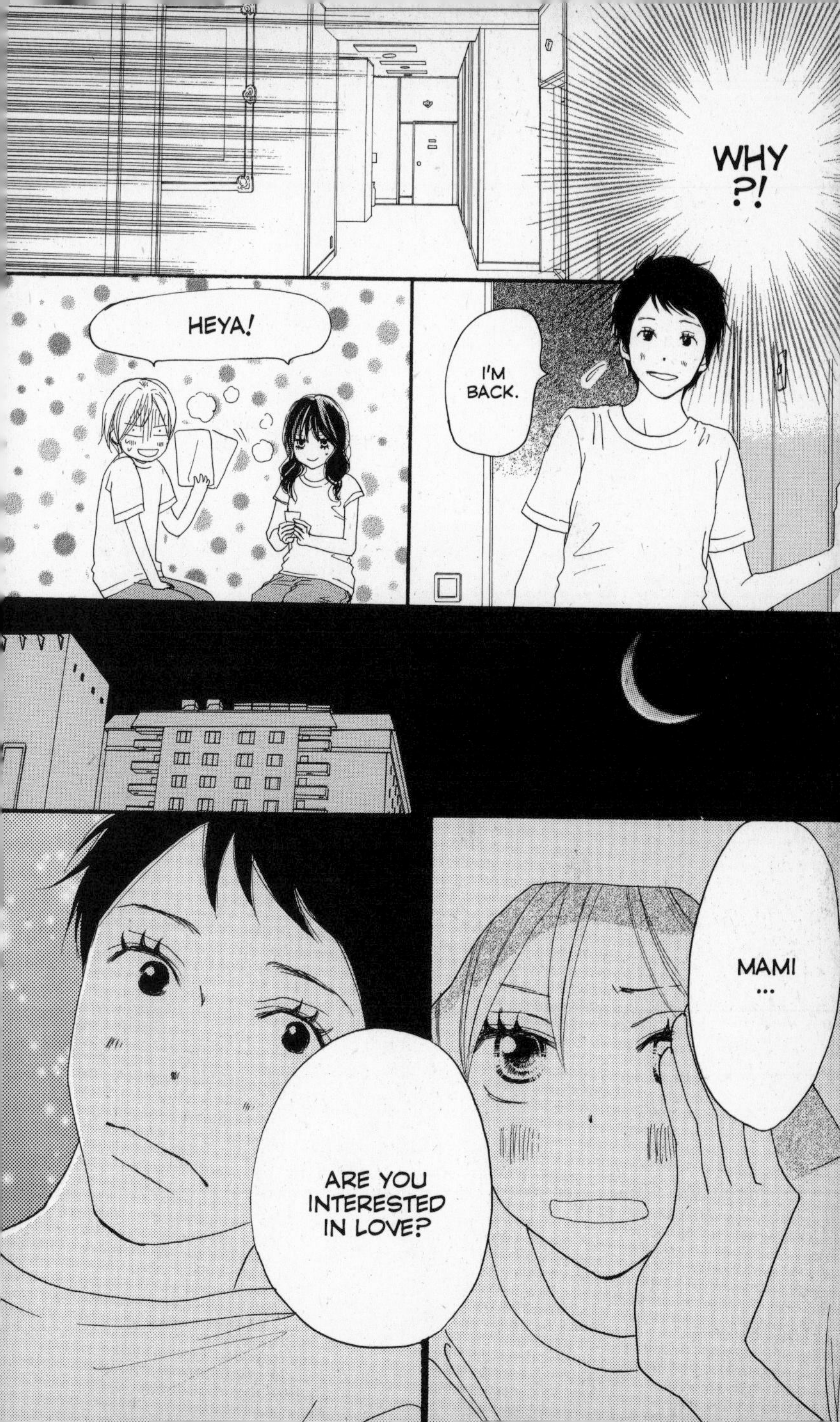
WHY ?!
I'M BACK.
HEYA!
MAMI ...
ARE YOU INTERESTED IN LOVE?

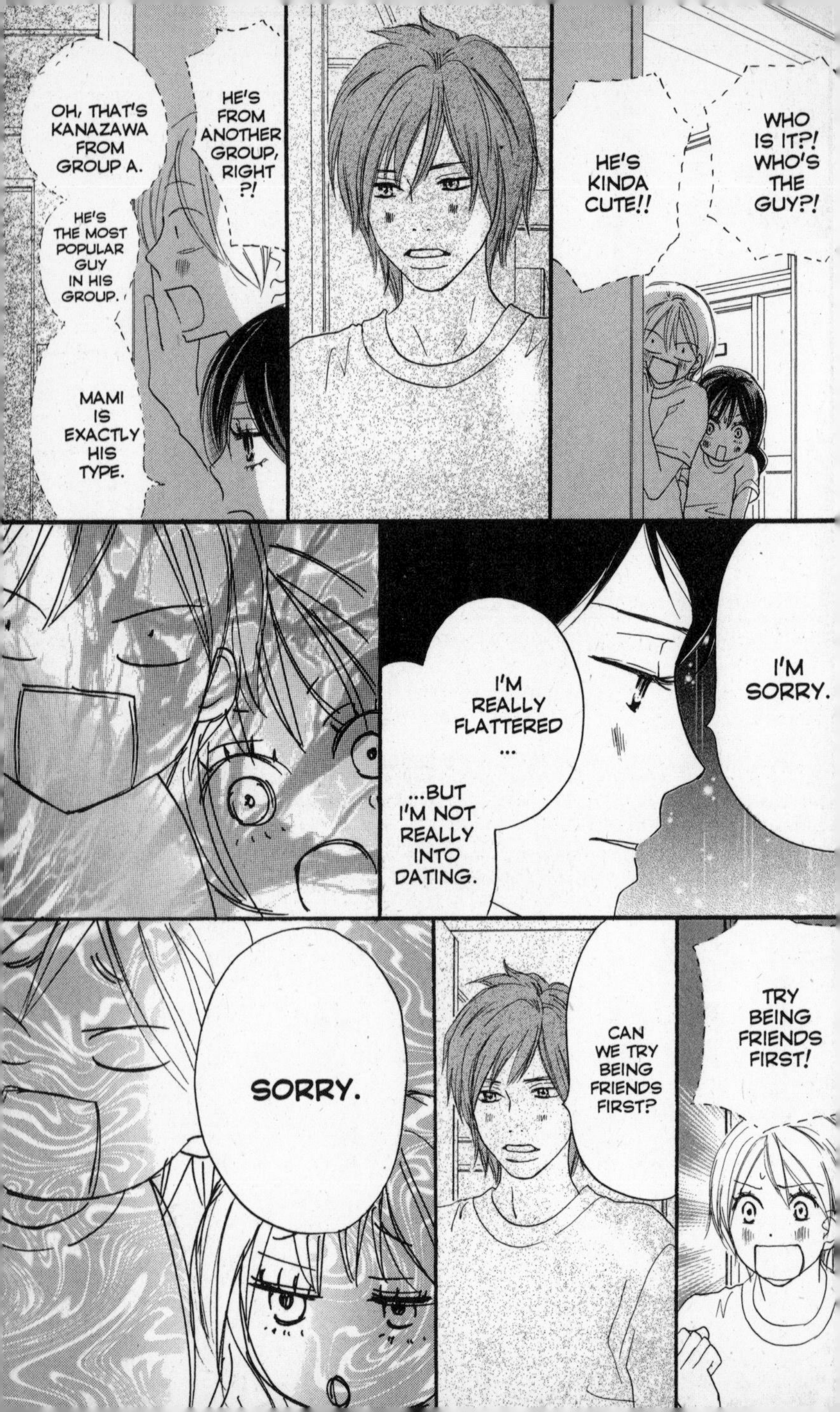
WHO IS IT?! WHO'S THE GUY?!
HE'S KINDA CUTE!!
HE'S FROM ANOTHER GROUP, RIGHT?!
OH, THAT'S KANAZAWA FROM GROUP A.
HE'S THE MOST POPULAR GUY IN HIS GROUP.
MAMI IS EXACTLY HIS TYPE.
I'M SORRY.
I'M REALLY FLATTERED ...
...BUT I'M NOT REALLY INTO DATING.
TRY BEING FRIENDS FIRST!
CAN WE TRY BEING FRIENDS FIRST?
SORRY.

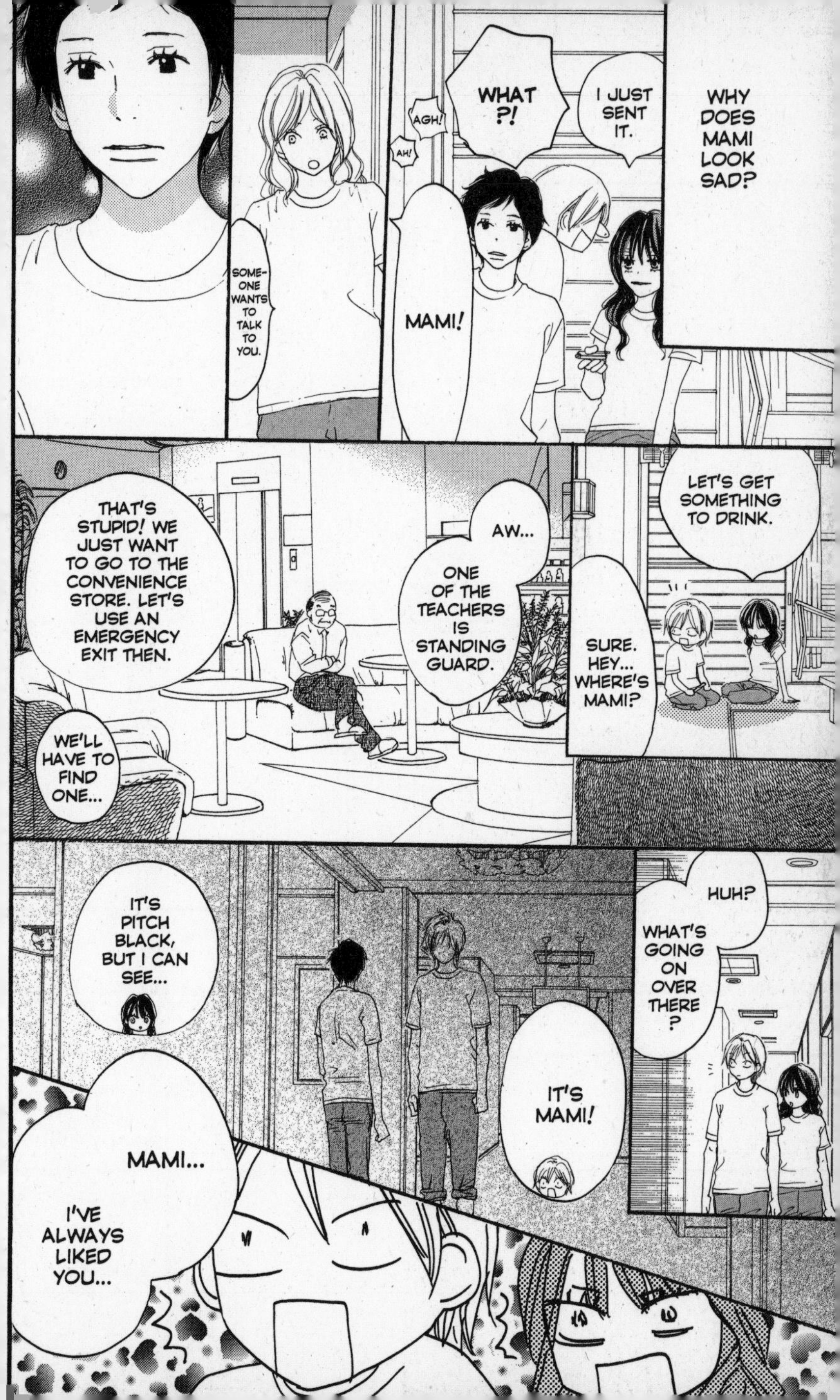
WHY DOES MAMI LOOK SAD?
I JUST SENT IT.
WHAT?!
AGH!
AH!
MAMI!
SOME-ONE WANTS TO TALK TO YOU.
LET'S GET SOMETHING TO DRINK.
SURE. HEY... WHERE'S MAMI?
AW...
ONE OF THE TEACHERS IS STANDING GUARD.
THAT'S STUPID! WE JUST WANT TO GO TO THE CONVENIENCE STORE. LET'S USE AN EMERGENCY EXIT THEN.
WE'LL HAVE TO FIND ONE...
HUH?
WHAT'S GOING ON OVER THERE?
IT'S MAMI!
IT'S PITCH BLACK, BUT I CAN SEE...
MAMI...
I'VE ALWAYS LIKED YOU...

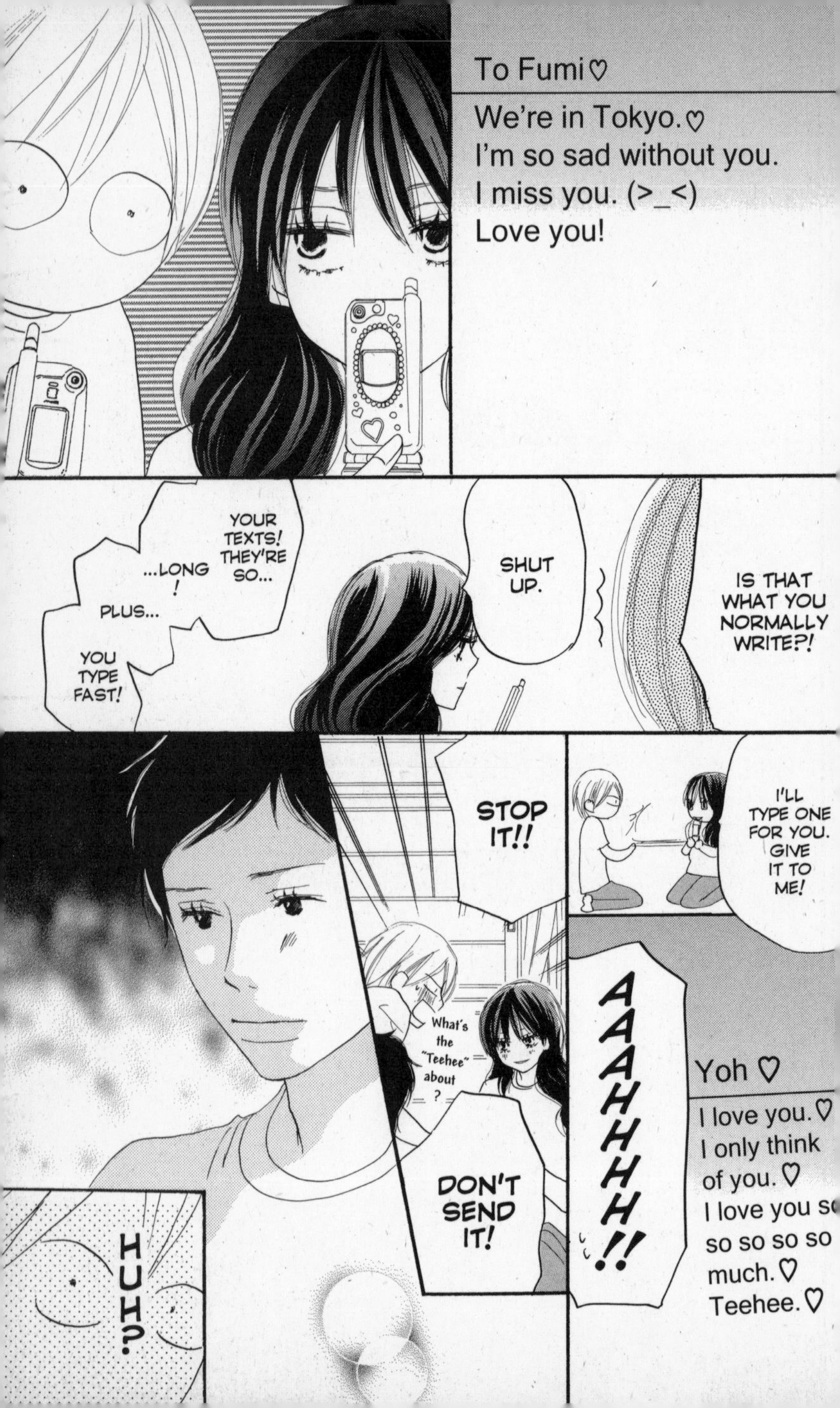
To Fumi♡
We're in Tokyo.♡
I'm so sad without you.
I miss you. (>_<)
Love you!
IS THAT WHAT YOU NORMALLY WRITE?!
SHUT UP.
YOUR TEXTS! THEY'RE SO...
...LONG!
PLUS...
YOU TYPE FAST!
I'LL TYPE ONE FOR YOU. GIVE IT TO ME!
Yoh♡
I love you.♡
I only think of you.♡
I love you s
so so so so
much.♡
Teehee.♡
AAAHHHHH!!
STOP IT!!
What's the "Teehee" about?
DON'T SEND IT!
HUH?

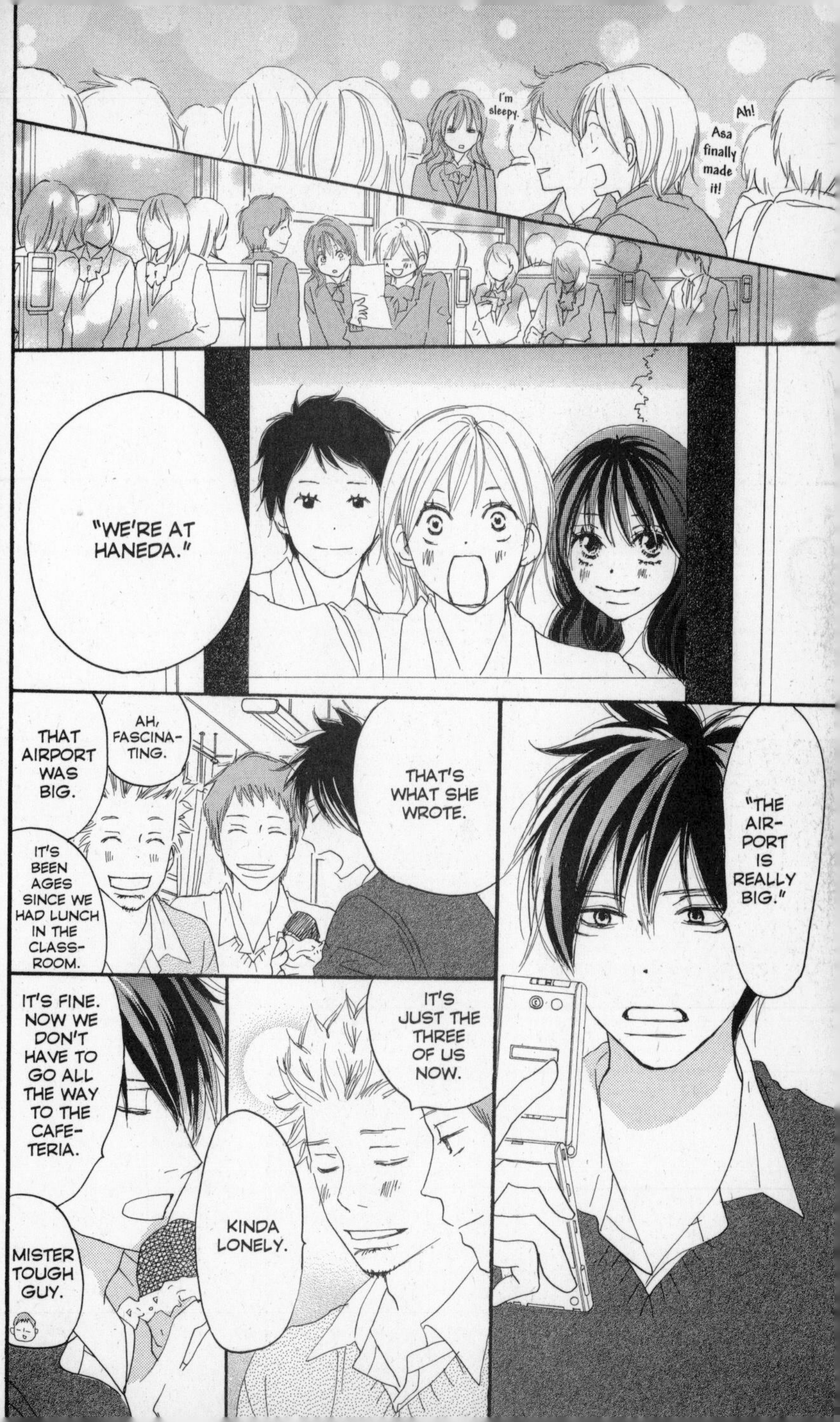
Ah! Asa finally made it!
I'm sleepy.
"WE'RE AT HANEDA."
"THE AIRPORT IS REALLY BIG."
THAT'S WHAT SHE WROTE.
AH, FASCINATING.
THAT AIRPORT WAS BIG.
IT'S BEEN AGES SINCE WE HAD LUNCH IN THE CLASSROOM.
IT'S JUST THE THREE OF US NOW.
KINDA LONELY.
IT'S FINE. NOW WE DON'T HAVE TO GO ALL THE WAY TO THE CAFETERIA.
MISTER TOUGH GUY.

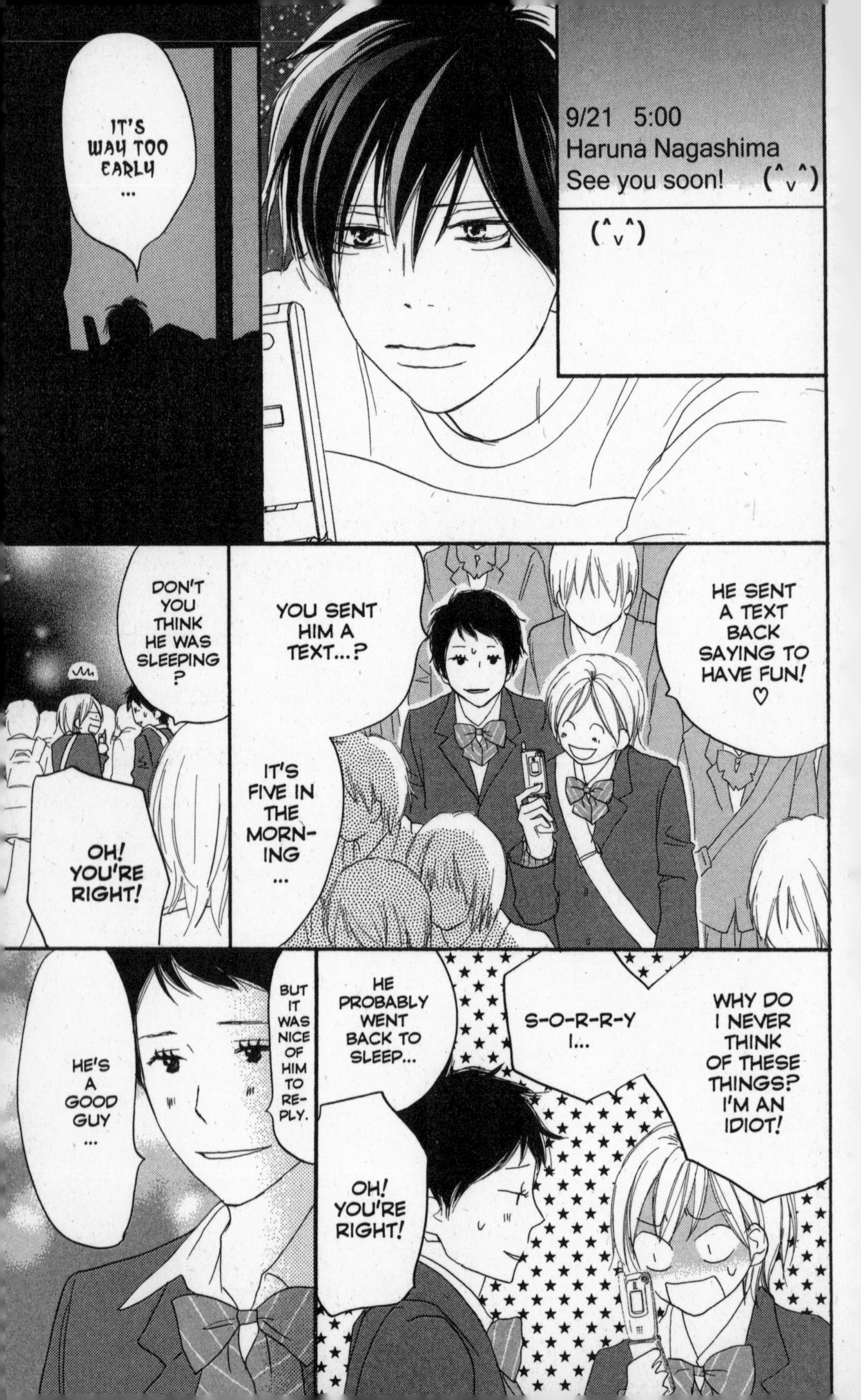
9/21 5:00
Haruna Nagashima
See you soon! (^v^)
(^v^)
IT'S WAY TOO EARLY ...
HE SENT A TEXT BACK SAYING TO HAVE FUN! ♡
YOU SENT HIM A TEXT...?
IT'S FIVE IN THE MORNING ...
DON'T YOU THINK HE WAS SLEEPING?
OH! YOU'RE RIGHT!
WHY DO I NEVER THINK OF THESE THINGS? I'M AN IDIOT!
S-O-R-R-Y I...
HE PROBABLY WENT BACK TO SLEEP...
OH! YOU'RE RIGHT!
BUT IT WAS NICE OF HIM TO RE-PLY.
HE'S A GOOD GUY ...

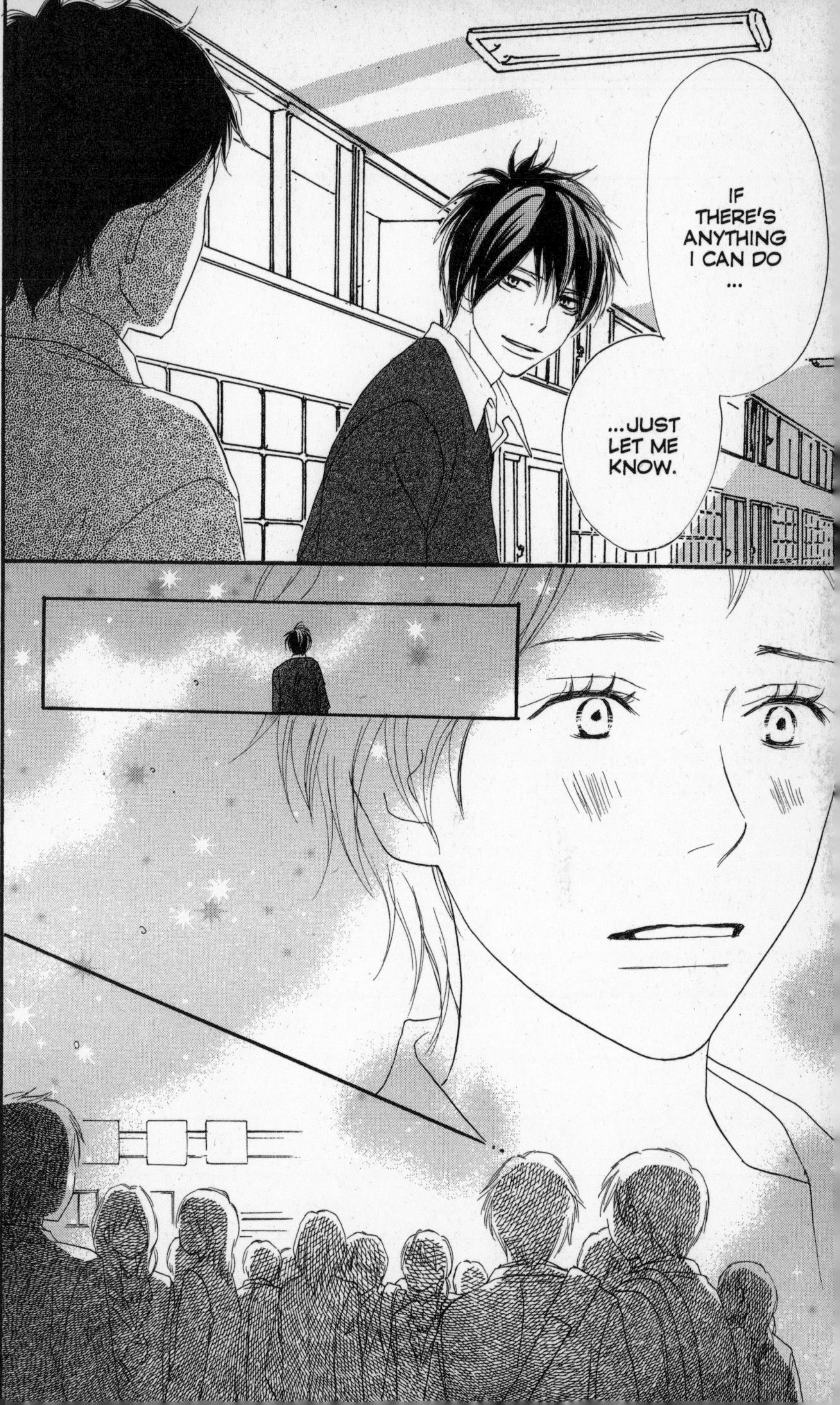
IF THERE'S ANYTHING I CAN DO ...
...JUST LET ME KNOW.

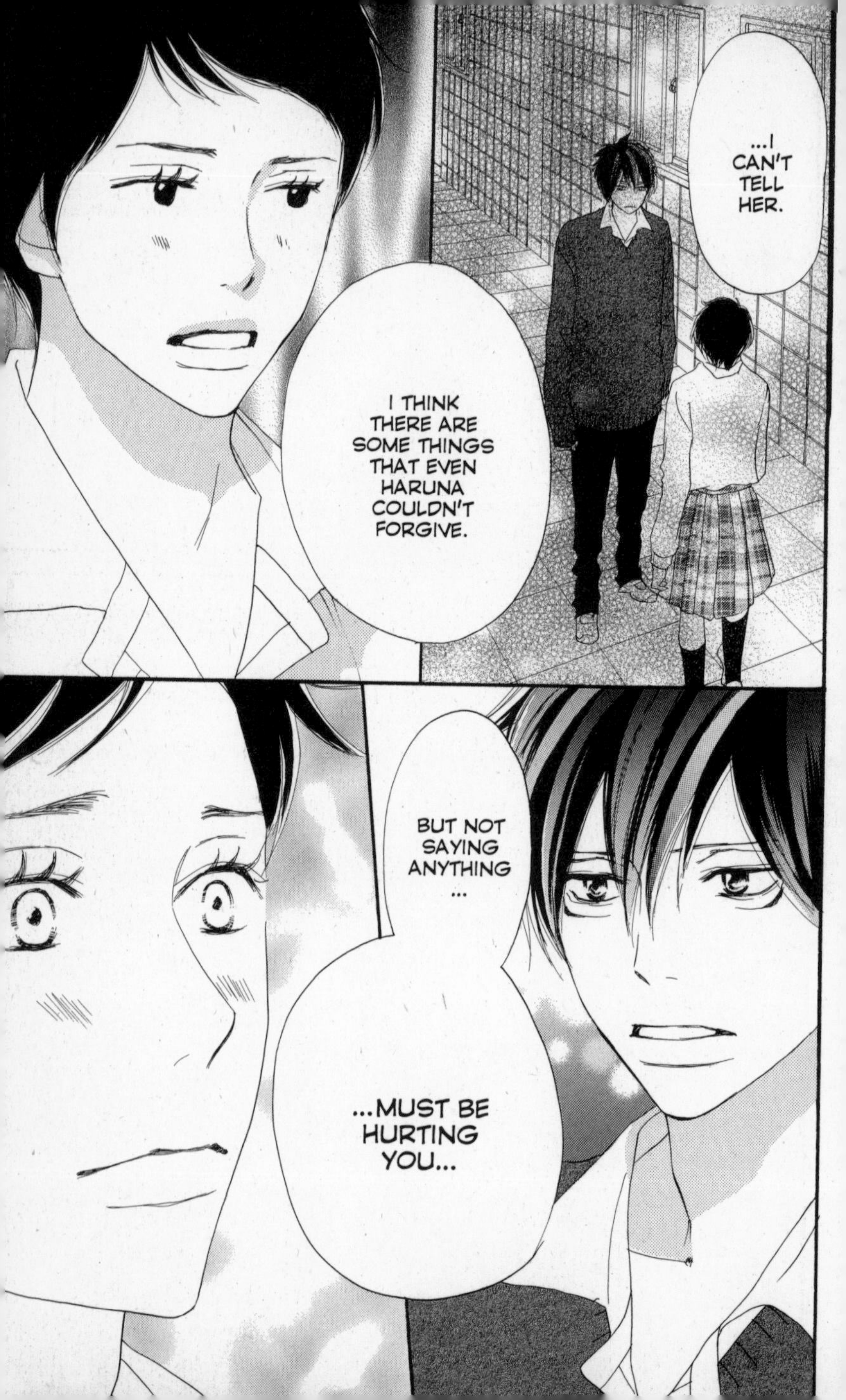
...I CAN'T TELL HER.
I THINK THERE ARE SOME THINGS THAT EVEN HARUNA COULDN'T FORGIVE.
BUT NOT SAYING ANYTHING ...
...MUST BE HURTING YOU...

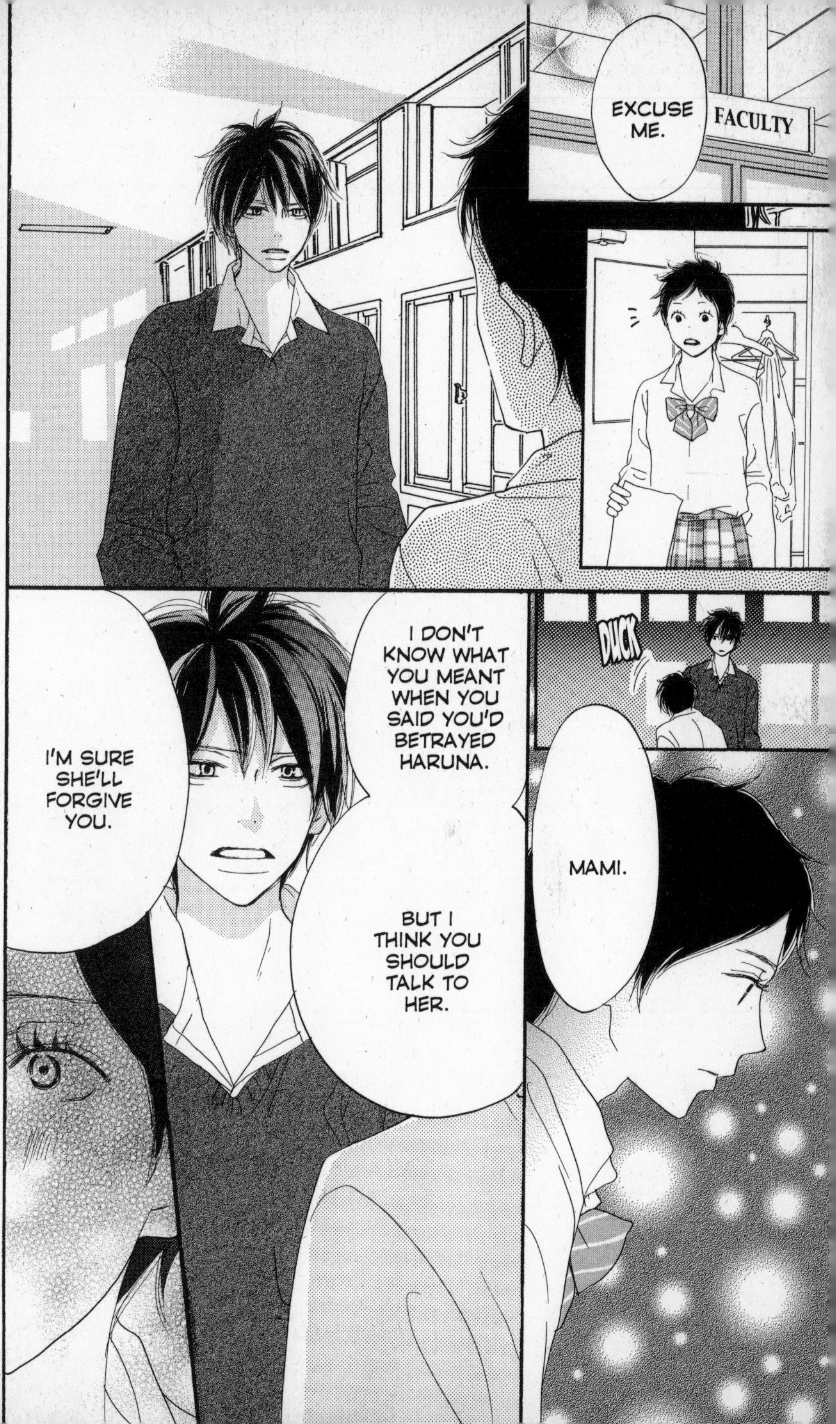
EXCUSE ME.
FACULTY
DUCK
MAMI.
I DON'T KNOW WHAT YOU MEANT WHEN YOU SAID YOU'D BETRAYED HARUNA.
BUT I THINK YOU SHOULD TALK TO HER.
I'M SURE SHE'LL FORGIVE YOU.

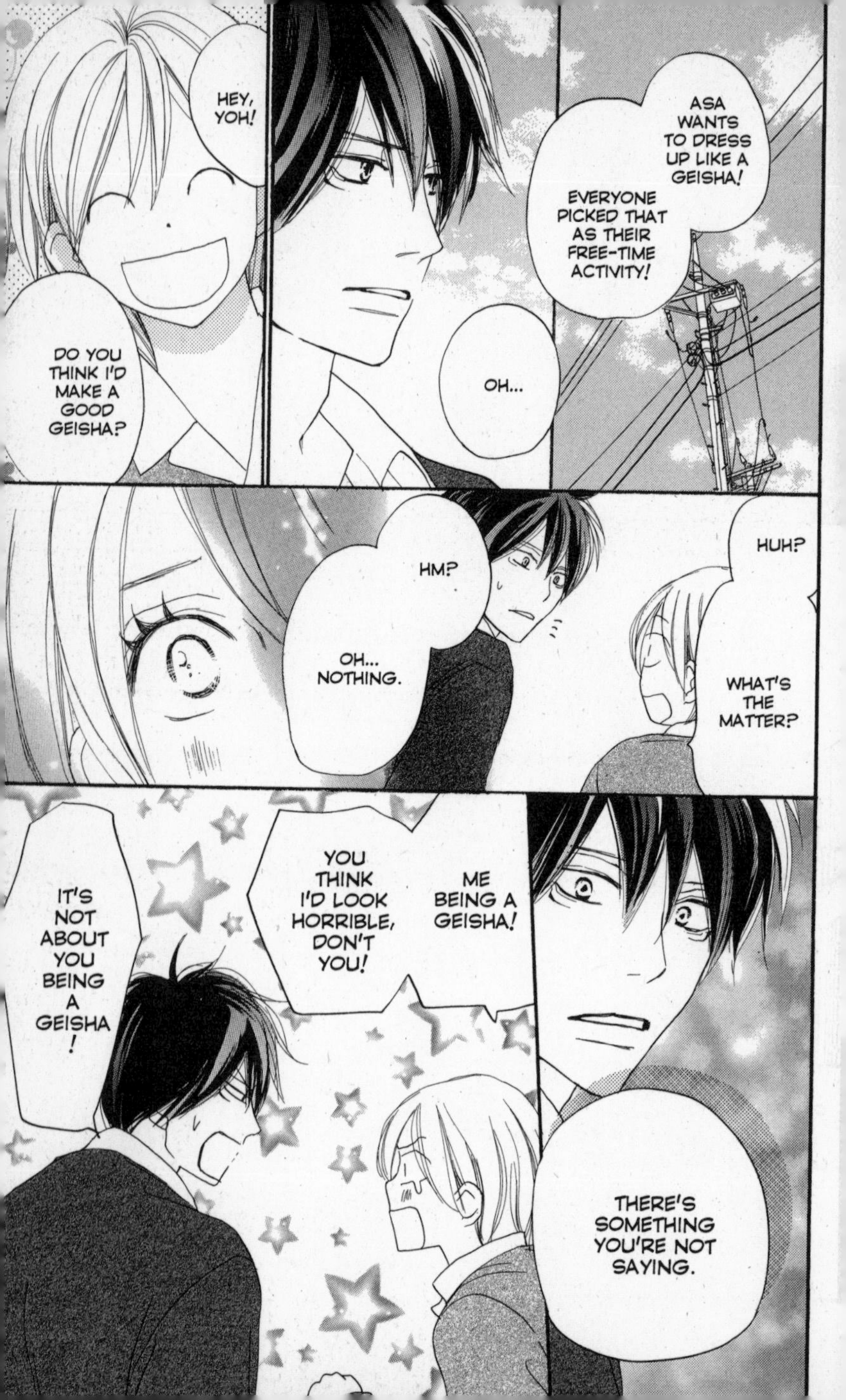
ASA WANTS TO DRESS UP LIKE A GEISHA!
EVERYONE PICKED THAT AS THEIR FREE-TIME ACTIVITY!
OH...
HEY, YOH!
DO YOU THINK I'D MAKE A GOOD GEISHA?
HUH?
WHAT'S THE MATTER?
HM?
OH... NOTHING.
THERE'S SOMETHING YOU'RE NOT SAYING.
YOU THINK I'D LOOK HORRIBLE, DON'T YOU! ME BEING A GEISHA!
IT'S NOT ABOUT YOU BEING A GEISHA!

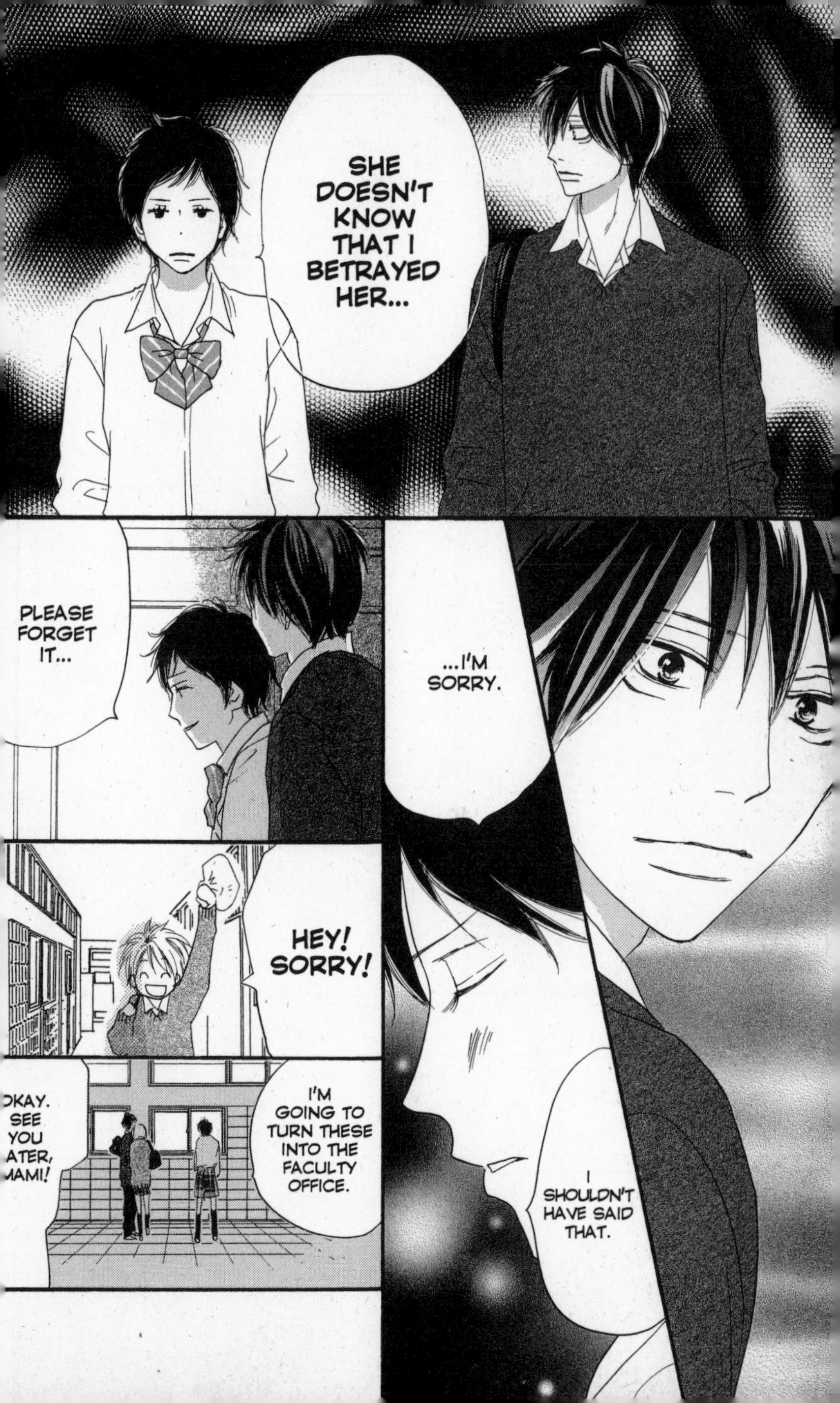
SHE DOESN'T KNOW THAT I BETRAYED HER...
...I'M SORRY.
I SHOULDN'T HAVE SAID THAT.
PLEASE FORGET IT...
HEY! SORRY!
I'M GOING TO TURN THESE INTO THE FACULTY OFFICE.
OKAY. SEE YOU LATER, MAMI!

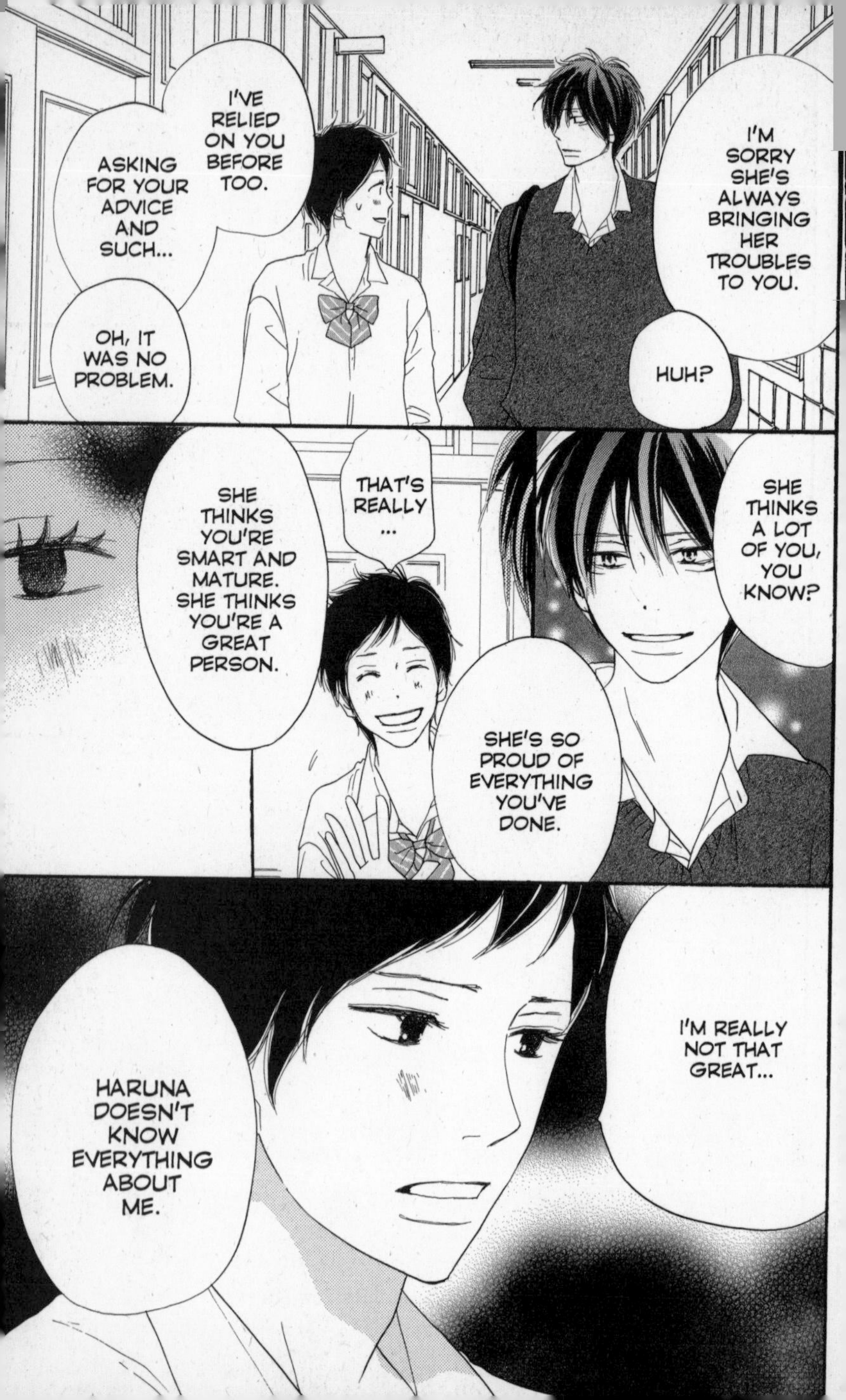
I'M SORRY SHE'S ALWAYS BRINGING HER TROUBLES TO YOU.
HUH?
I'VE RELIED ON YOU BEFORE TOO.
ASKING FOR YOUR ADVICE AND SUCH...
OH, IT WAS NO PROBLEM.
SHE THINKS A LOT OF YOU, YOU KNOW?
SHE'S SO PROUD OF EVERYTHING YOU'VE DONE.
THAT'S REALLY...
SHE THINKS YOU'RE SMART AND MATURE. SHE THINKS YOU'RE A GREAT PERSON.
I'M REALLY NOT THAT GREAT...
HARUNA DOESN'T KNOW EVERYTHING ABOUT ME.

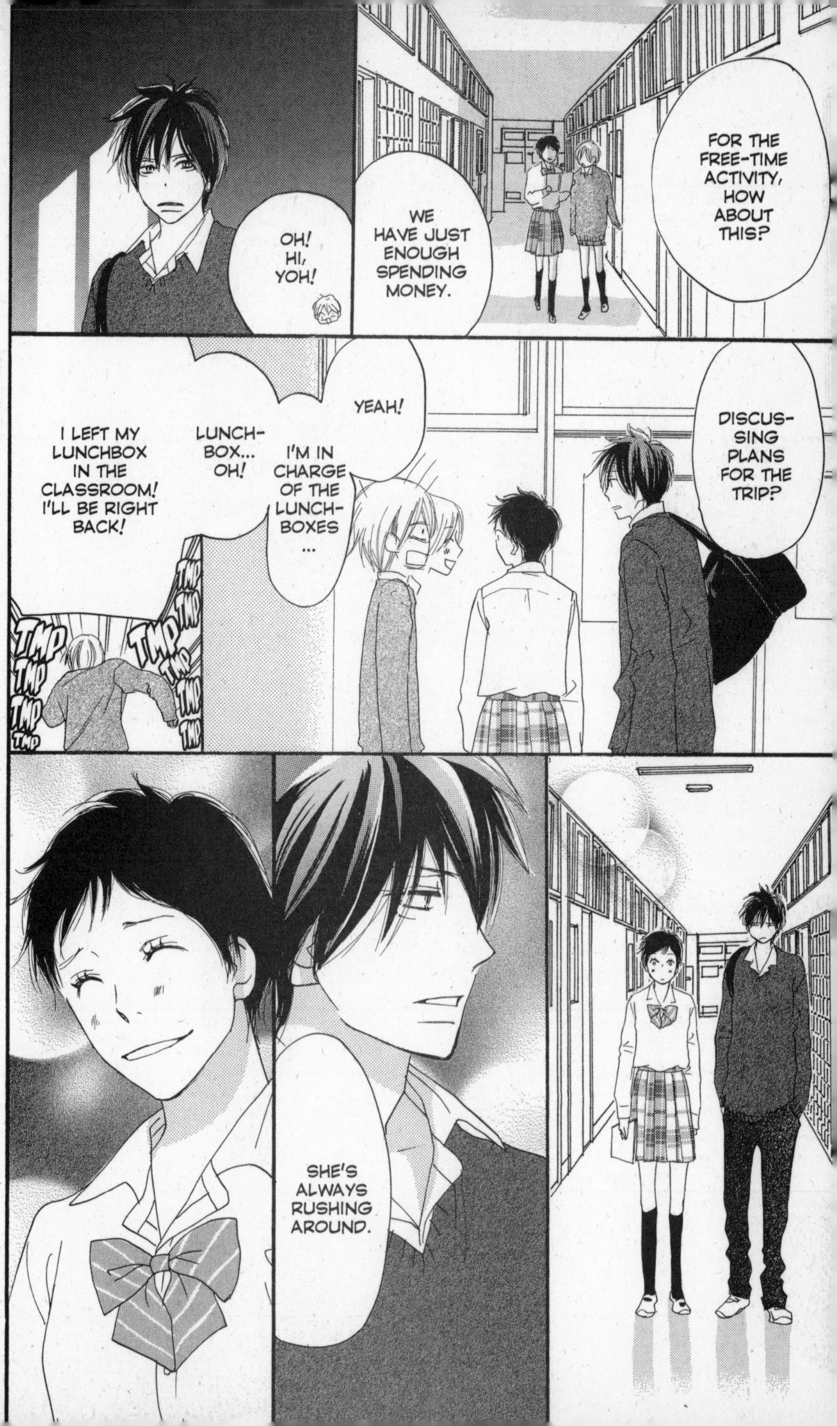
FOR THE FREE-TIME ACTIVITY, HOW ABOUT THIS?
WE HAVE JUST ENOUGH SPENDING MONEY.
OH! HI, YOH!
DISCUS-SING PLANS FOR THE TRIP?
YEAH!
I'M IN CHARGE OF THE LUNCH-BOXES ...
LUNCH-BOX... OH!
I LEFT MY LUNCHBOX IN THE CLASSROOM! I'LL BE RIGHT BACK!
TMP TMP TMP TMP TMP TMP TMP TMP TMP TMP TMP
SHE'S ALWAYS RUSHING AROUND.

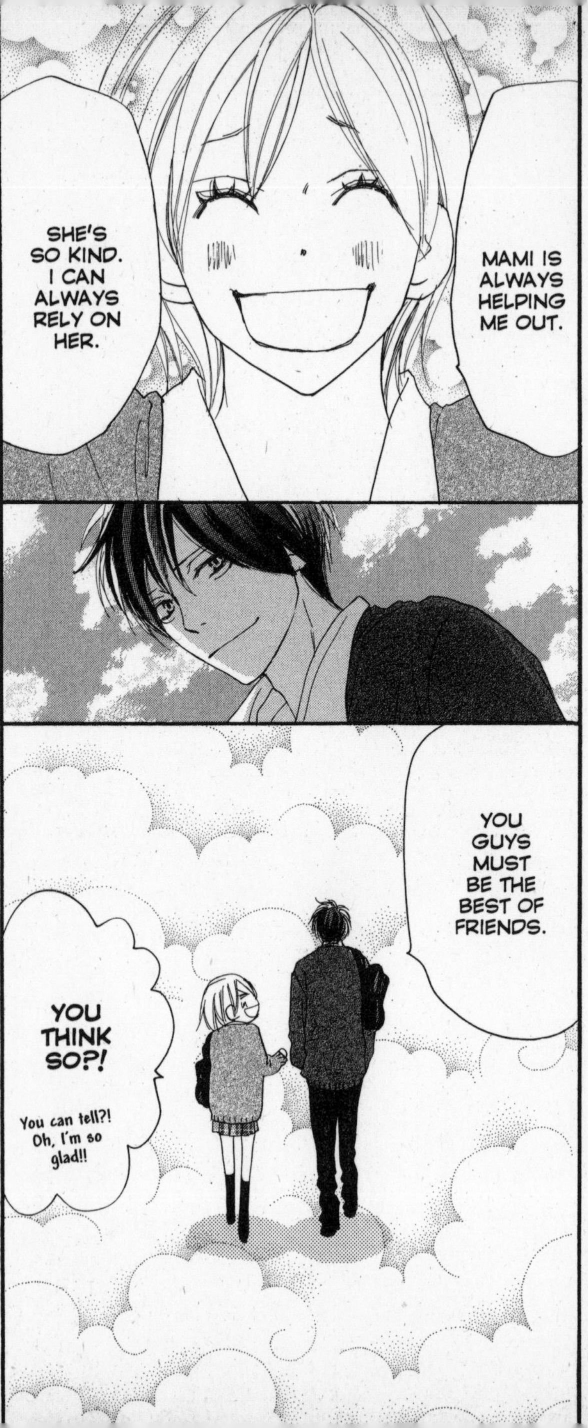
MAMI IS ALWAYS HELPING ME OUT.
SHE'S SO KIND. I CAN ALWAYS RELY ON HER.
YOU GUYS MUST BE THE BEST OF FRIENDS.
YOU THINK SO?!
You can tell?! Oh, I'm so glad!!

2

This isn't relevant to anything, but when kids are playing superheroes, I like to get involved.

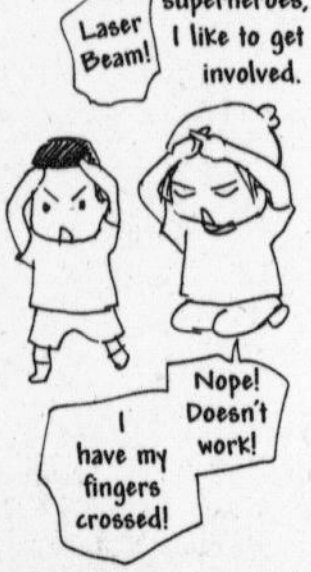
Laser Beam!
Nope! Doesn't work!
I have my fingers crossed!

Parents seem to get tired of their kids' games, but I don't think I could ever get bored of this.

※Kung-fu Games

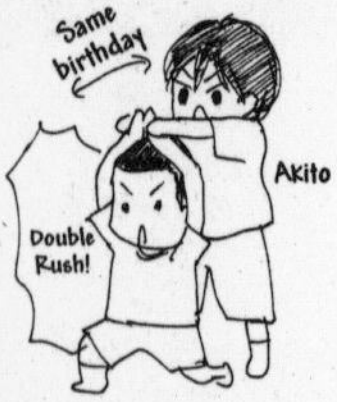
Same birthday
Akito
Double Rush!

Children playing together are so cute! Adults just can't compare.

This happened recently with my niece:

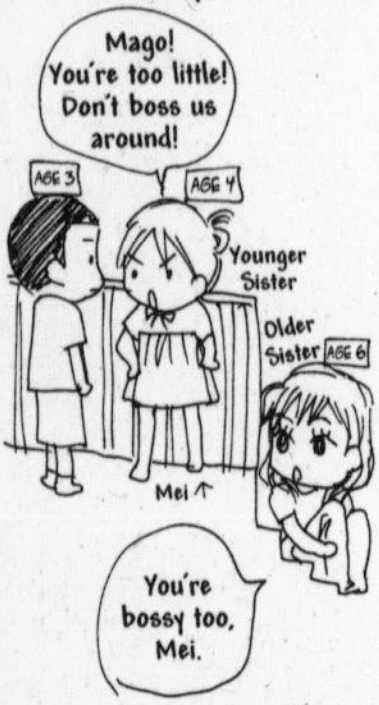
Mago! You're too little! Don't boss us around!
AGE 3
AGE 4
Younger Sister
Older Sister
AGE 6
Mei ↑
You're bossy too, Mei.

I'm not good at writing kids' speech.

See you in the next volume!

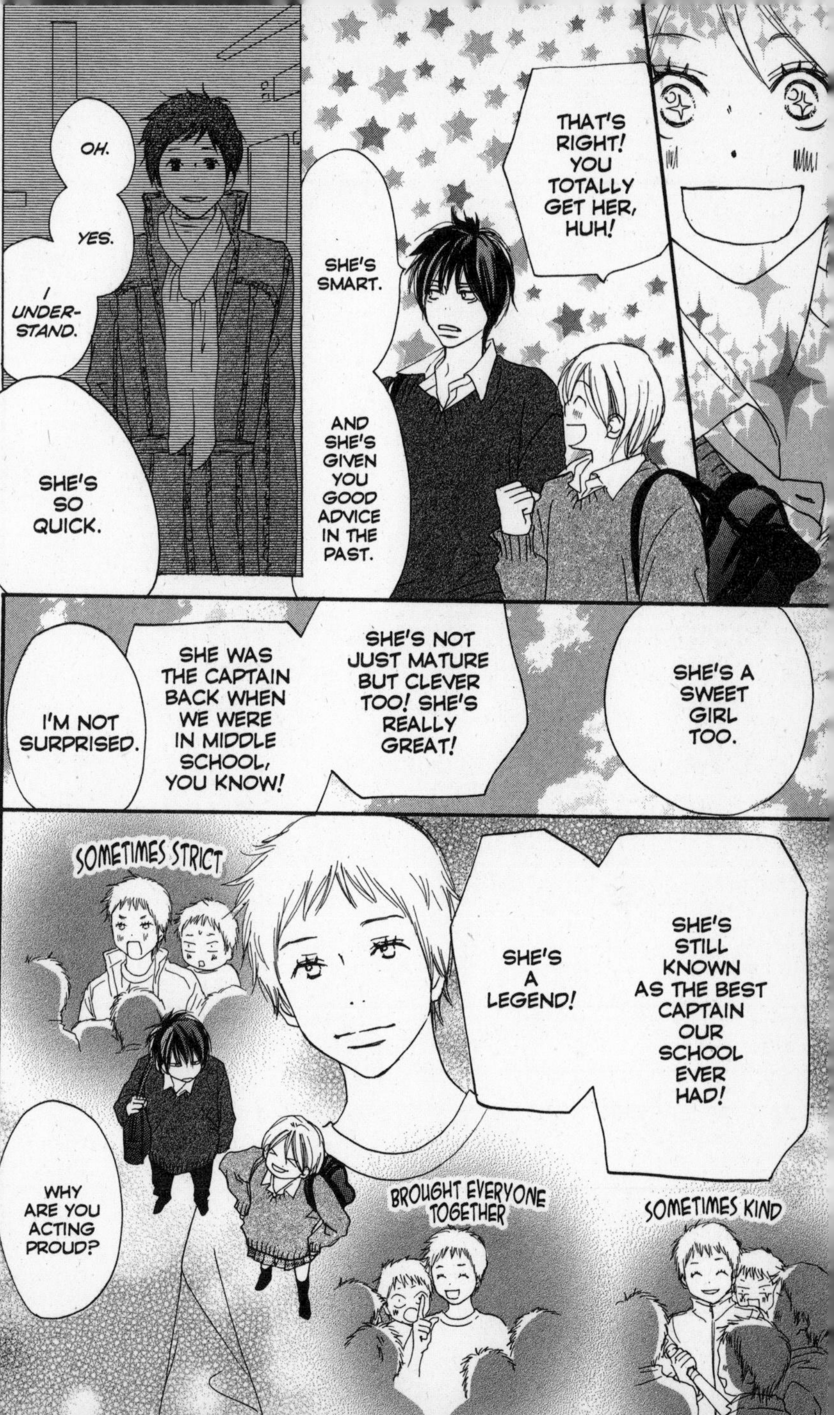
THAT'S RIGHT! YOU TOTALLY GET HER, HUH!
SHE'S SMART.
AND SHE'S GIVEN YOU GOOD ADVICE IN THE PAST.
OH.
YES.
I UNDERSTAND.
SHE'S SO QUICK.
SHE'S A SWEET GIRL TOO.
SHE'S NOT JUST MATURE BUT CLEVER TOO! SHE'S REALLY GREAT!
SHE WAS THE CAPTAIN BACK WHEN WE WERE IN MIDDLE SCHOOL, YOU KNOW!
I'M NOT SURPRISED.
SHE'S STILL KNOWN AS THE BEST CAPTAIN OUR SCHOOL EVER HAD!
SHE'S A LEGEND!
SOMETIMES STRICT
SOMETIMES KIND
BROUGHT EVERYONE TOGETHER
WHY ARE YOU ACTING PROUD?

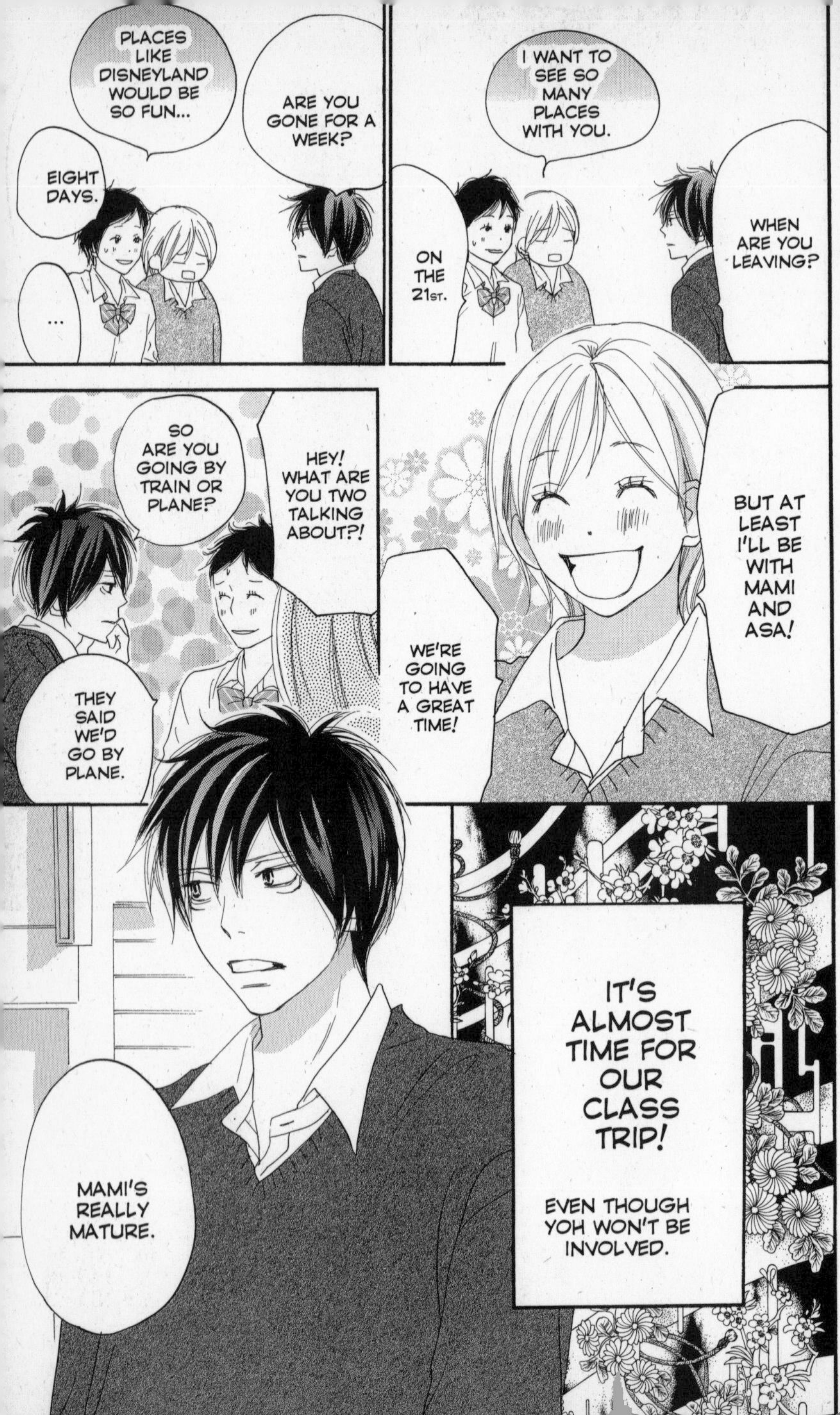
I WANT TO SEE SO MANY PLACES WITH YOU.
WHEN ARE YOU LEAVING?
ON THE 21ST.
PLACES LIKE DISNEYLAND WOULD BE SO FUN...
ARE YOU GONE FOR A WEEK?
EIGHT DAYS.
...
BUT AT LEAST I'LL BE WITH MAMI AND ASA!
WE'RE GOING TO HAVE A GREAT TIME!
HEY! WHAT ARE YOU TWO TALKING ABOUT?!
SO ARE YOU GOING BY TRAIN OR PLANE?
THEY SAID WE'D GO BY PLANE.
IT'S ALMOST TIME FOR OUR CLASS TRIP!
EVEN THOUGH YOH WON'T BE INVOLVED.
MAMI'S REALLY MATURE.

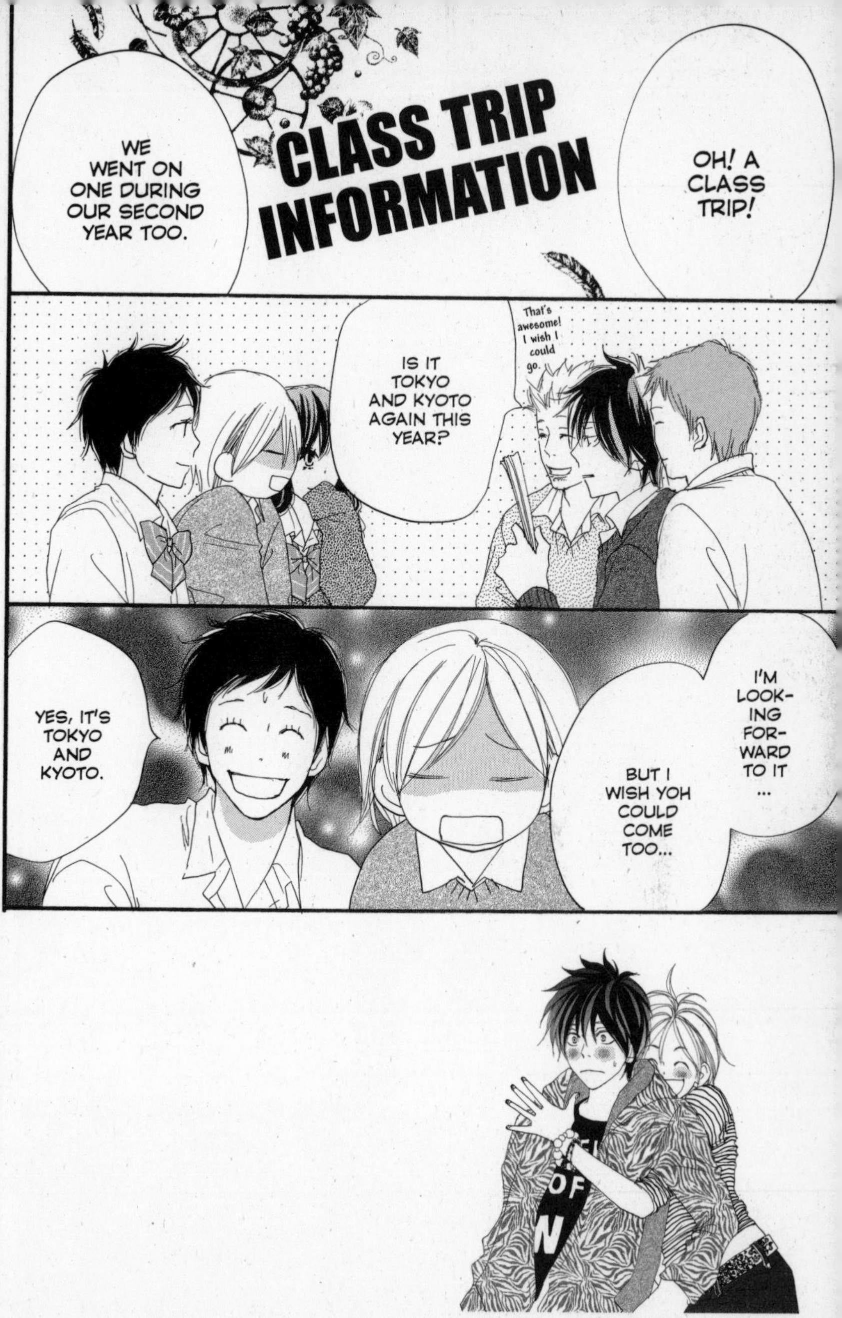
OH! A CLASS TRIP!
CLASS TRIP INFORMATION
WE WENT ON ONE DURING OUR SECOND YEAR TOO.
That's awesome! I wish I could go.
IS IT TOKYO AND KYOTO AGAIN THIS YEAR?
I'M LOOKING-FORWARD TO IT...
BUT I WISH YOH COULD COME TOO...
YES, IT'S TOKYO AND KYOTO.

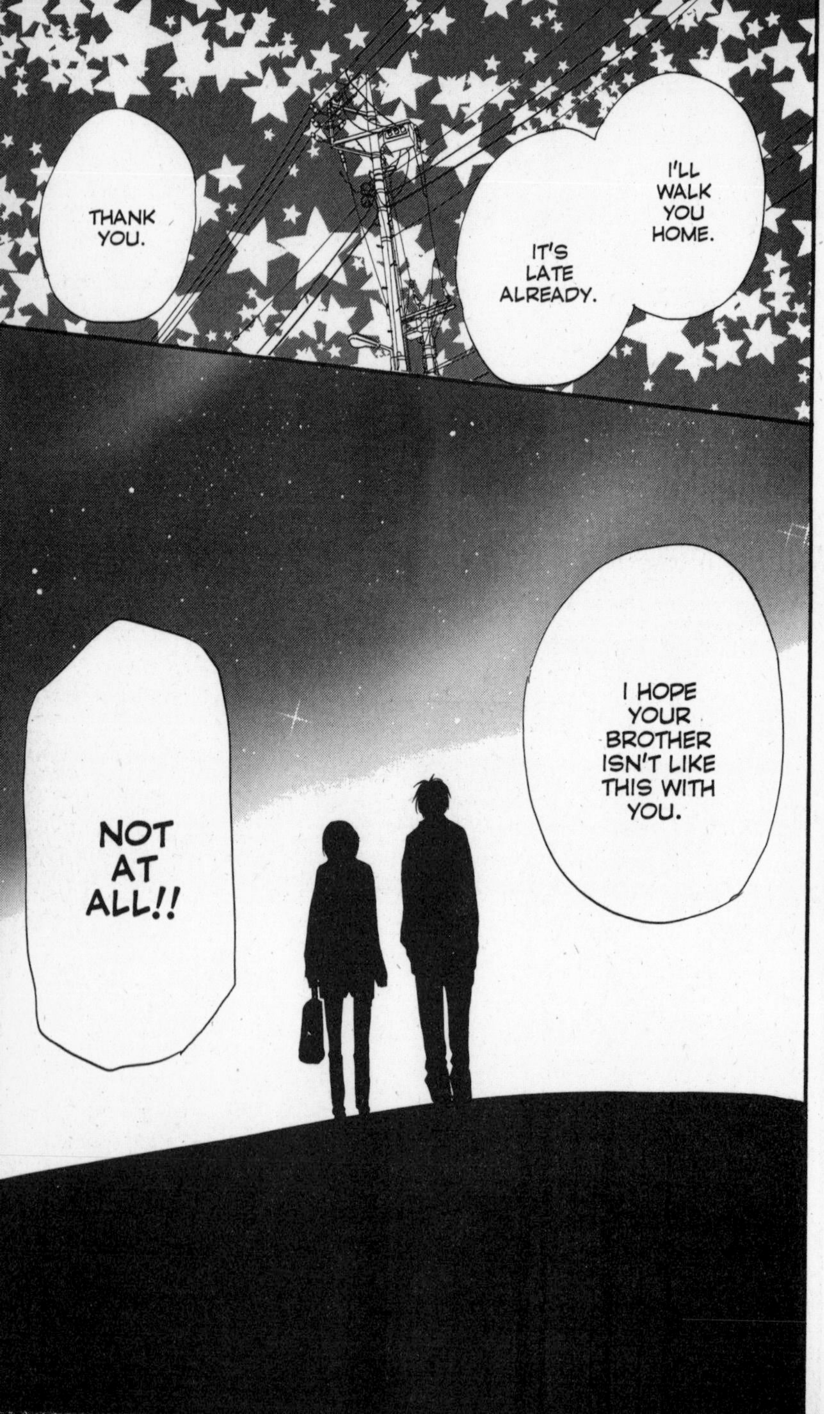
I'LL WALK YOU HOME.
IT'S LATE ALREADY.
THANK YOU.
I HOPE YOUR BROTHER ISN'T LIKE THIS WITH YOU.
NOT AT ALL!!

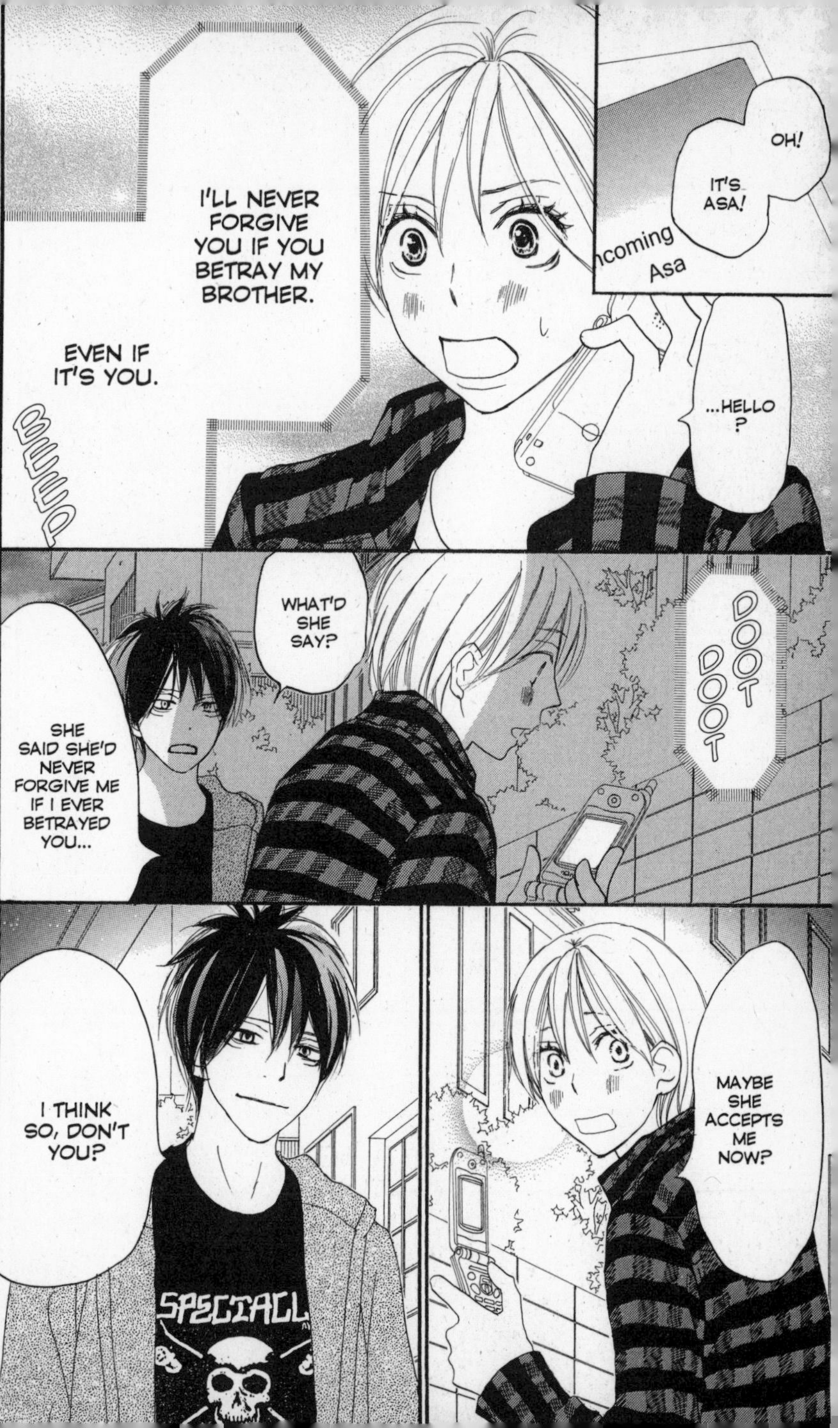
OH!
IT'S ASA!
ncoming
Asa
...HELLO?
I'LL NEVER FORGIVE YOU IF YOU BETRAY MY BROTHER.
EVEN IF IT'S YOU.
BEEP
DOOT DOOT
DOOT DOOT
WHAT'D SHE SAY?
SHE SAID SHE'D NEVER FORGIVE ME IF I EVER BETRAYED YOU...
MAYBE SHE ACCEPTS ME NOW?
I THINK SO, DON'T YOU?
SPECIALL

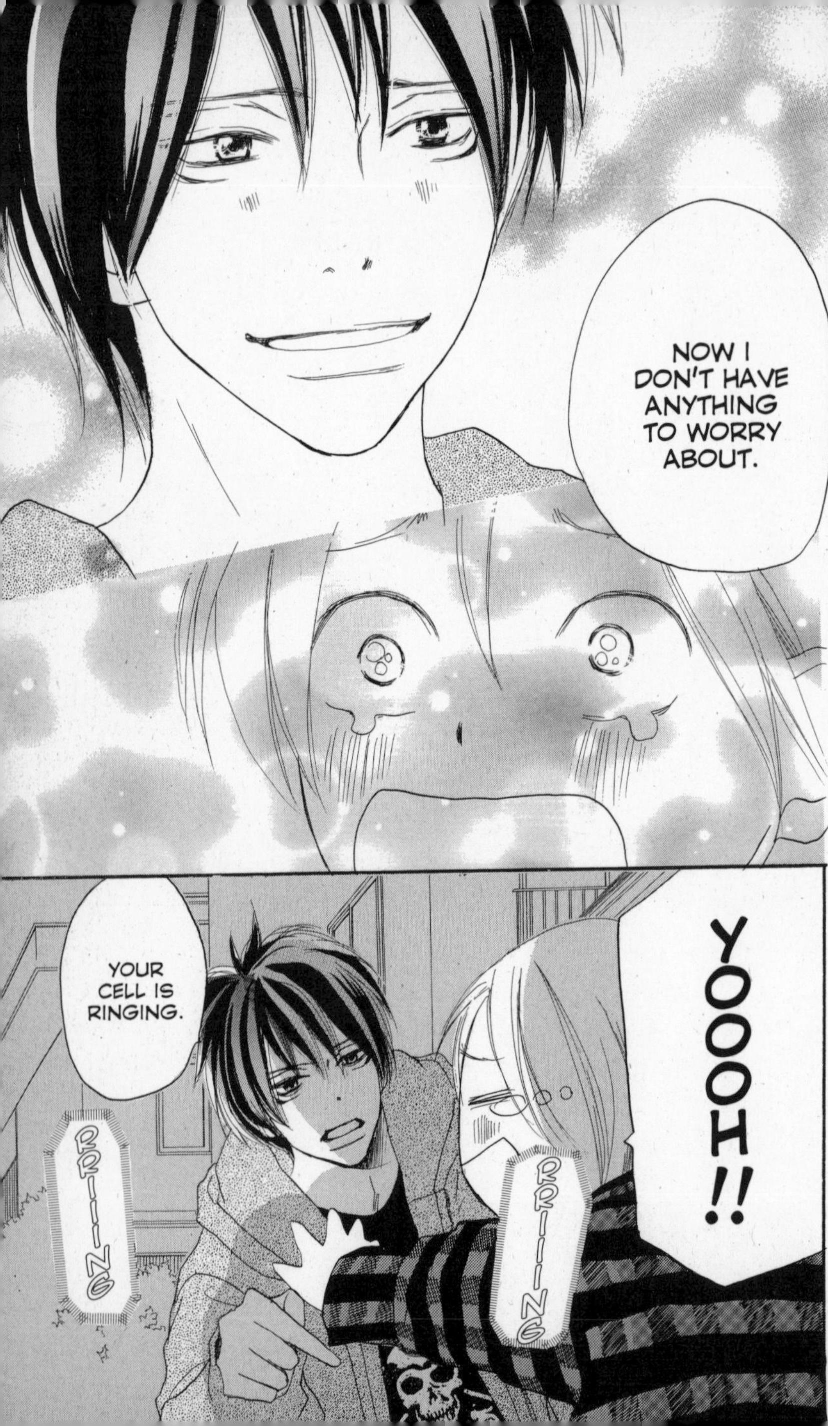
NOW I DON'T HAVE ANYTHING TO WORRY ABOUT.
YOOOOH!!
RRIIING
YOUR CELL IS RINGING.
RRIIING

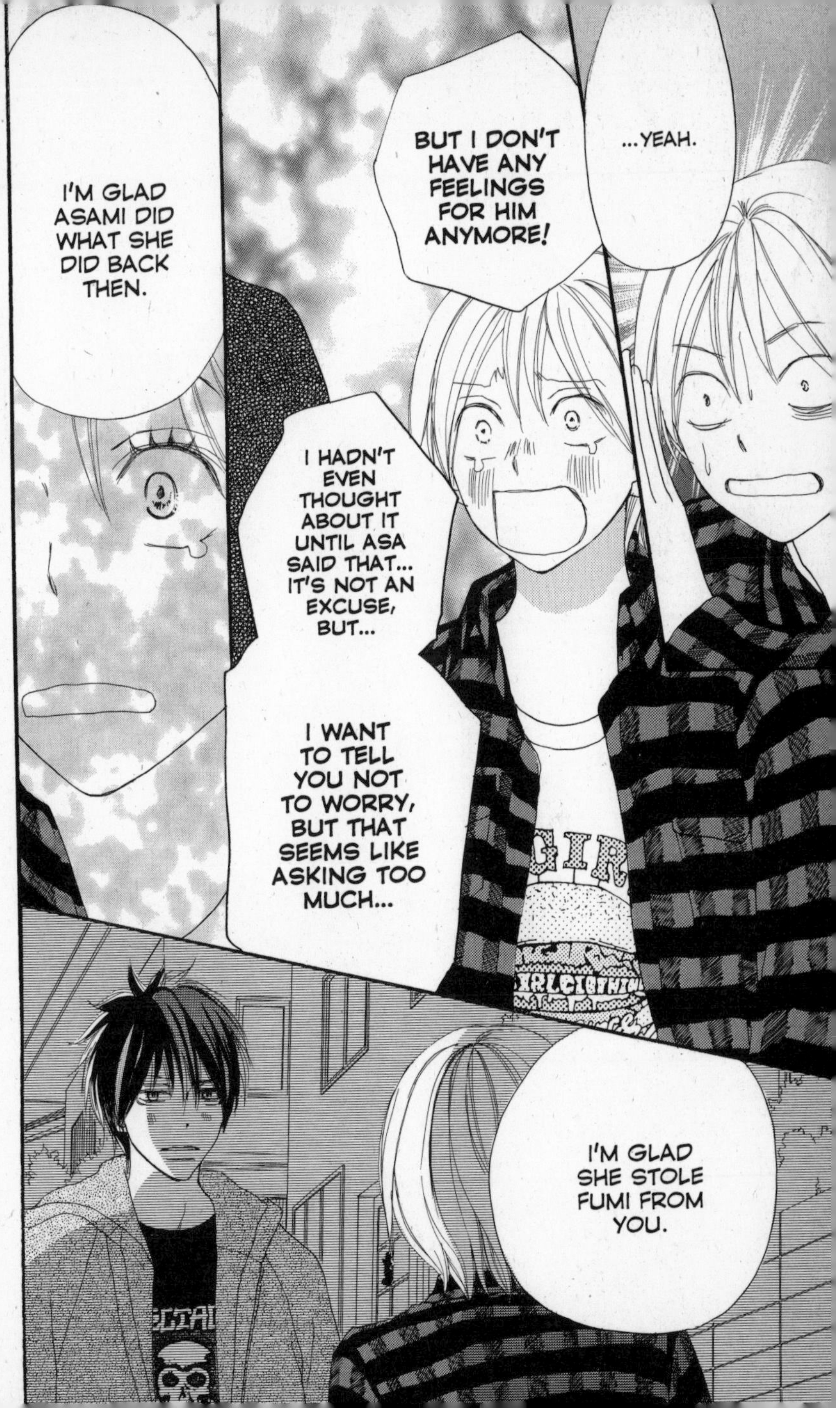
...YEAH.
BUT I DON'T HAVE ANY FEELINGS FOR HIM ANYMORE!
I HADN'T EVEN THOUGHT ABOUT IT UNTIL ASA SAID THAT... IT'S NOT AN EXCUSE, BUT...
I WANT TO TELL YOU NOT TO WORRY, BUT THAT SEEMS LIKE ASKING TOO MUCH...
I'M GLAD ASAMI DID WHAT SHE DID BACK THEN.
I'M GLAD SHE STOLE FUMI FROM YOU.

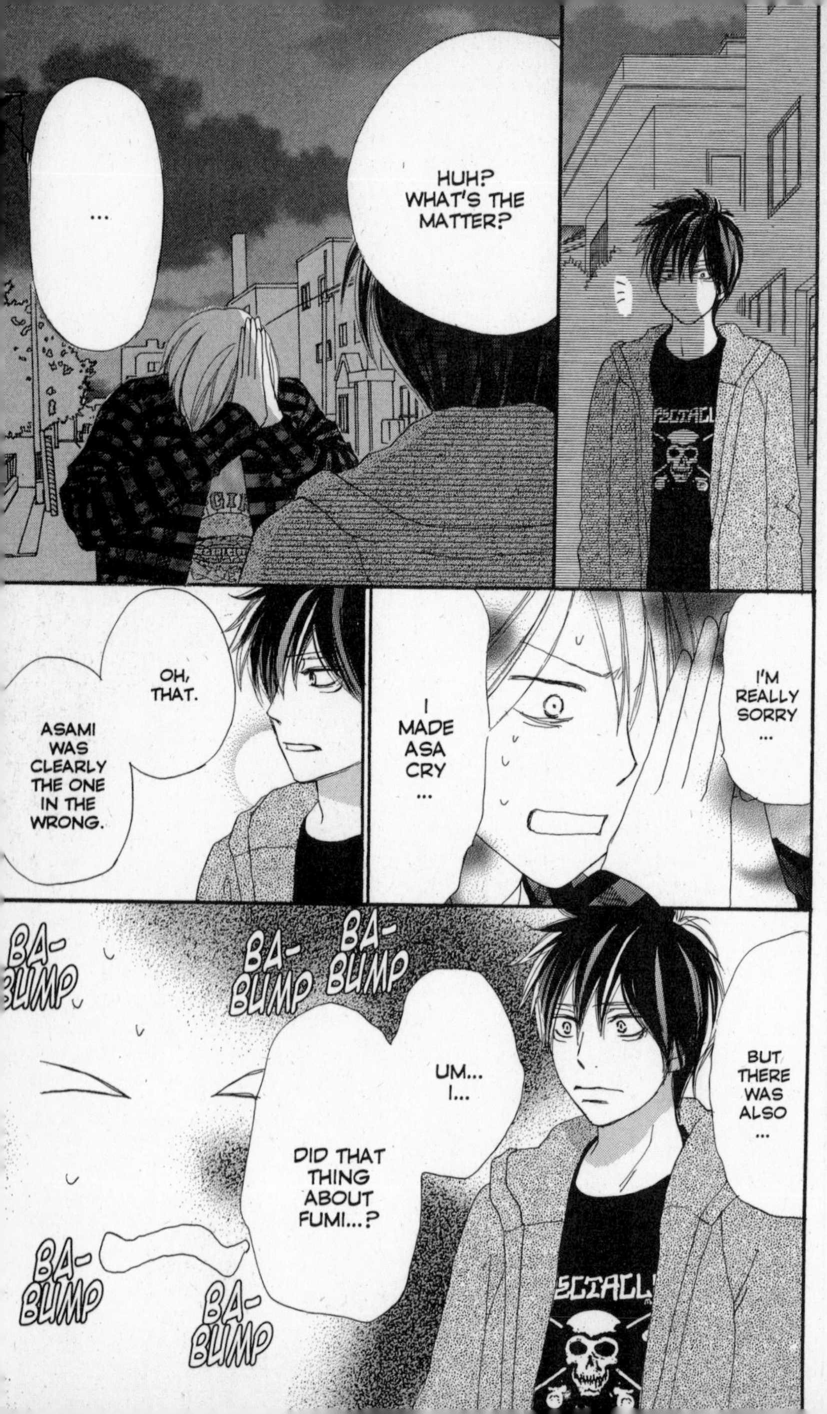
HUH? WHAT'S THE MATTER?
...
I'M REALLY SORRY...
I MADE ASA CRY...
OH, THAT.
ASAMI WAS CLEARLY THE ONE IN THE WRONG.
BUT THERE WAS ALSO...
BA-BUMP BA-BUMP
UM... I...
DID THAT THING ABOUT FUMI...?
BA-BUMP
BA-BUMP
BA-BUMP

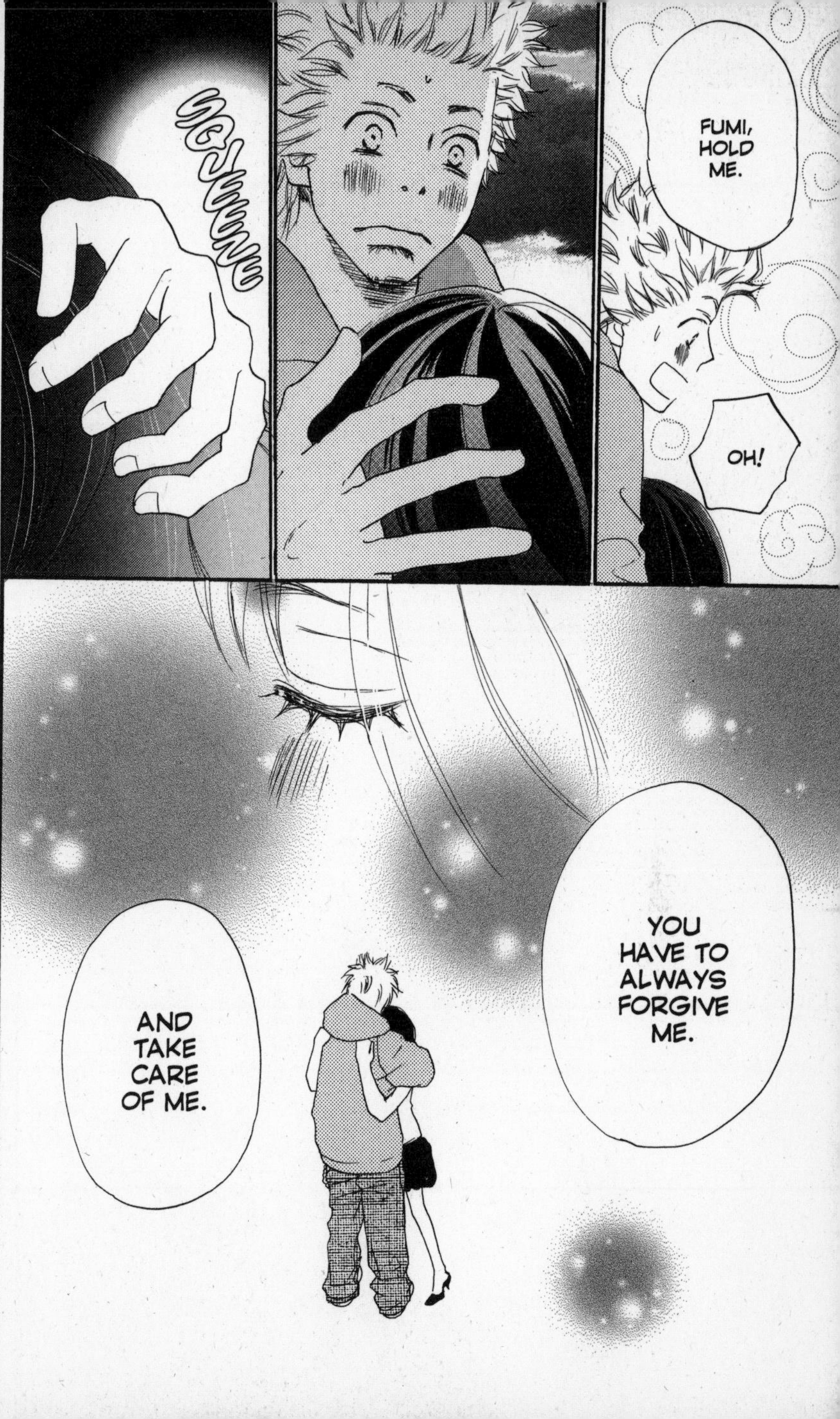
FUMI, HOLD ME.
OH!
SQUEEZE
YOU HAVE TO ALWAYS FORGIVE ME.
AND TAKE CARE OF ME.

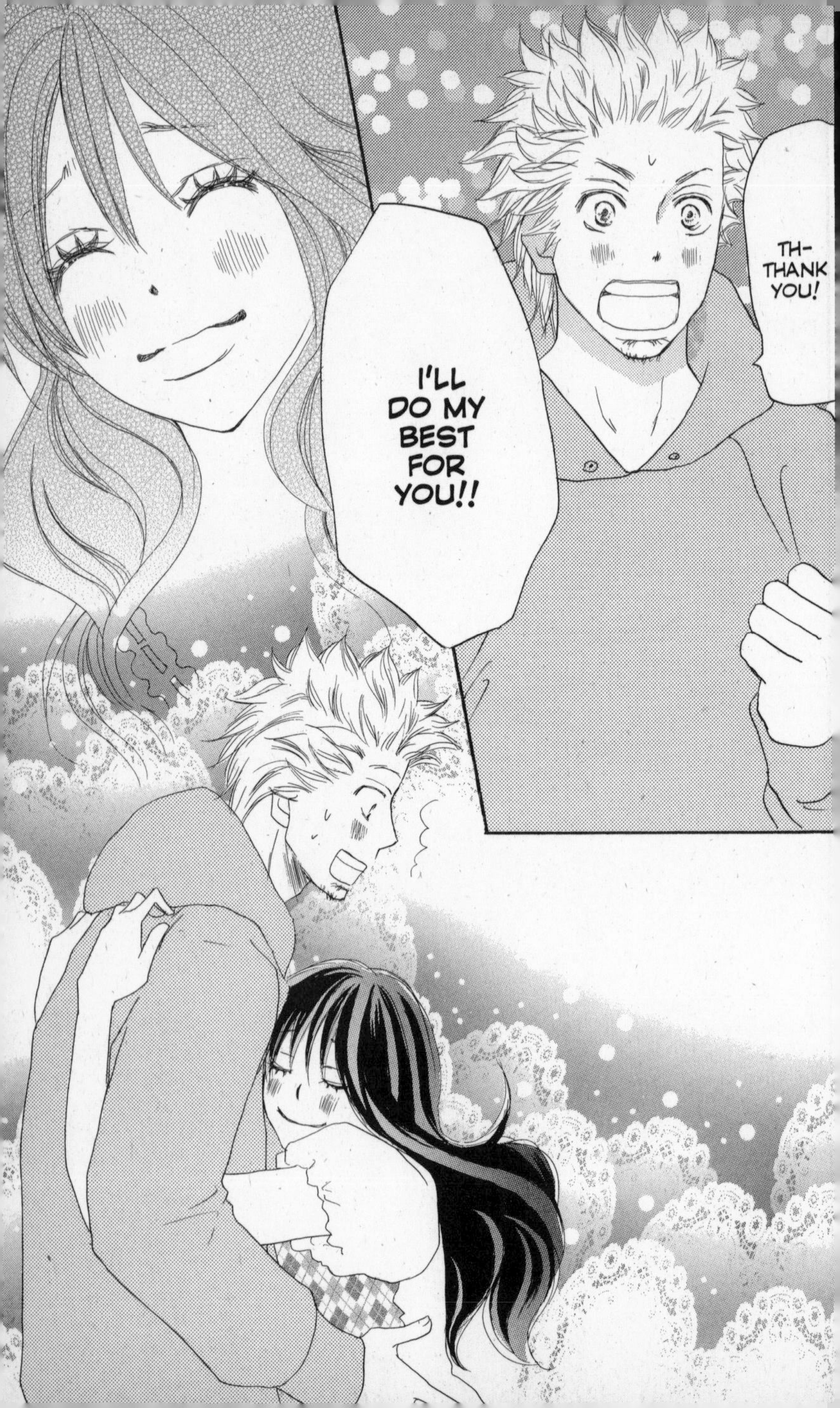
TH- THANK YOU!
I'LL DO MY BEST FOR YOU!!

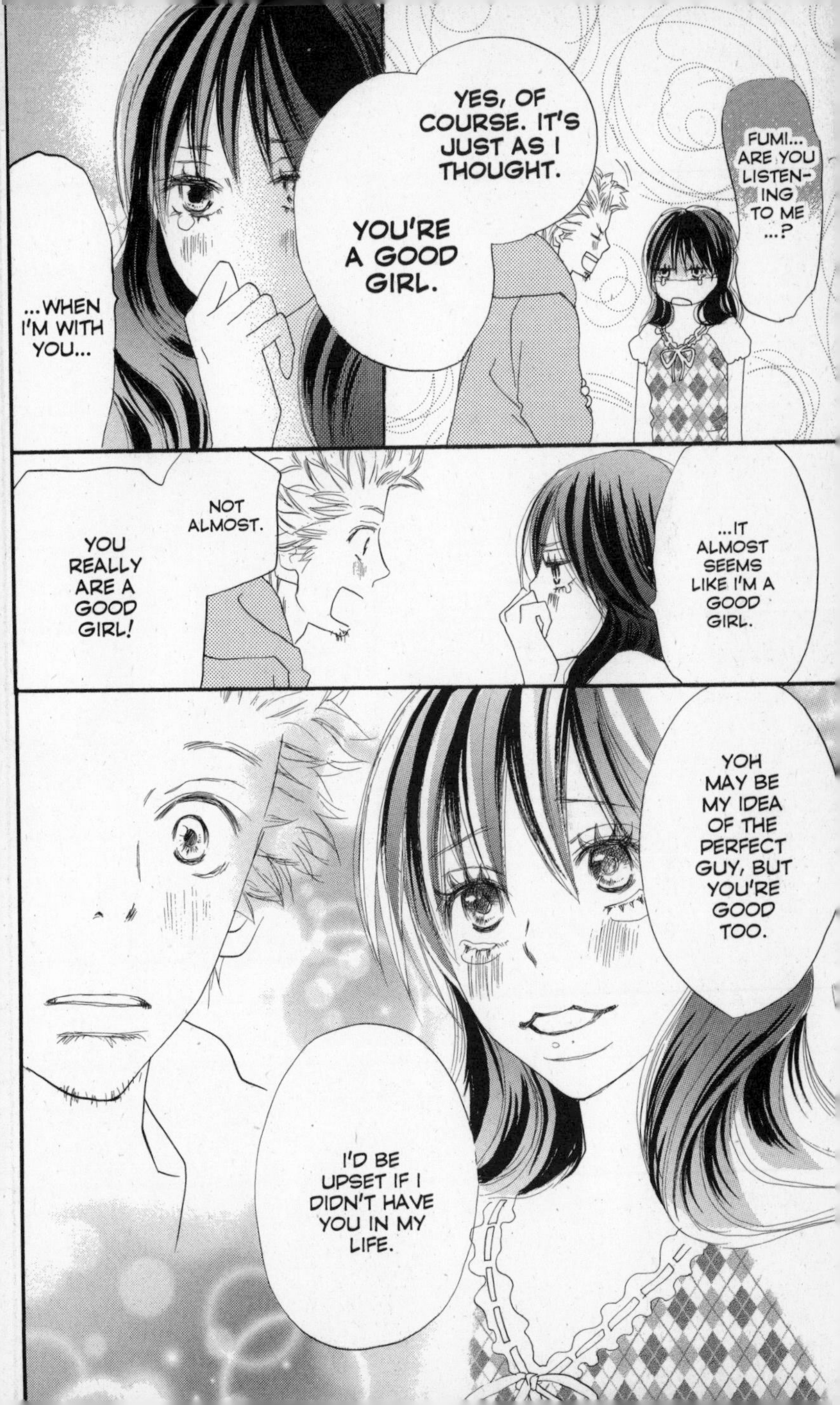
FUMI... ARE YOU LISTENING TO ME ...?
YES, OF COURSE. IT'S JUST AS I THOUGHT.
YOU'RE A GOOD GIRL.
...WHEN I'M WITH YOU...
...IT ALMOST SEEMS LIKE I'M A GOOD GIRL.
NOT ALMOST.
YOU REALLY ARE A GOOD GIRL!
YOH MAY BE MY IDEA OF THE PERFECT GUY, BUT YOU'RE GOOD TOO.
I'D BE UPSET IF I DIDN'T HAVE YOU IN MY LIFE.

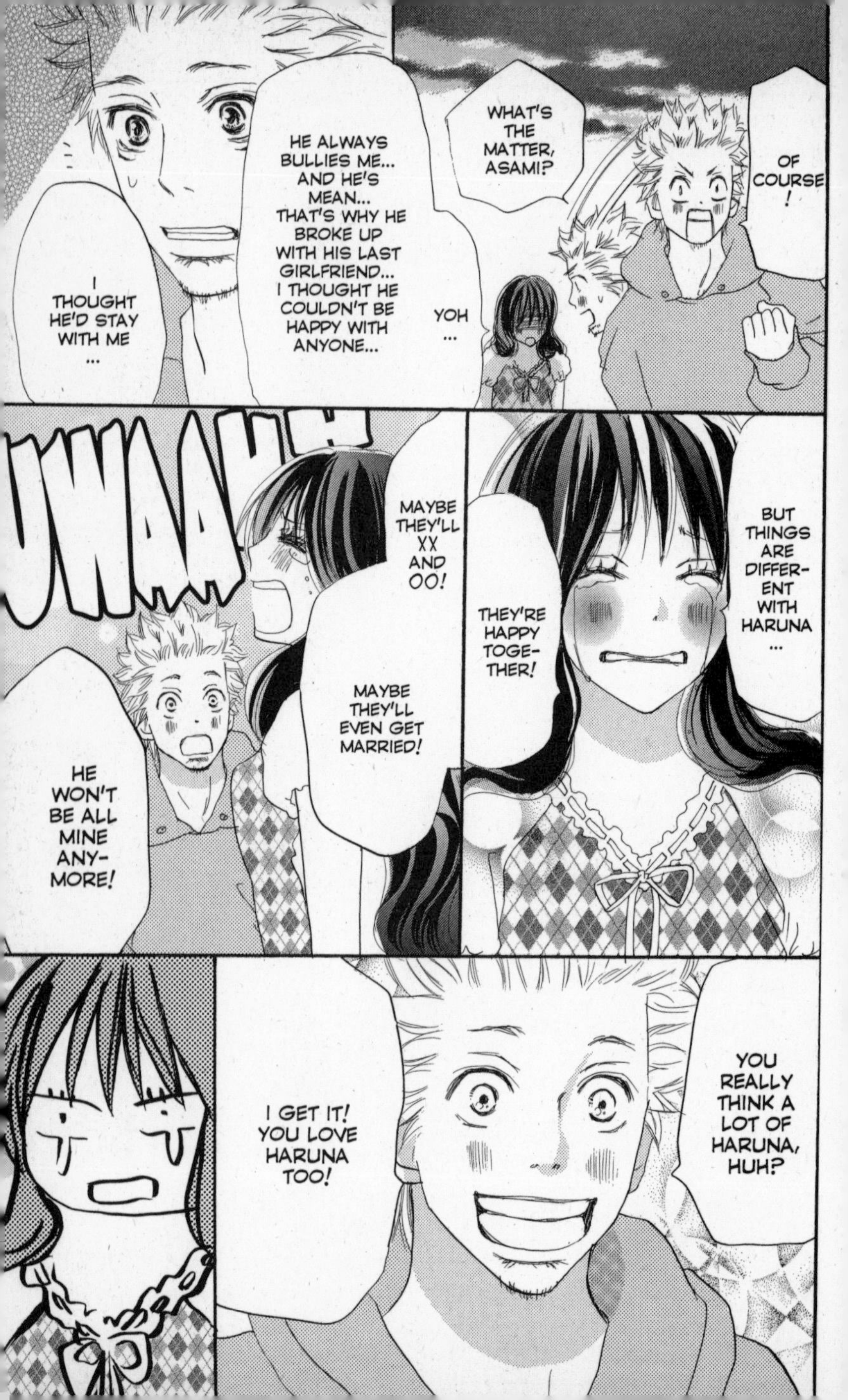
OF COURSE!
WHAT'S THE MATTER, ASAMI?
YOH...
HE ALWAYS BULLIES ME... AND HE'S MEAN... THAT'S WHY HE BROKE UP WITH HIS LAST GIRLFRIEND... I THOUGHT HE COULDN'T BE HAPPY WITH ANYONE...
I THOUGHT HE'D STAY WITH ME...
BUT THINGS ARE DIFFERENT WITH HARUNA...
THEY'RE HAPPY TOGETHER!
MAYBE THEY'LL XX AND OO!
MAYBE THEY'LL EVEN GET MARRIED!
UWAAH!
HE WON'T BE ALL MINE ANYMORE!
YOU REALLY THINK A LOT OF HARUNA, HUH?
I GET IT! YOU LOVE HARUNA TOO!

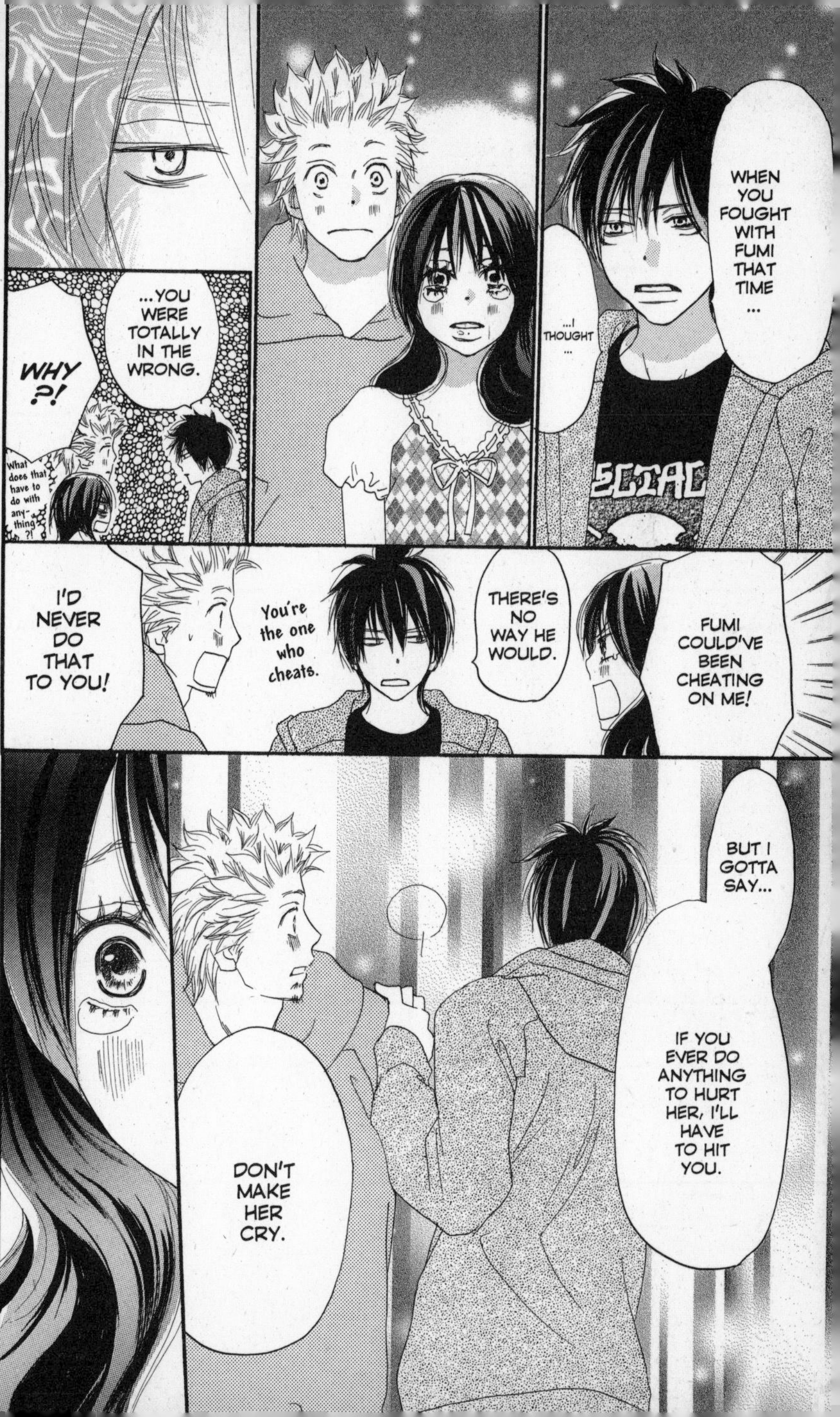
WHEN YOU FOUGHT WITH FUMI THAT TIME ...
...I THOUGHT ...
...YOU WERE TOTALLY IN THE WRONG.
WHY ?!
What does that have to do with anything ?!
FUMI COULD'VE BEEN CHEATING ON ME!
THERE'S NO WAY HE WOULD.
You're the one who cheats.
I'D NEVER DO THAT TO YOU!
BUT I GOTTA SAY...
IF YOU EVER DO ANYTHING TO HURT HER, I'LL HAVE TO HIT YOU.
DON'T MAKE HER CRY.

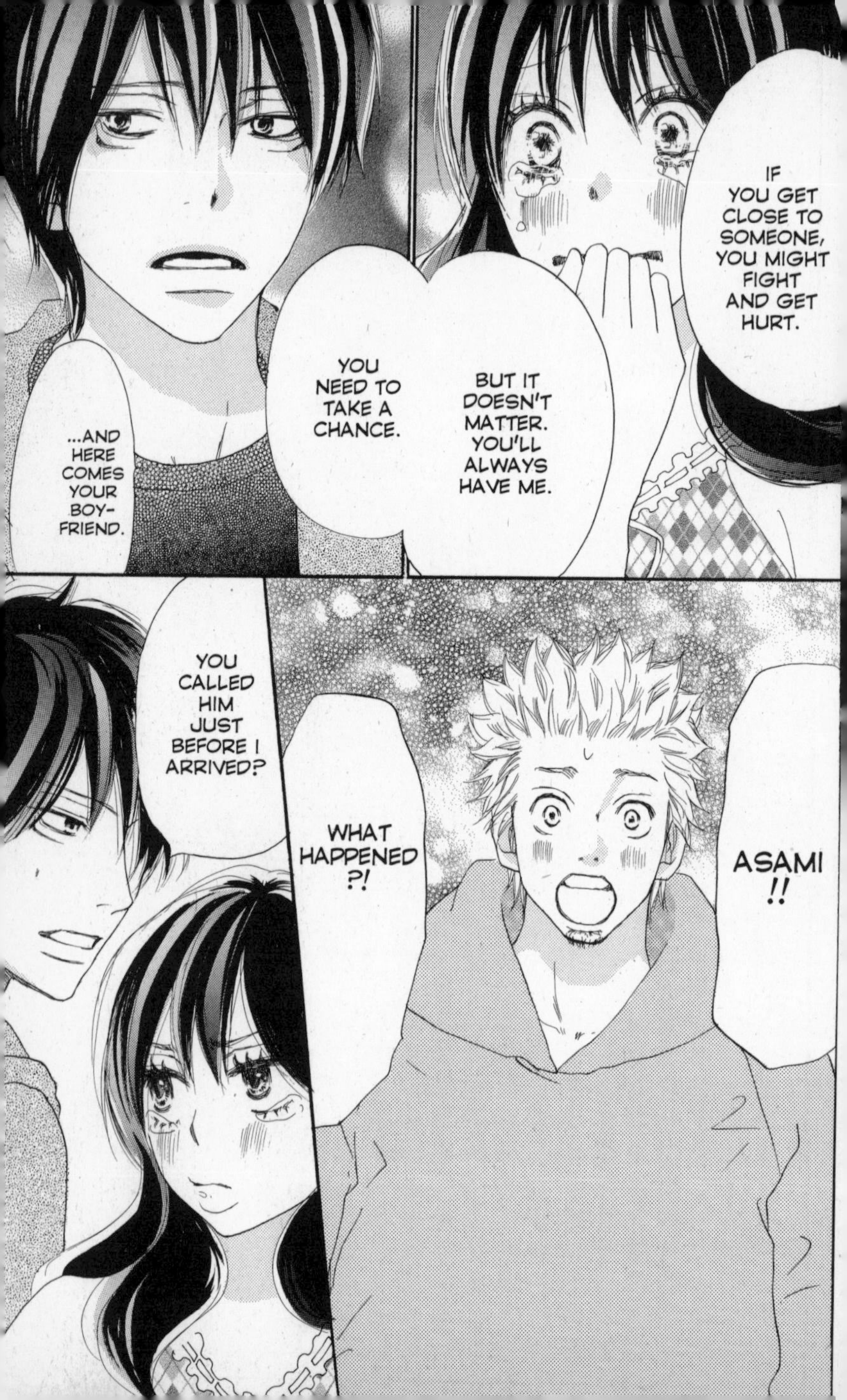
IF YOU GET CLOSE TO SOMEONE, YOU MIGHT FIGHT AND GET HURT.
BUT IT DOESN'T MATTER. YOU'LL ALWAYS HAVE ME.
YOU NEED TO TAKE A CHANCE.
...AND HERE COMES YOUR BOY-FRIEND.
ASAMI!!
WHAT HAPPENED?!
YOU CALLED HIM JUST BEFORE I ARRIVED?

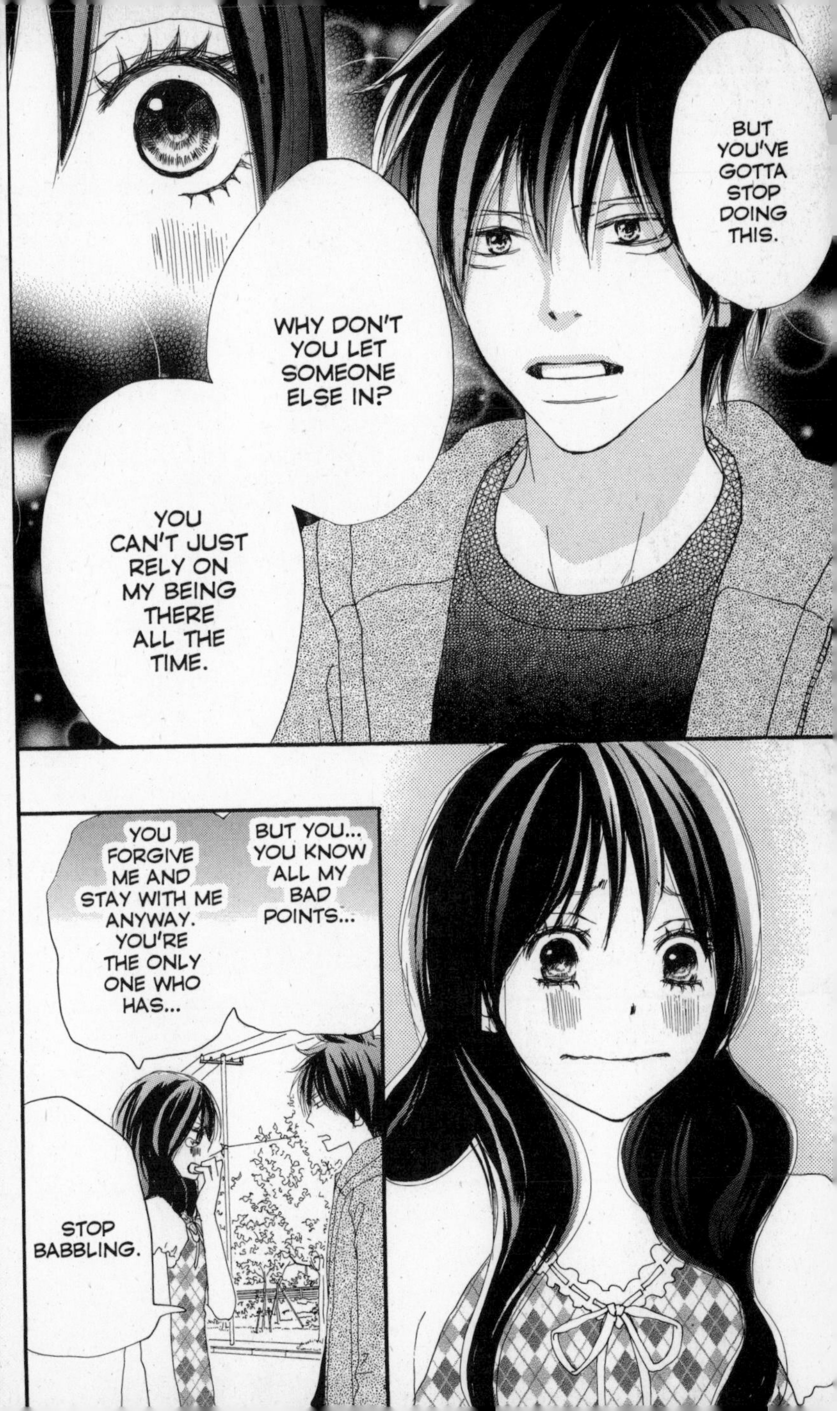
BUT YOU'VE GOTTA STOP DOING THIS.
WHY DON'T YOU LET SOMEONE ELSE IN?
YOU CAN'T JUST RELY ON MY BEING THERE ALL THE TIME.
BUT YOU... YOU KNOW ALL MY BAD POINTS...
YOU FORGIVE ME AND STAY WITH ME ANYWAY. YOU'RE THE ONLY ONE WHO HAS...
STOP BABBLING.

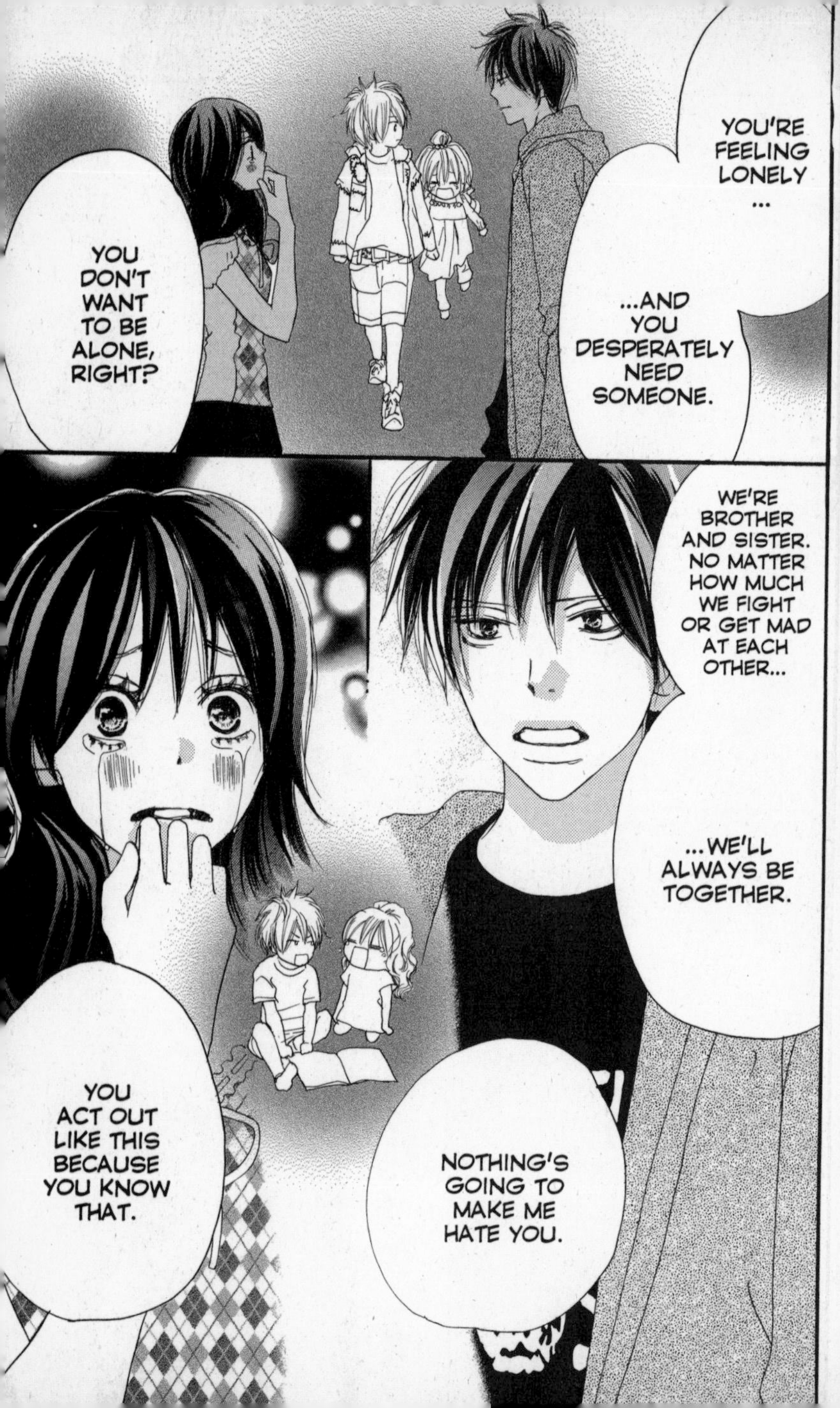
YOU'RE FEELING LONELY ...
...AND YOU DESPERATELY NEED SOMEONE.
YOU DON'T WANT TO BE ALONE, RIGHT?
WE'RE BROTHER AND SISTER. NO MATTER HOW MUCH WE FIGHT OR GET MAD AT EACH OTHER...
...WE'LL ALWAYS BE TOGETHER.
NOTHING'S GOING TO MAKE ME HATE YOU.
YOU ACT OUT LIKE THIS BECAUSE YOU KNOW THAT.

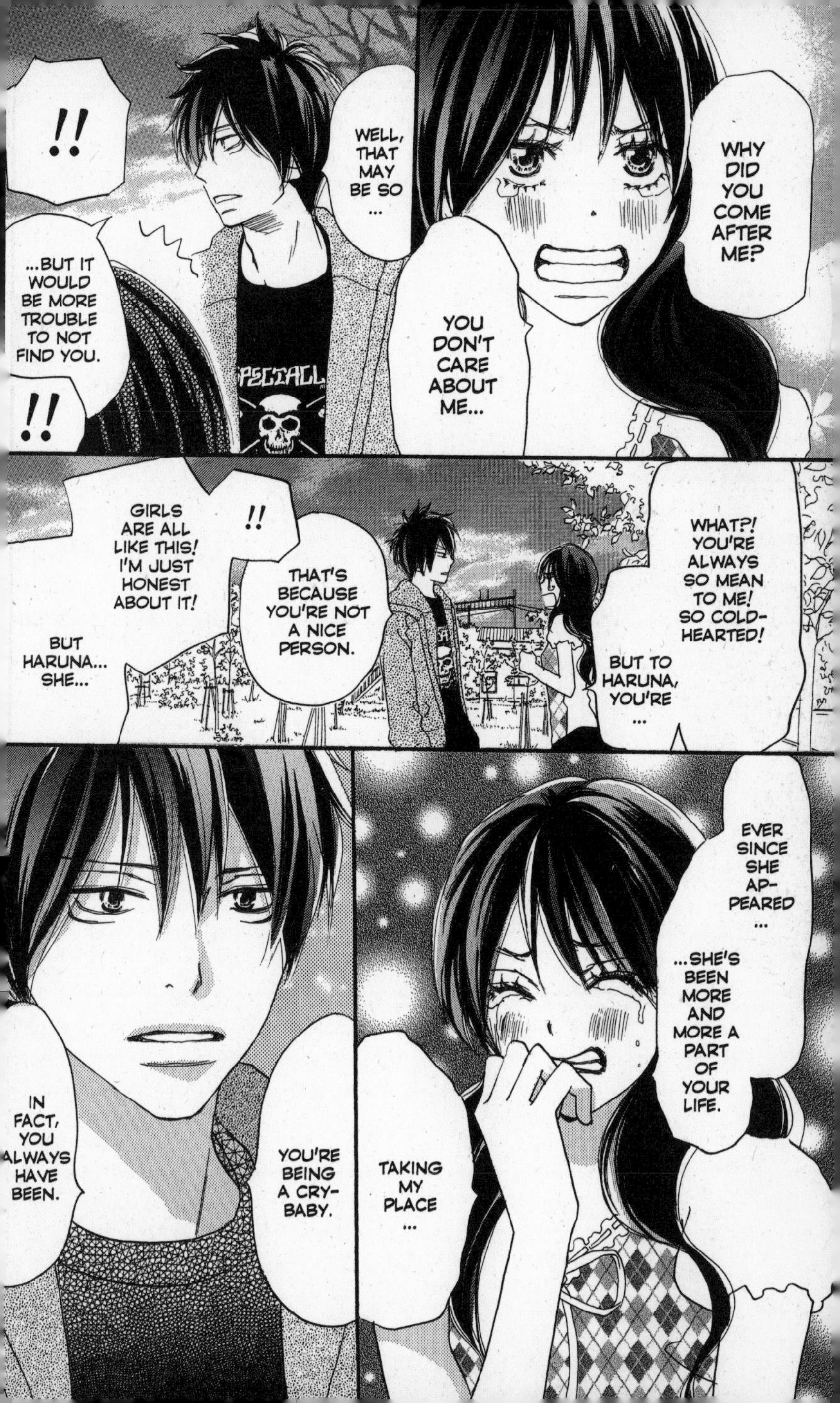
WHY DID YOU COME AFTER ME?
YOU DON'T CARE ABOUT ME...
WELL, THAT MAY BE SO ...
!!
...BUT IT WOULD BE MORE TROUBLE TO NOT FIND YOU.
!!
WHAT?! YOU'RE ALWAYS SO MEAN TO ME! SO COLD-HEARTED!
BUT TO HARUNA, YOU'RE ...
!!
THAT'S BECAUSE YOU'RE NOT A NICE PERSON.
GIRLS ARE ALL LIKE THIS! I'M JUST HONEST ABOUT IT!
BUT HARUNA... SHE...
EVER SINCE SHE AP-PEARED ...
...SHE'S BEEN MORE AND MORE A PART OF YOUR LIFE.
TAKING MY PLACE ...
YOU'RE BEING A CRY-BABY.
IN FACT, YOU ALWAYS HAVE BEEN.

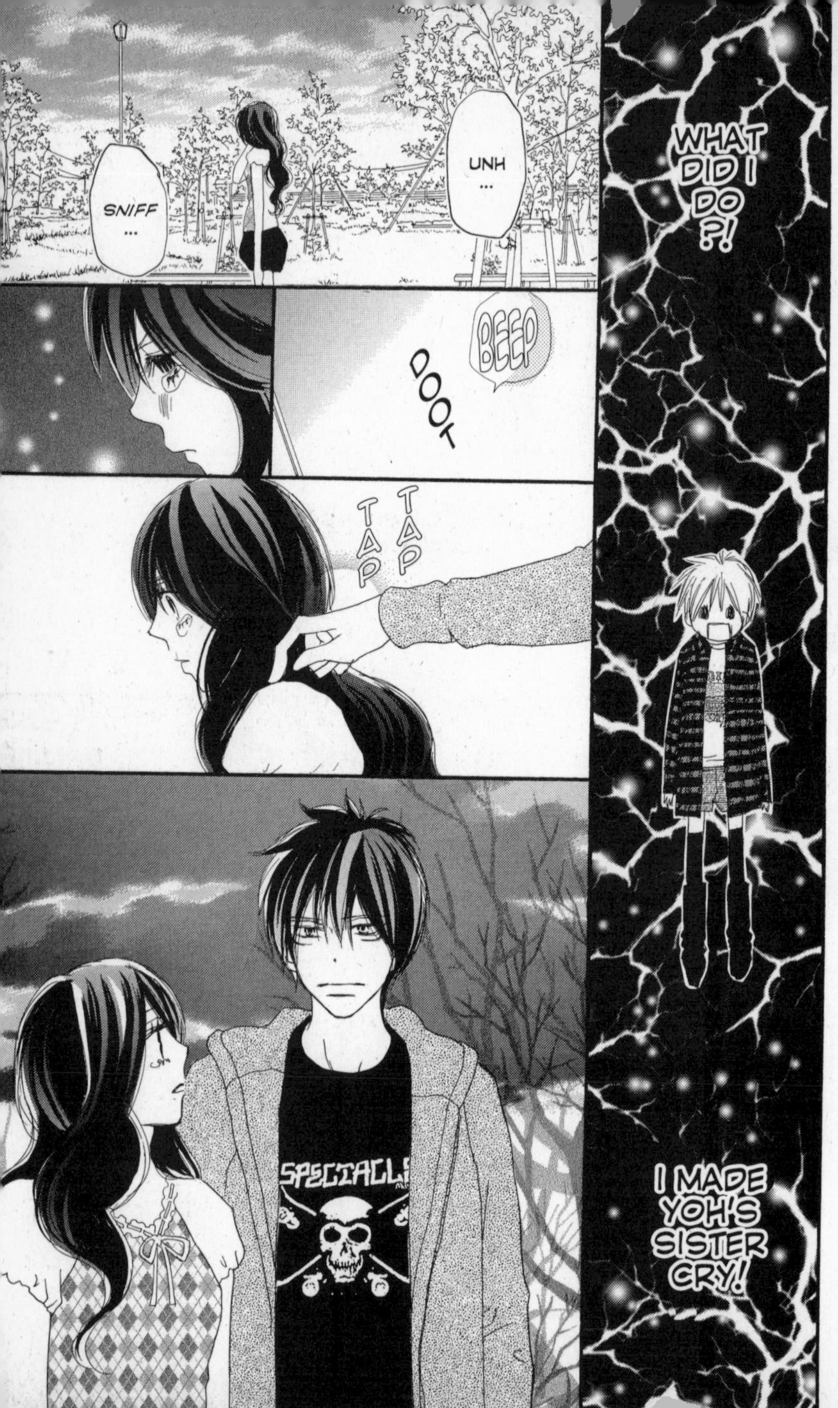

WHAT DID I DO ?!
I MADE YOH'S SISTER CRY!
UNH ...
SNIFF ...
BEEP
DOOT
TAP TAP

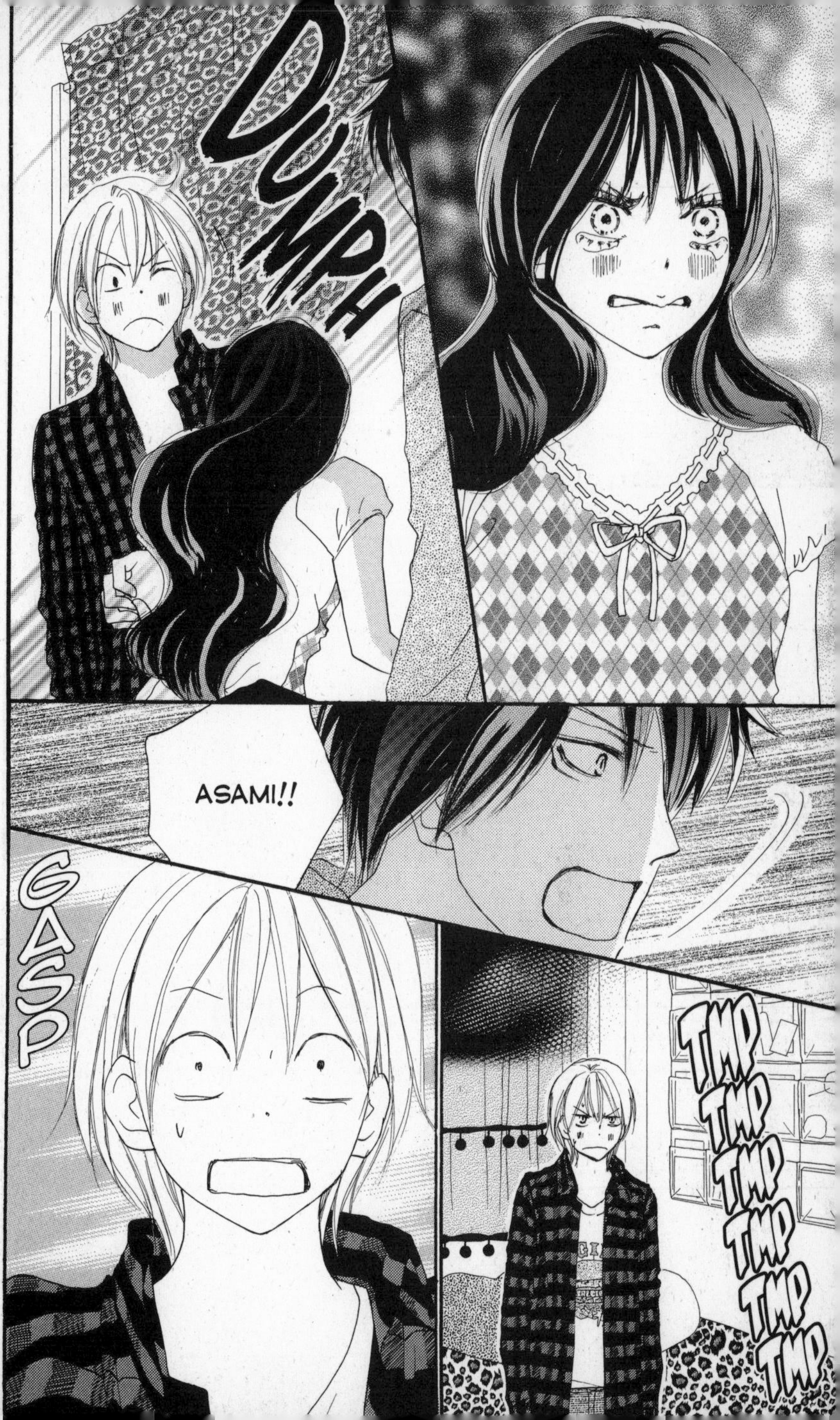
DUMPH
ASAMI!!
TMP TMP TMP TMP TMP TMP
GASP

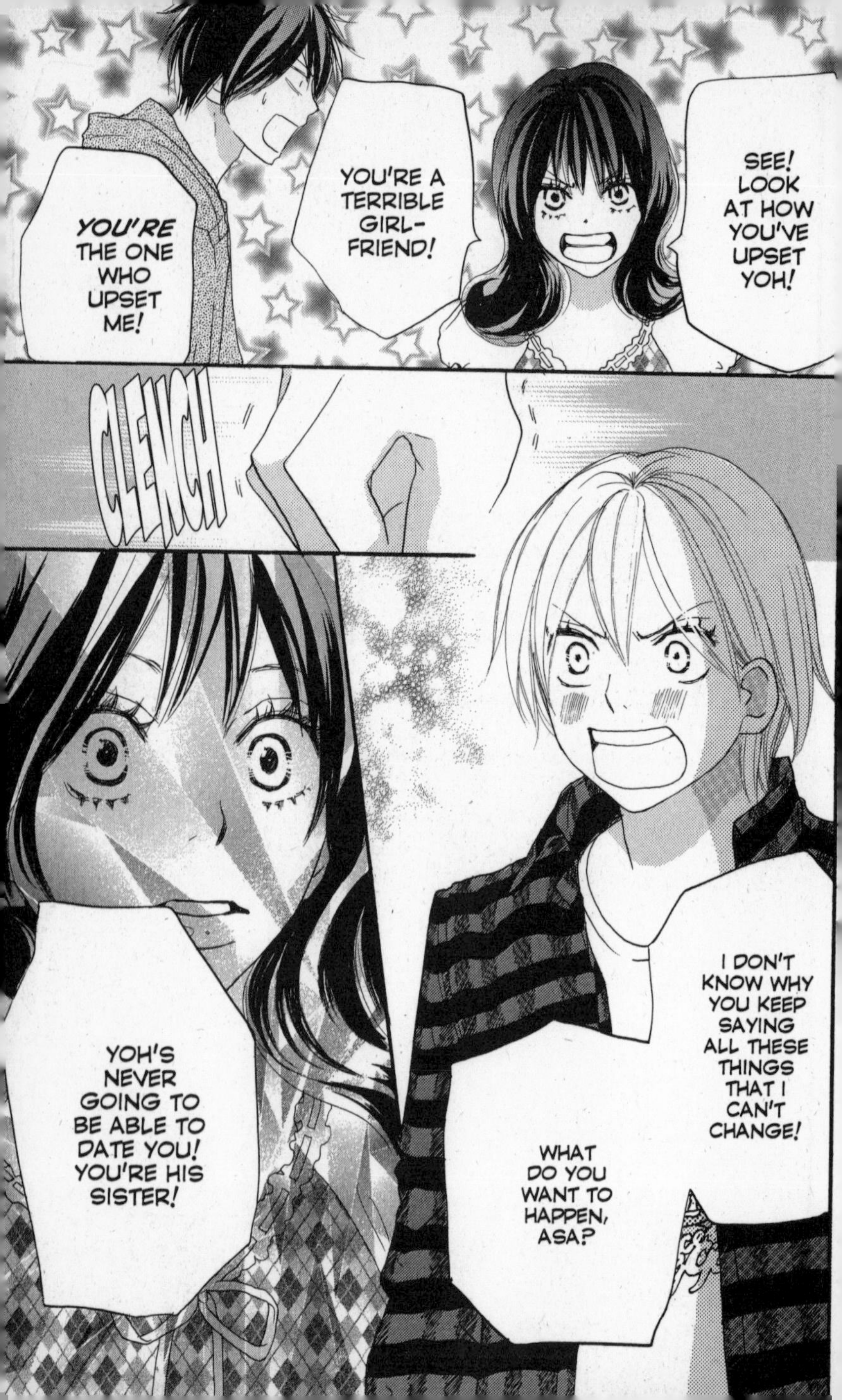
SEE! LOOK AT HOW YOU'VE UPSET YOH!
YOU'RE A TERRIBLE GIRL-FRIEND!
YOU'RE THE ONE WHO UPSET ME!
CLENCH
I DON'T KNOW WHY YOU KEEP SAYING ALL THESE THINGS THAT I CAN'T CHANGE!
WHAT DO YOU WANT TO HAPPEN, ASA?
YOH'S NEVER GOING TO BE ABLE TO DATE YOU! YOU'RE HIS SISTER!

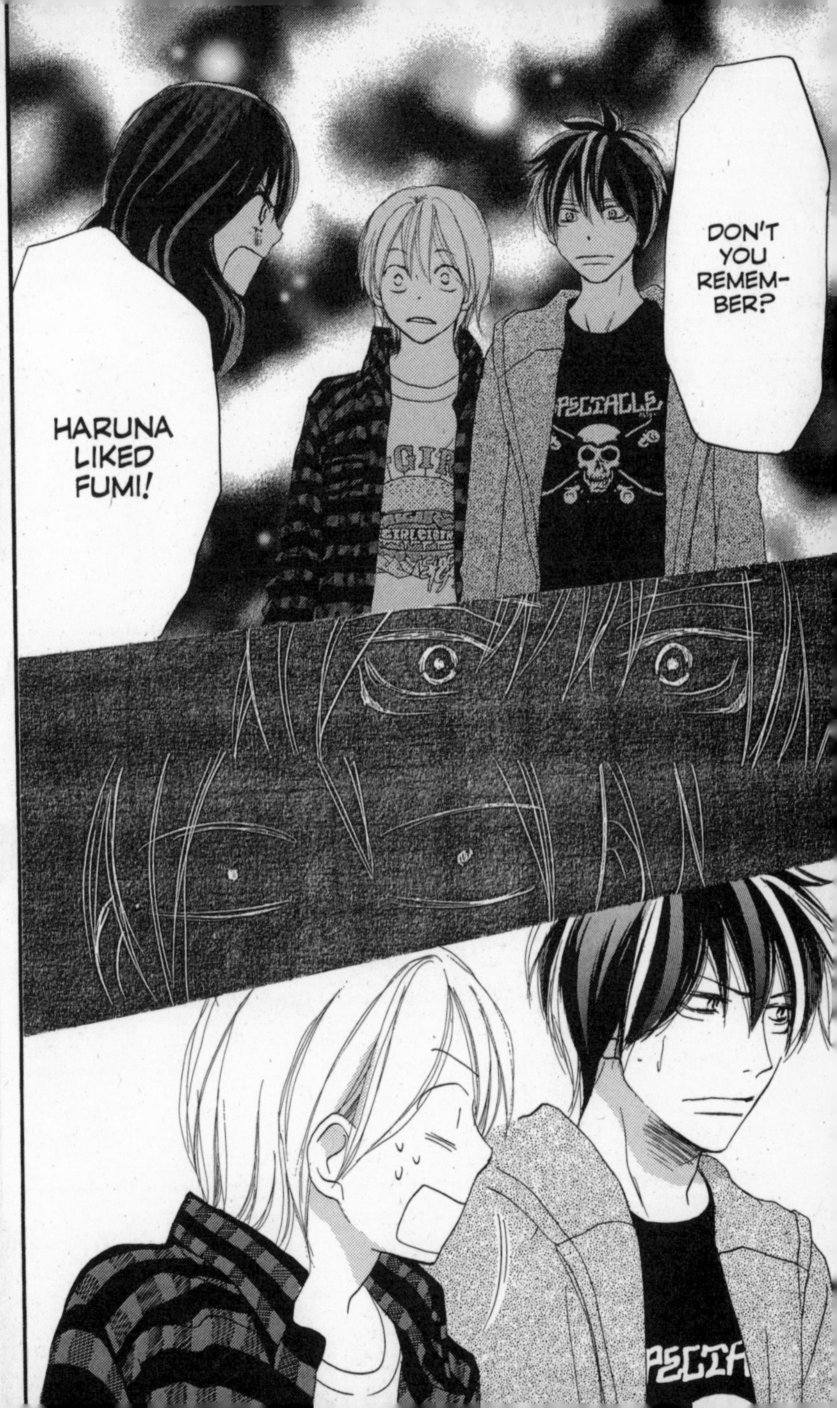
DON'T YOU REMEMBER?
HARUNA LIKED FUMI!

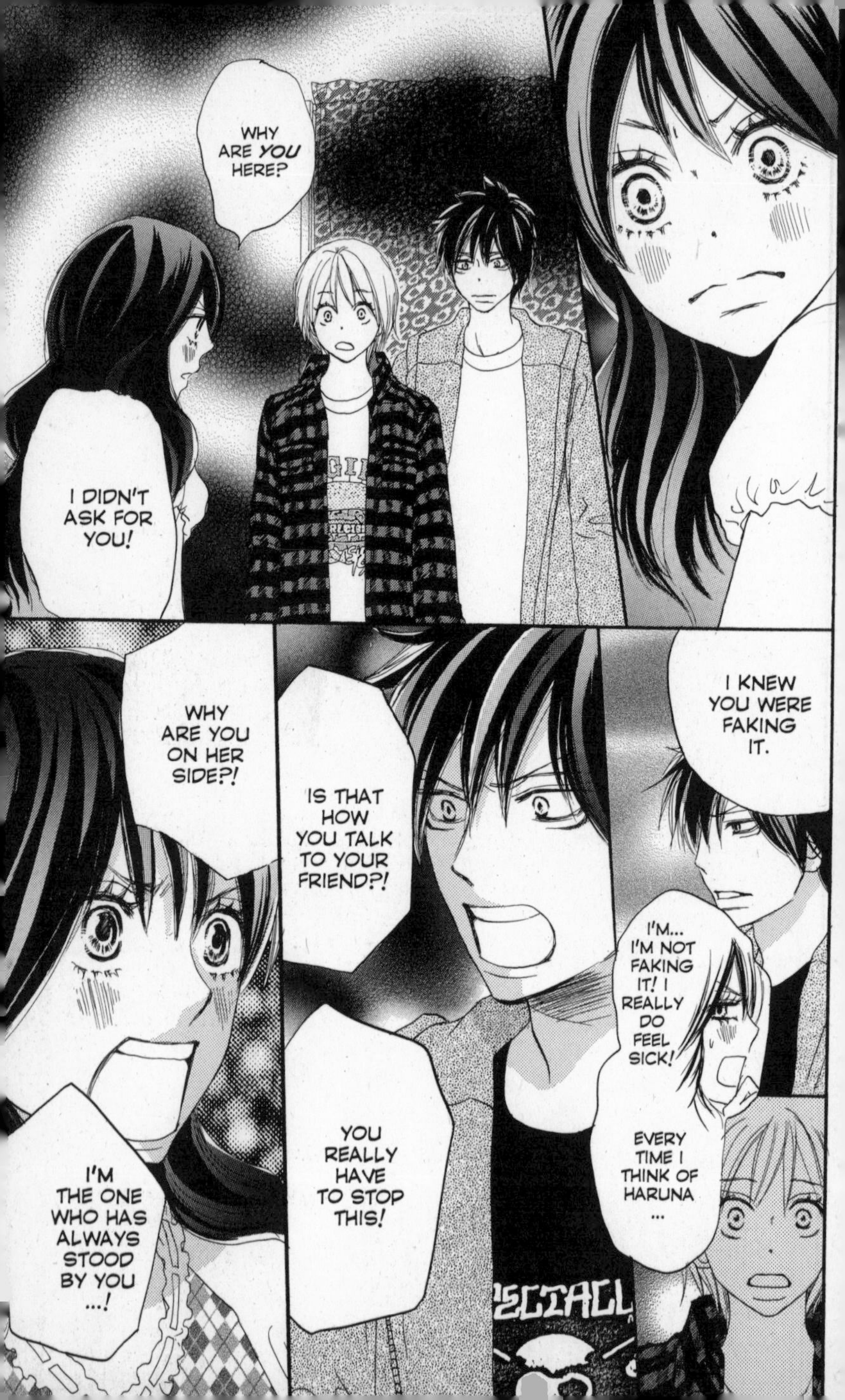
WHY ARE *YOU* HERE?
I DIDN'T ASK FOR YOU!
I KNEW YOU WERE FAKING IT.
I'M... I'M NOT FAKING IT! I REALLY DO FEEL SICK!
EVERY TIME I THINK OF HARUNA ...
IS THAT HOW YOU TALK TO YOUR FRIEND?!
YOU REALLY HAVE TO STOP THIS!
WHY ARE YOU ON HER SIDE?!
I'M THE ONE WHO HAS ALWAYS STOOD BY YOU ...!

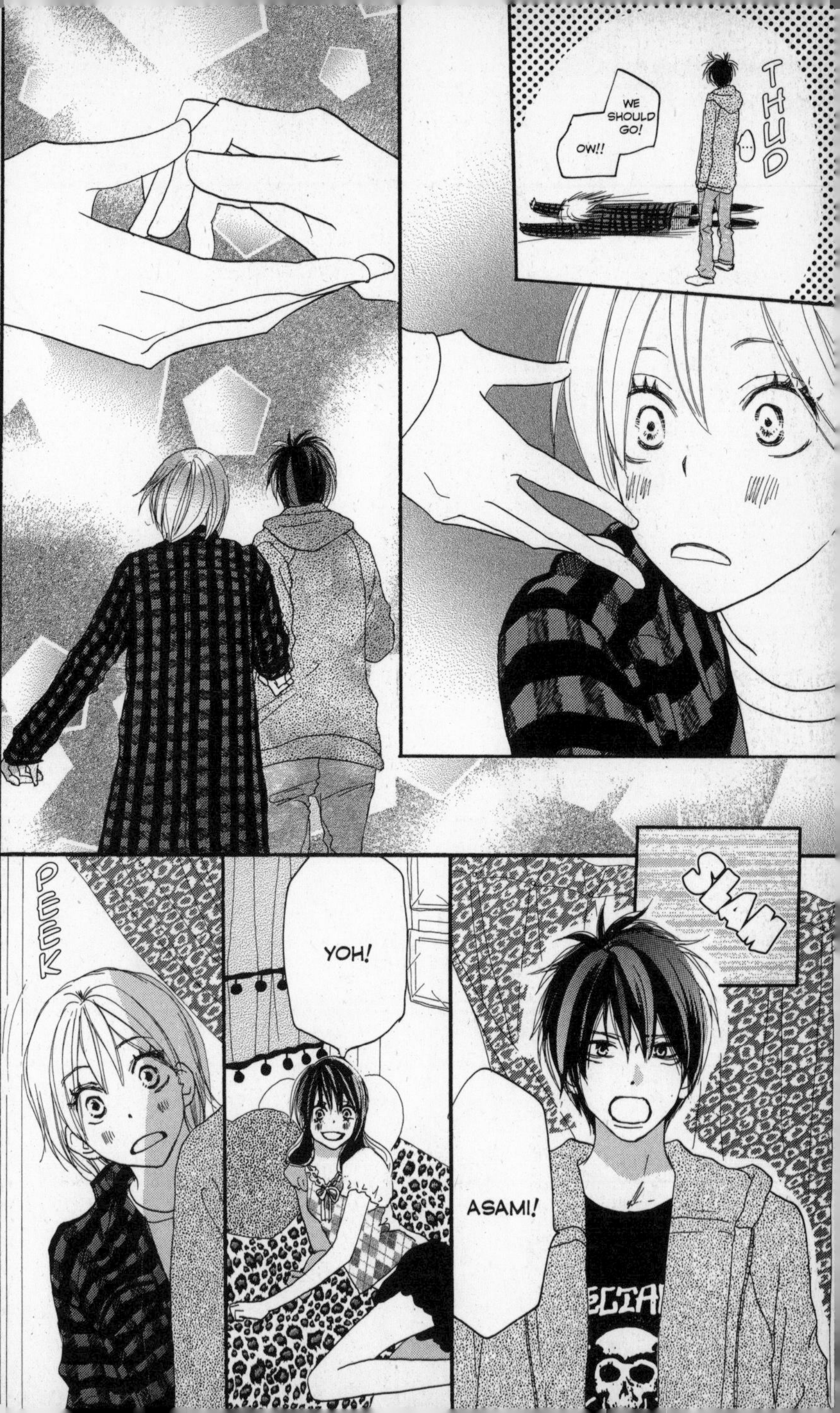

THUD
...
WE SHOULD GO!
OW!!
SLAM
ASAMI!
YOH!
PEEK

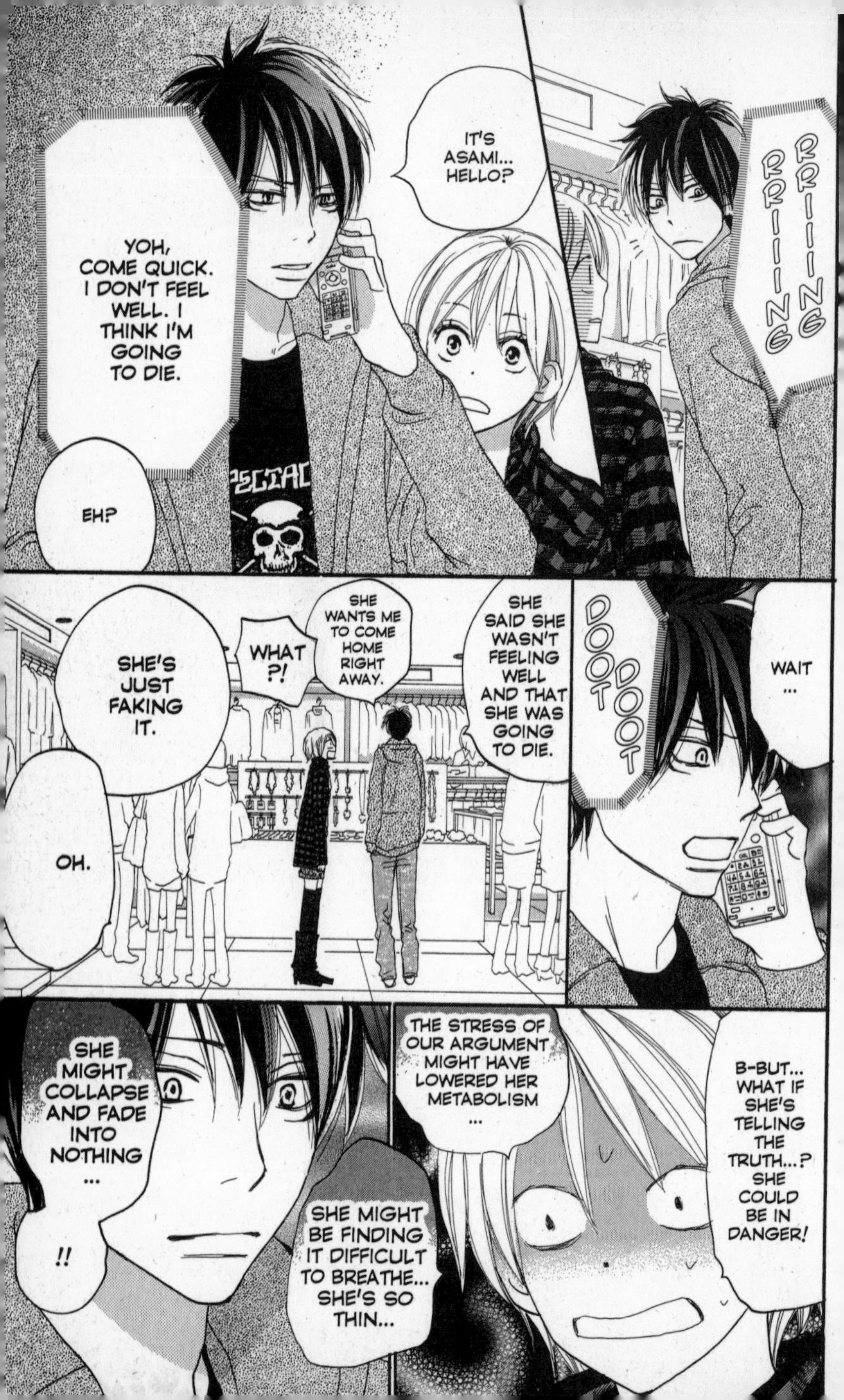
RRIIING RRIIING
IT'S ASAMI... HELLO?
YOH, COME QUICK. I DON'T FEEL WELL. I THINK I'M GOING TO DIE.
EH?
DOOT DOOT
WAIT ...
SHE SAID SHE WASN'T FEELING WELL AND THAT SHE WAS GOING TO DIE.
SHE WANTS ME TO COME HOME RIGHT AWAY.
WHAT?!
SHE'S JUST FAKING IT.
OH.
B-BUT... WHAT IF SHE'S TELLING THE TRUTH...? SHE COULD BE IN DANGER!
THE STRESS OF OUR ARGUMENT MIGHT HAVE LOWERED HER METABOLISM ...
SHE MIGHT BE FINDING IT DIFFICULT TO BREATHE... SHE'S SO THIN...
SHE MIGHT COLLAPSE AND FADE INTO NOTHING ...
!!

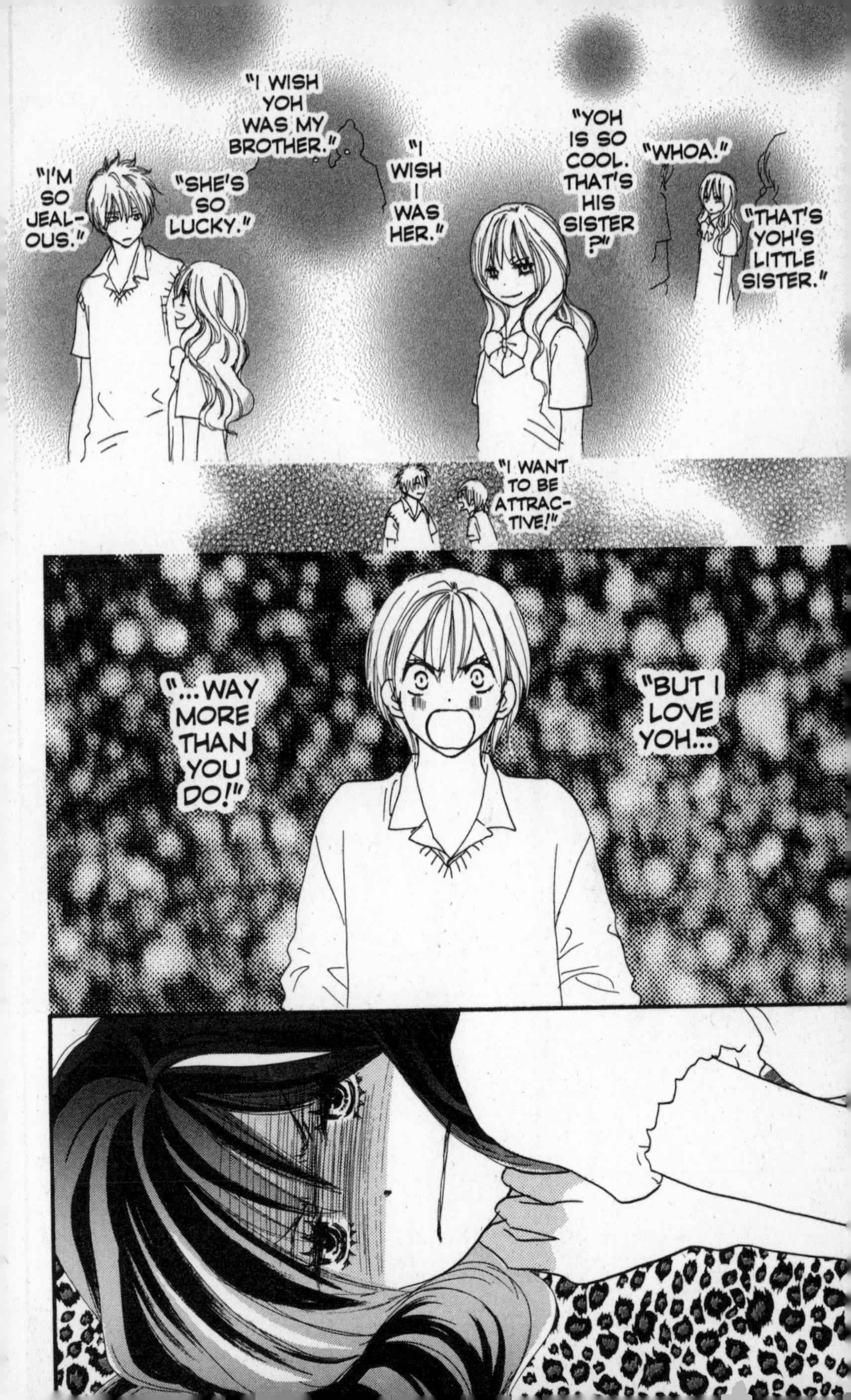
"THAT'S YOH'S LITTLE SISTER."
"WHOA."
"YOH IS SO COOL. THAT'S HIS SISTER?!"
"I WISH I WAS HER."
"I WISH YOH WAS MY BROTHER."
"SHE'S SO LUCKY."
"I'M SO JEAL-OUS."
"I WANT TO BE ATTRAC-TIVE!"
"BUT I LOVE YOH...
...WAY MORE THAN YOU DO!"

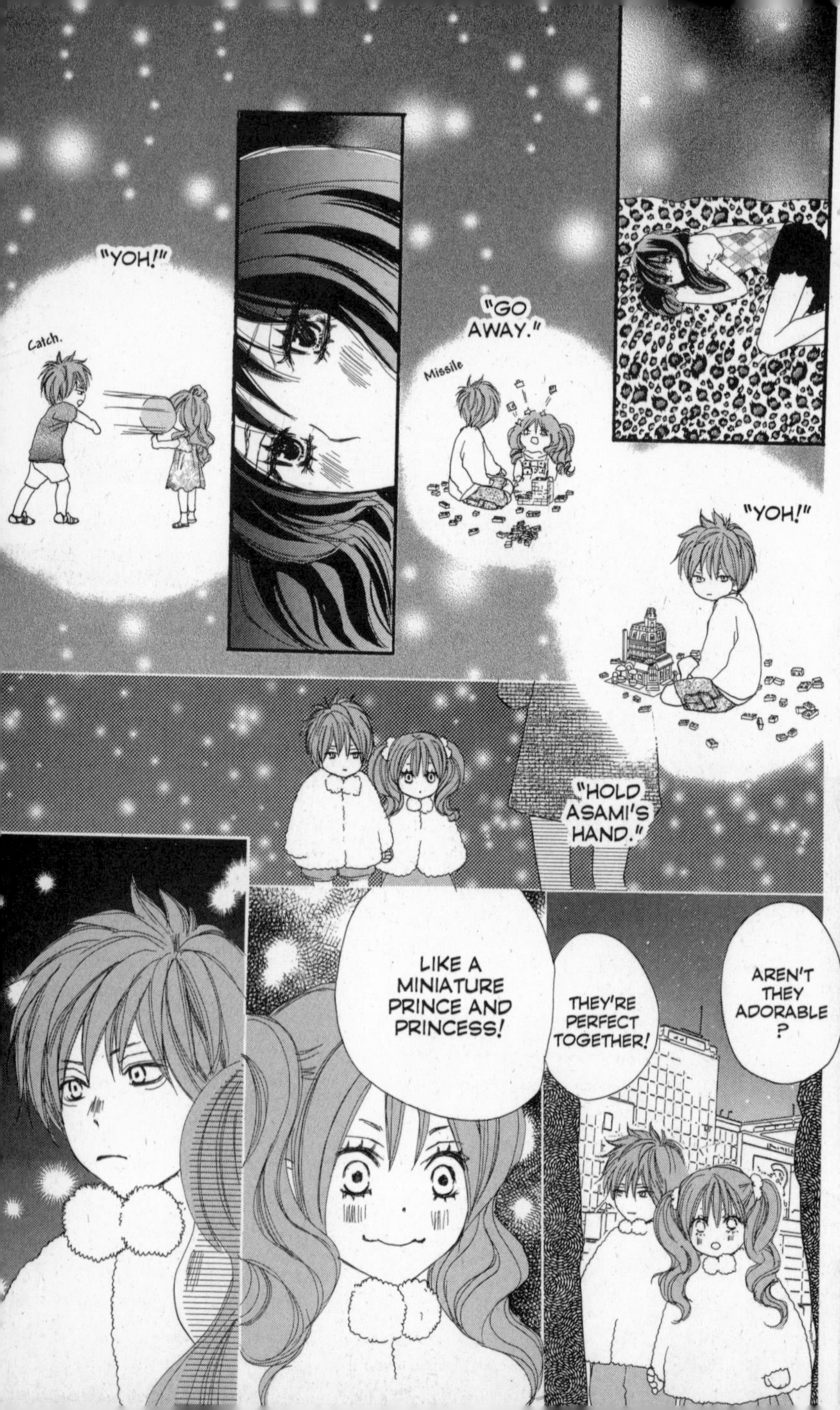

"YOH!"
"GO AWAY."
Missile
"YOH!"
Catch.
"HOLD ASAMI'S HAND."
AREN'T THEY ADORABLE?
THEY'RE PERFECT TOGETHER!
LIKE A MINIATURE PRINCE AND PRINCESS!

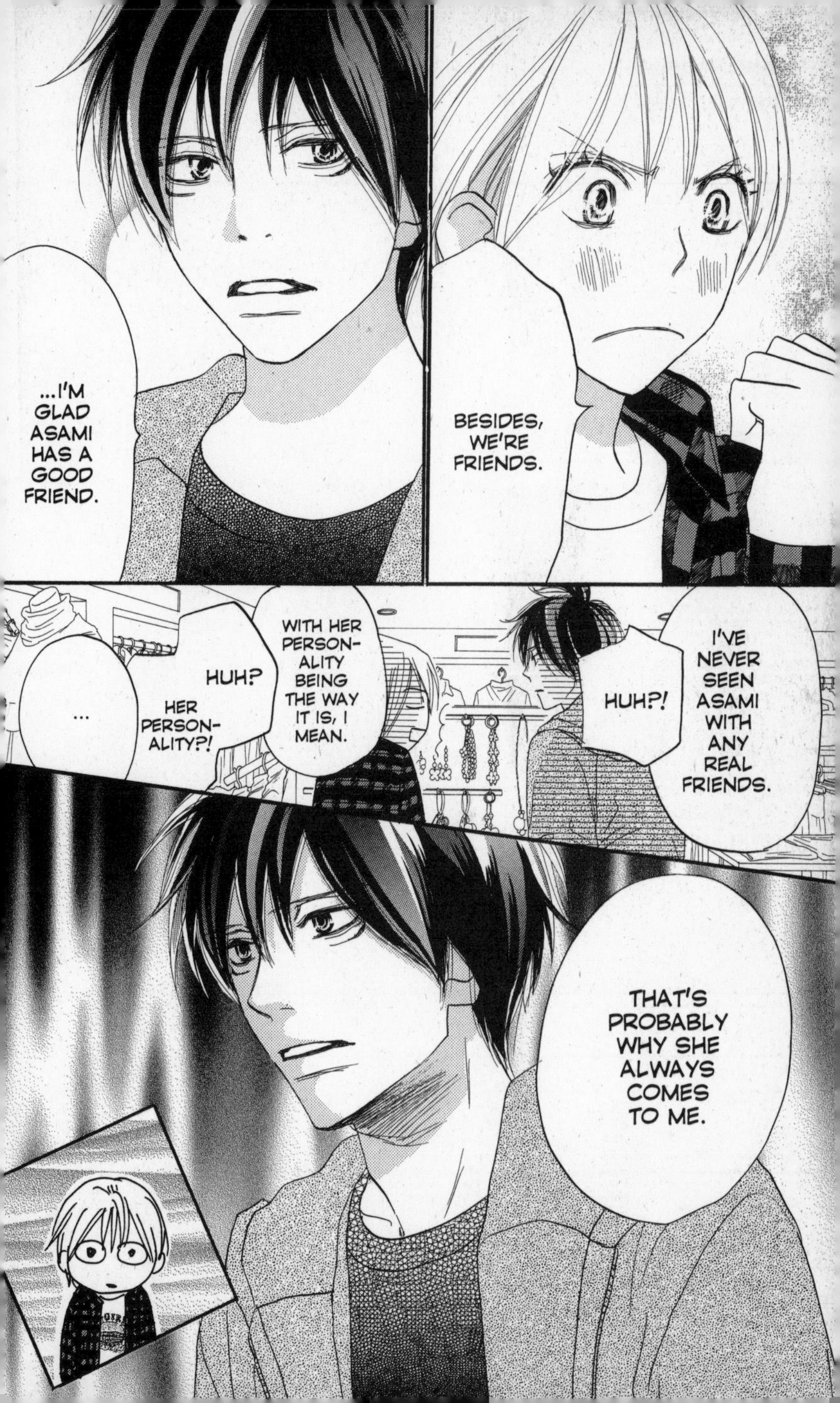
BESIDES, WE'RE FRIENDS.
...I'M GLAD ASAMI HAS A GOOD FRIEND.
I'VE NEVER SEEN ASAMI WITH ANY REAL FRIENDS.
HUH?!
WITH HER PERSONALITY BEING THE WAY IT IS, I MEAN.
HUH?
HER PERSONALITY?!
...
THAT'S PROBABLY WHY SHE ALWAYS COMES TO ME.

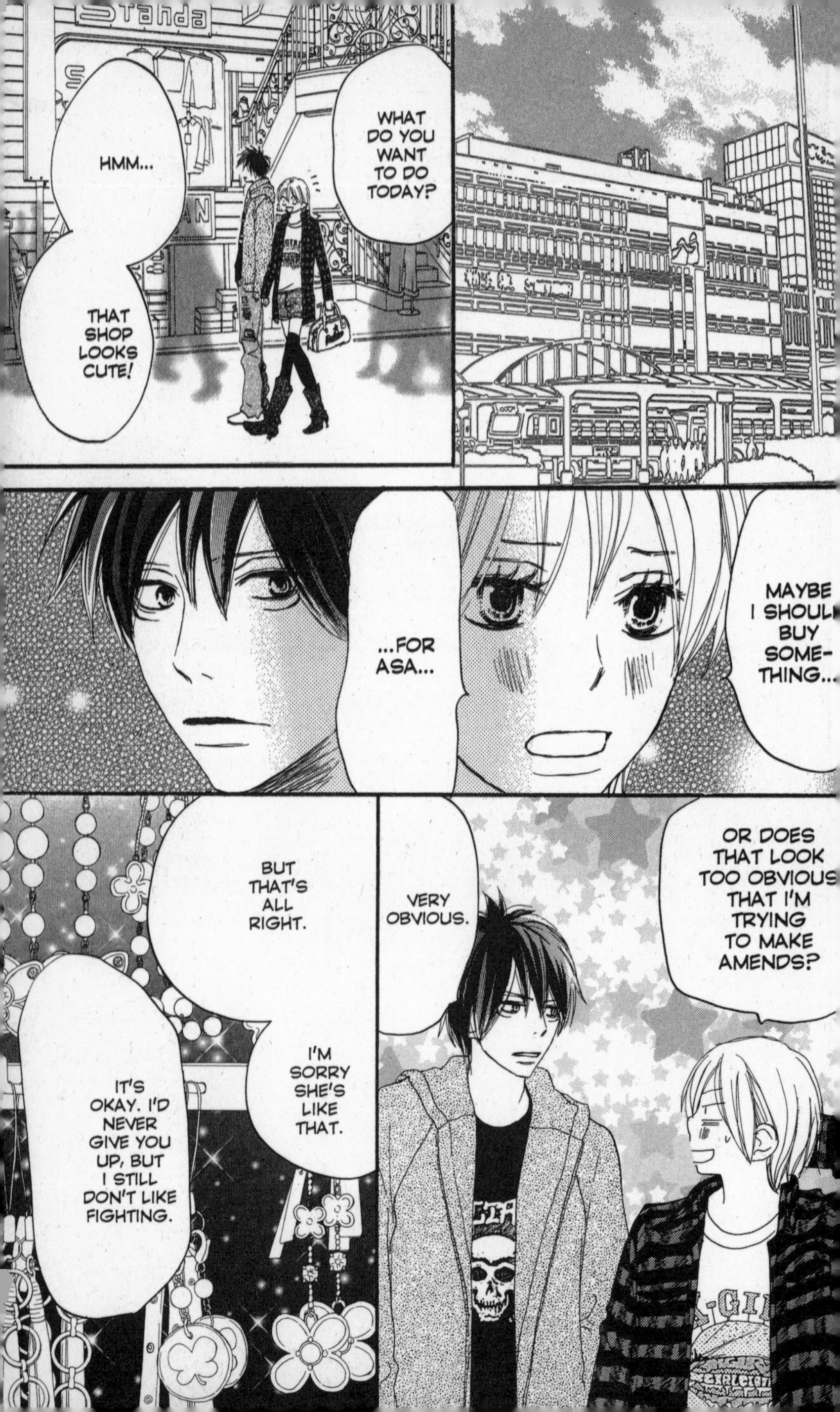
WHAT DO YOU WANT TO DO TODAY?
HMM...
THAT SHOP LOOKS CUTE!
MAYBE I SHOUL BUY SOME-THING...
...FOR ASA...
OR DOES THAT LOOK TOO OBVIOUS THAT I'M TRYING TO MAKE AMENDS?
VERY OBVIOUS.
BUT THAT'S ALL RIGHT.
I'M SORRY SHE'S LIKE THAT.
IT'S OKAY. I'D NEVER GIVE YOU UP, BUT I STILL DON'T LIKE FIGHTING.

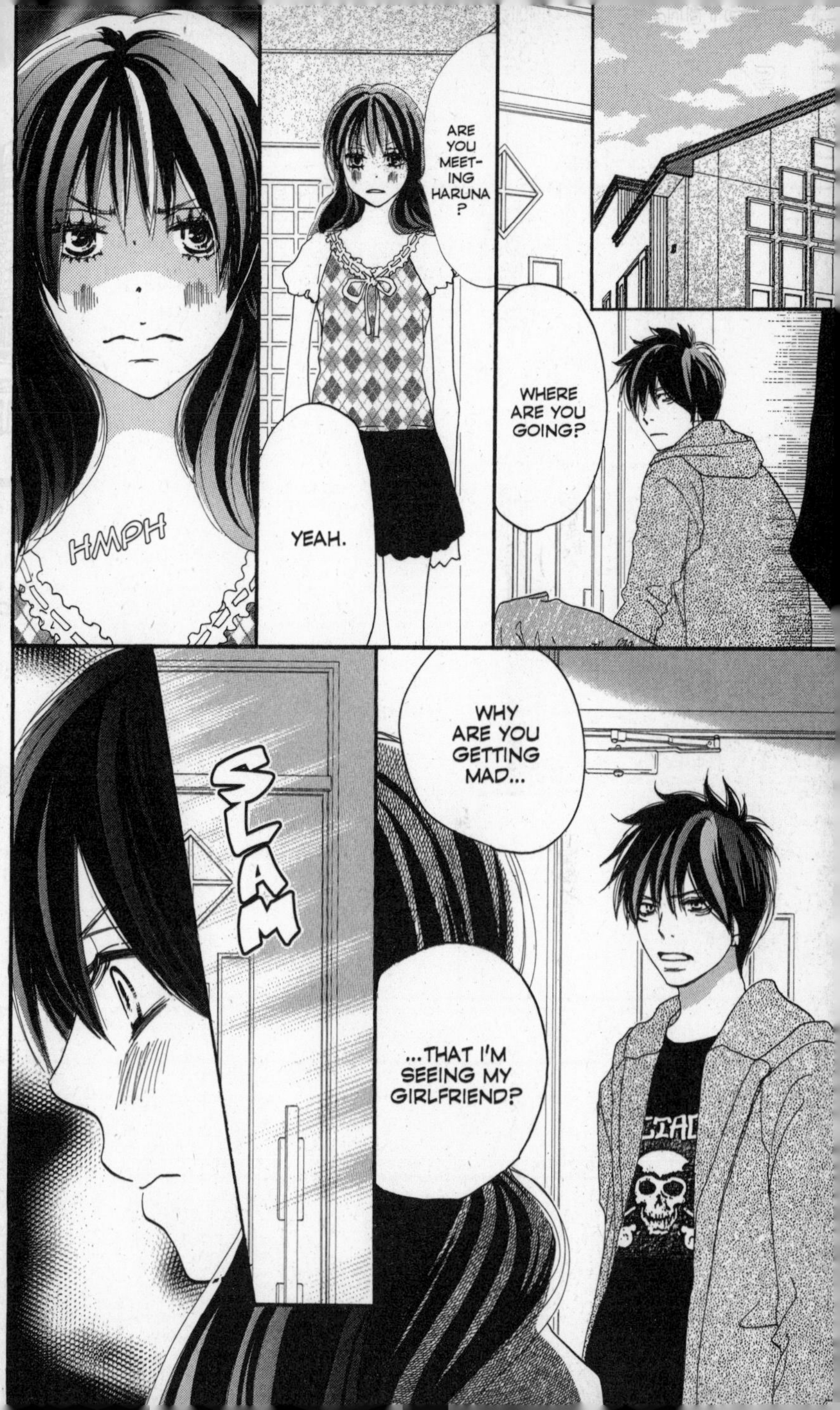
WHERE ARE YOU GOING?
ARE YOU MEET-ING HARUNA?
YEAH.
HMPH
WHY ARE YOU GETTING MAD...
...THAT I'M SEEING MY GIRLFRIEND?
SLAM

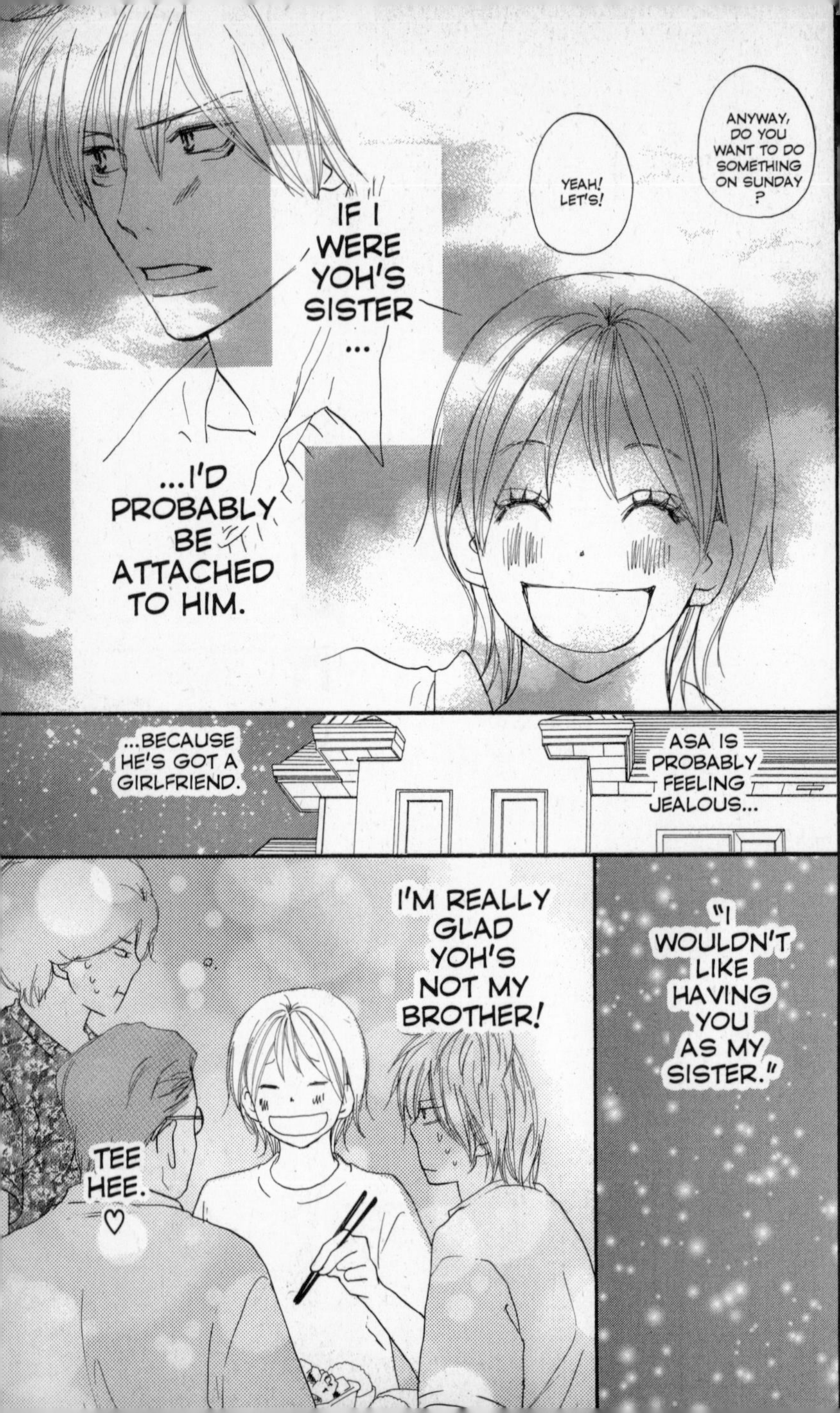
ANYWAY, DO YOU WANT TO DO SOMETHING ON SUNDAY?
YEAH! LET'S!
IF I WERE YOH'S SISTER...
...I'D PROBABLY BE ATTACHED TO HIM.
ASA IS PROBABLY FEELING JEALOUS...
...BECAUSE HE'S GOT A GIRLFRIEND.
"I WOULDN'T LIKE HAVING YOU AS MY SISTER."
I'M REALLY GLAD YOH'S NOT MY BROTHER!
TEE HEE. ♡

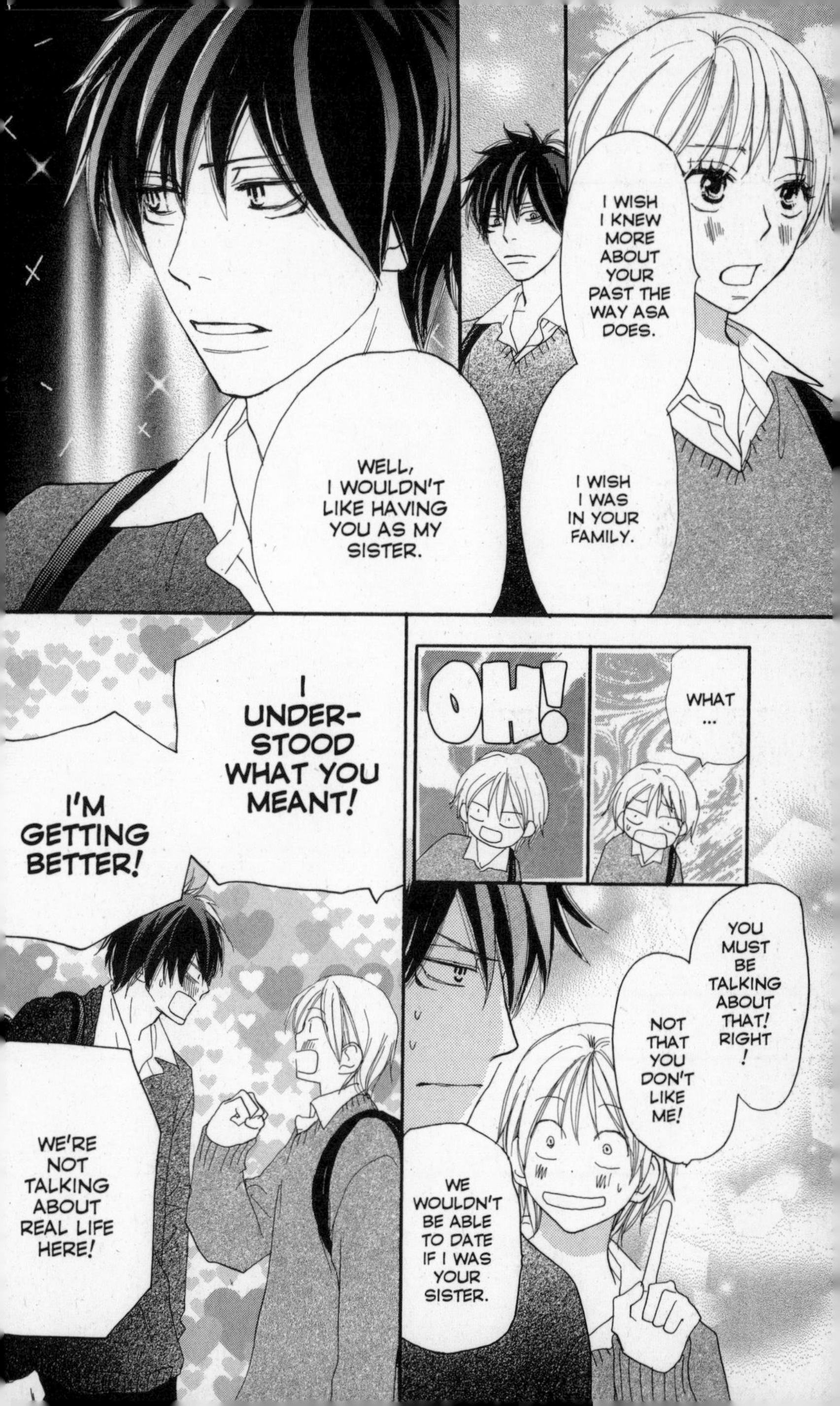
I WISH I KNEW MORE ABOUT YOUR PAST THE WAY ASA DOES.
I WISH I WAS IN YOUR FAMILY.
WELL, I WOULDN'T LIKE HAVING YOU AS MY SISTER.
WHAT ...
OH!
YOU MUST BE TALKING ABOUT THAT! RIGHT!
NOT THAT YOU DON'T LIKE ME!
WE WOULDN'T BE ABLE TO DATE IF I WAS YOUR SISTER.
I UNDERSTOOD WHAT YOU MEANT!
I'M GETTING BETTER!
WE'RE NOT TALKING ABOUT REAL LIFE HERE!

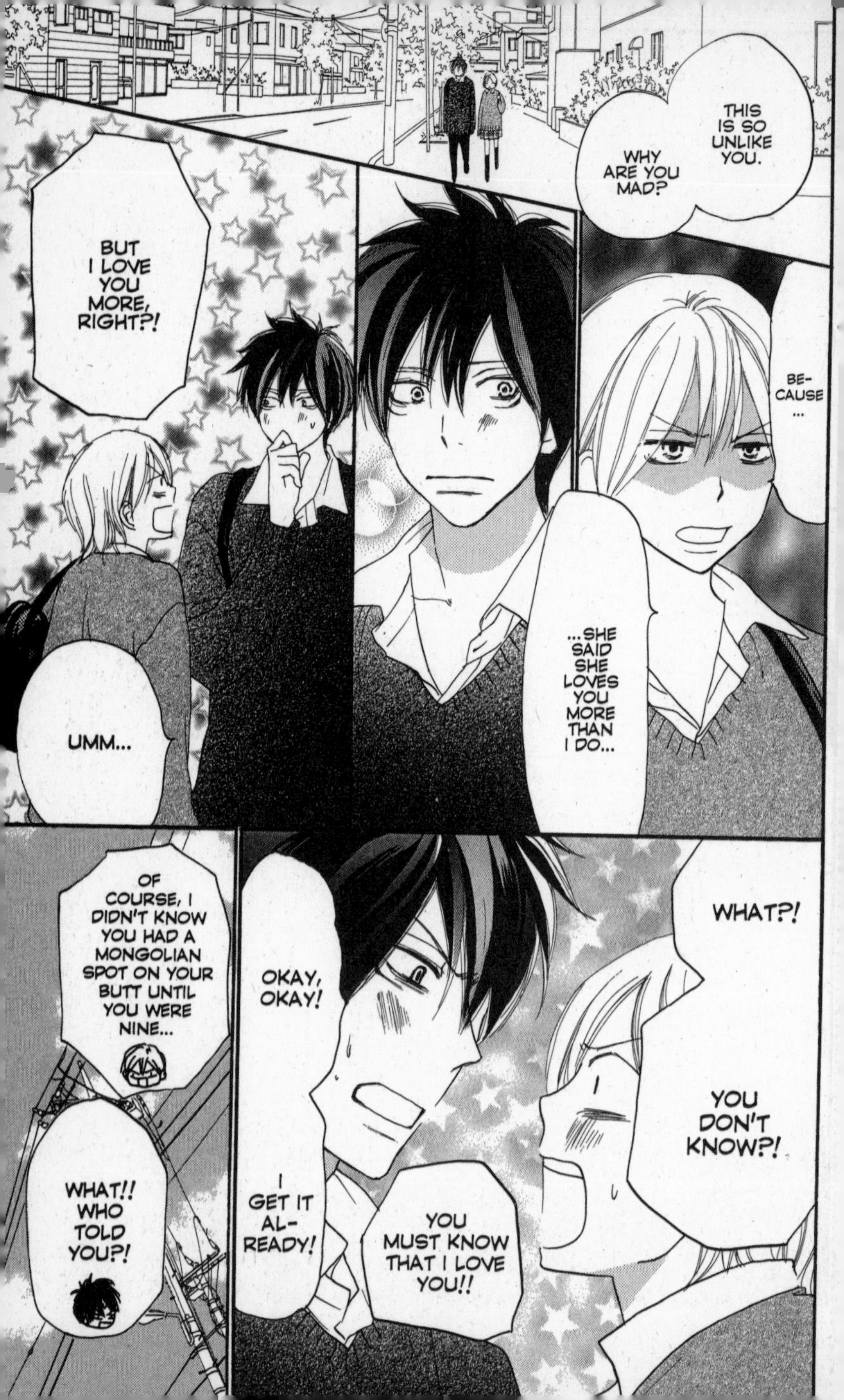
THIS IS SO UNLIKE YOU.
WHY ARE YOU MAD?
BE-CAUSE...
...SHE SAID SHE LOVES YOU MORE THAN I DO...
BUT I LOVE YOU MORE, RIGHT?!
UMM...
WHAT?!
YOU DON'T KNOW?!
YOU MUST KNOW THAT I LOVE YOU!!
OKAY, OKAY!
I GET IT AL-READY!
OF COURSE, I DIDN'T KNOW YOU HAD A MONGOLIAN SPOT ON YOUR BUTT UNTIL YOU WERE NINE...
WHAT!! WHO TOLD YOU?!

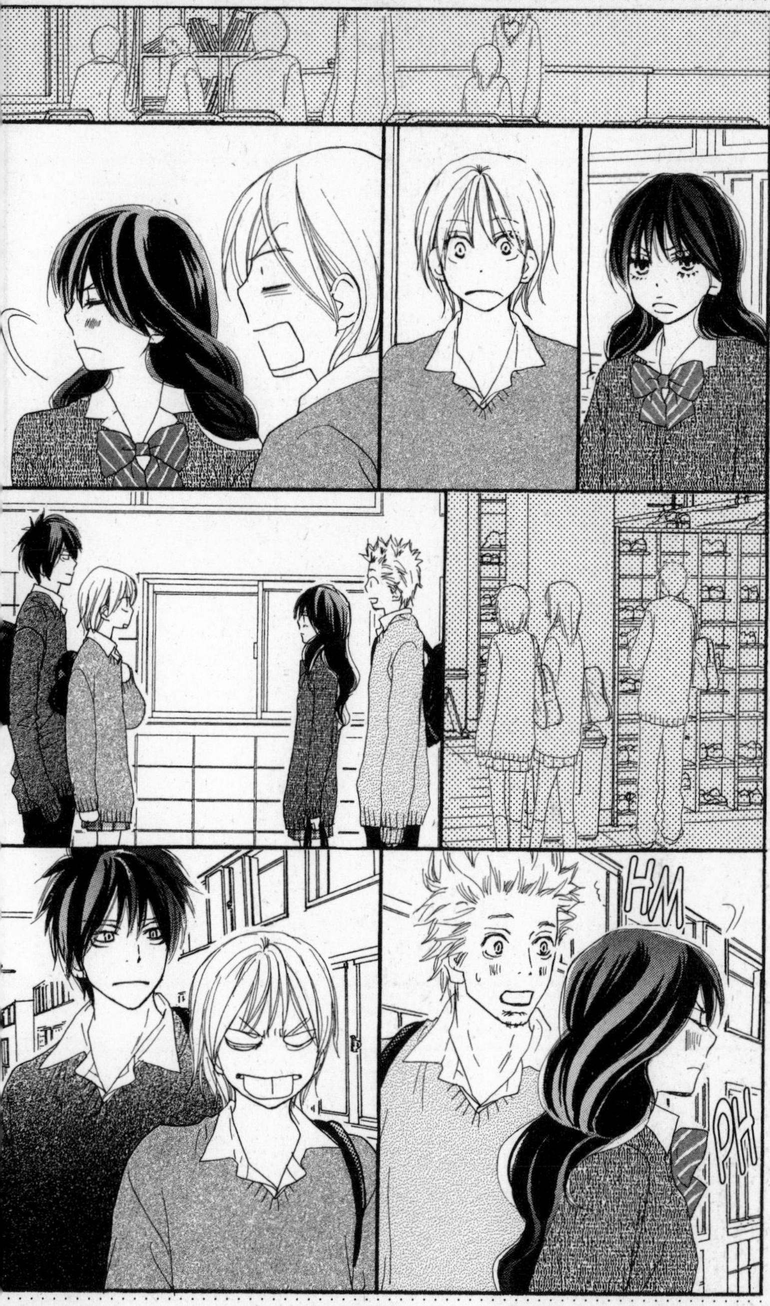
HM
PH

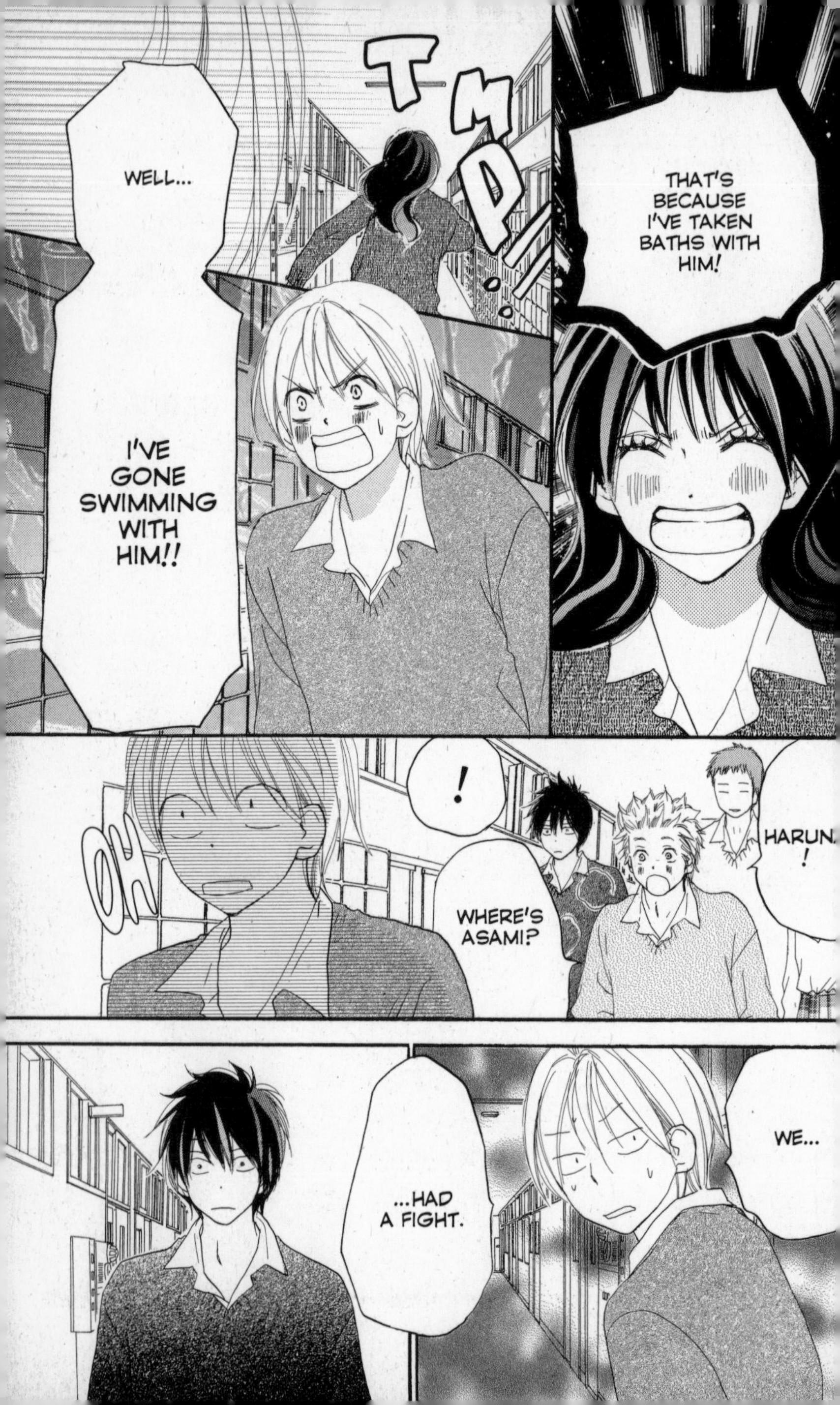
THAT'S BECAUSE I'VE TAKEN BATHS WITH HIM!
TMP
WELL...
I'VE GONE SWIMMING WITH HIM!!
HARUN. !
!
WHERE'S ASAMI?
OH
WE...
...HAD A FIGHT.

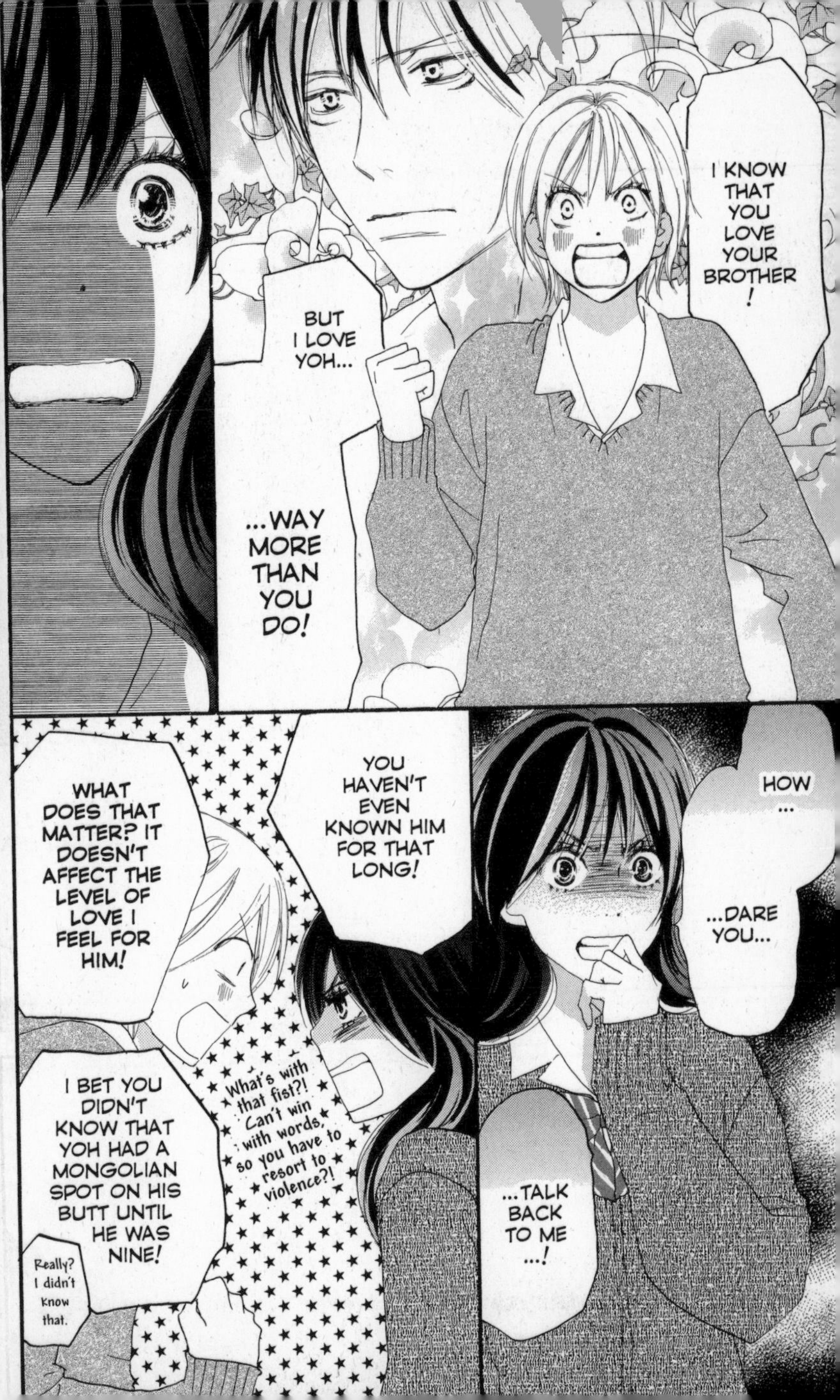
I KNOW THAT YOU LOVE YOUR BROTHER!
BUT I LOVE YOH...
...WAY MORE THAN YOU DO!
HOW...
...DARE YOU...
...TALK BACK TO ME...!
YOU HAVEN'T EVEN KNOWN HIM FOR THAT LONG!
WHAT DOES THAT MATTER? IT DOESN'T AFFECT THE LEVEL OF LOVE I FEEL FOR HIM!
What's with that fist?! Can't win with words, so you have to resort to violence?!
I BET YOU DIDN'T KNOW THAT YOH HAD A MONGOLIAN SPOT ON HIS BUTT UNTIL HE WAS NINE!
Really? I didn't know that.

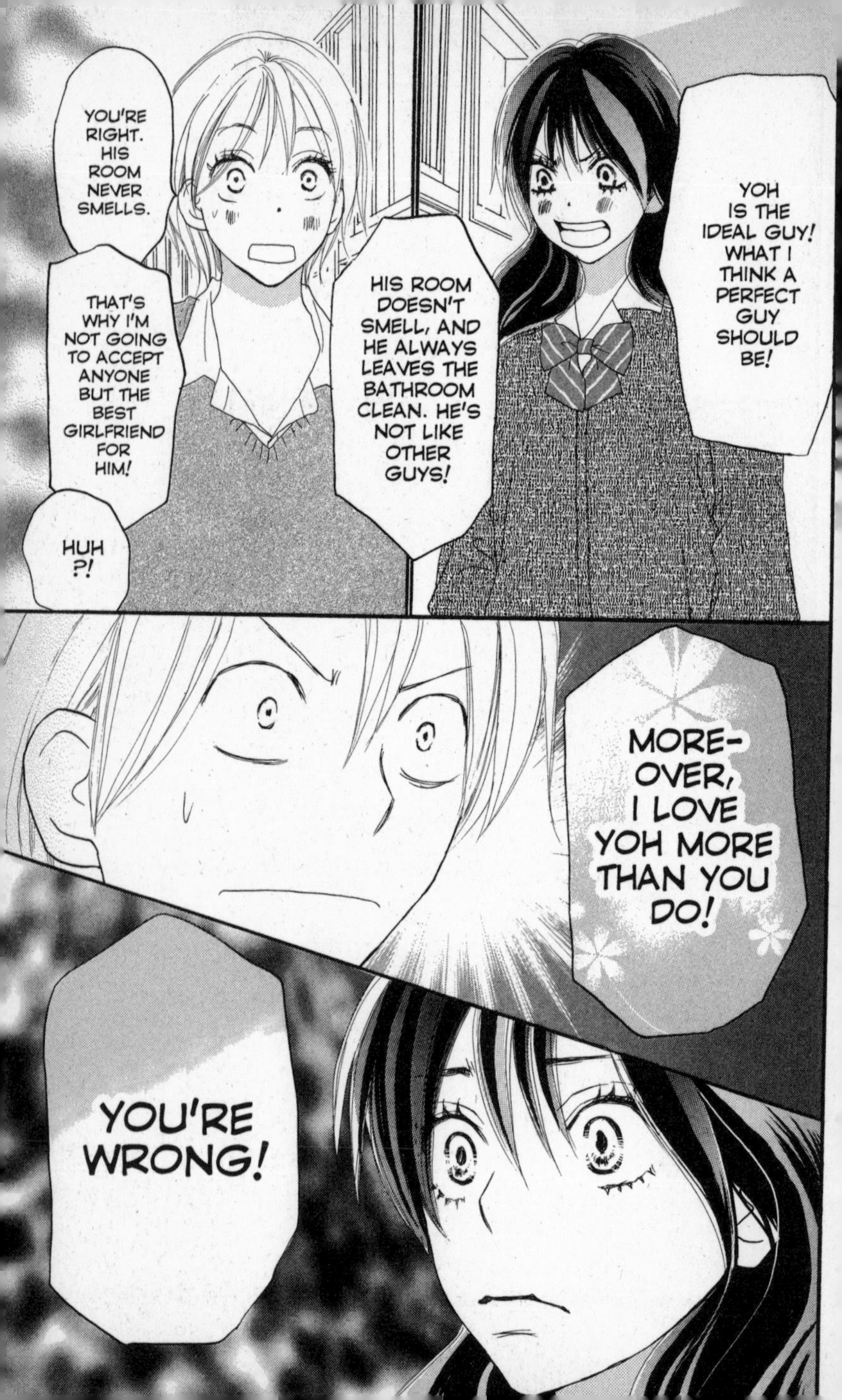
YOH IS THE IDEAL GUY! WHAT I THINK A PERFECT GUY SHOULD BE!
HIS ROOM DOESN'T SMELL, AND HE ALWAYS LEAVES THE BATHROOM CLEAN. HE'S NOT LIKE OTHER GUYS!
YOU'RE RIGHT. HIS ROOM NEVER SMELLS.
THAT'S WHY I'M NOT GOING TO ACCEPT ANYONE BUT THE BEST GIRLFRIEND FOR HIM!
HUH?!
MORE-OVER, I LOVE YOH MORE THAN YOU DO!
YOU'RE WRONG!

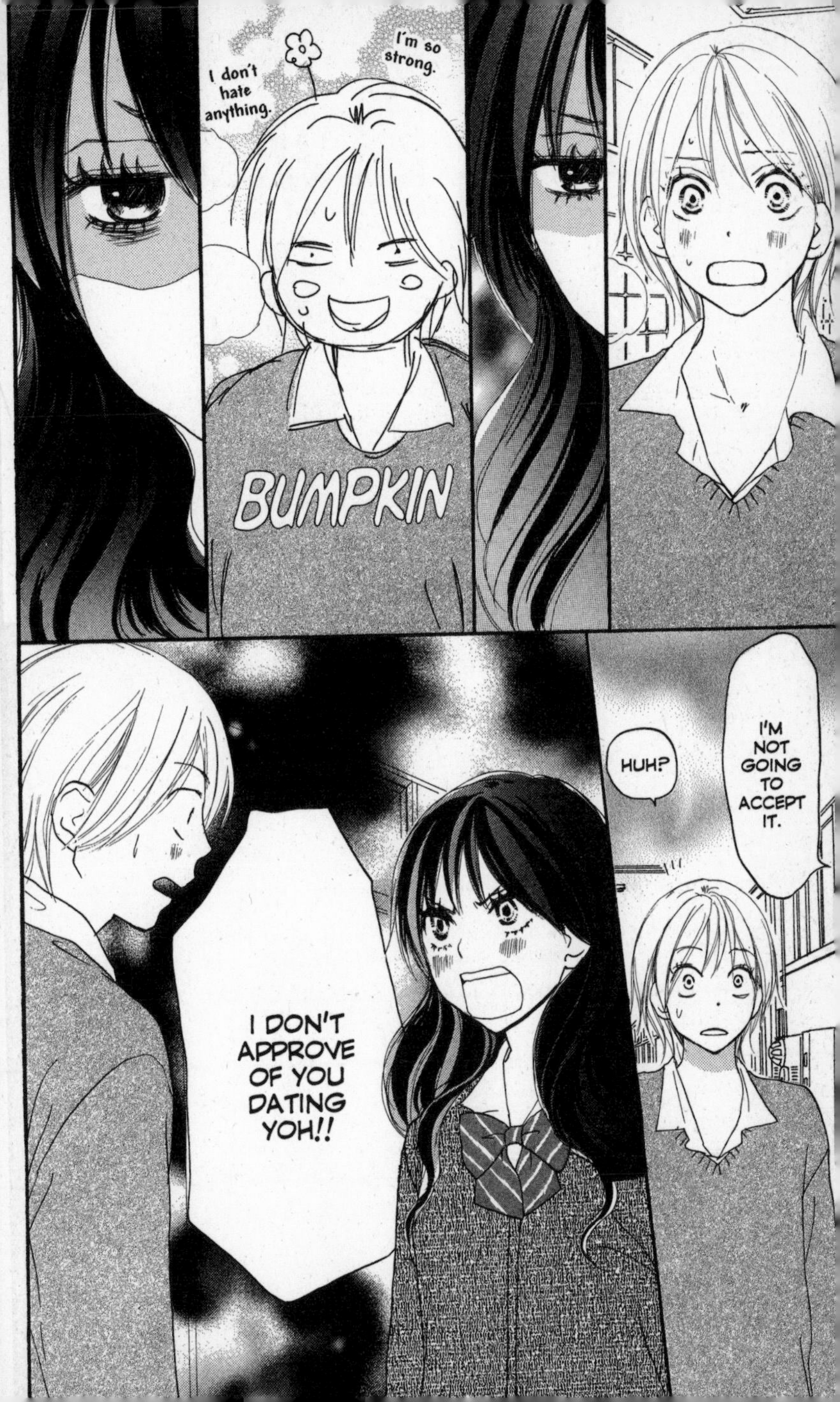
I'm so strong.
I don't hate anything.
BUMPKIN
I'M NOT GOING TO ACCEPT IT.
HUH?
I DON'T APPROVE OF YOU DATING YOH!!

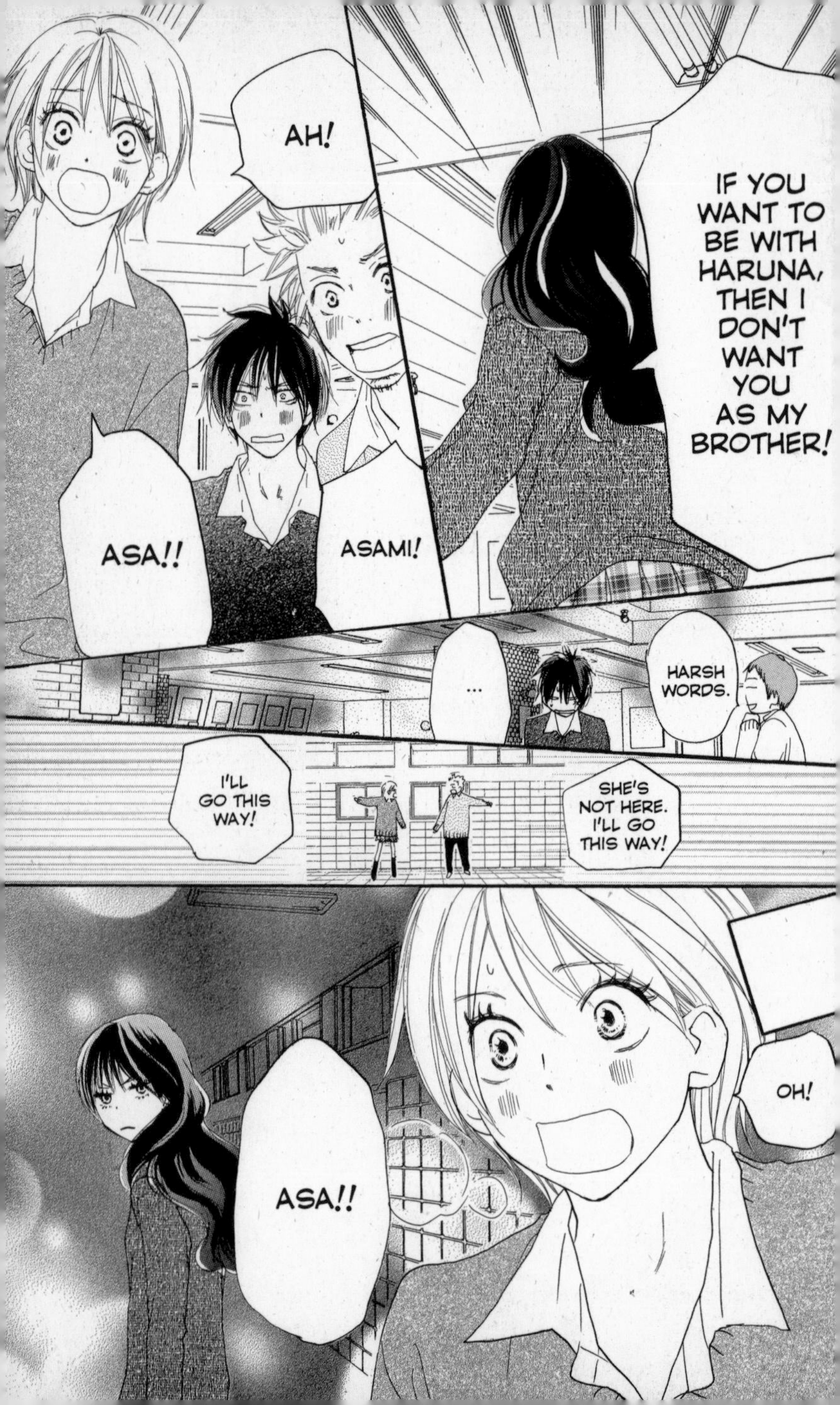
IF YOU WANT TO BE WITH HARUNA, THEN I DON'T WANT YOU AS MY BROTHER!
AH!
ASAMI!
ASA!!
HARSH WORDS.
...
SHE'S NOT HERE. I'LL GO THIS WAY!
I'LL GO THIS WAY!
OH!
ASA!!

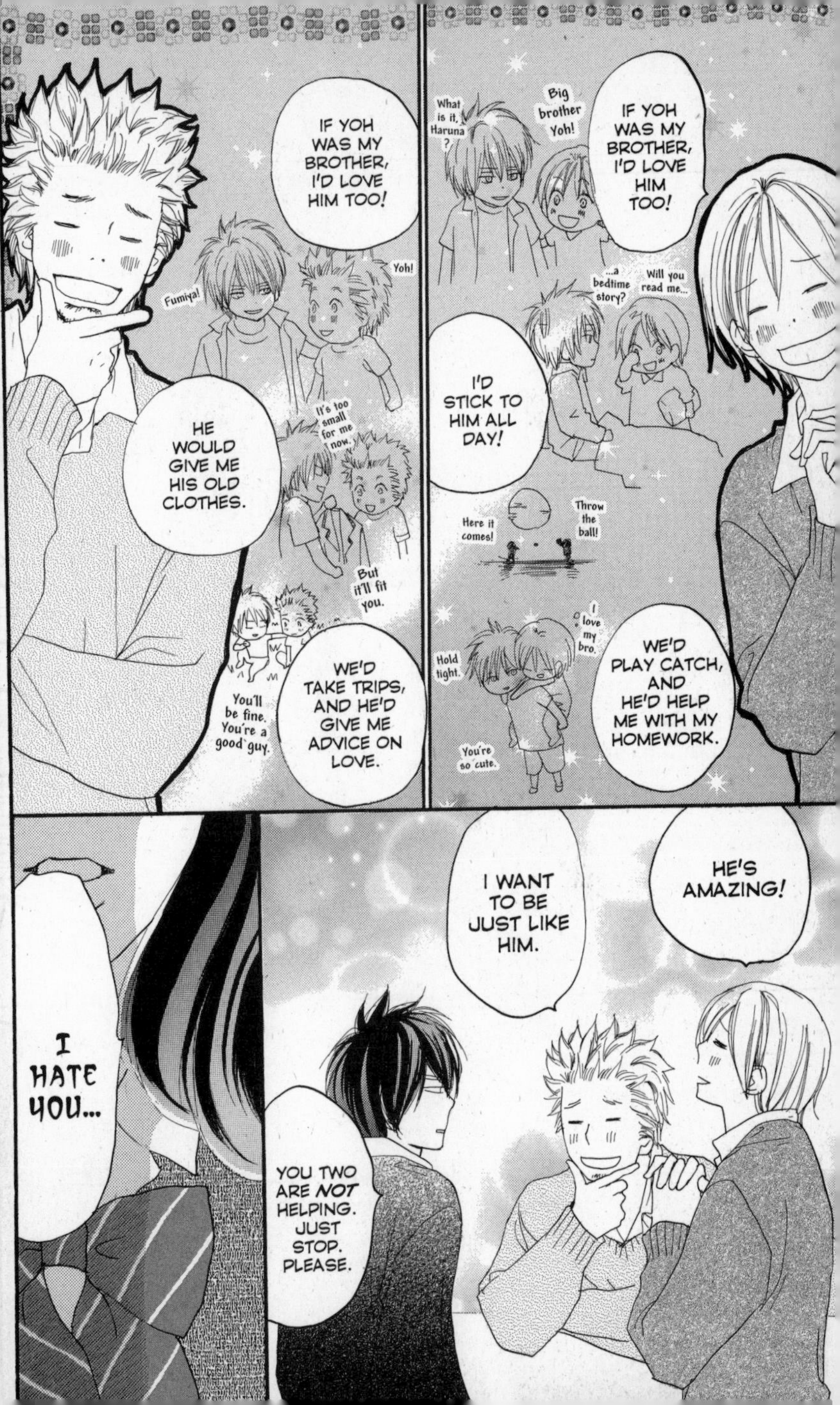
IF YOH WAS MY BROTHER, I'D LOVE HIM TOO!
Big brother Yoh!
What is it, Haruna?
Will you read me...
...a bedtime story?
I'D STICK TO HIM ALL DAY!
Throw the ball!
Here it comes!
I love my bro.
Hold tight.
WE'D PLAY CATCH, AND HE'D HELP ME WITH MY HOMEWORK.
You're so cute.
IF YOH WAS MY BROTHER, I'D LOVE HIM TOO!
Yoh!
Fumiya!
HE WOULD GIVE ME HIS OLD CLOTHES.
It's too small for me now.
But it'll fit you.
WE'D TAKE TRIPS, AND HE'D GIVE ME ADVICE ON LOVE.
You'll be fine. You're a good guy.
HE'S AMAZING!
I WANT TO BE JUST LIKE HIM.
YOU TWO ARE *NOT* HELPING. JUST STOP. PLEASE.
I HATE YOU...

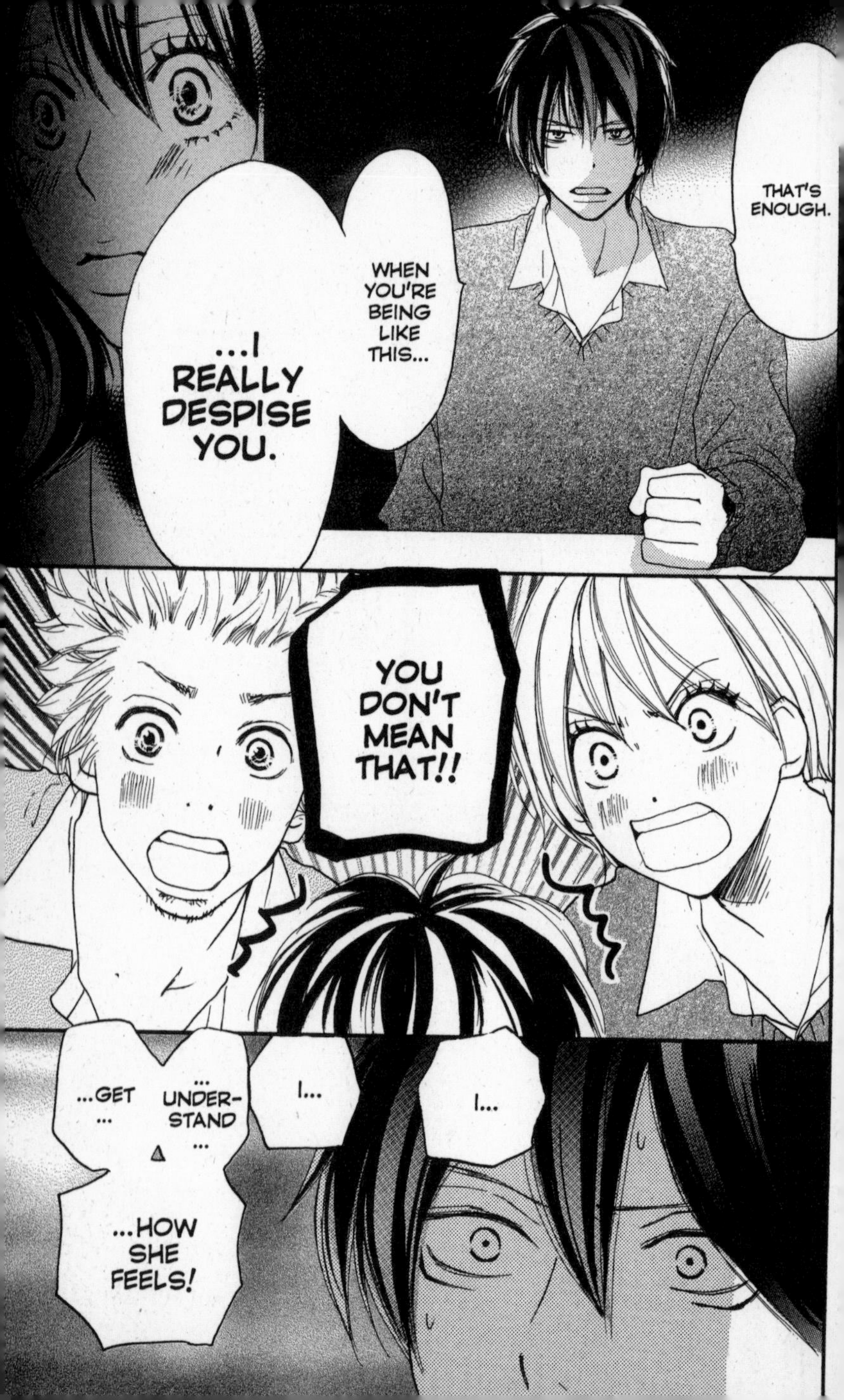
THAT'S ENOUGH.
WHEN YOU'RE BEING LIKE THIS...
...I REALLY DESPISE YOU.
YOU DON'T MEAN THAT!!
I...
I...
... UNDER-STAND ...
...GET ...
...HOW SHE FEELS!

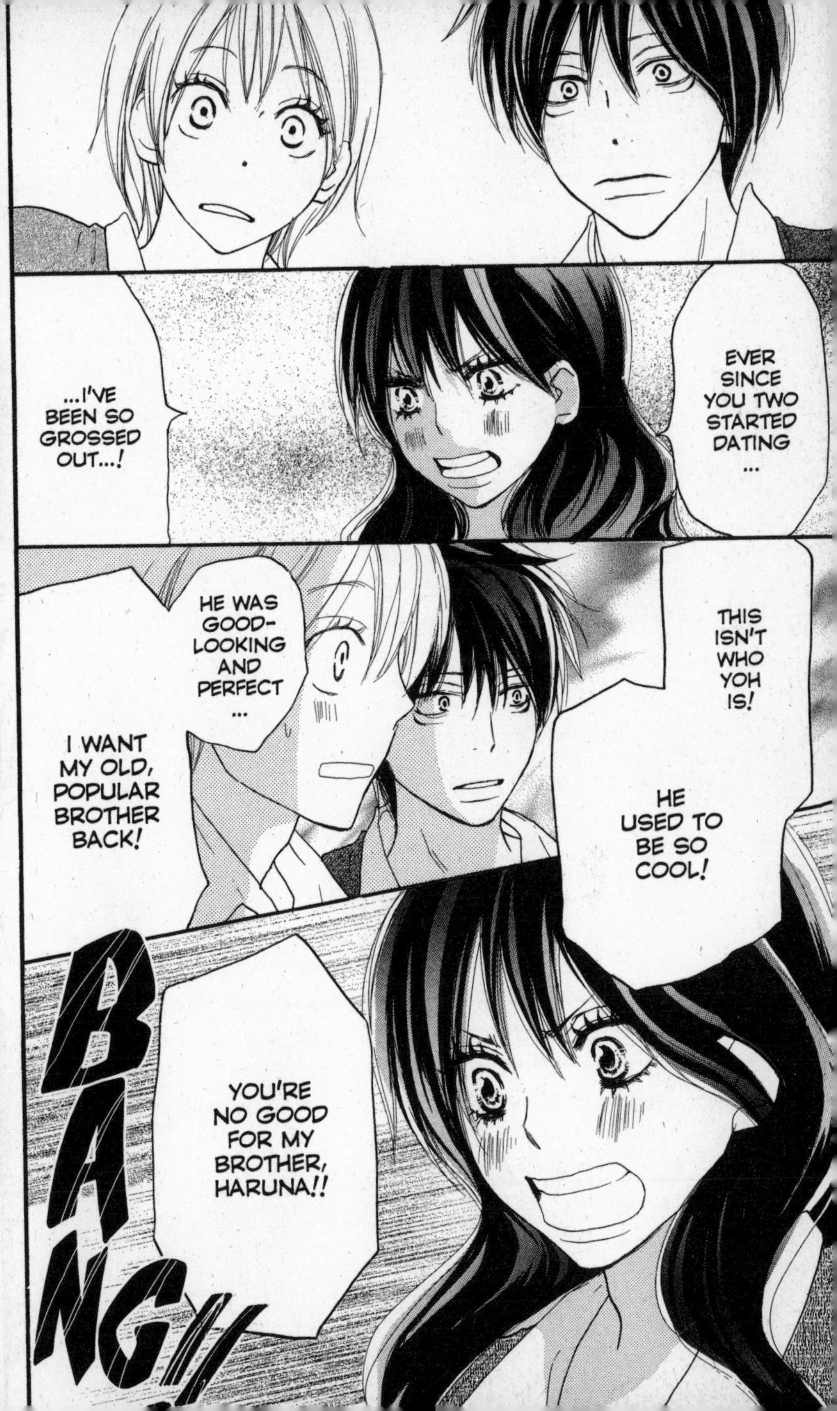
EVER SINCE YOU TWO STARTED DATING...
...I'VE BEEN SO GROSSED OUT...!
THIS ISN'T WHO YOH IS!
HE USED TO BE SO COOL!
HE WAS GOOD-LOOKING AND PERFECT...
I WANT MY OLD, POPULAR BROTHER BACK!
YOU'RE NO GOOD FOR MY BROTHER, HARUNA!!
BANG!!

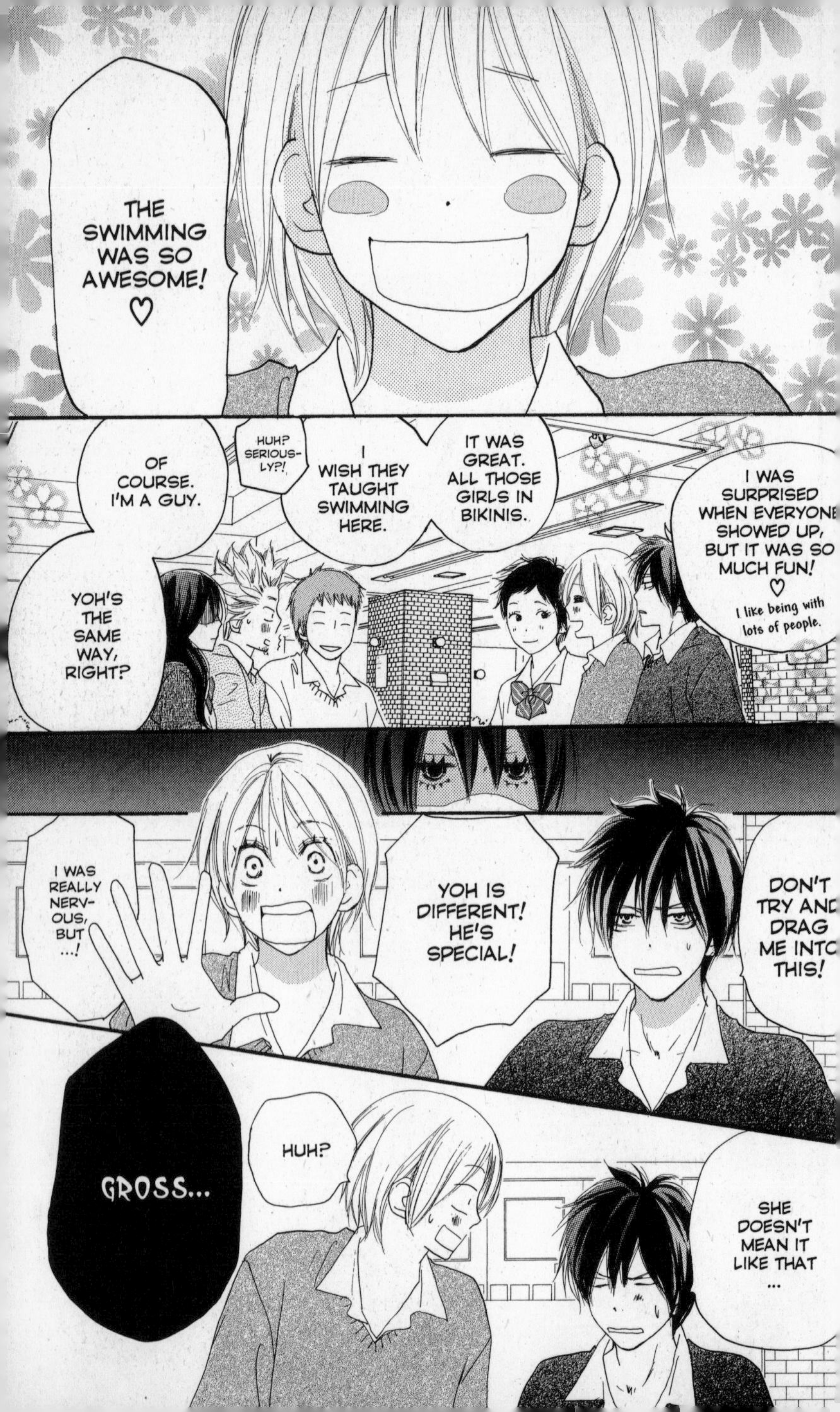
THE SWIMMING WAS SO AWESOME! ♡
I WAS SURPRISED WHEN EVERYONE SHOWED UP, BUT IT WAS SO MUCH FUN! ♡
I like being with lots of people.
IT WAS GREAT. ALL THOSE GIRLS IN BIKINIS.
I WISH THEY TAUGHT SWIMMING HERE.
HUH? SERIOUSLY?!
OF COURSE. I'M A GUY.
YOH'S THE SAME WAY, RIGHT?
DON'T TRY AND DRAG ME INTO THIS!
YOH IS DIFFERENT! HE'S SPECIAL!
I WAS REALLY NERVOUS, BUT ...!
SHE DOESN'T MEAN IT LIKE THAT ...
HUH?
GROSS...

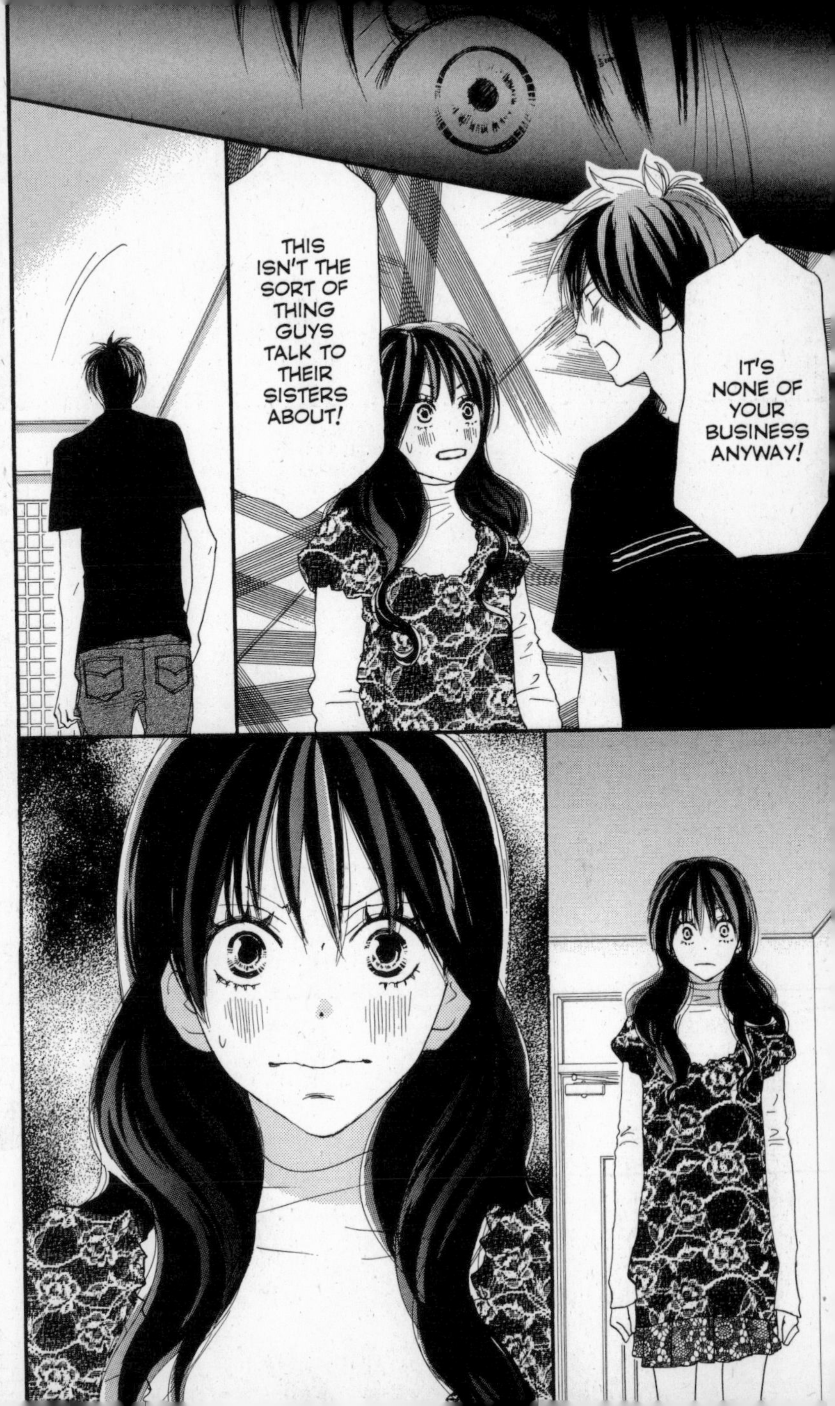
THIS ISN'T THE SORT OF THING GUYS TALK TO THEIR SISTERS ABOUT!
IT'S NONE OF YOUR BUSINESS ANYWAY!

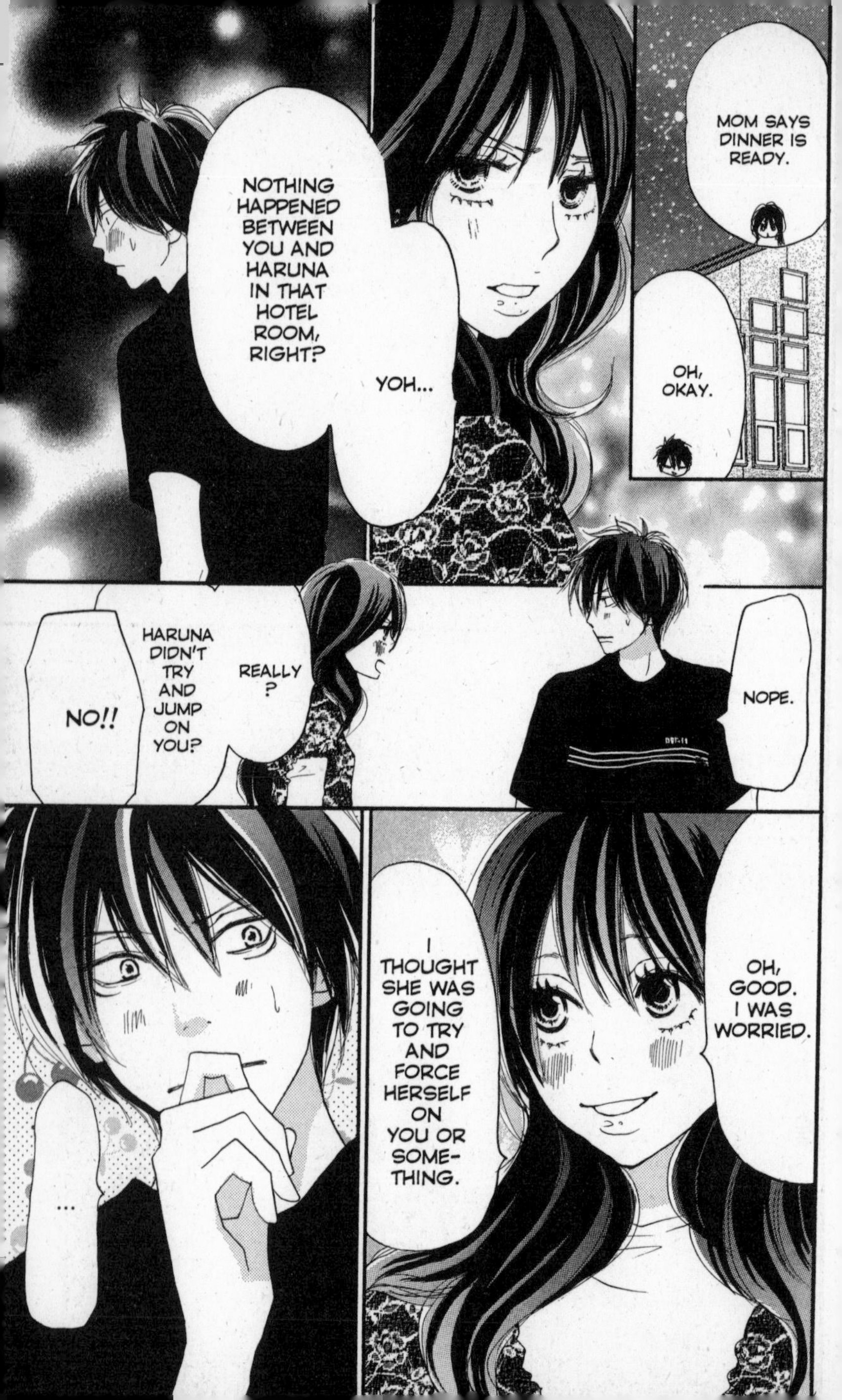
MOM SAYS DINNER IS READY.
OH, OKAY.
YOH...
NOTHING HAPPENED BETWEEN YOU AND HARUNA IN THAT HOTEL ROOM, RIGHT?
NOPE.
REALLY?
HARUNA DIDN'T TRY AND JUMP ON YOU?
NO!!
OH, GOOD. I WAS WORRIED.
I THOUGHT SHE WAS GOING TO TRY AND FORCE HERSELF ON YOU OR SOME-THING.
...

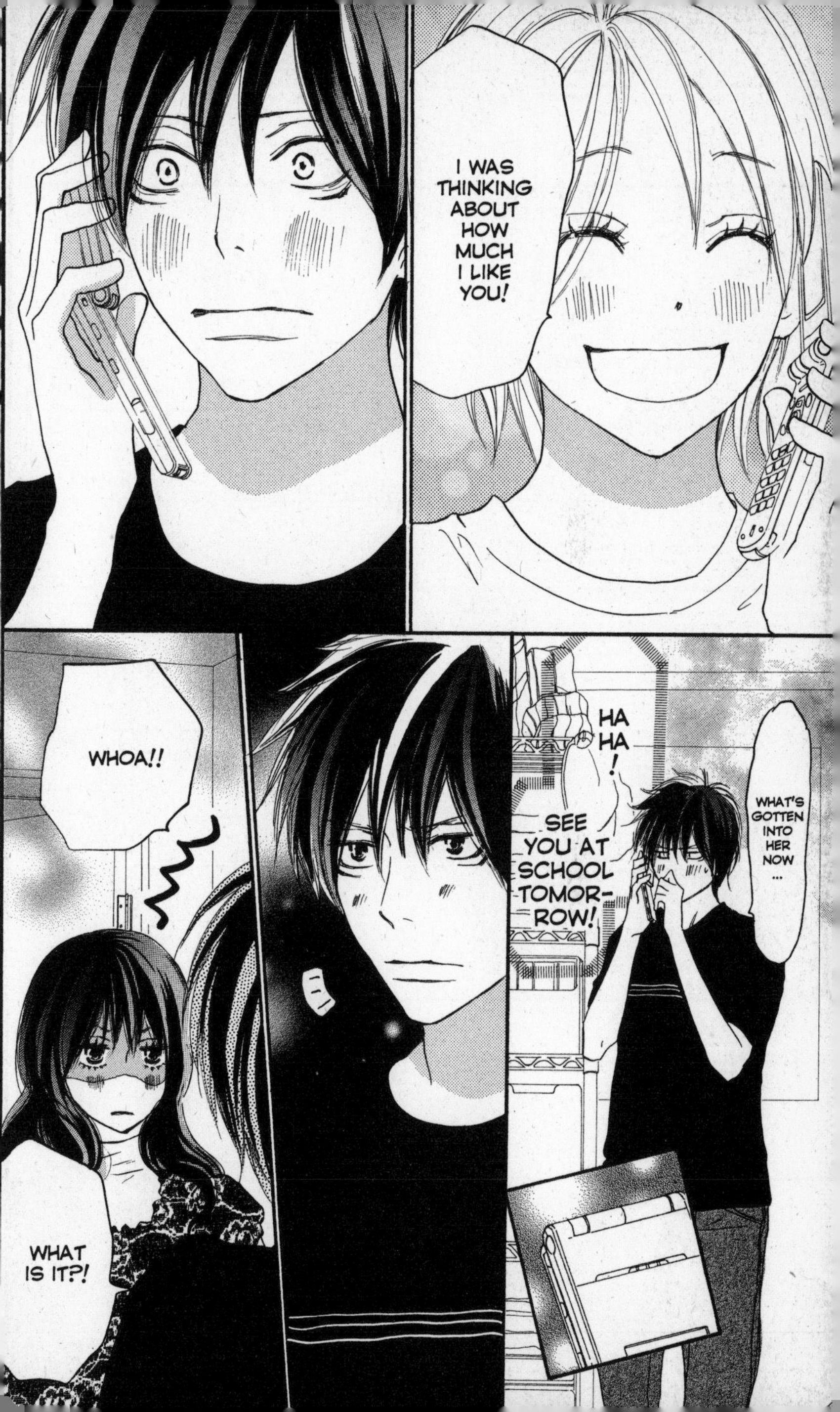
I WAS THINKING ABOUT HOW MUCH I LIKE YOU!
HA HA!
SEE YOU AT SCHOOL TOMORROW!
WHAT'S GOTTEN INTO HER NOW...
WHOA!!
WHAT IS IT?!

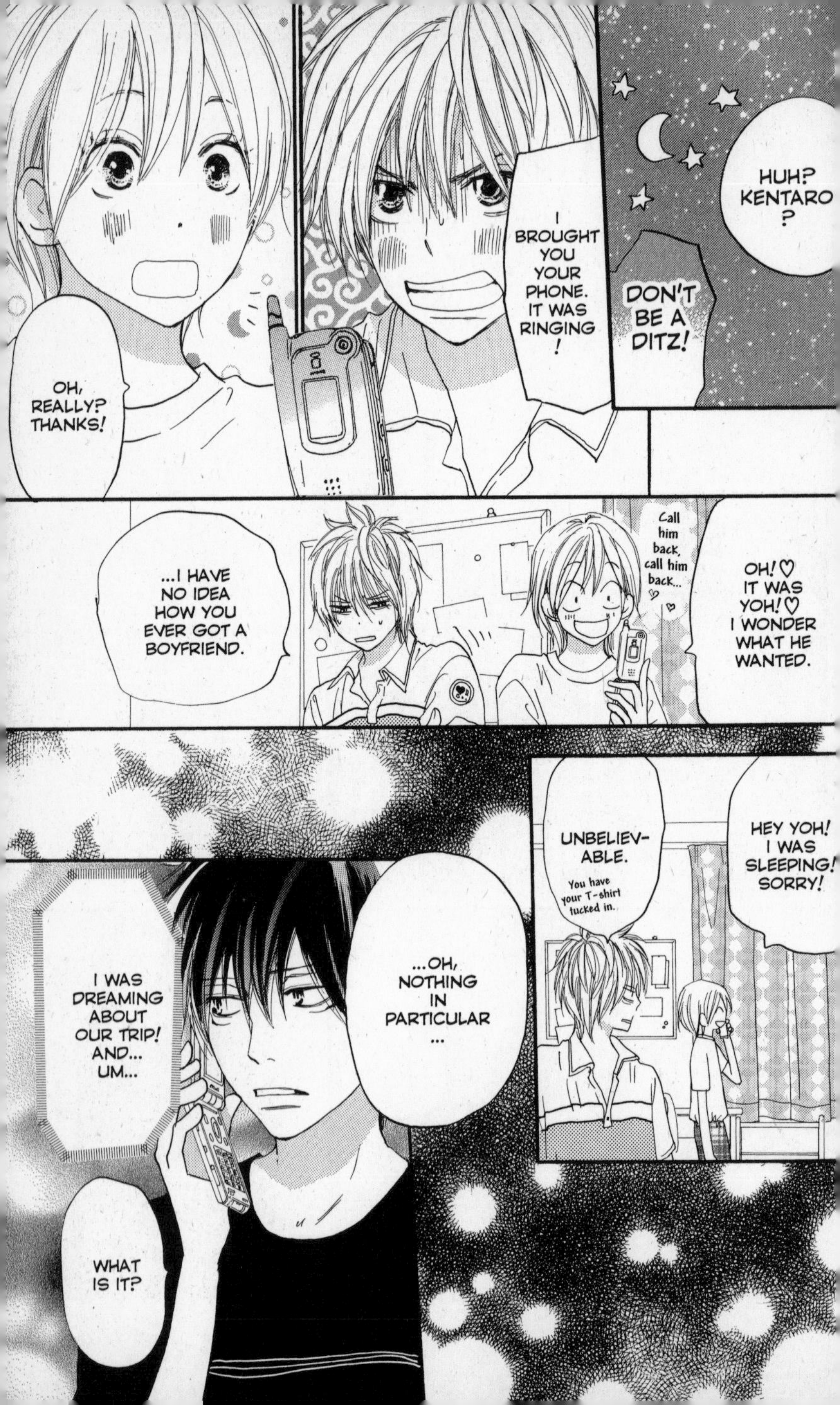
HUH? KENTARO?
DON'T BE A DITZ!
I BROUGHT YOU YOUR PHONE. IT WAS RINGING!
OH, REALLY? THANKS!
OH! ♡ IT WAS YOH! ♡ I WONDER WHAT HE WANTED.
Call him back, call him back... ♡ ♡
...I HAVE NO IDEA HOW YOU EVER GOT A BOYFRIEND.
HEY YOH! I WAS SLEEPING! SORRY!
UNBELIEV-ABLE.
You have your T-shirt tucked in.
...OH, NOTHING IN PARTICULAR...
I WAS DREAMING ABOUT OUR TRIP! AND... UM...
WHAT IS IT?

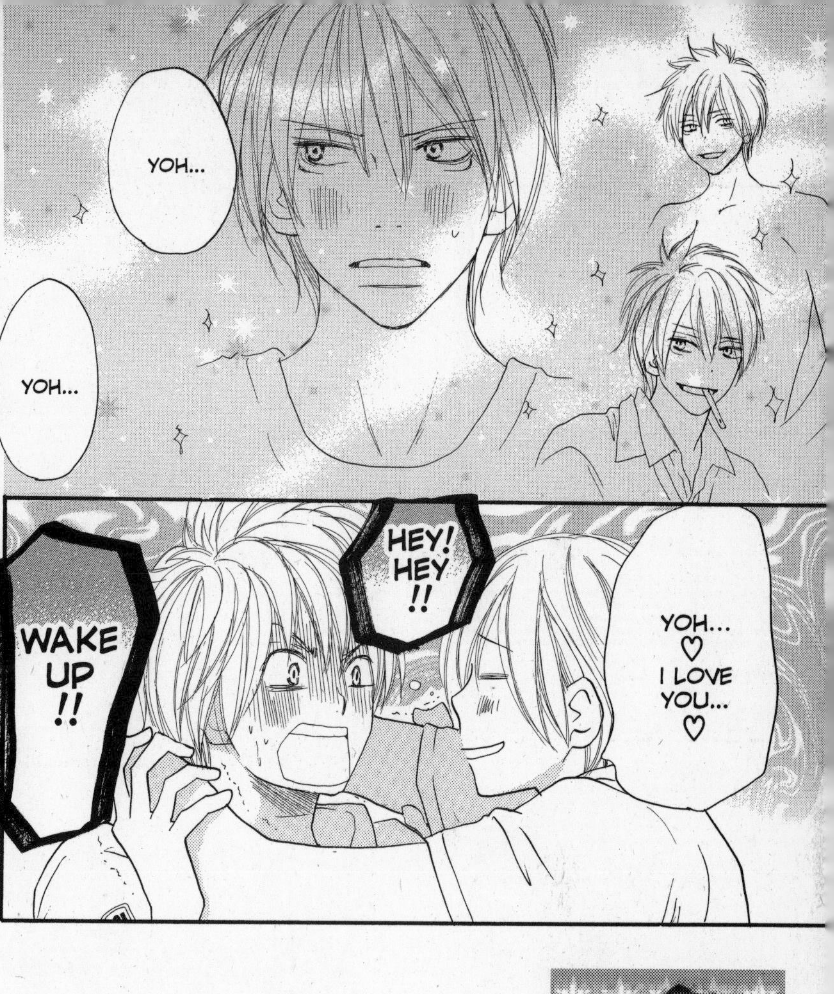
YOH...
YOH...
YOH... ♡ I LOVE YOU... ♡
HEY! HEY !!
WAKE UP !!

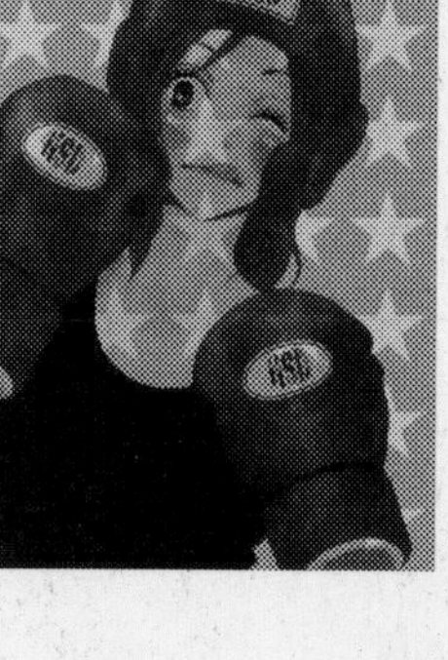

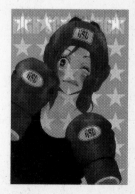

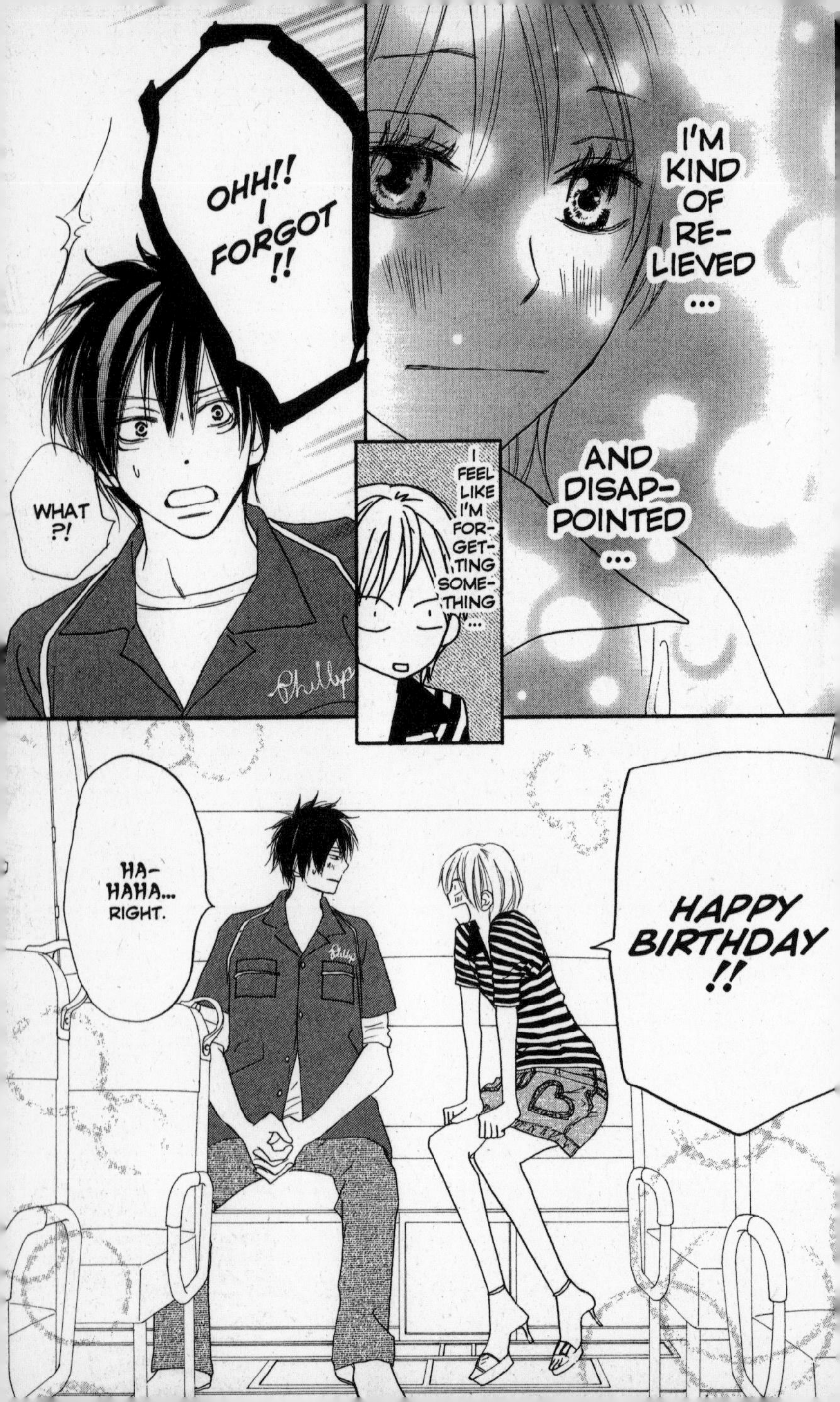
I'M KIND OF RE-LIEVED...
AND DISAP-POINTED...
I FEEL LIKE I'M FOR-GET-TING SOME-THING...
OHH!! I FORGOT!!
WHAT?!
HAPPY BIRTHDAY!!
HA-HAHA... RIGHT.

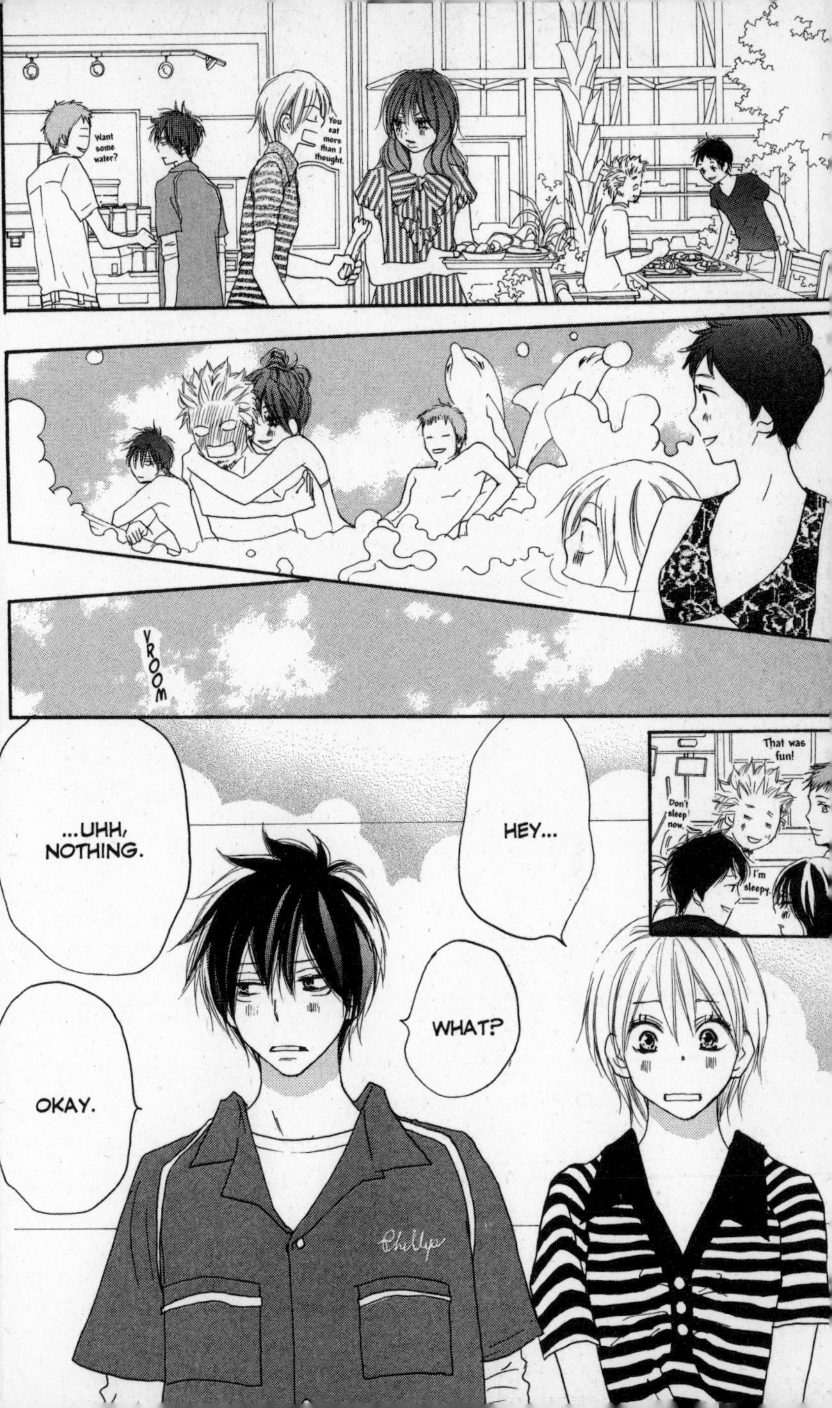
You eat more than I thought.
Want some water?
VROOM
That was fun!
Don't sleep now.
I'm sleepy.
HEY...
WHAT?
...UHH, NOTHING.
OKAY.

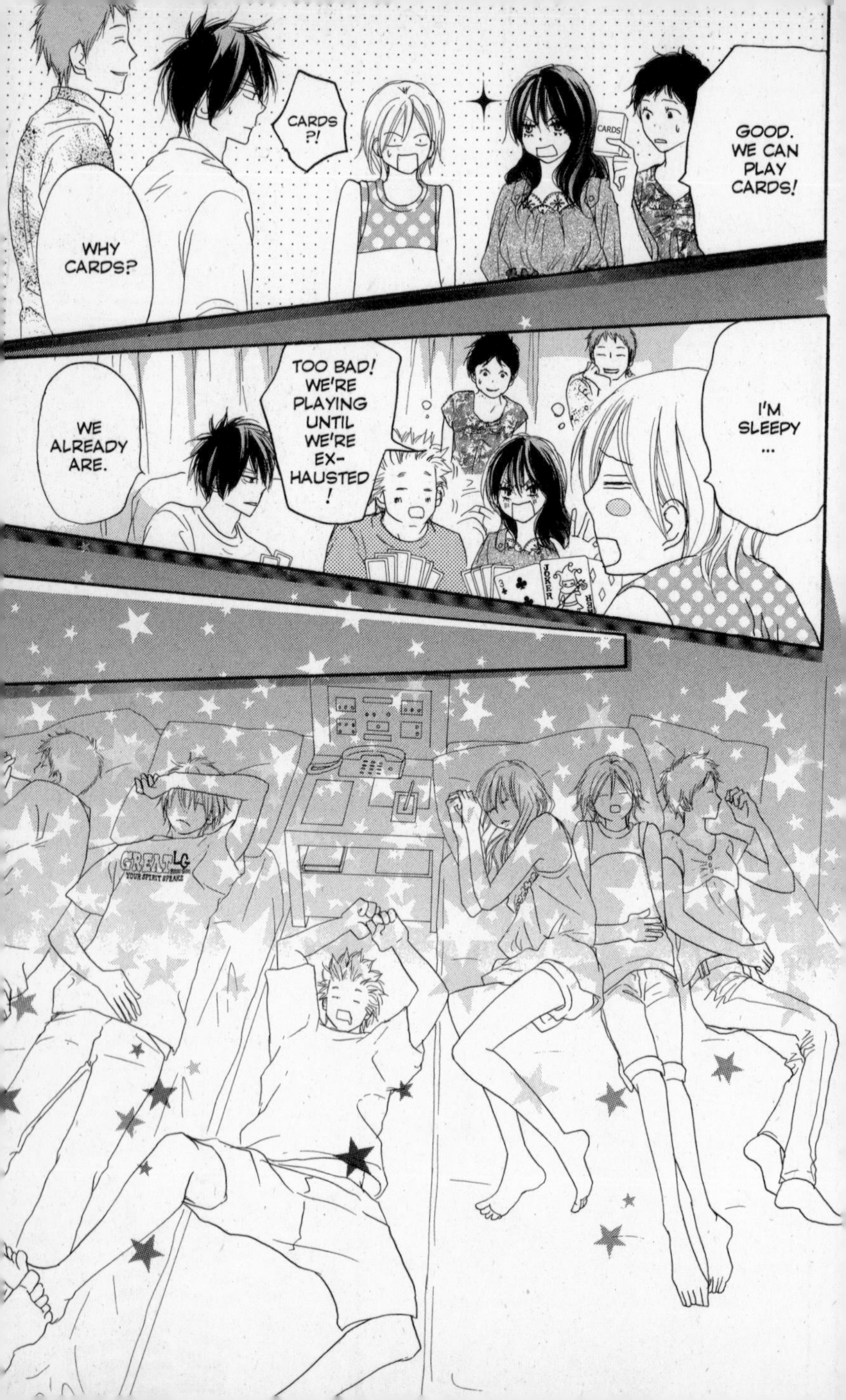
GOOD. WE CAN PLAY CARDS!
CARDS
CARDS ?!
WHY CARDS?
I'M SLEEPY ...
TOO BAD! WE'RE PLAYING UNTIL WE'RE EX-HAUSTED!
WE ALREADY ARE.
JOKER
GREAT LG
YOUR SPIRIT SPEAKS

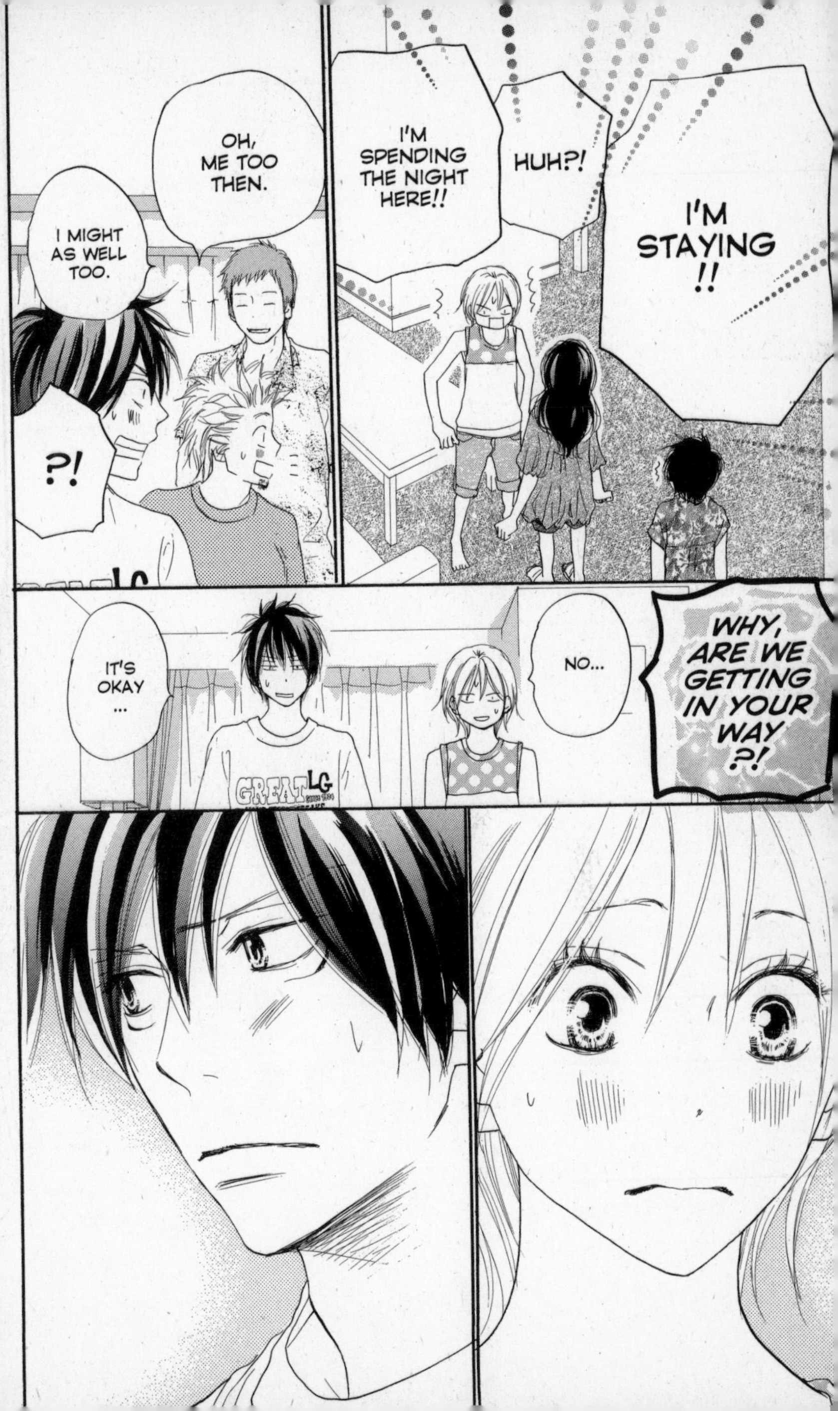
I'M STAYING!!
HUH?!
I'M SPENDING THE NIGHT HERE!!
OH, ME TOO THEN.
I MIGHT AS WELL TOO.
?!
WHY, ARE WE GETTING IN YOUR WAY?!
NO...
IT'S OKAY ...

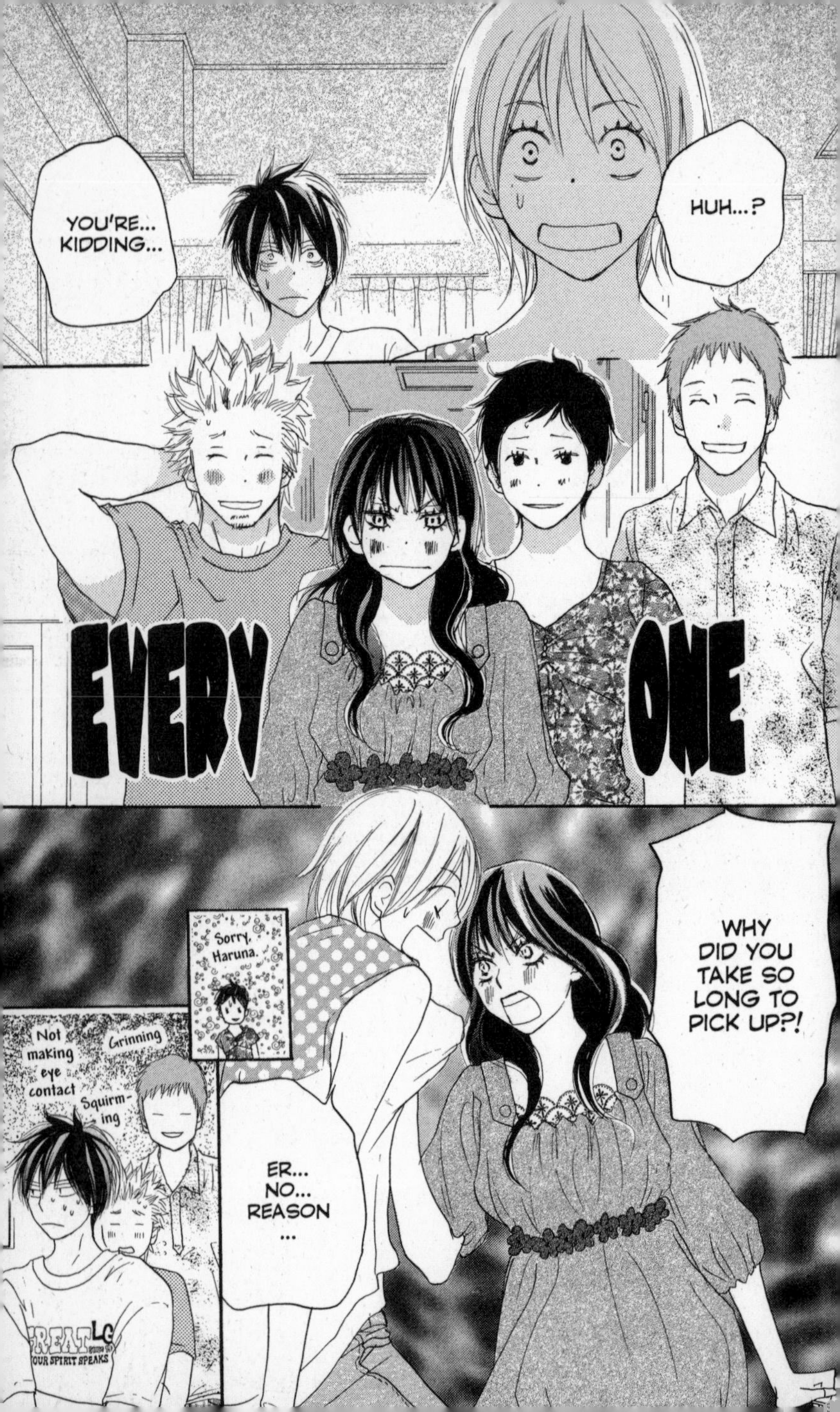
HUH...?
YOU'RE... KIDDING...
EVERY ONE
WHY DID YOU TAKE SO LONG TO PICK UP?!
Sorry, Haruna.
ER... NO... REASON...
Grinning
Not making eye contact
Squirm-ing

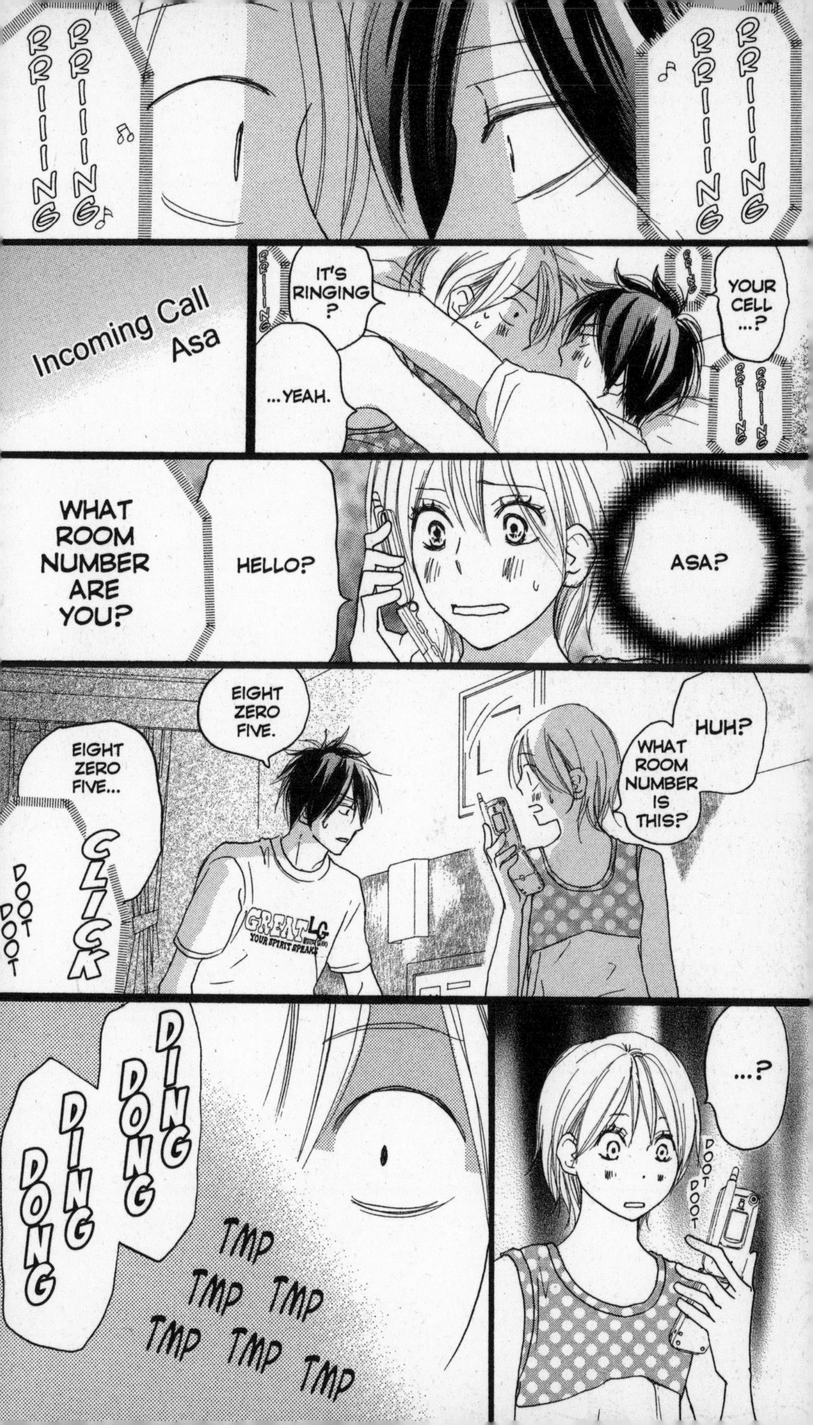
RRIIING
RRIIING
RRIIING
RRIIING
YOUR CELL ...?
IT'S RINGING ?
...YEAH.
Incoming Call
Asa
ASA?
HELLO?
WHAT ROOM NUMBER ARE YOU?
HUH?
WHAT ROOM NUMBER IS THIS?
EIGHT ZERO FIVE.
EIGHT ZERO FIVE...
CLICK
DOOT DOOT
...?
DOOT DOOT
DING DONG
DING DONG
TMP
TMP TMP
TMP TMP TMP

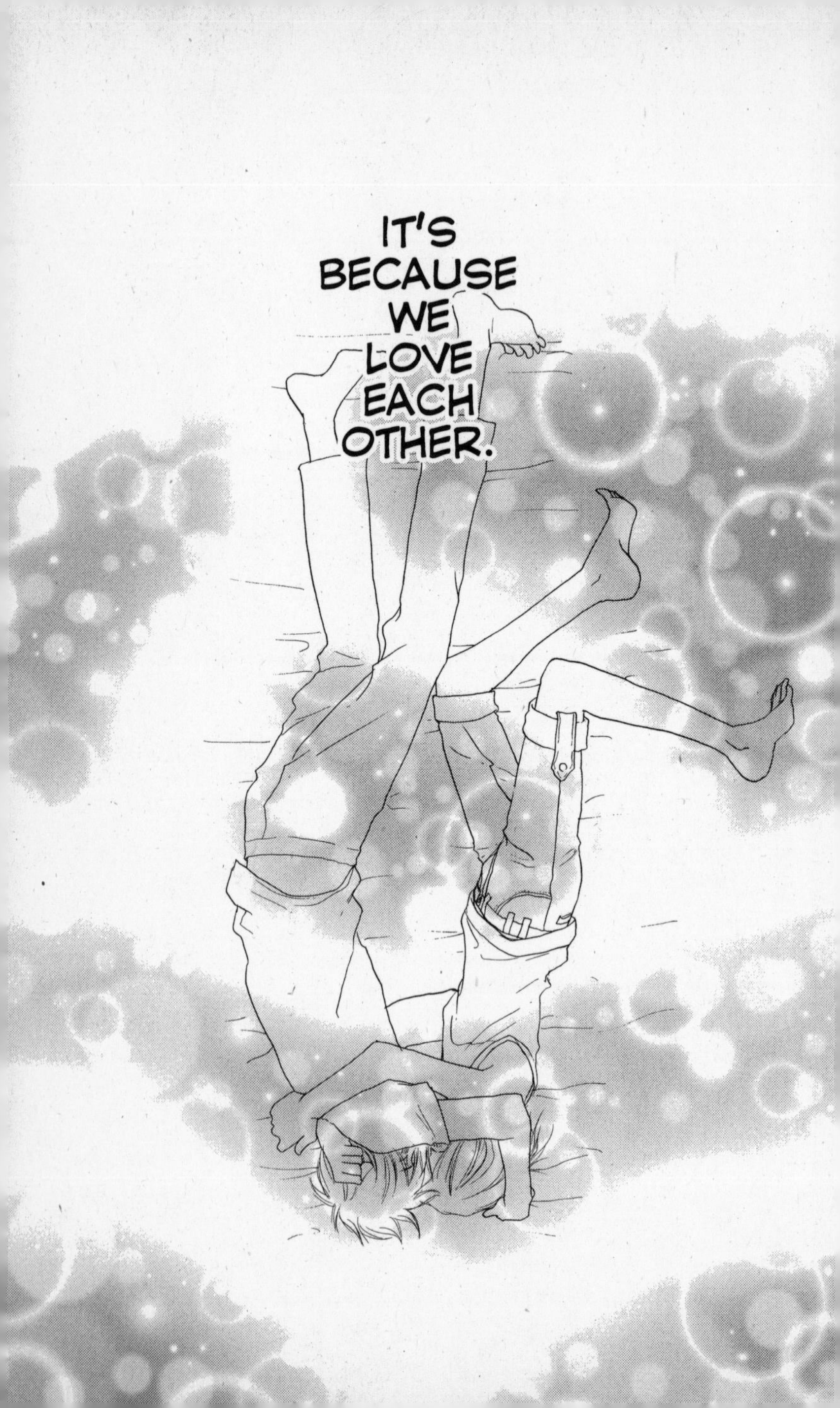
IT'S BECAUSE WE LOVE EACH OTHER.

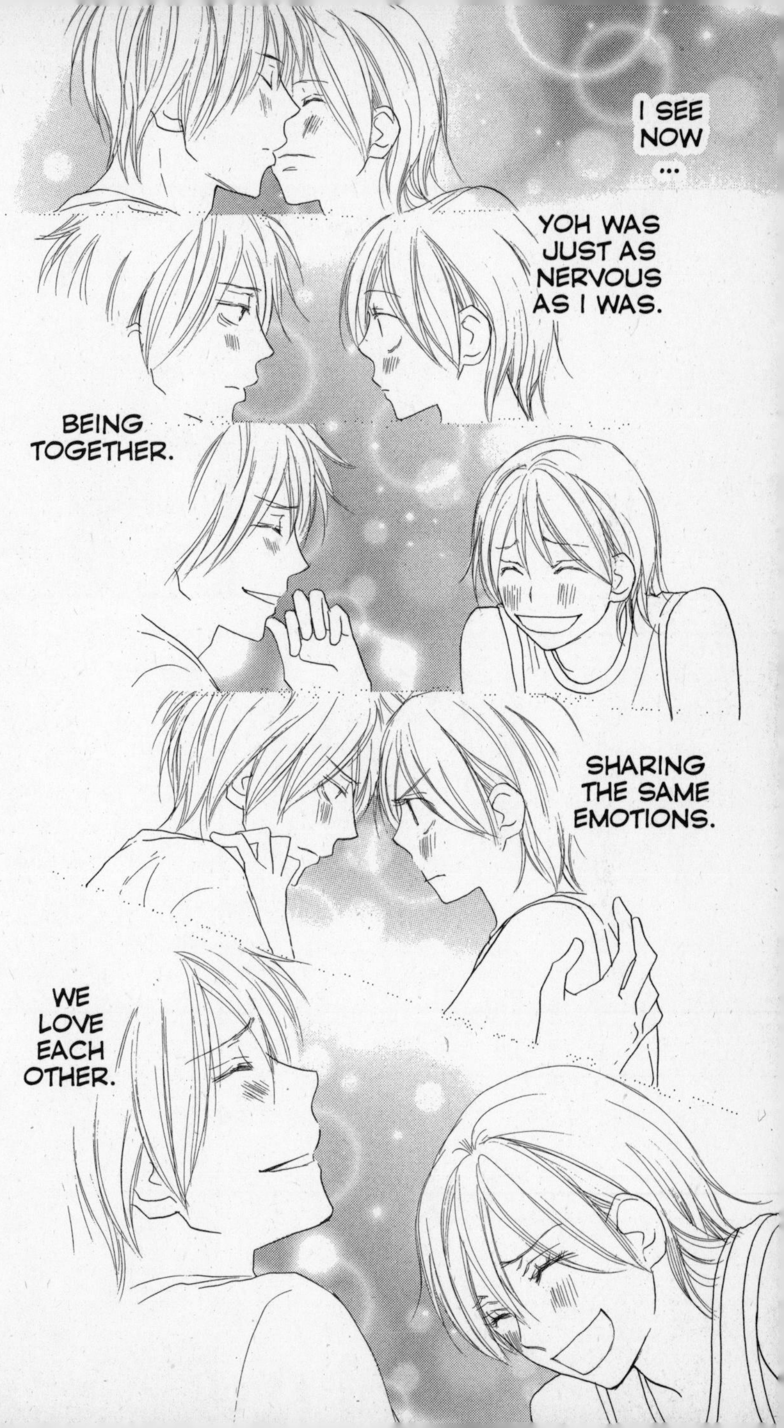
I SEE NOW ...
YOH WAS JUST AS NERVOUS AS I WAS.
BEING TOGETHER.
SHARING THE SAME EMOTIONS.
WE LOVE EACH OTHER.

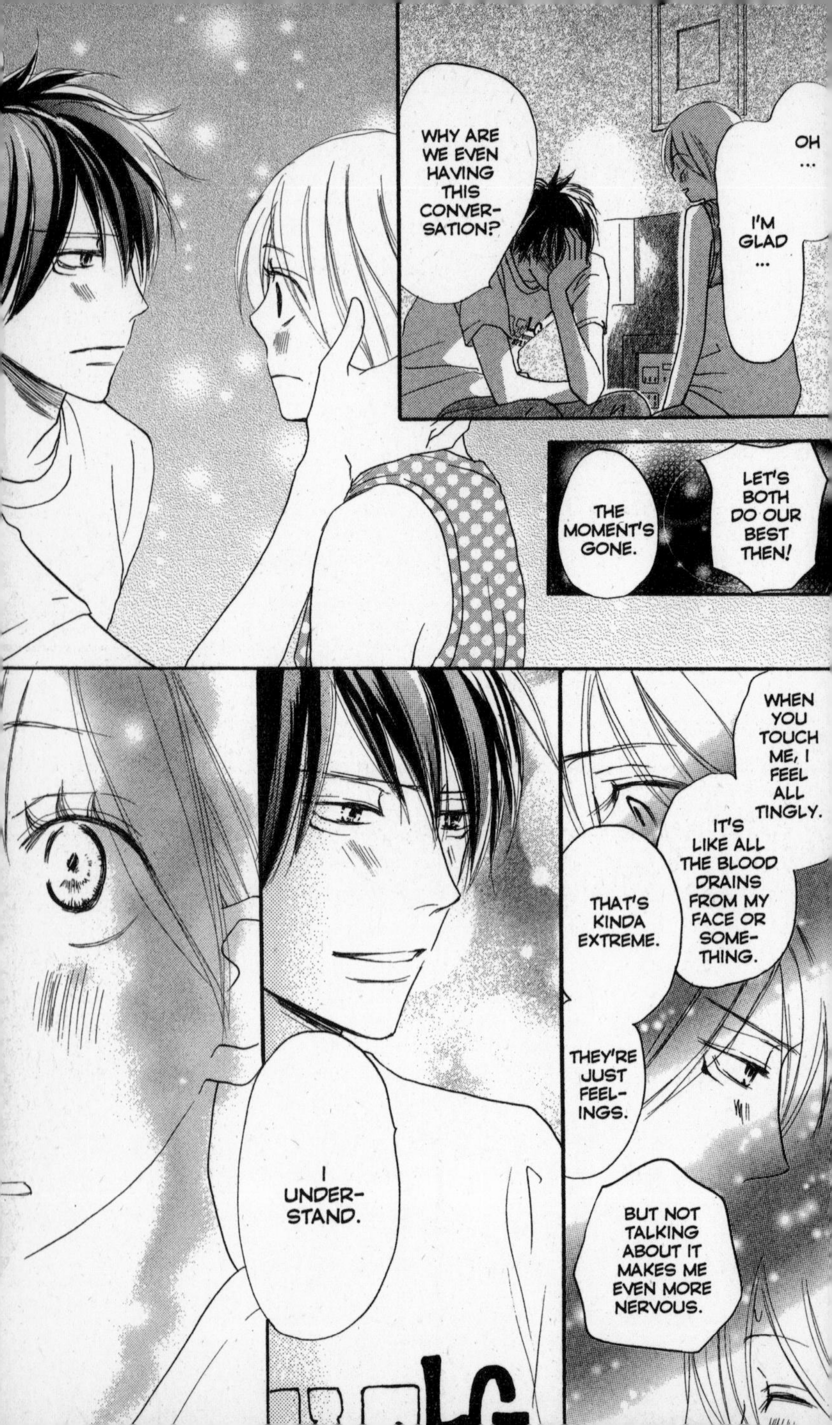
OH ... I'M GLAD ...
WHY ARE WE EVEN HAVING THIS CONVER-SATION?
LET'S BOTH DO OUR BEST THEN!
THE MOMENT'S GONE.
WHEN YOU TOUCH ME, I FEEL ALL TINGLY.
IT'S LIKE ALL THE BLOOD DRAINS FROM MY FACE OR SOME-THING.
THAT'S KINDA EXTREME.
THEY'RE JUST FEEL-INGS.
BUT NOT TALKING ABOUT IT MAKES ME EVEN MORE NERVOUS.
I UNDER-STAND.

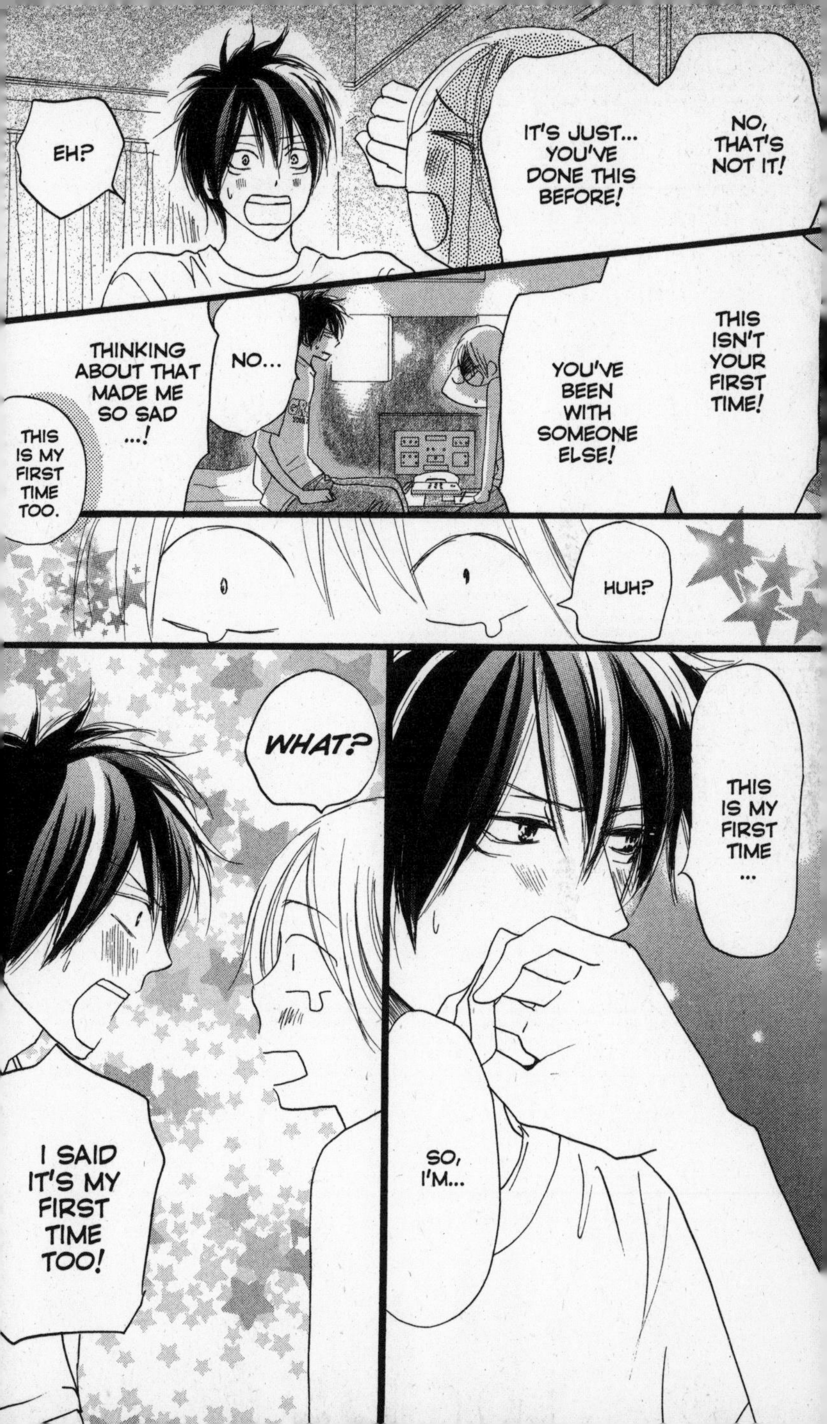
NO, THAT'S NOT IT!
IT'S JUST... YOU'VE DONE THIS BEFORE!
EH?
THIS ISN'T YOUR FIRST TIME!
YOU'VE BEEN WITH SOMEONE ELSE!
NO...
THINKING ABOUT THAT MADE ME SO SAD ...!
THIS IS MY FIRST TIME TOO.
HUH?
THIS IS MY FIRST TIME ...
SO, I'M...
WHAT?
I SAID IT'S MY FIRST TIME TOO!

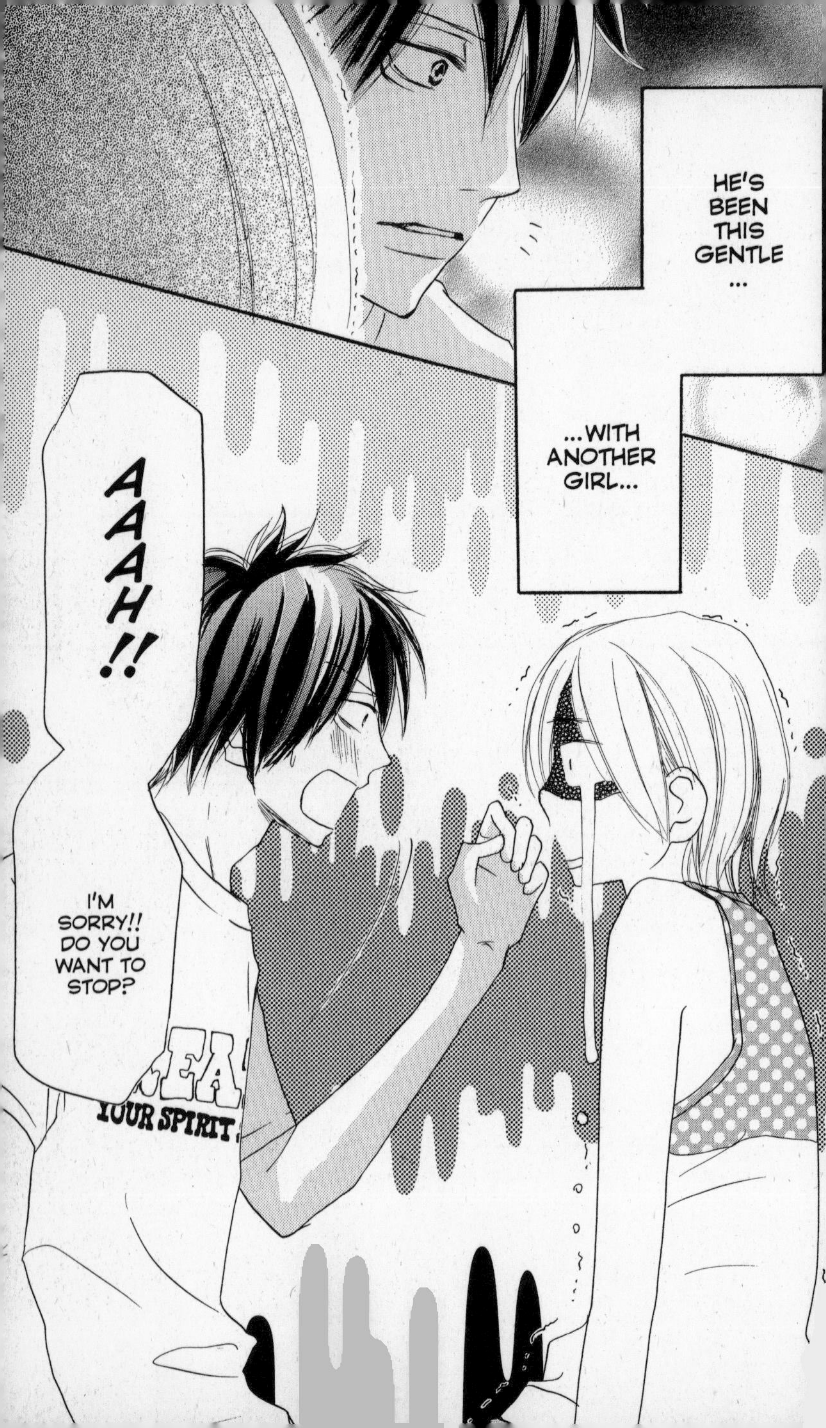
HE'S BEEN THIS GENTLE ...
...WITH ANOTHER GIRL...
AAAAH!!
I'M SORRY!! DO YOU WANT TO STOP?
YOUR SPIRIT

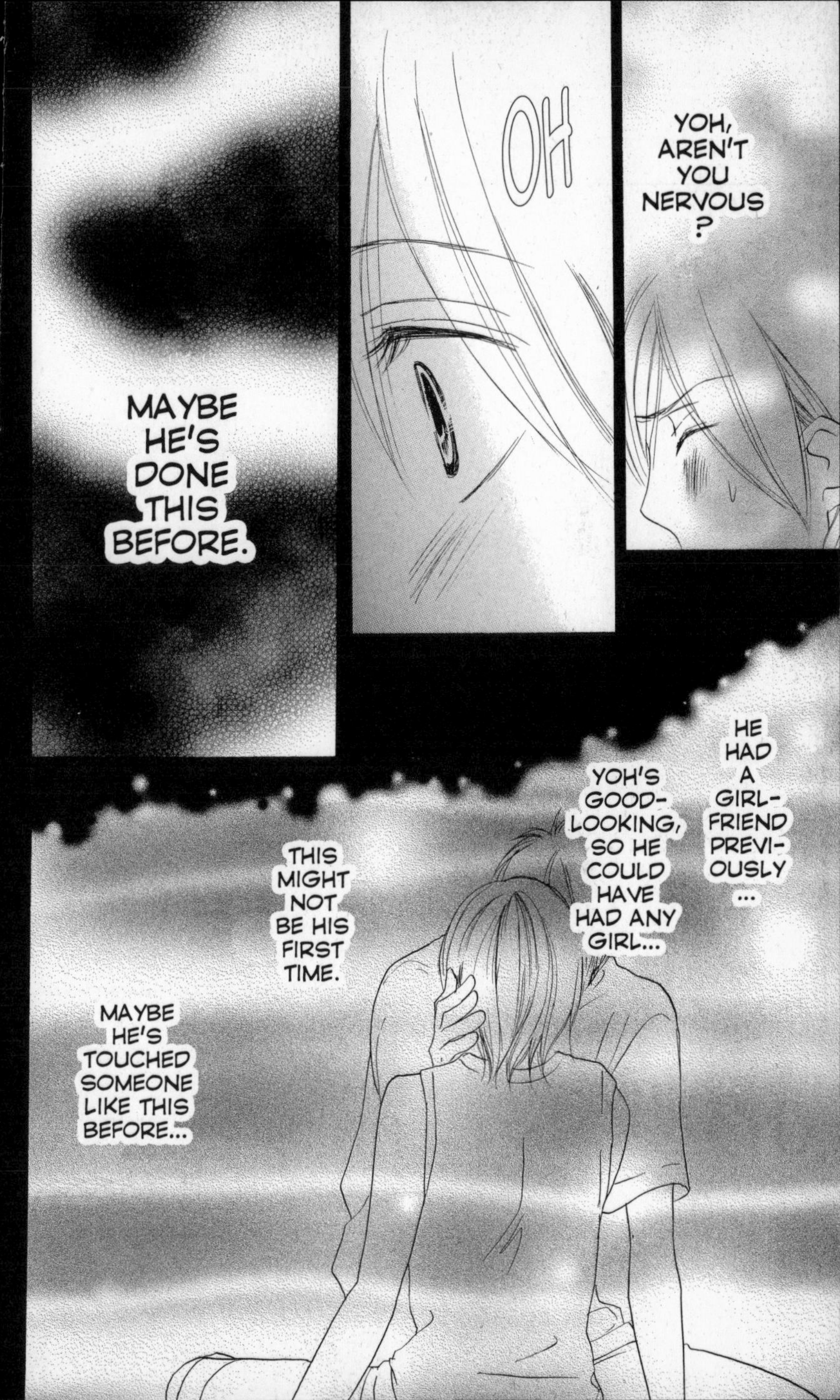
YOH, AREN'T YOU NERVOUS?
OH
MAYBE HE'S DONE THIS BEFORE.
HE HAD A GIRL-FRIEND PREVI-OUSLY...
YOH'S GOOD-LOOKING, SO HE COULD HAVE HAD ANY GIRL...
THIS MIGHT NOT BE HIS FIRST TIME.
MAYBE HE'S TOUCHED SOMEONE LIKE THIS BEFORE...

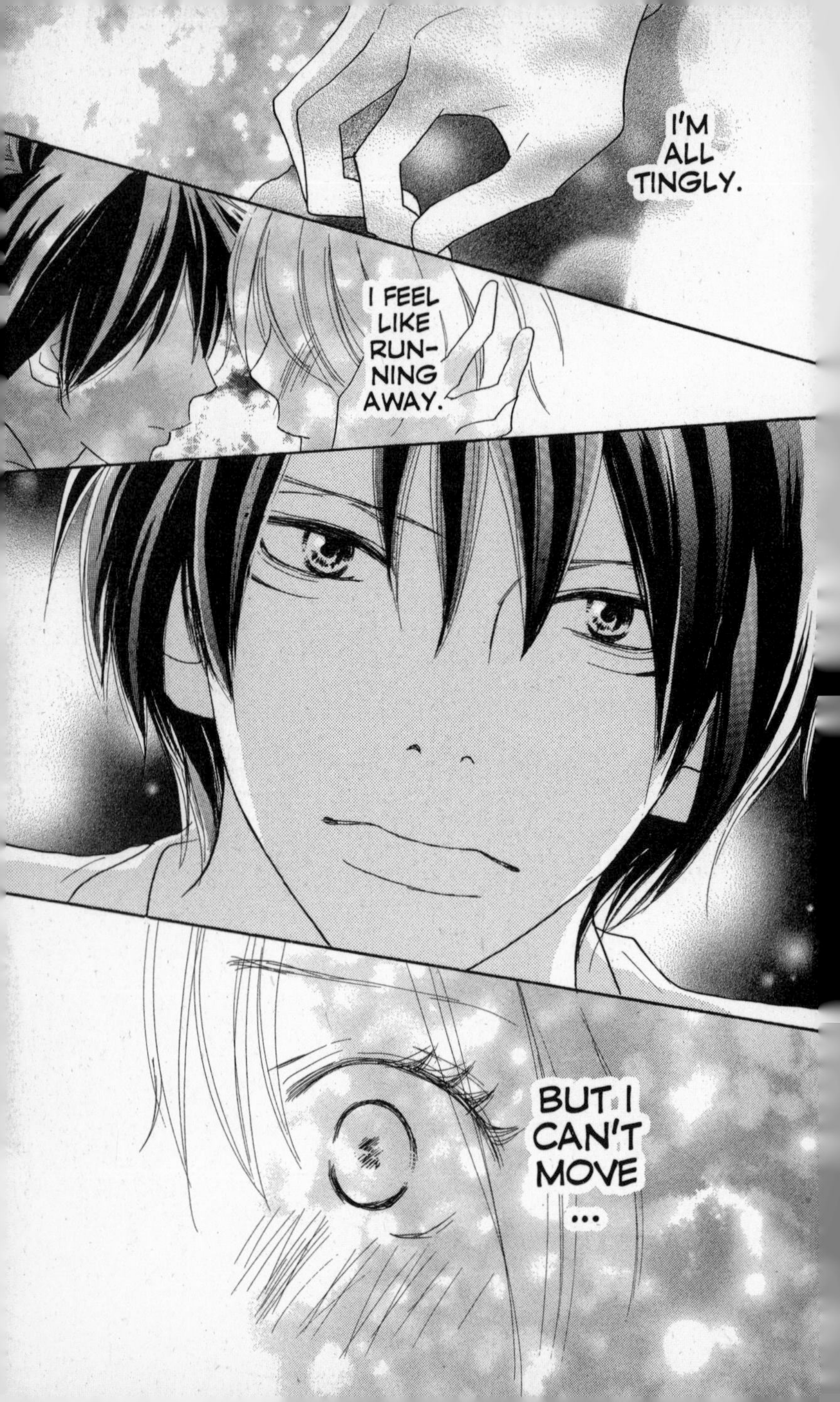
I'M ALL TINGLY.
I FEEL LIKE RUN-NING AWAY.
BUT I CAN'T MOVE ...

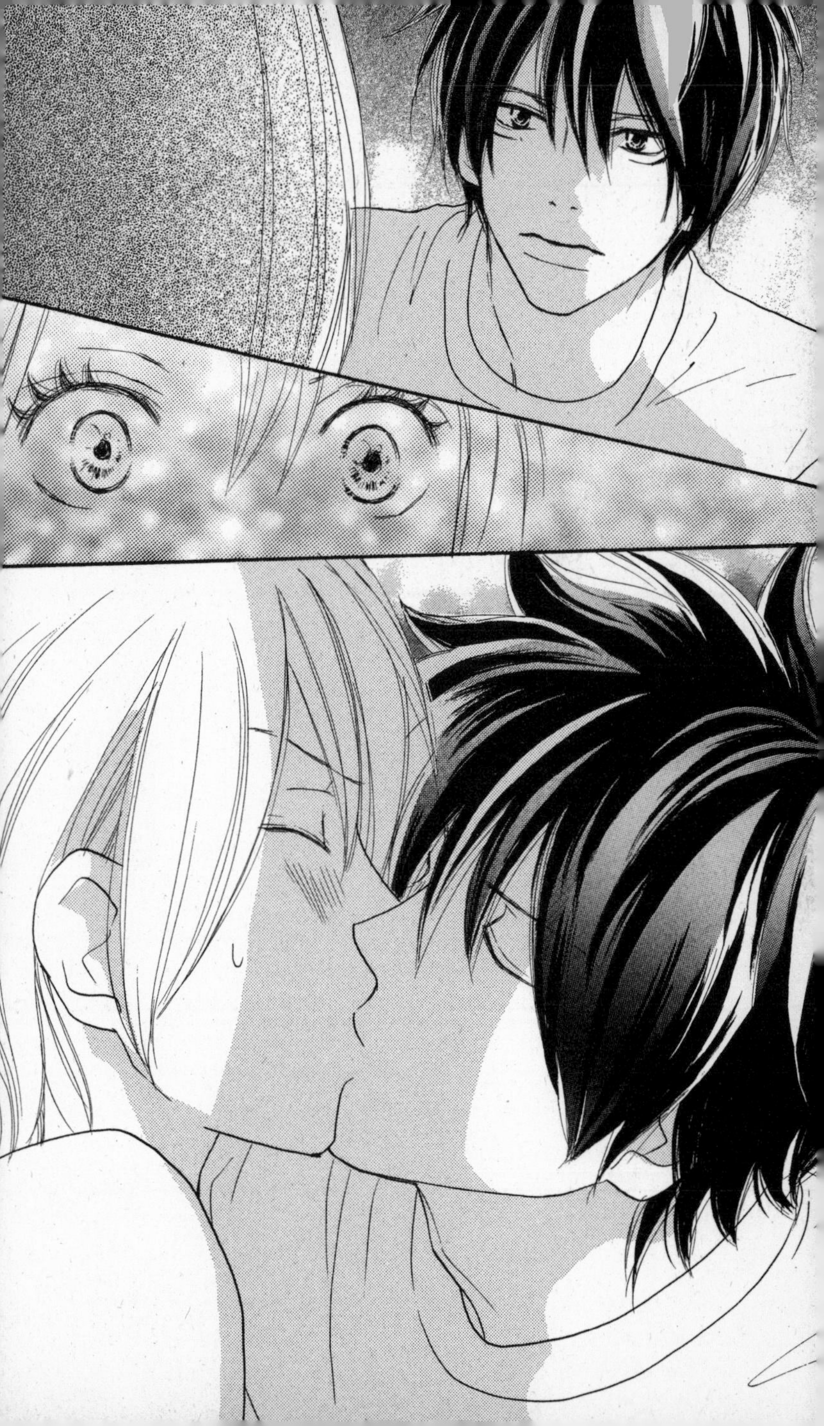

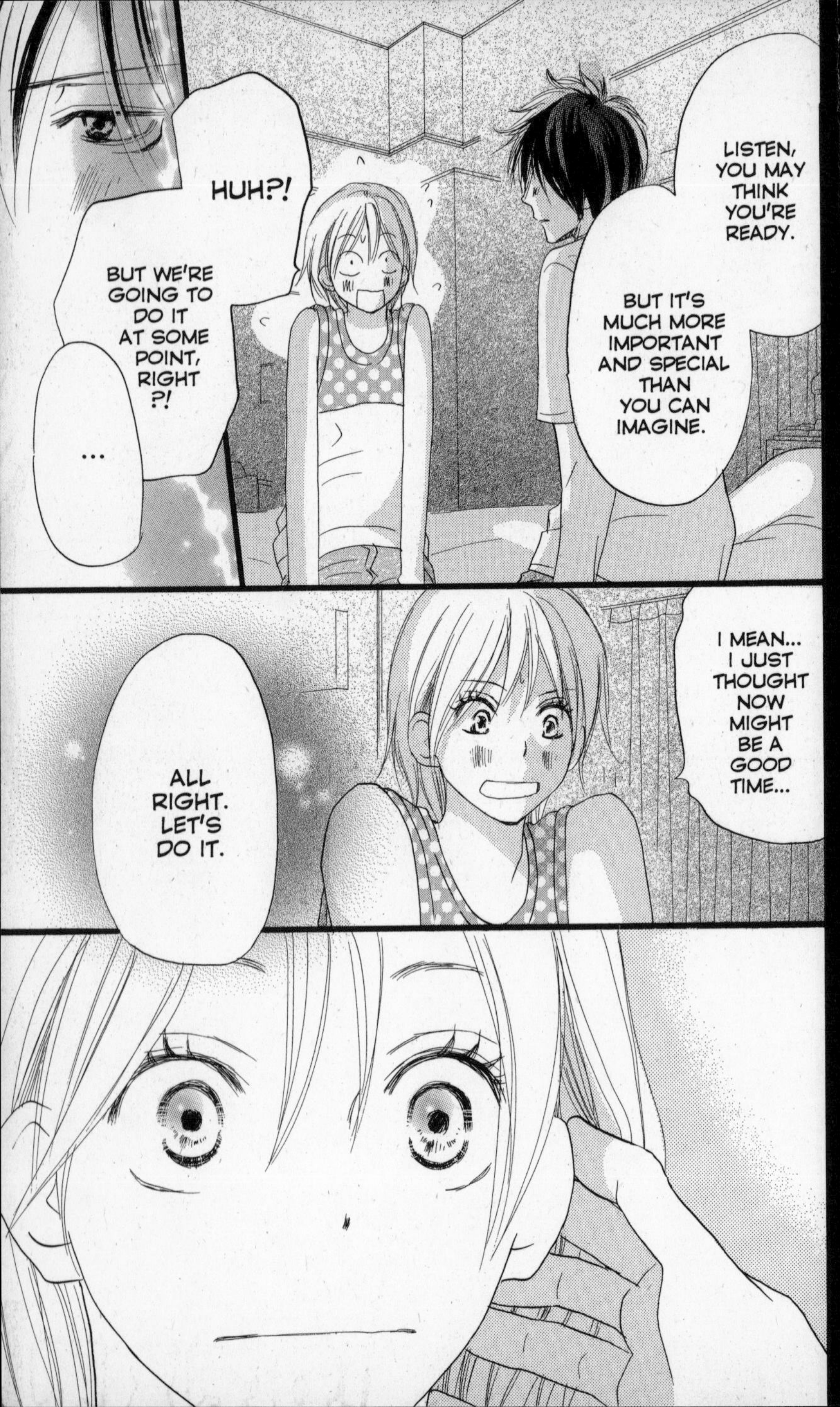
LISTEN, YOU MAY THINK YOU'RE READY.
BUT IT'S MUCH MORE IMPORTANT AND SPECIAL THAN YOU CAN IMAGINE.
HUH?!
BUT WE'RE GOING TO DO IT AT SOME POINT, RIGHT ?!
...
I MEAN... I JUST THOUGHT NOW MIGHT BE A GOOD TIME...
ALL RIGHT. LET'S DO IT.

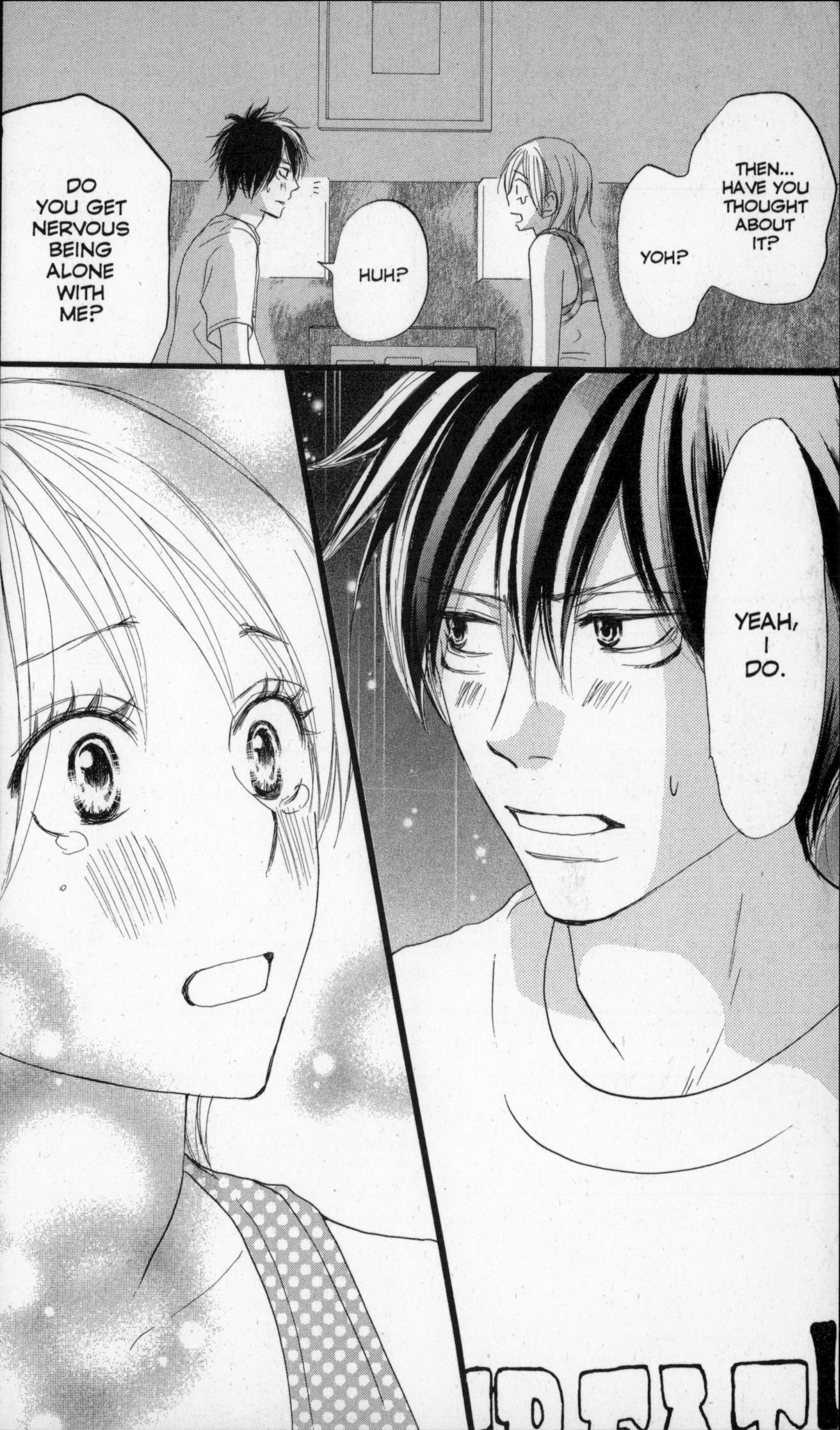
THEN... HAVE YOU THOUGHT ABOUT IT?
YOH?
HUH?
DO YOU GET NERVOUS BEING ALONE WITH ME?
YEAH, I DO.

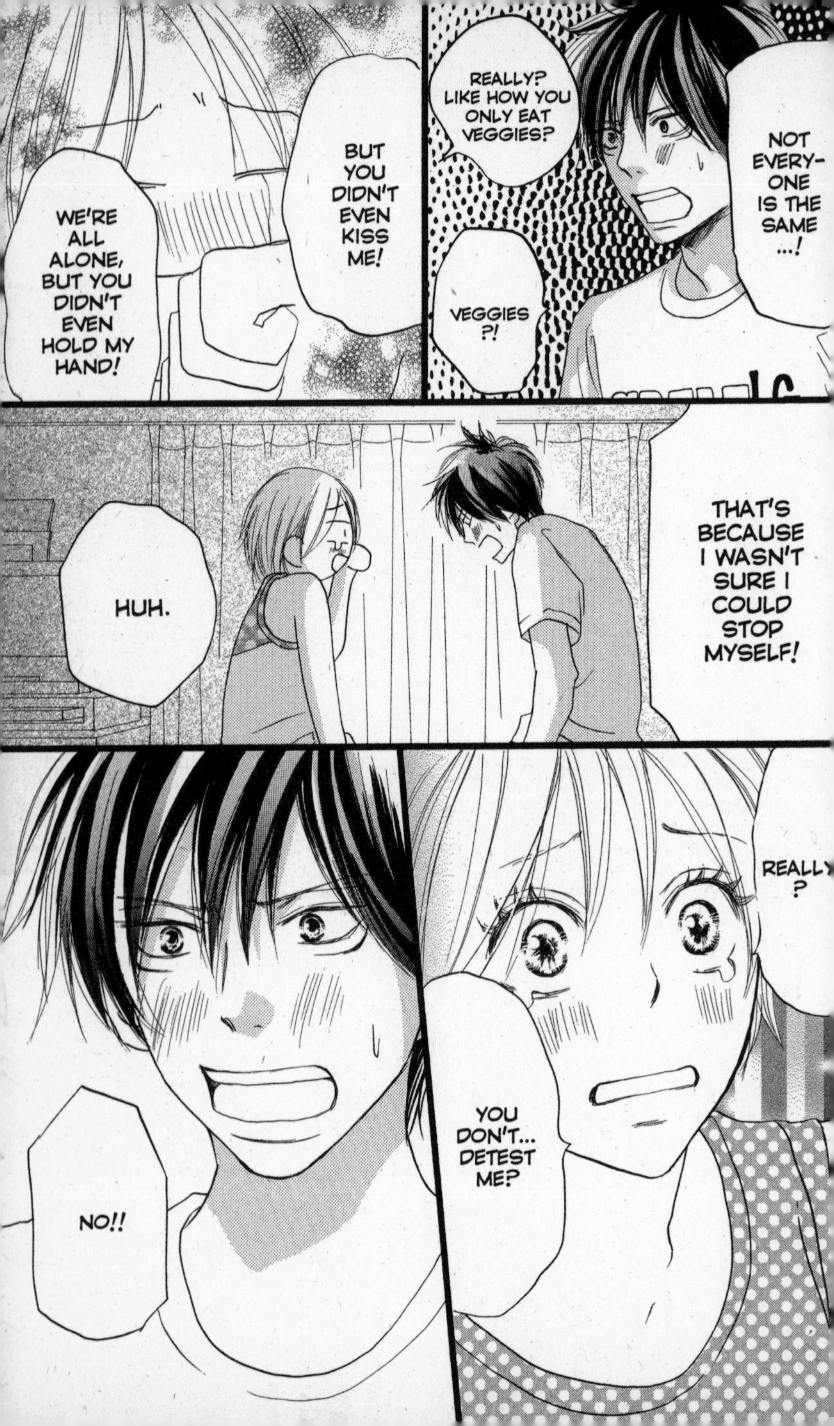
NOT EVERY-ONE IS THE SAME ...!
REALLY? LIKE HOW YOU ONLY EAT VEGGIES?
VEGGIES?!
BUT YOU DIDN'T EVEN KISS ME!
WE'RE ALL ALONE, BUT YOU DIDN'T EVEN HOLD MY HAND!
THAT'S BECAUSE I WASN'T SURE I COULD STOP MYSELF!
HUH.
REALLY?
YOU DON'T... DETEST ME?
NO!!

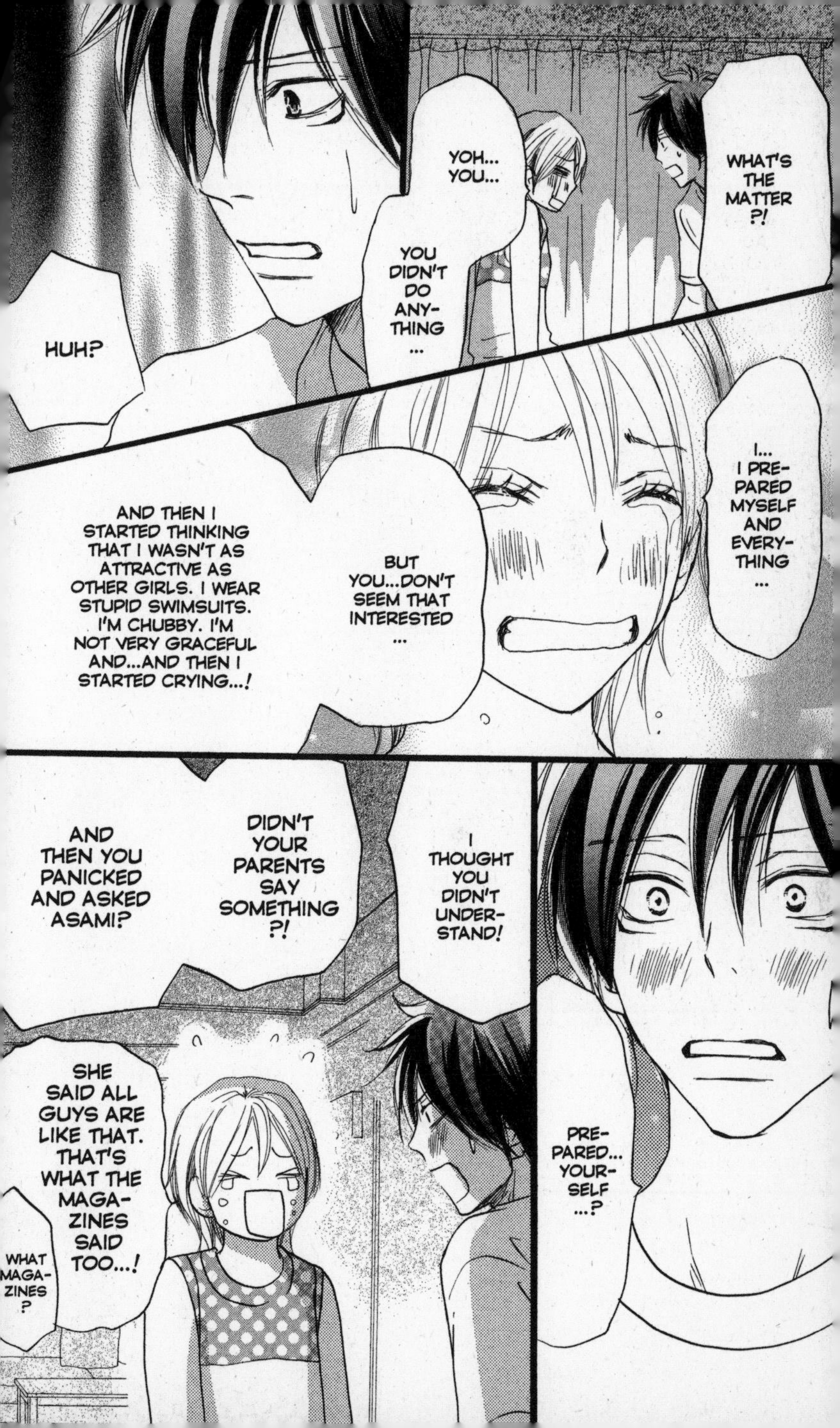
WHAT'S THE MATTER ?!
YOH... YOU...
YOU DIDN'T DO ANY-THING ...
HUH?
I... I PRE-PARED MYSELF AND EVERY-THING ...
BUT YOU...DON'T SEEM THAT INTERESTED ...
AND THEN I STARTED THINKING THAT I WASN'T AS ATTRACTIVE AS OTHER GIRLS. I WEAR STUPID SWIMSUITS. I'M CHUBBY. I'M NOT VERY GRACEFUL AND...AND THEN I STARTED CRYING...!
PRE-PARED... YOUR-SELF ...?
I THOUGHT YOU DIDN'T UNDER-STAND!
DIDN'T YOUR PARENTS SAY SOMETHING ?!
AND THEN YOU PANICKED AND ASKED ASAMI?
SHE SAID ALL GUYS ARE LIKE THAT. THAT'S WHAT THE MAGA-ZINES SAID TOO...!
WHAT MAGA-ZINES ?

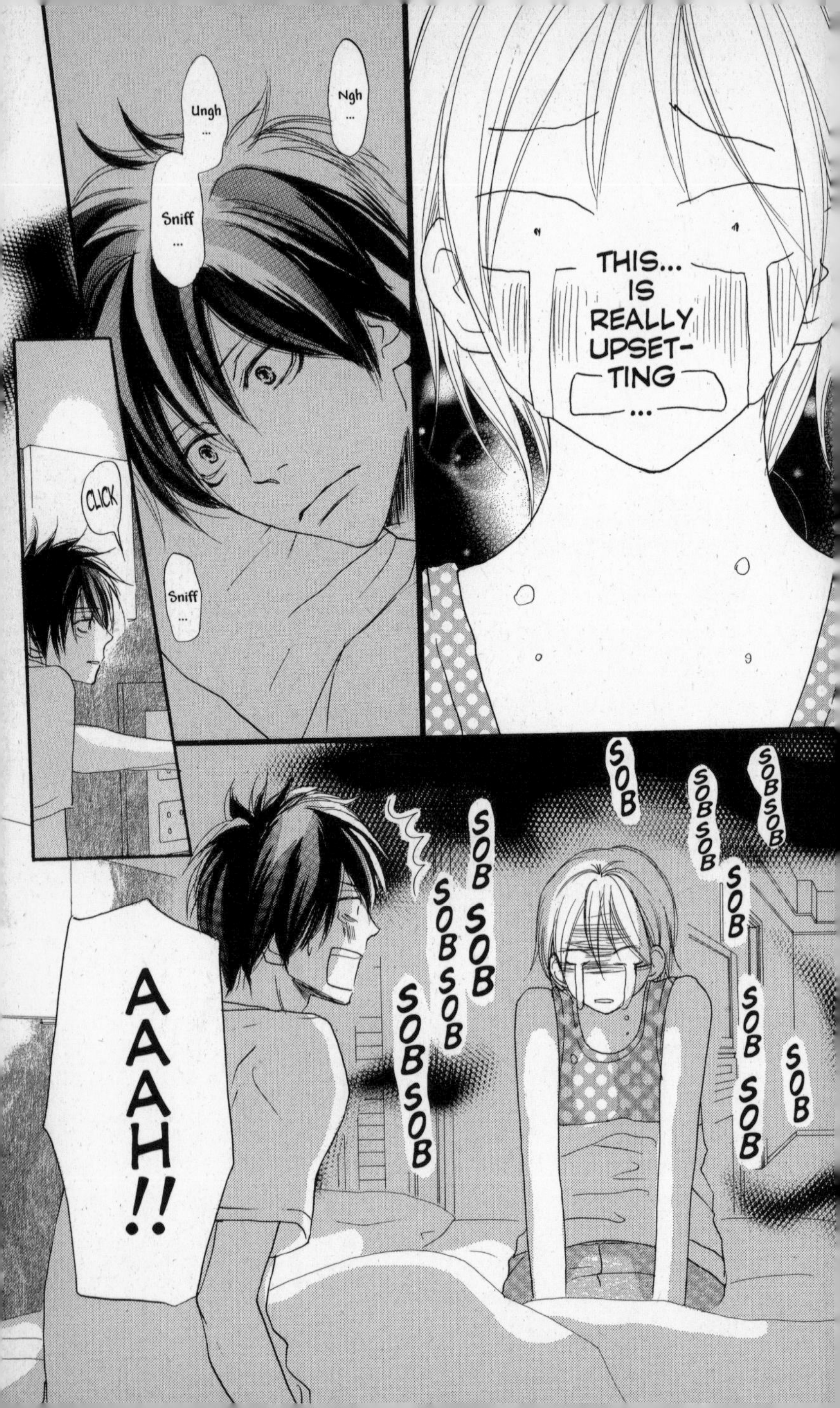
THIS... IS REALLY UPSET-TING...
Ngh...
Ungh...
Sniff...
Sniff...
CLICK
SOB SOB
SOB SOB
SOB
SOB
SOB
SOB SOB
SOB SOB
SOB SOB SOB
SOB SOB
SOB SOB
AAAH!!

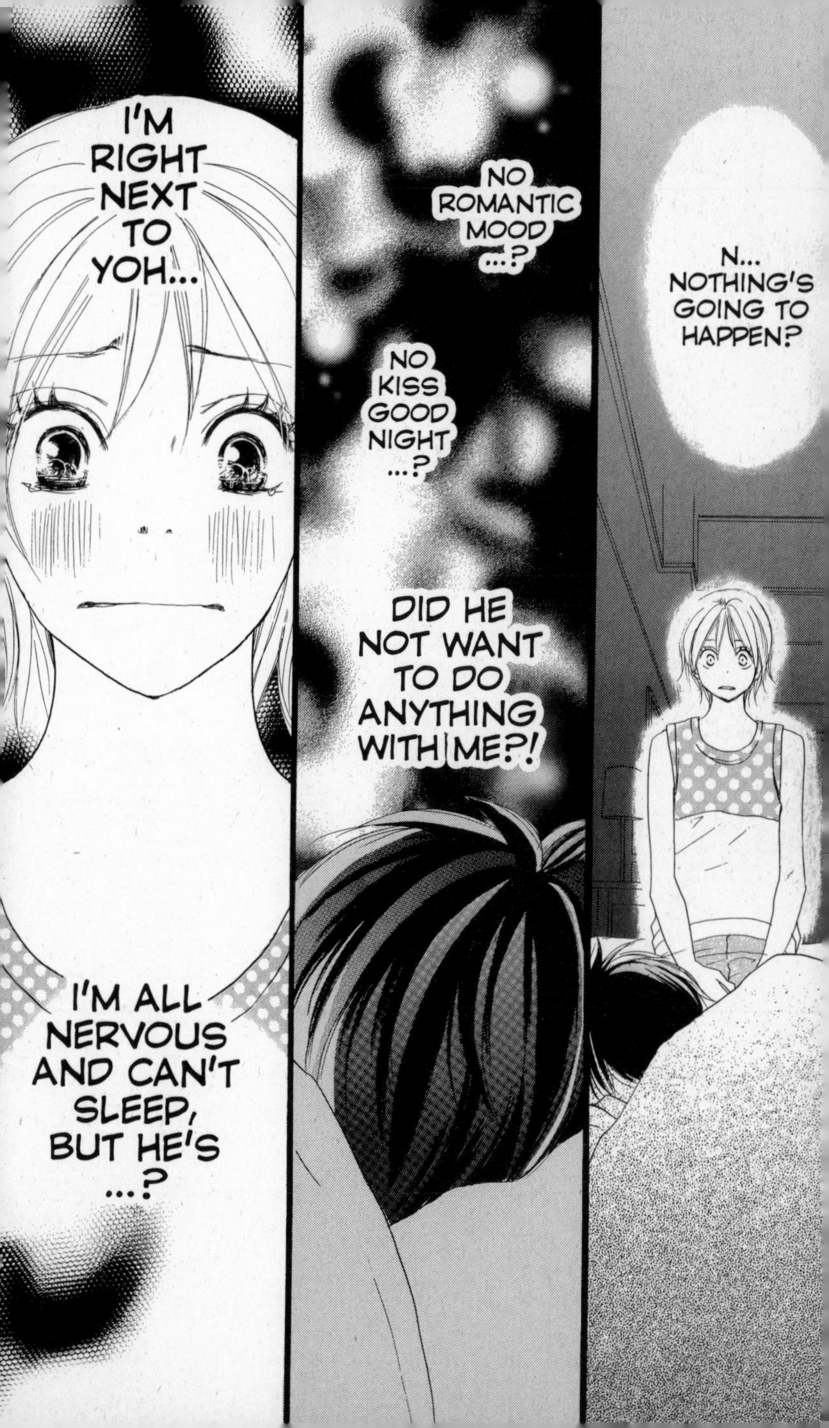
N... NOTHING'S GOING TO HAPPEN?
NO ROMANTIC MOOD ...?
NO KISS GOOD NIGHT ...?
DID HE NOT WANT TO DO ANYTHING WITH ME?!
I'M RIGHT NEXT TO YOH...
I'M ALL NERVOUS AND CAN'T SLEEP, BUT HE'S ...?

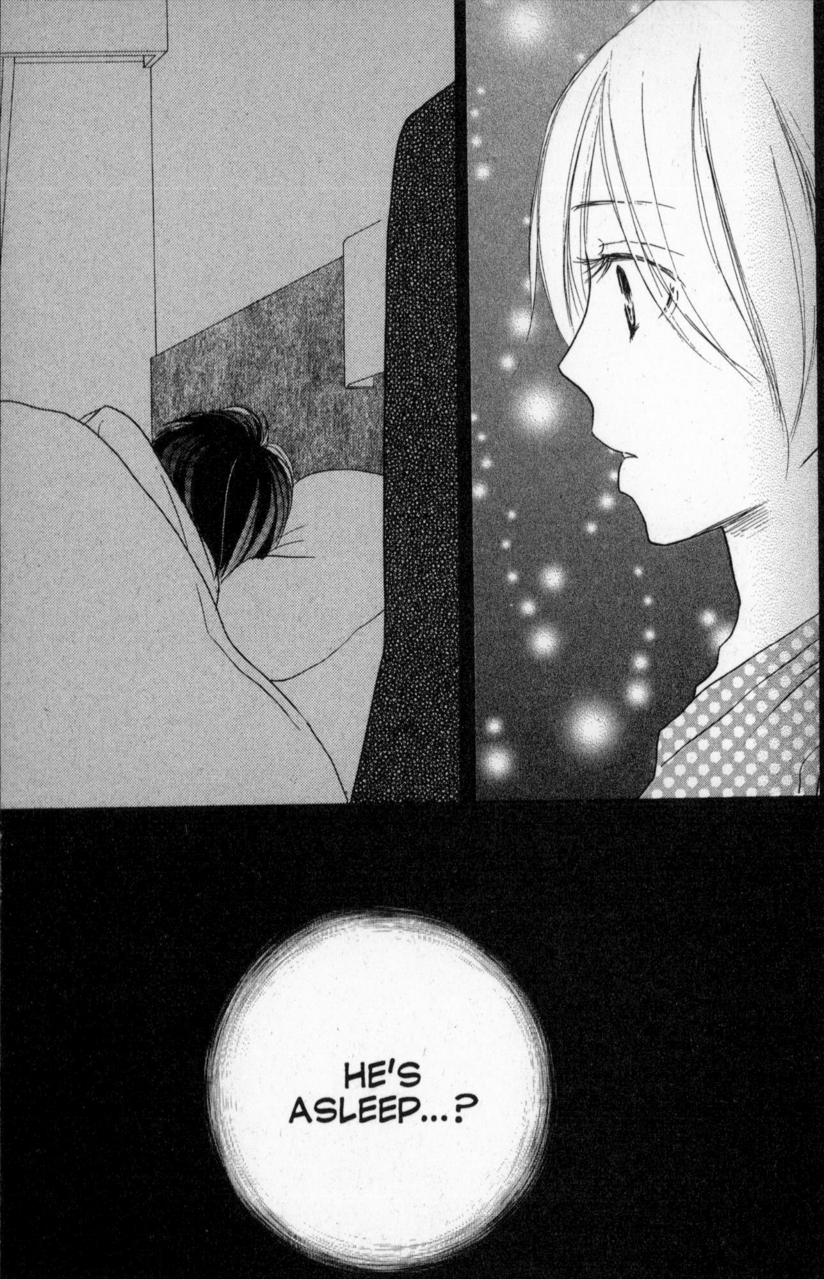
HE'S ASLEEP...?

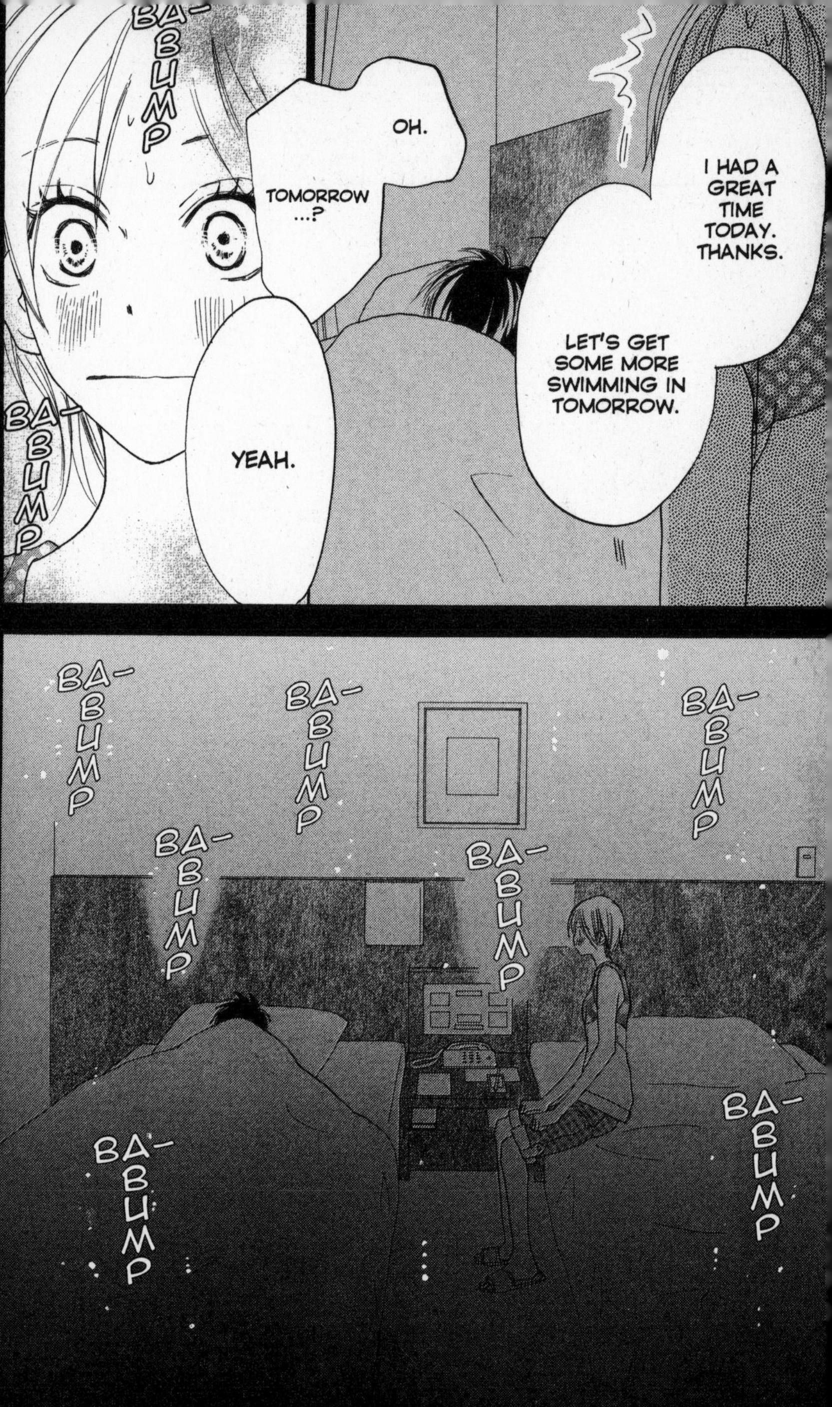
I HAD A GREAT TIME TODAY. THANKS.
LET'S GET SOME MORE SWIMMING IN TOMORROW.
OH.
TOMORROW ...?
BA-BUMP
YEAH.
BA-BUMP
BA-BUMP
BA-BUMP
BA-BUMP
BA-BUMP
BA-BUMP
BA-BUMP
BA-BUMP

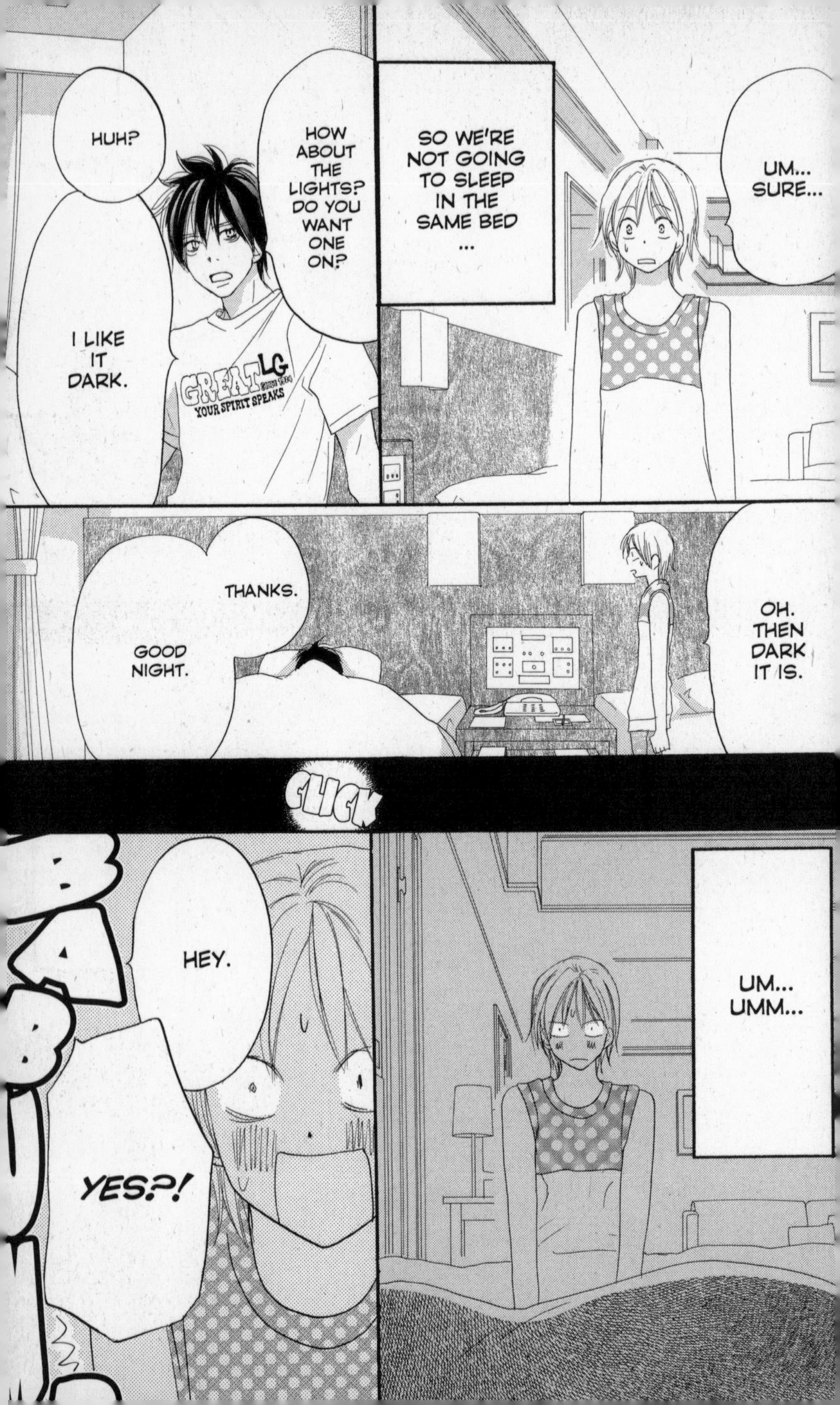
UM... SURE...
SO WE'RE NOT GOING TO SLEEP IN THE SAME BED ...
HOW ABOUT THE LIGHTS? DO YOU WANT ONE ON?
HUH?
I LIKE IT DARK.
OH. THEN DARK IT IS.
THANKS.
GOOD NIGHT.
CLICK
UM... UMM...
HEY.
YES?!

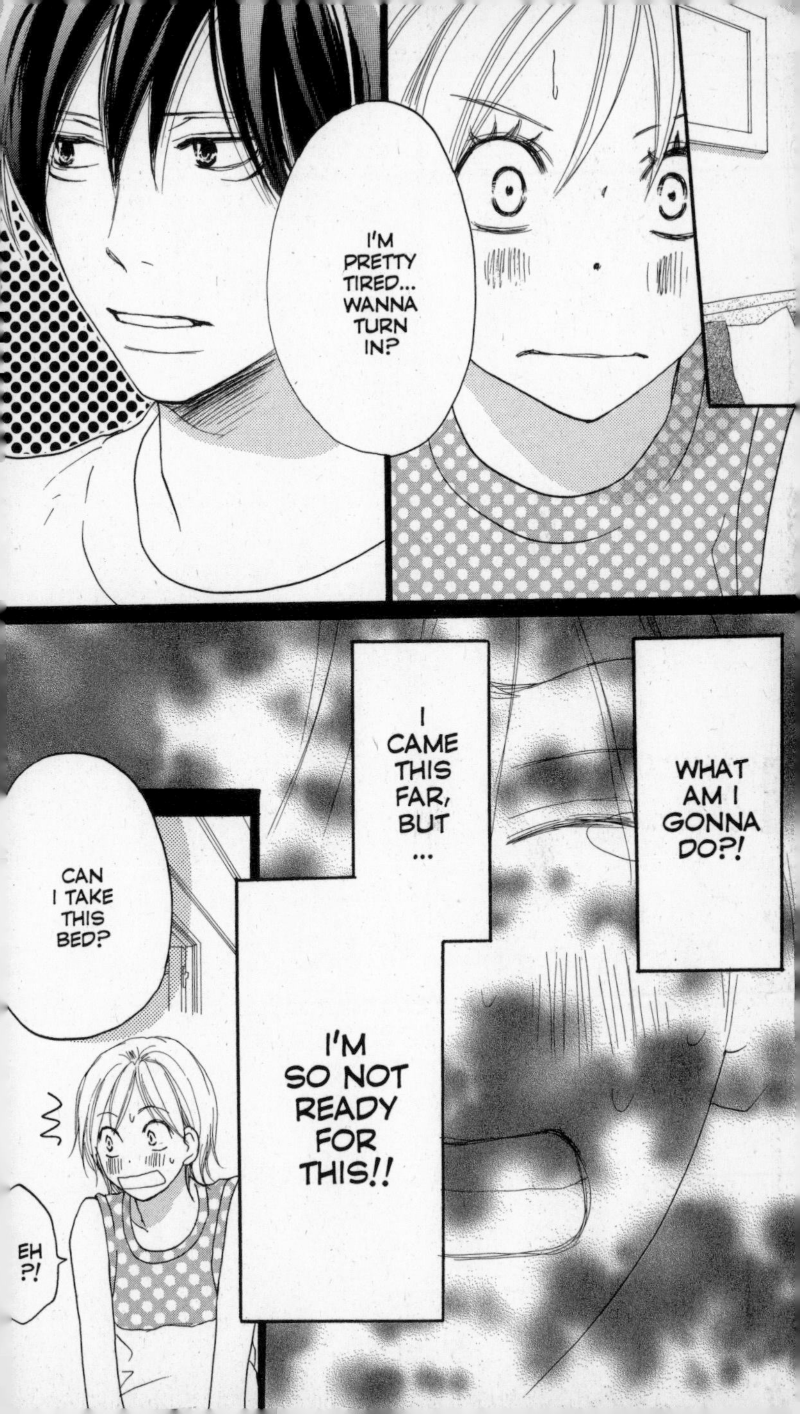
I'M PRETTY TIRED... WANNA TURN IN?
WHAT AM I GONNA DO?!
I CAME THIS FAR, BUT ...
I'M SO NOT READY FOR THIS!!
CAN I TAKE THIS BED?
EH?!

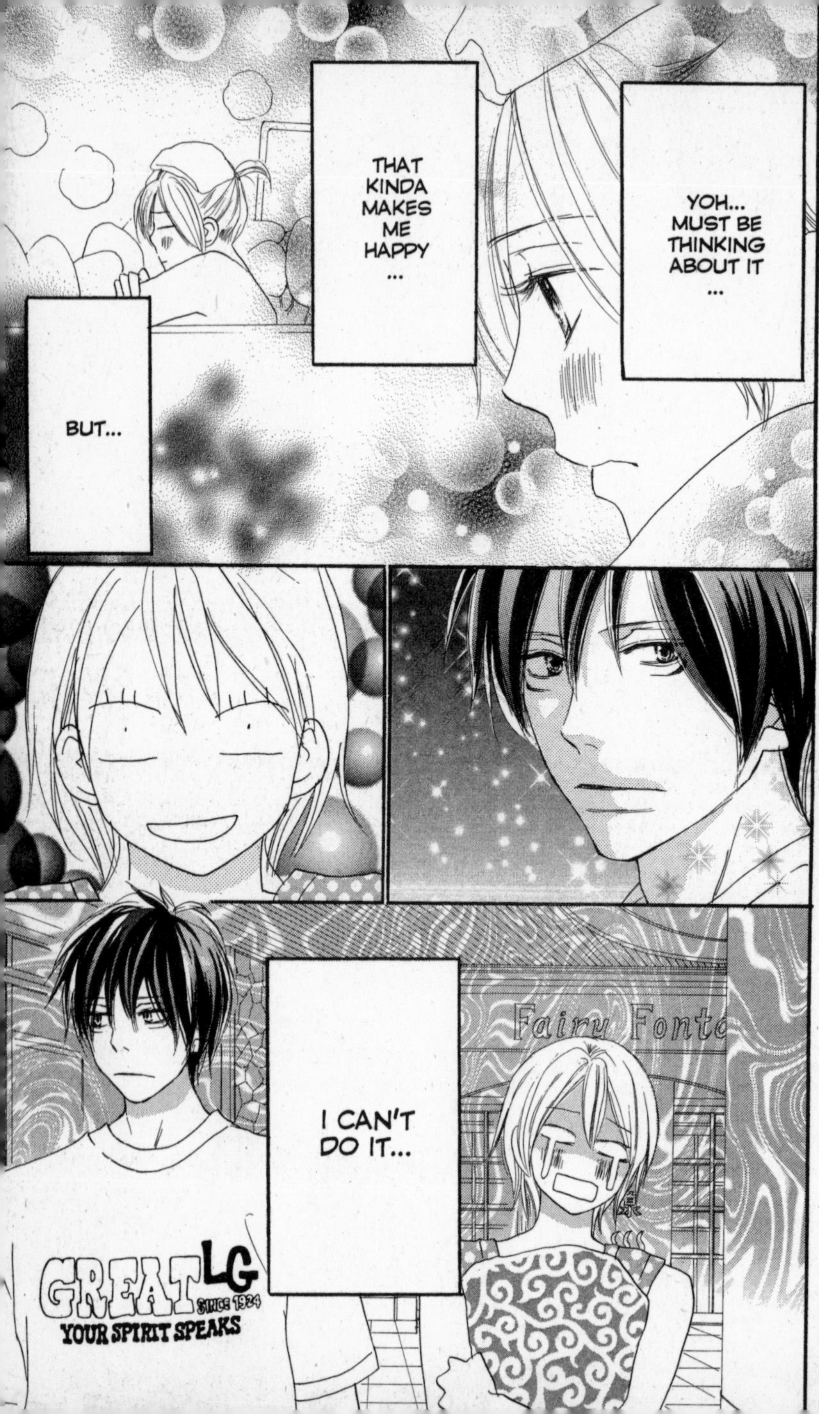
YOH... MUST BE THINKING ABOUT IT ...
THAT KINDA MAKES ME HAPPY ...
BUT...
Fairy Fonte
I CAN'T DO IT...
GREAT LG SINCE 1924
YOUR SPIRIT SPEAKS

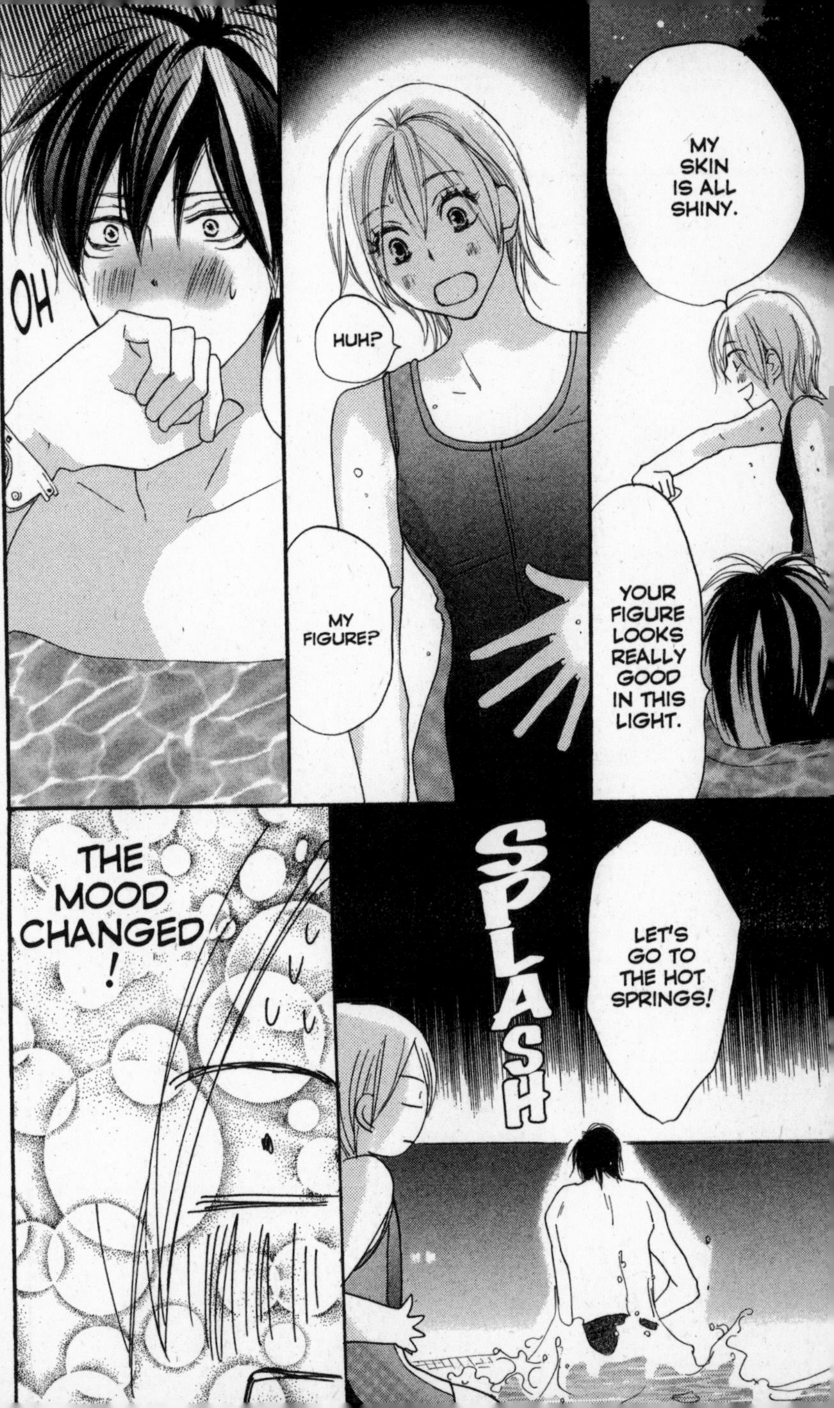
MY SKIN IS ALL SHINY.
YOUR FIGURE LOOKS REALLY GOOD IN THIS LIGHT.
HUH?
MY FIGURE?
OH
LET'S GO TO THE HOT SPRINGS!
SPLASH
THE MOOD CHANGED!

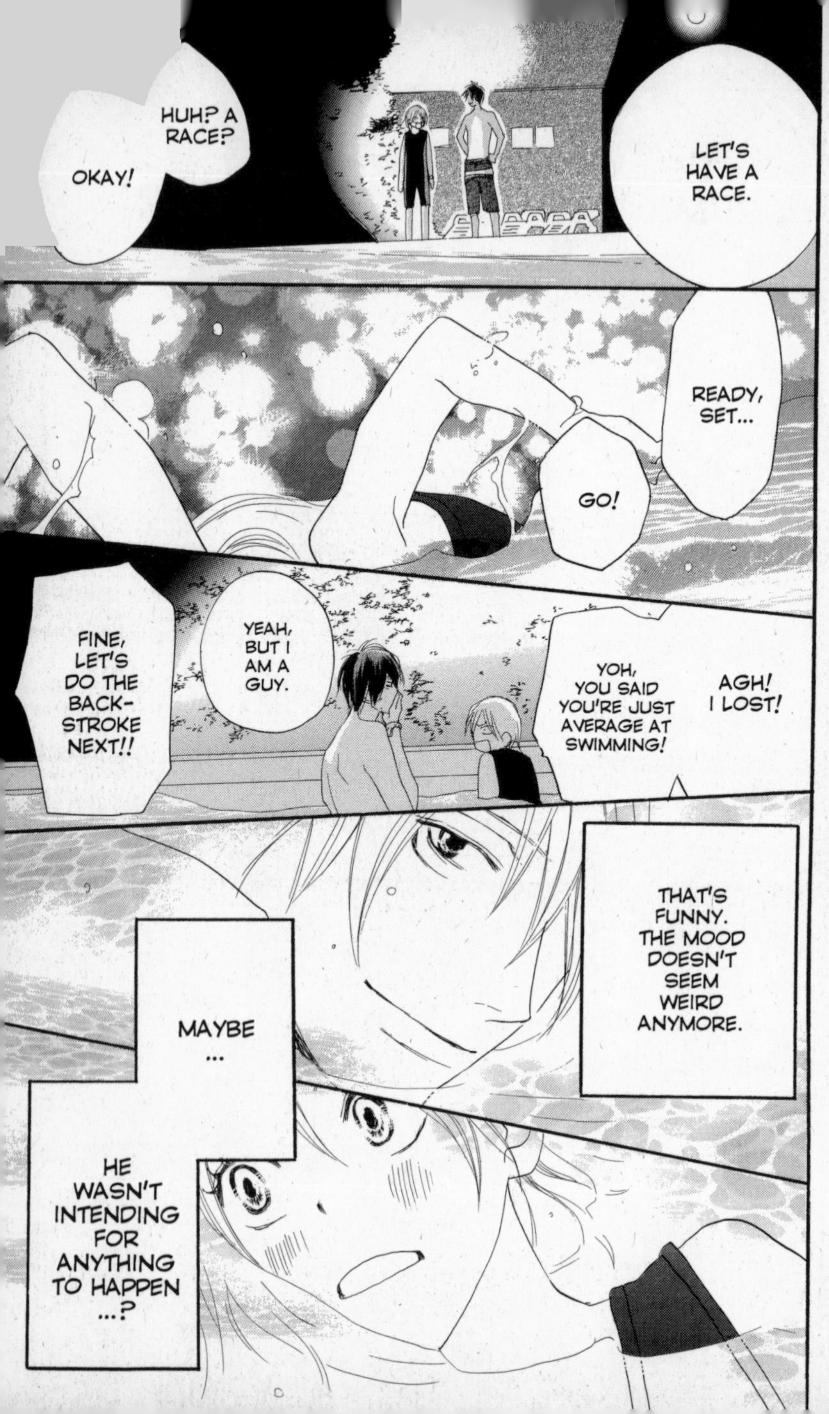
LET'S HAVE A RACE.
HUH? A RACE?
OKAY!
READY, SET...
GO!
AGH! I LOST!
YOH, YOU SAID YOU'RE JUST AVERAGE AT SWIMMING!
YEAH, BUT I AM A GUY.
FINE, LET'S DO THE BACK-STROKE NEXT!!
THAT'S FUNNY. THE MOOD DOESN'T SEEM WEIRD ANYMORE.
MAYBE ...
HE WASN'T INTENDING FOR ANYTHING TO HAPPEN ...?

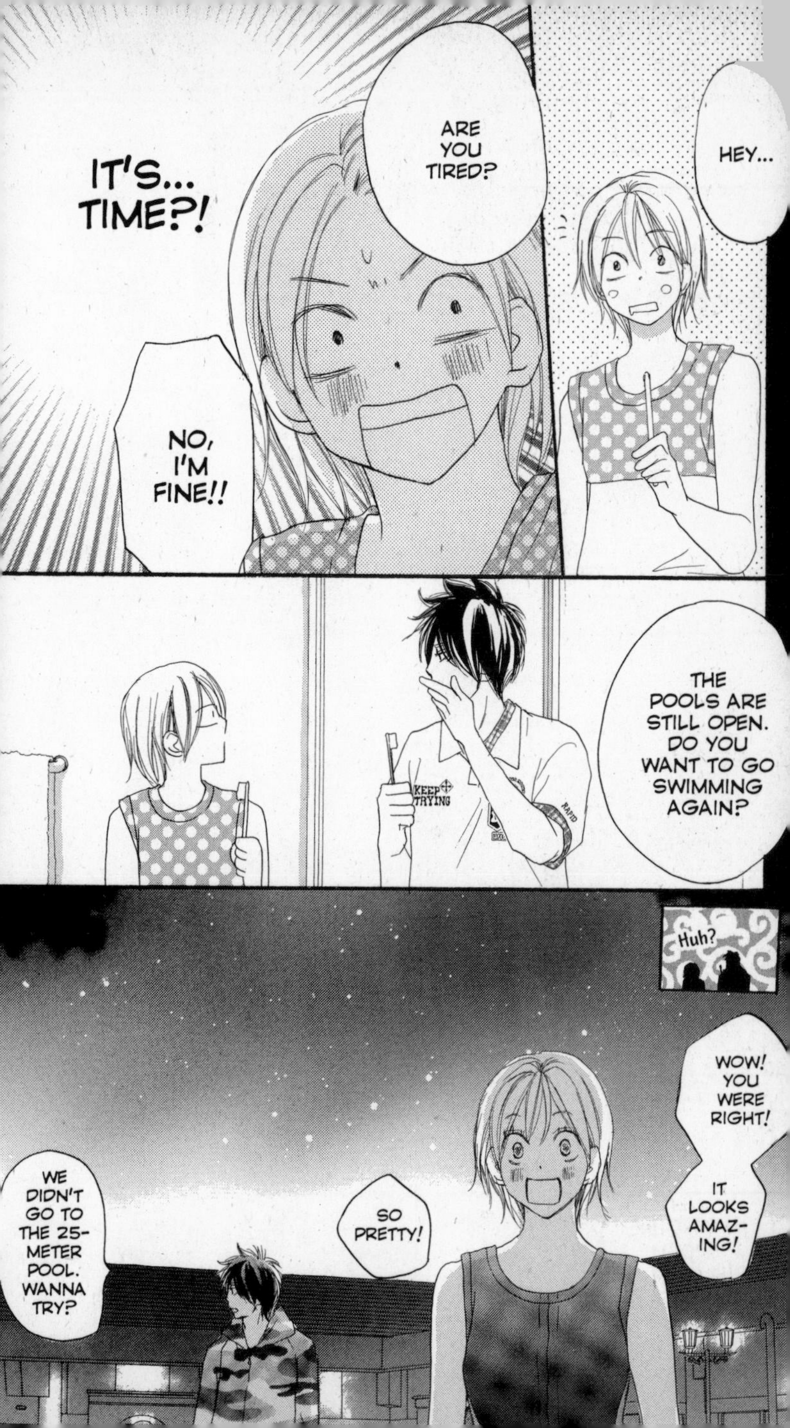
HEY...
ARE YOU TIRED?
IT'S... TIME?!
NO, I'M FINE!!
THE POOLS ARE STILL OPEN. DO YOU WANT TO GO SWIMMING AGAIN?
KEEP TRYING
Huh?
WOW! YOU WERE RIGHT!
IT LOOKS AMAZ-ING!
SO PRETTY!
WE DIDN'T GO TO THE 25-METER POOL. WANNA TRY?

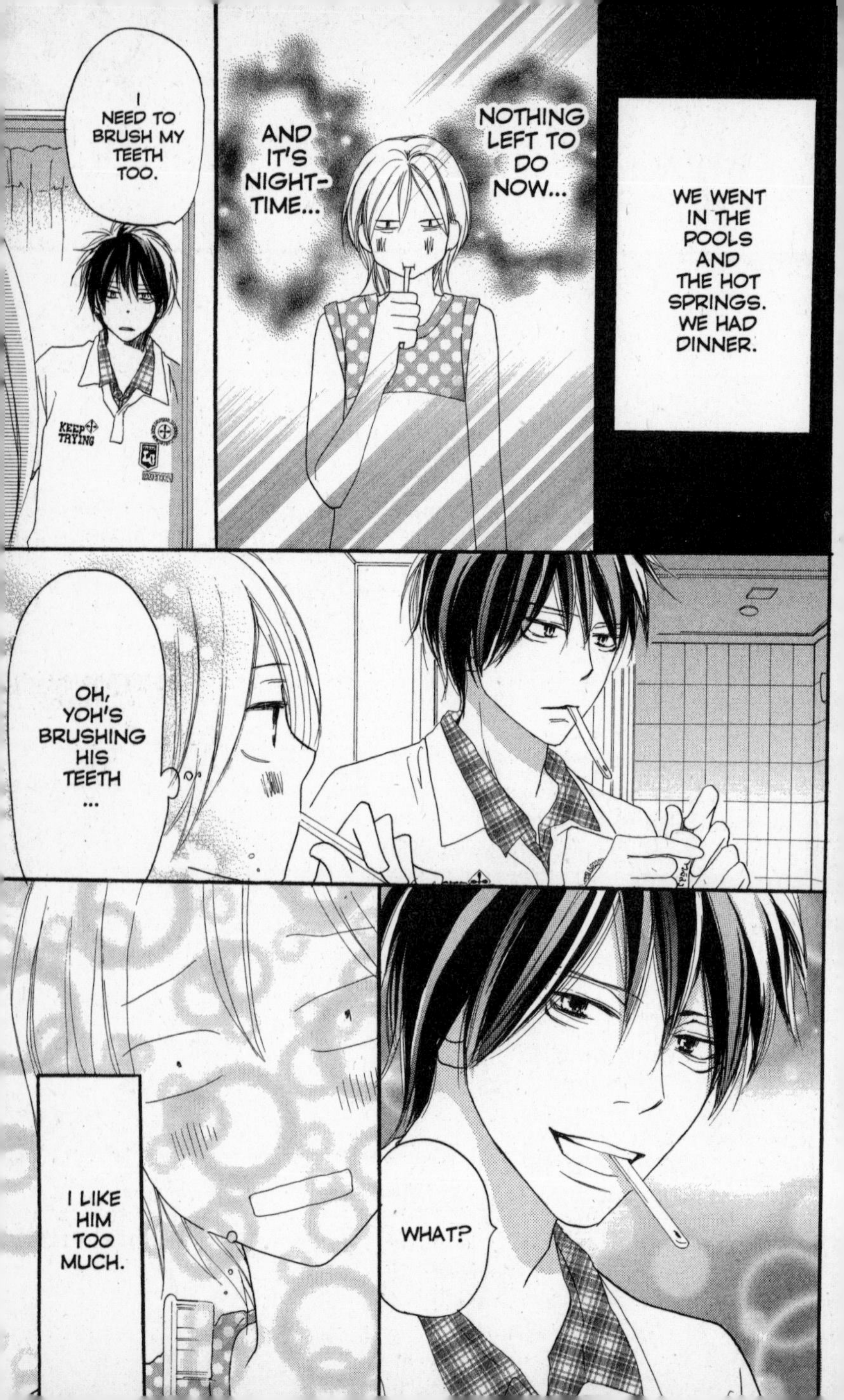
WE WENT IN THE POOLS AND THE HOT SPRINGS. WE HAD DINNER.
NOTHING LEFT TO DO NOW...
AND IT'S NIGHT-TIME...
I NEED TO BRUSH MY TEETH TOO.
KEEP TRYING
OH, YOH'S BRUSHING HIS TEETH ...
WHAT?
I LIKE HIM TOO MUCH.

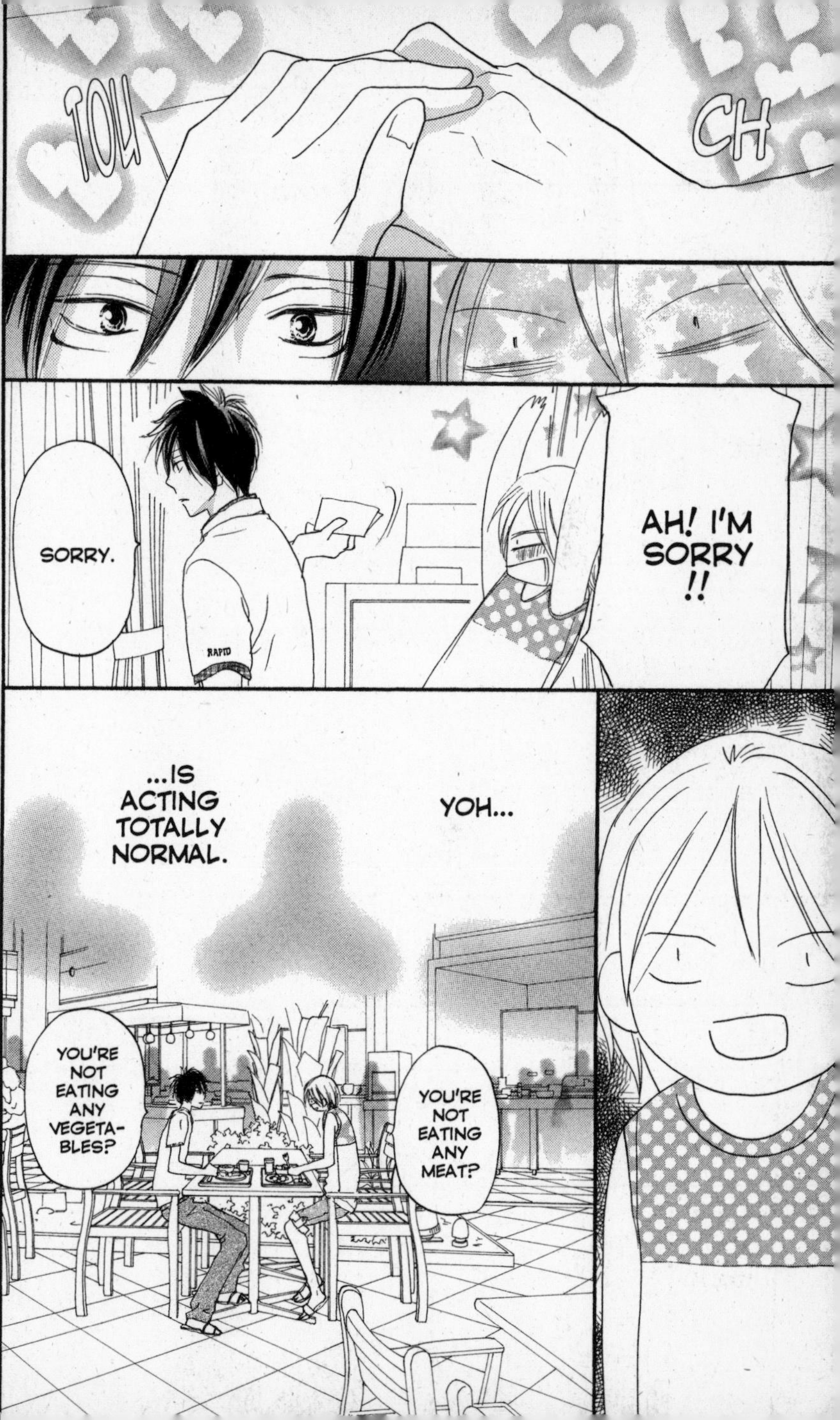
TOU CH
AH! I'M SORRY !!
SORRY.
YOH...
...IS ACTING TOTALLY NORMAL.
YOU'RE NOT EATING ANY MEAT?
YOU'RE NOT EATING ANY VEGETA-BLES?
RAPID

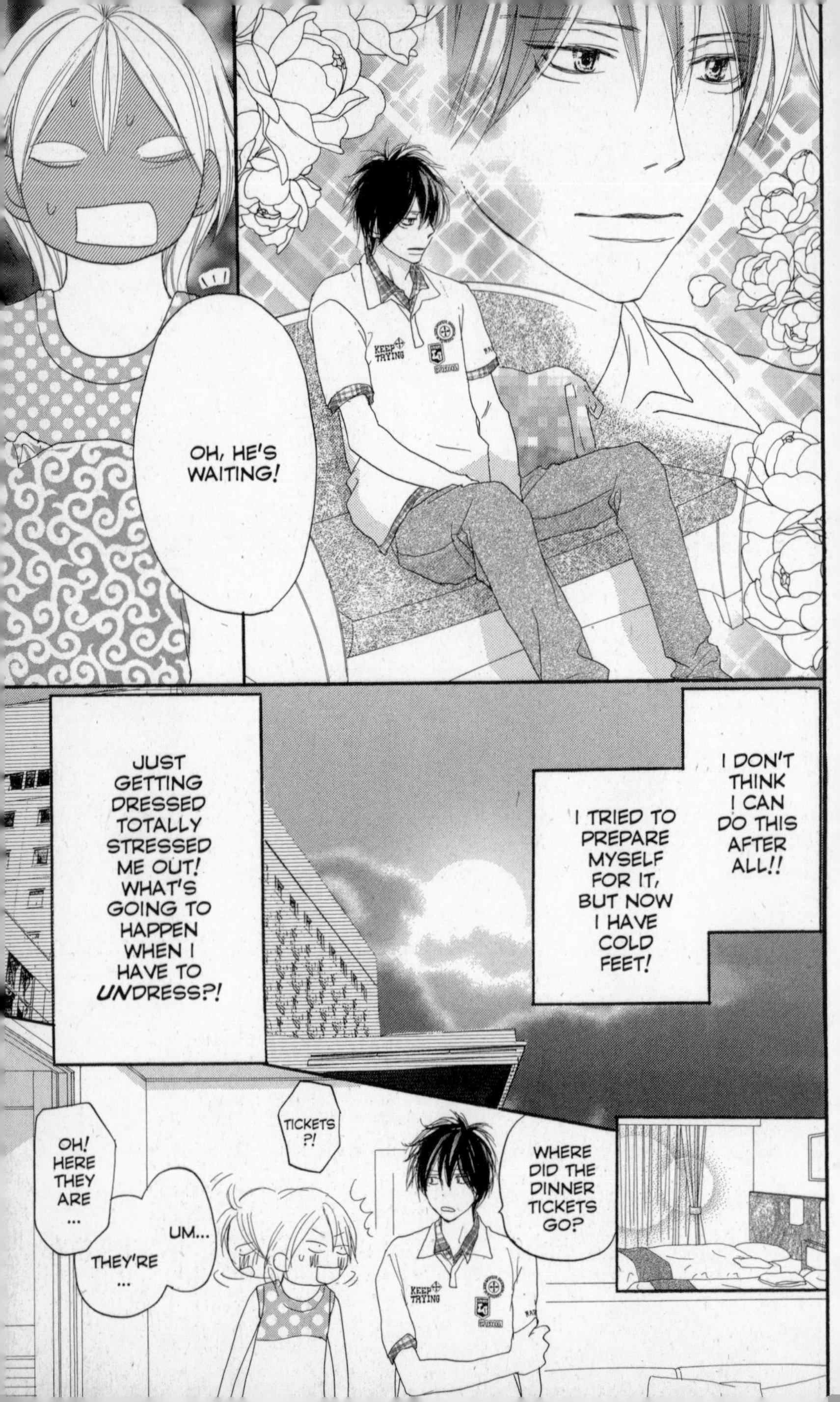
OH, HE'S WAITING!
I DON'T THINK I CAN DO THIS AFTER ALL!!
I TRIED TO PREPARE MYSELF FOR IT, BUT NOW I HAVE COLD FEET!
JUST GETTING DRESSED TOTALLY STRESSED ME OUT! WHAT'S GOING TO HAPPEN WHEN I HAVE TO *UN*DRESS?!
WHERE DID THE DINNER TICKETS GO?
TICKETS ?!
OH! HERE THEY ARE ...
UM...
THEY'RE ...

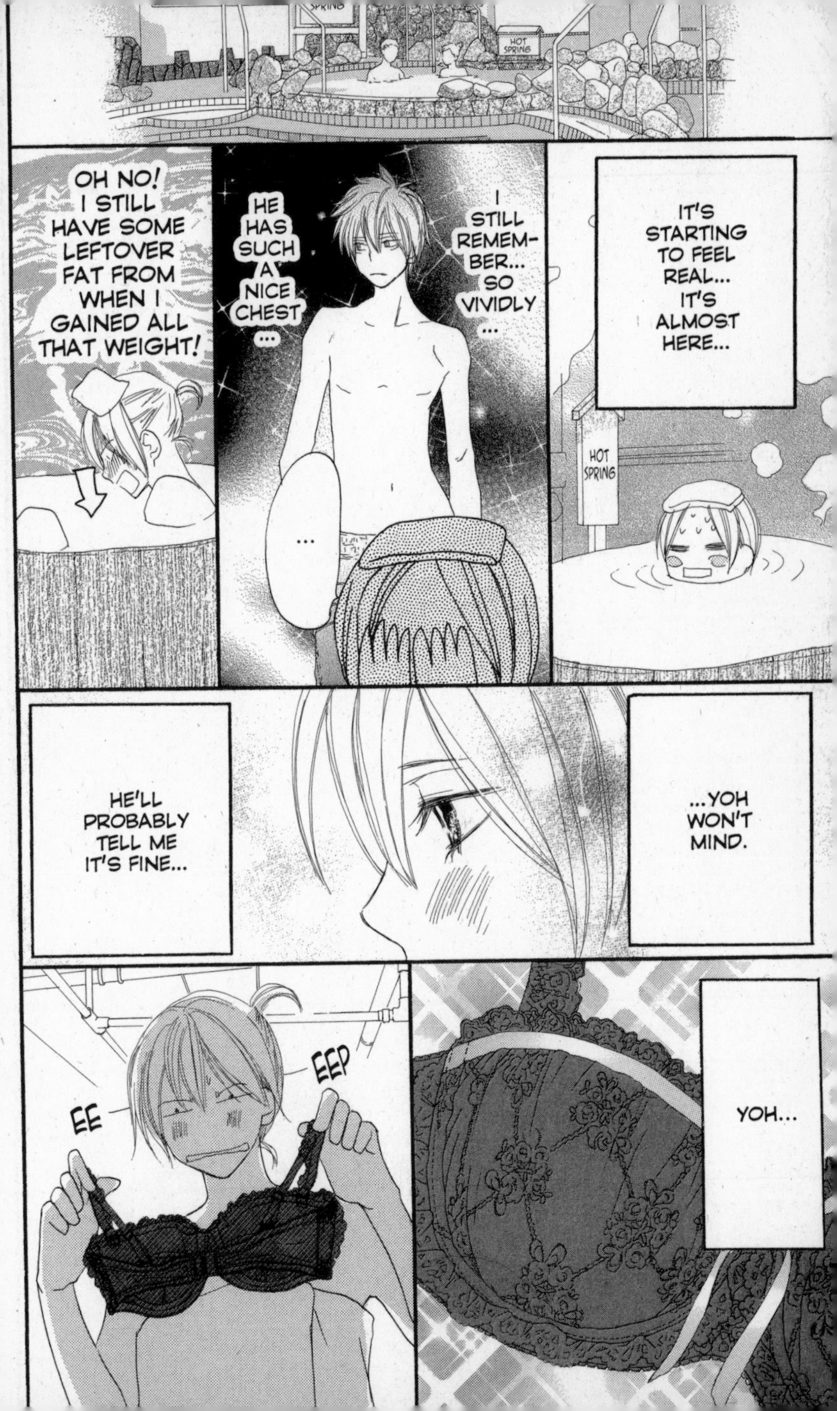

SPRING
HOT SPRING
IT'S STARTING TO FEEL REAL... IT'S ALMOST HERE...
HOT SPRING
I STILL REMEMBER... SO VIVIDLY...
HE HAS SUCH A NICE CHEST...
...
OH NO! I STILL HAVE SOME LEFTOVER FAT FROM WHEN I GAINED ALL THAT WEIGHT!
...YOH WON'T MIND.
HE'LL PROBABLY TELL ME IT'S FINE...
YOH...
EEP
EE

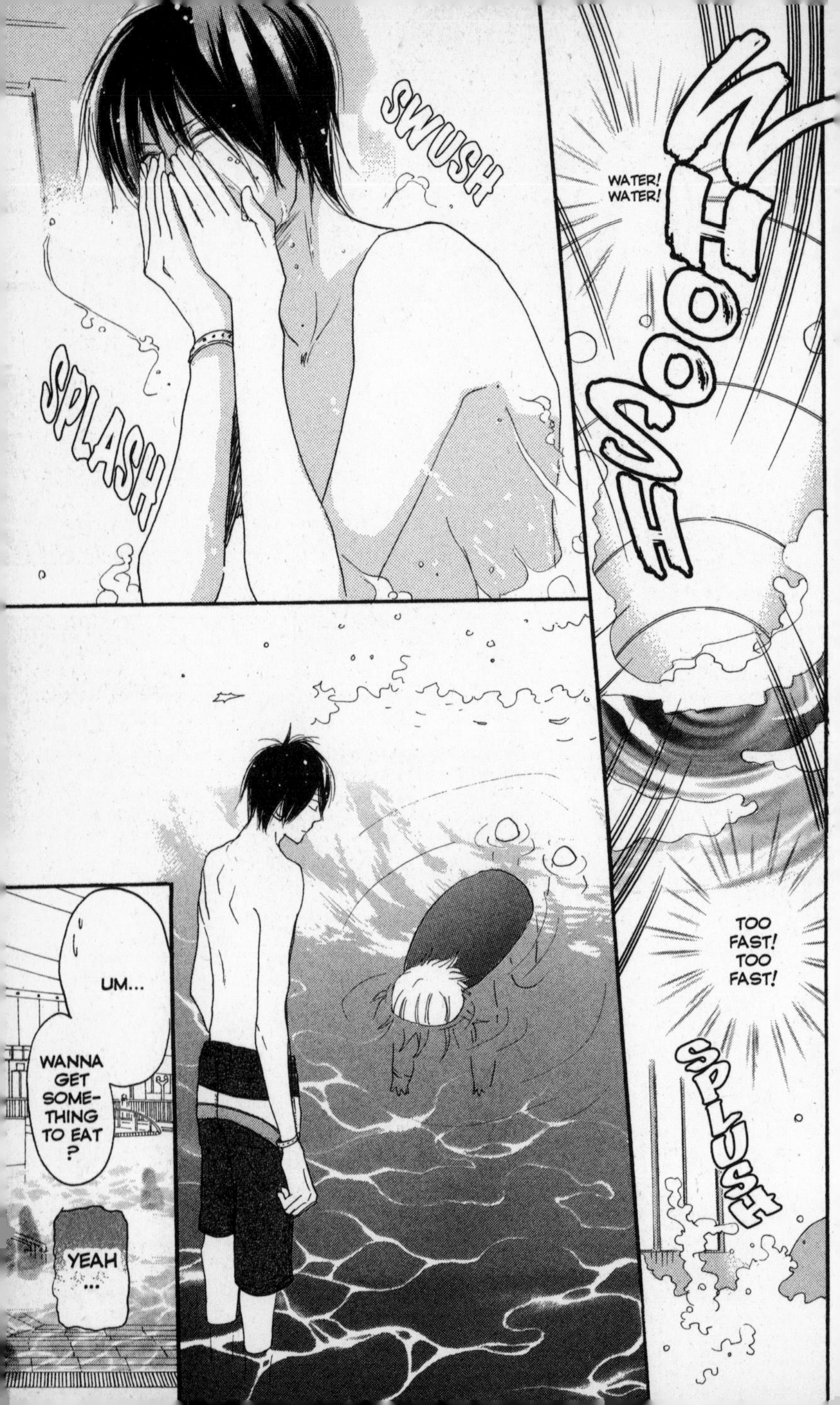
WHOOSH
WATER! WATER!
TOO FAST! TOO FAST!
SPLUSH
SWUSH
SPLASH
UM...
WANNA GET SOME-THING TO EAT?
YEAH...

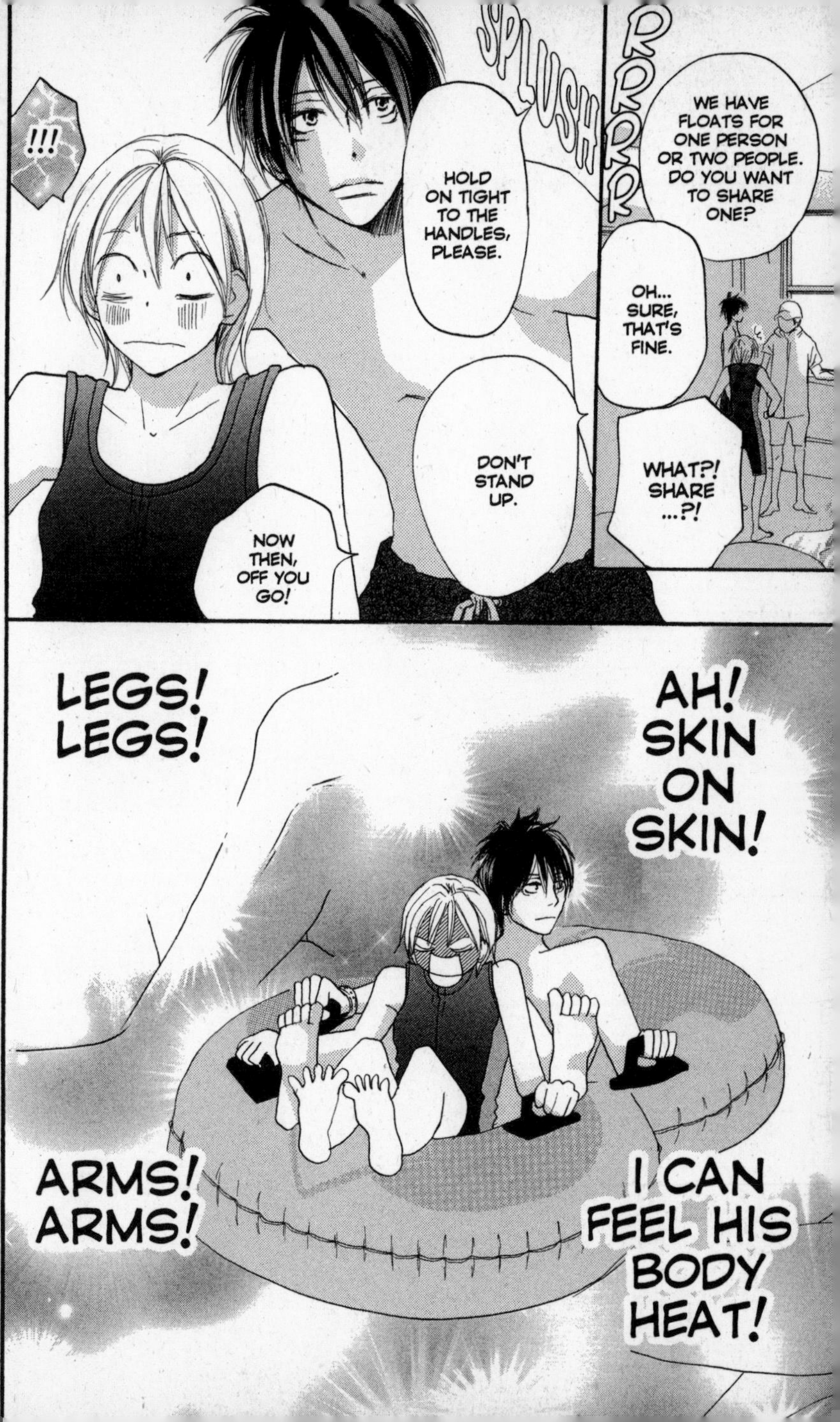
RRRRR
WE HAVE FLOATS FOR ONE PERSON OR TWO PEOPLE. DO YOU WANT TO SHARE ONE?
OH... SURE, THAT'S FINE.
WHAT?! SHARE ...?!
SPLUSH
HOLD ON TIGHT TO THE HANDLES, PLEASE.
!!!
DON'T STAND UP.
NOW THEN, OFF YOU GO!
AH! SKIN ON SKIN!
LEGS! LEGS!
I CAN FEEL HIS BODY HEAT!
ARMS! ARMS!

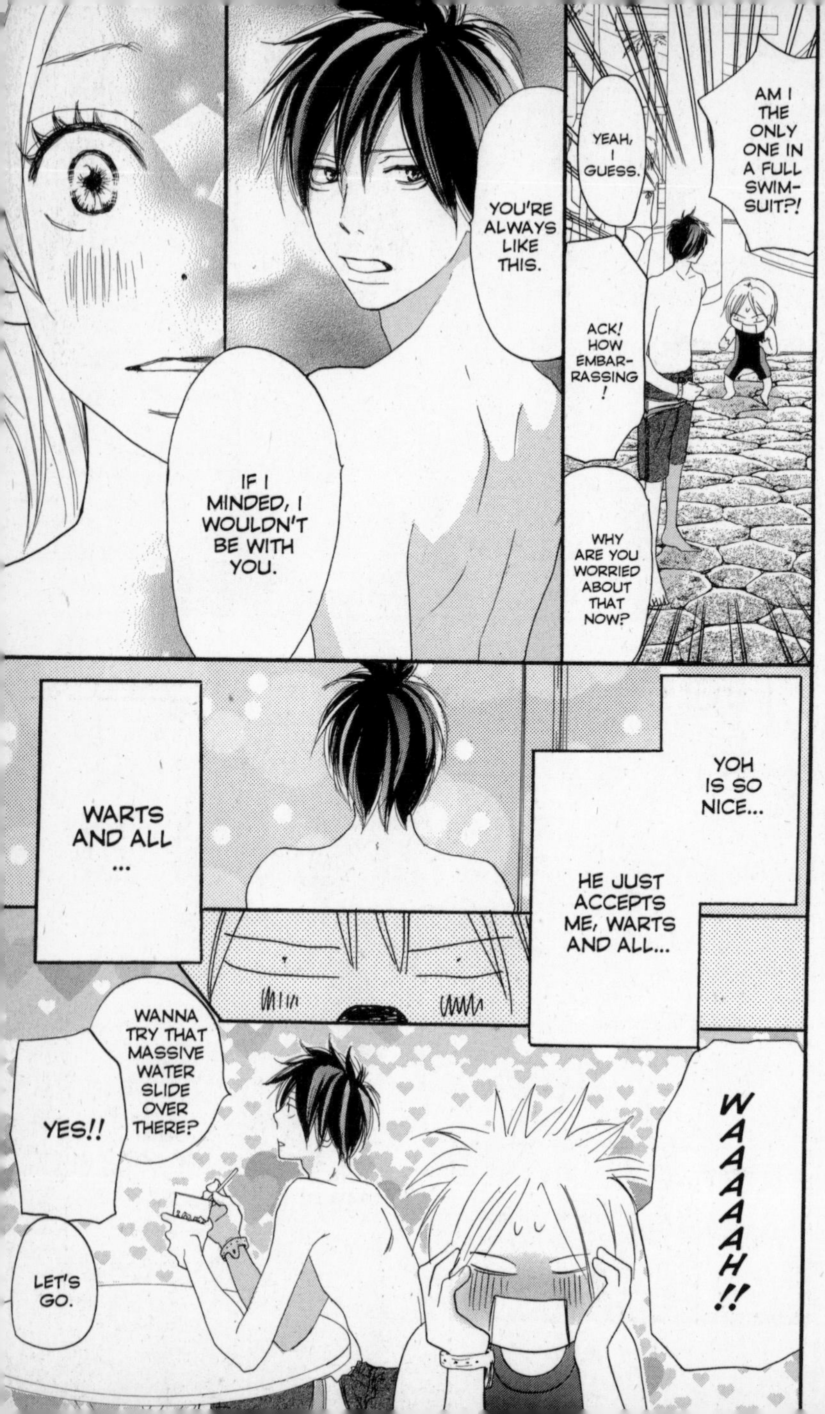
AM I THE ONLY ONE IN A FULL SWIM-SUIT?!
YEAH, I GUESS.
ACK! HOW EMBARRASSING!
WHY ARE YOU WORRIED ABOUT THAT NOW?
YOU'RE ALWAYS LIKE THIS.
IF I MINDED, I WOULDN'T BE WITH YOU.
YOH IS SO NICE...
HE JUST ACCEPTS ME, WARTS AND ALL...
WARTS AND ALL ...
WAAAAAAH!!
WANNA TRY THAT MASSIVE WATER SLIDE OVER THERE?
YES!!
LET'S GO.

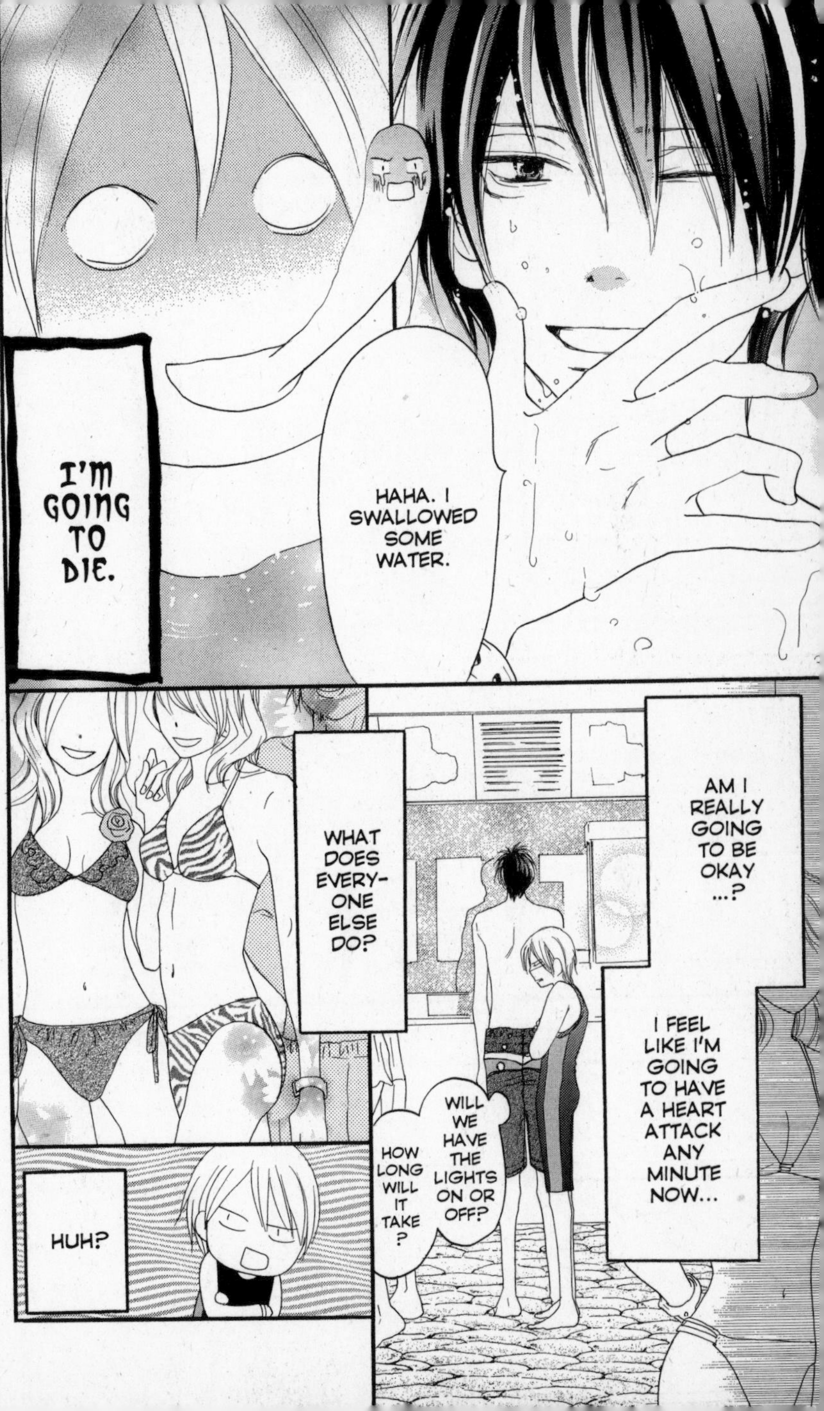
HAHA. I SWALLOWED SOME WATER.
I'M GOING TO DIE.
AM I REALLY GOING TO BE OKAY ...?
I FEEL LIKE I'M GOING TO HAVE A HEART ATTACK ANY MINUTE NOW...
WILL WE HAVE THE LIGHTS ON OR OFF?
HOW LONG WILL IT TAKE?
WHAT DOES EVERY-ONE ELSE DO?
HUH?

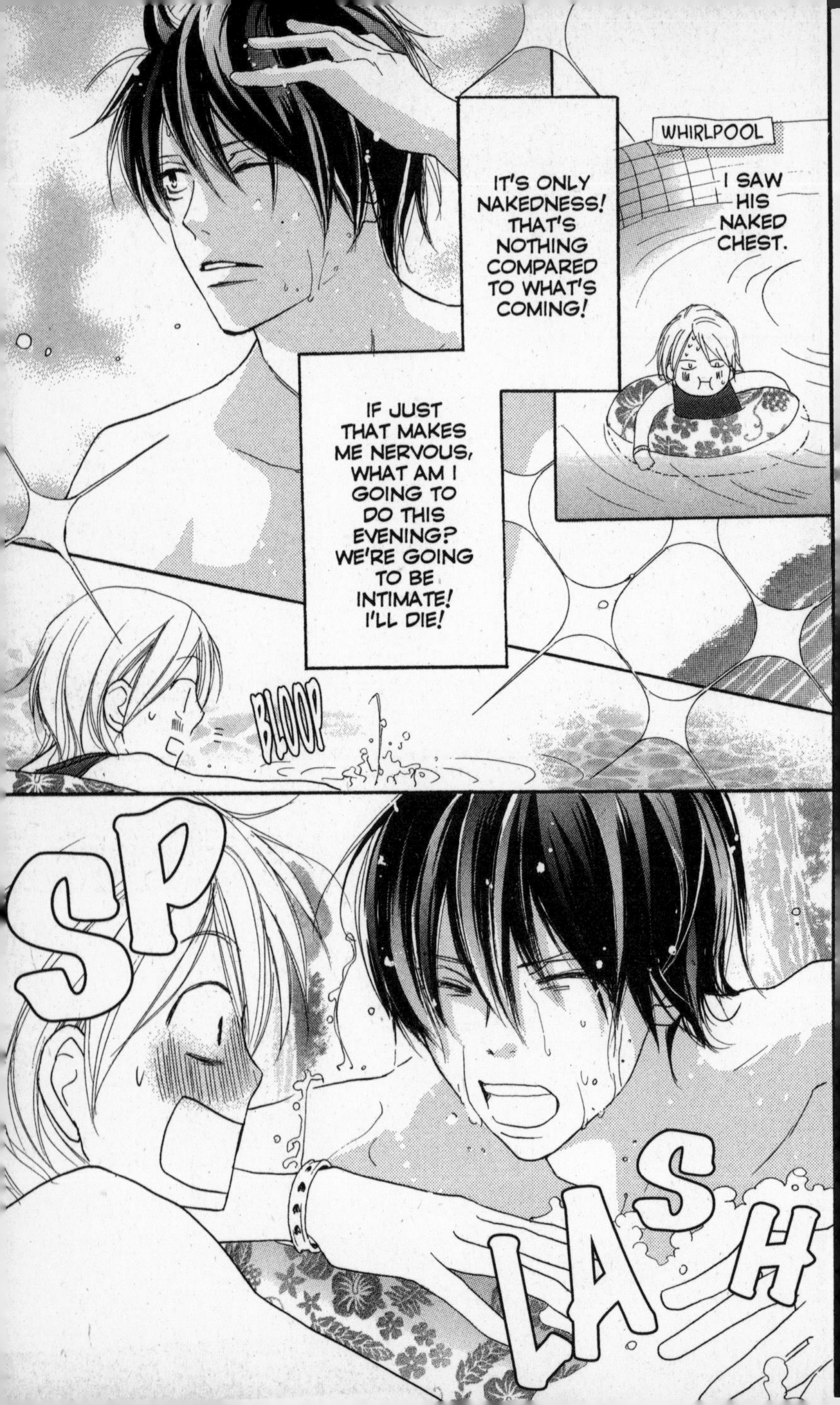
WHIRLPOOL
I SAW HIS NAKED CHEST.
IT'S ONLY NAKEDNESS! THAT'S NOTHING COMPARED TO WHAT'S COMING!
IF JUST THAT MAKES ME NERVOUS, WHAT AM I GOING TO DO THIS EVENING? WE'RE GOING TO BE INTIMATE! I'LL DIE!
BLOOP
SPLASH

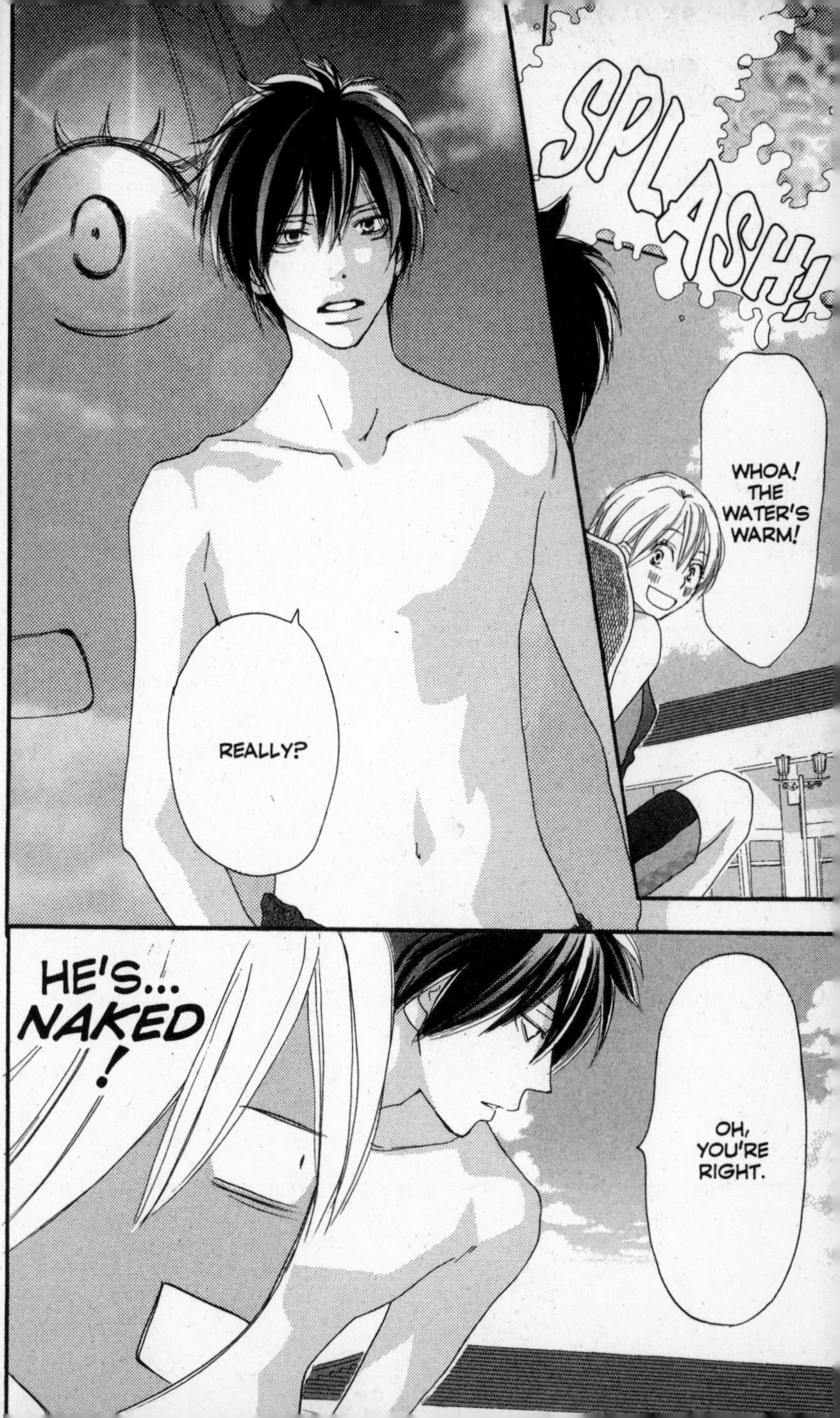
SPLASH!!
WHOA! THE WATER'S WARM!
REALLY?
OH, YOU'RE RIGHT.
HE'S... NAKED!

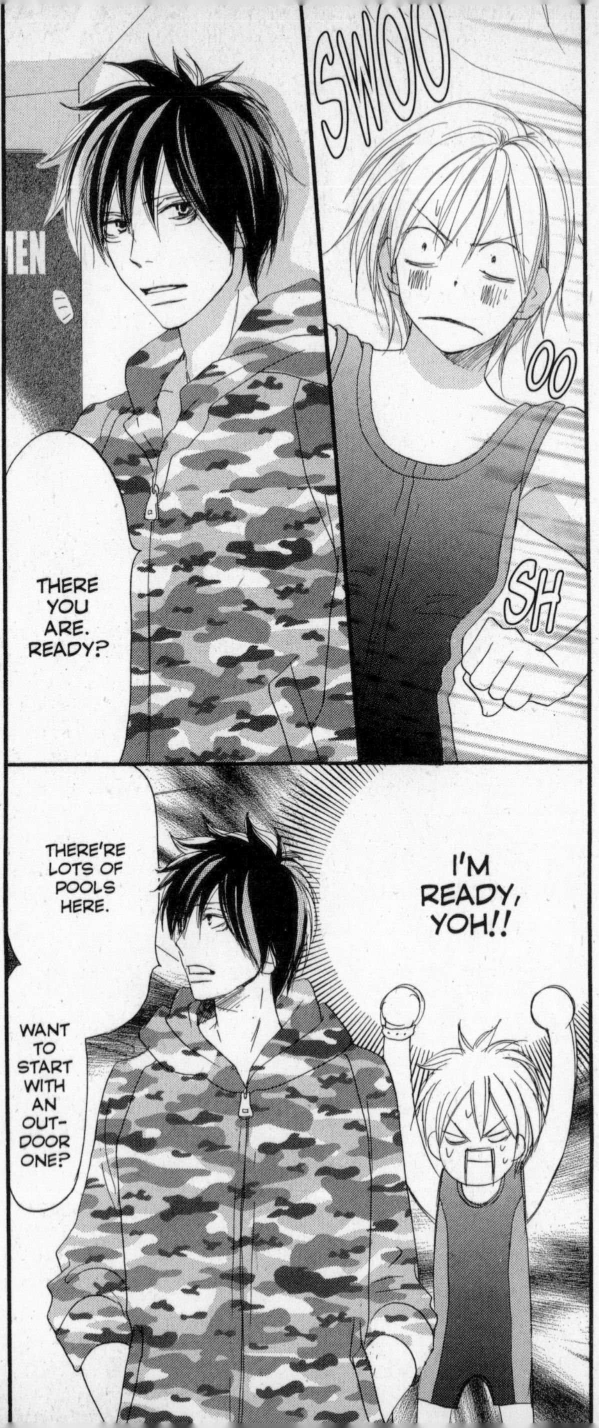
SWOO
OO
SH
THERE YOU ARE. READY?
I'M READY, YOH!!
THERE'RE LOTS OF POOLS HERE.
WANT TO START WITH AN OUT-DOOR ONE?

Hello! 1 There're only two spaces to write in for this volume.

How are you all? The other day I was invited to a manga friend's wedding. We were all enjoying some tea tasting. (The bridegroom works at .) It was a lot of fun!

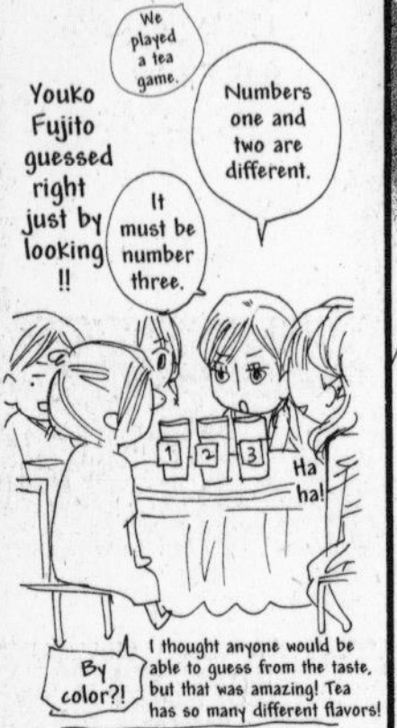
We played a tea game.
Youko Fujito guessed right just by looking !!
Numbers one and two are different.
It must be number three.
1
2
3
Ha ha!
By color?!
I thought anyone would be able to guess from the taste, but that was amazing! Tea has so many different flavors!

During the wedding, my friends' kids were like this:

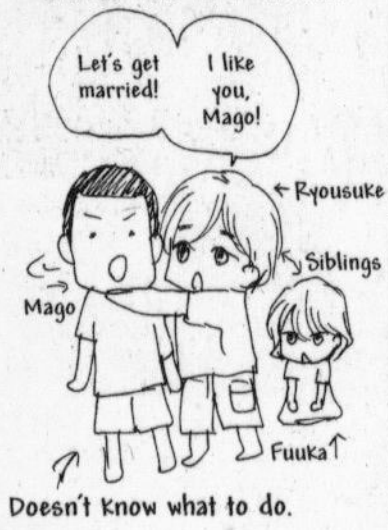
Let's get married!
I like you, Mago!
← Ryousuke
Siblings
Mago
Fuuka ↑
Doesn't know what to do.

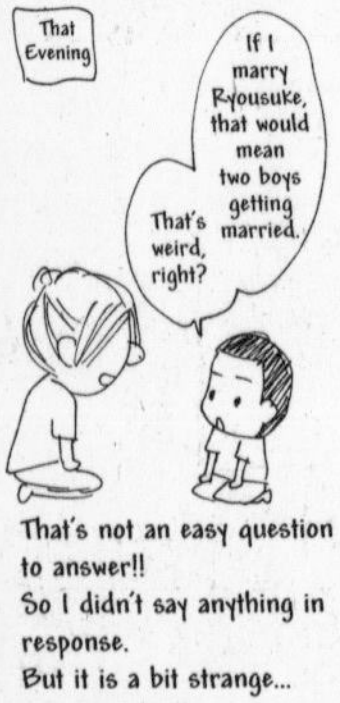
That Evening
If I marry Ryousuke, that would mean two boys getting married.
That's weird, right?

That's not an easy question to answer!!
So I didn't say anything in response.
But it is a bit strange...

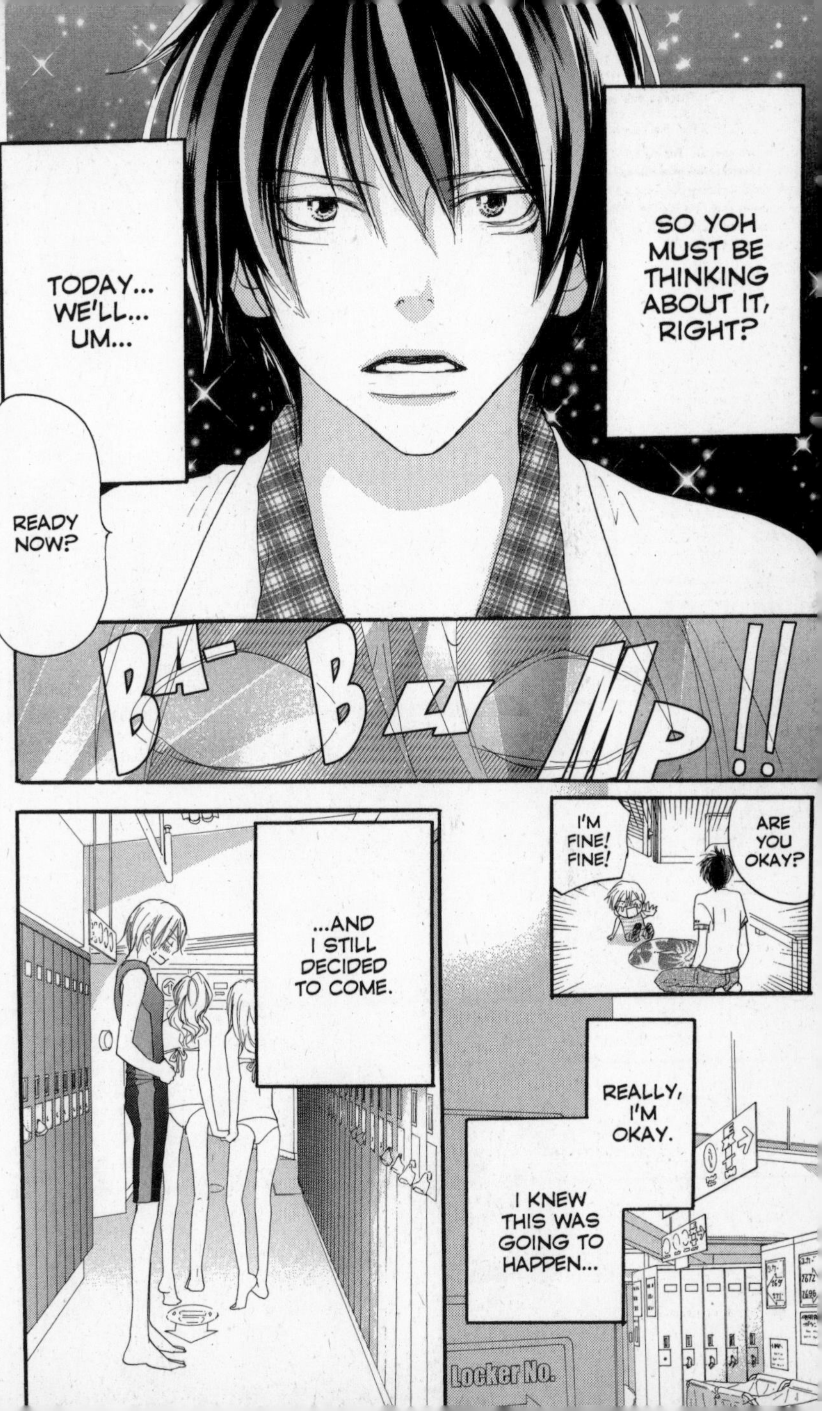
SO YOH MUST BE THINKING ABOUT IT, RIGHT?
TODAY... WE'LL... UM...
READY NOW?
BA-BUMP!!
ARE YOU OKAY?
I'M FINE! FINE!
REALLY, I'M OKAY.
I KNEW THIS WAS GOING TO HAPPEN...
Locker No.
...AND I STILL DECIDED TO COME.

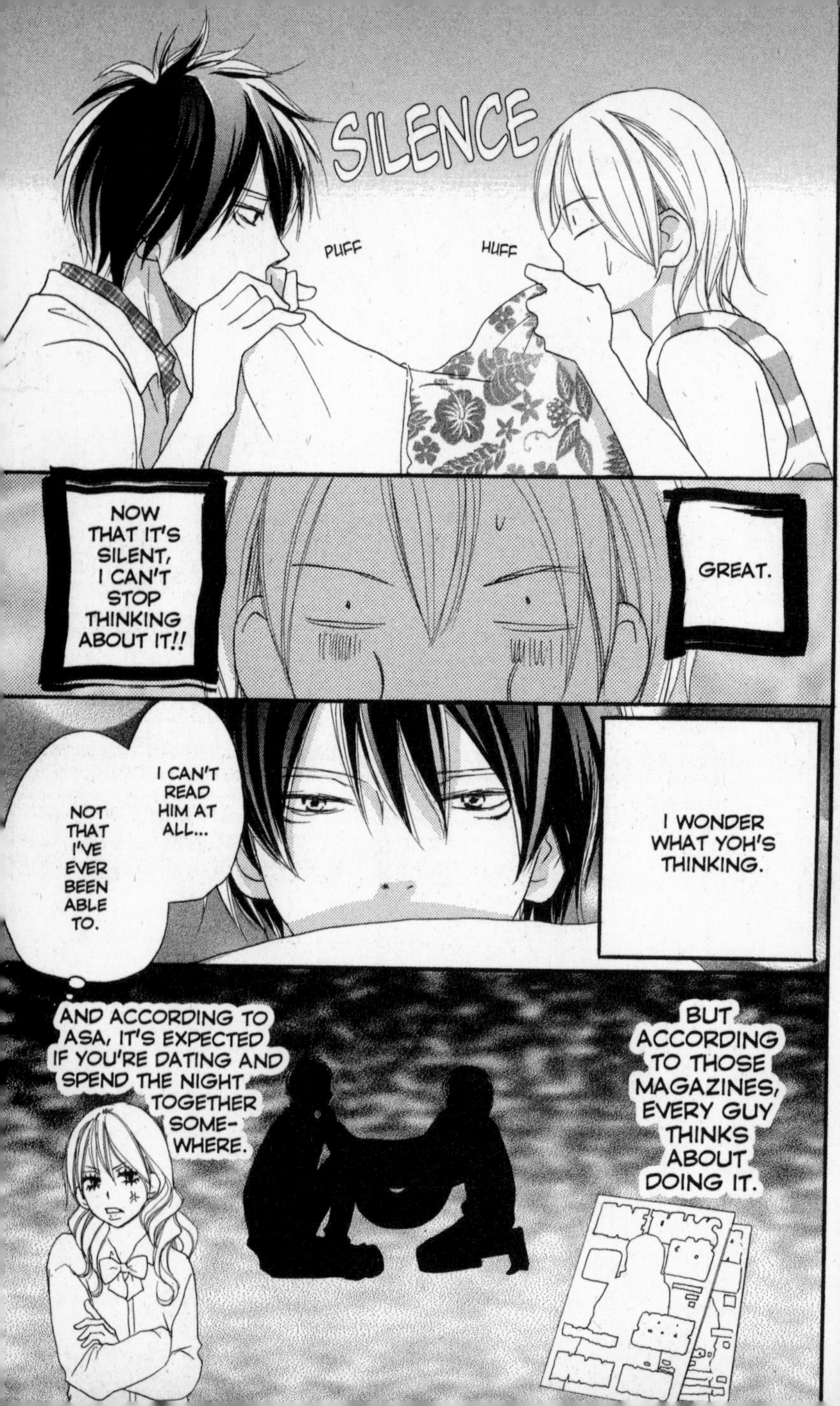
SILENCE
HUFF
PUFF
GREAT.
NOW THAT IT'S SILENT, I CAN'T STOP THINKING ABOUT IT!!
I WONDER WHAT YOH'S THINKING.
I CAN'T READ HIM AT ALL...
NOT THAT I'VE EVER BEEN ABLE TO.
BUT ACCORDING TO THOSE MAGAZINES, EVERY GUY THINKS ABOUT DOING IT.
AND ACCORDING TO ASA, IT'S EXPECTED IF YOU'RE DATING AND SPEND THE NIGHT TOGETHER SOME-WHERE.

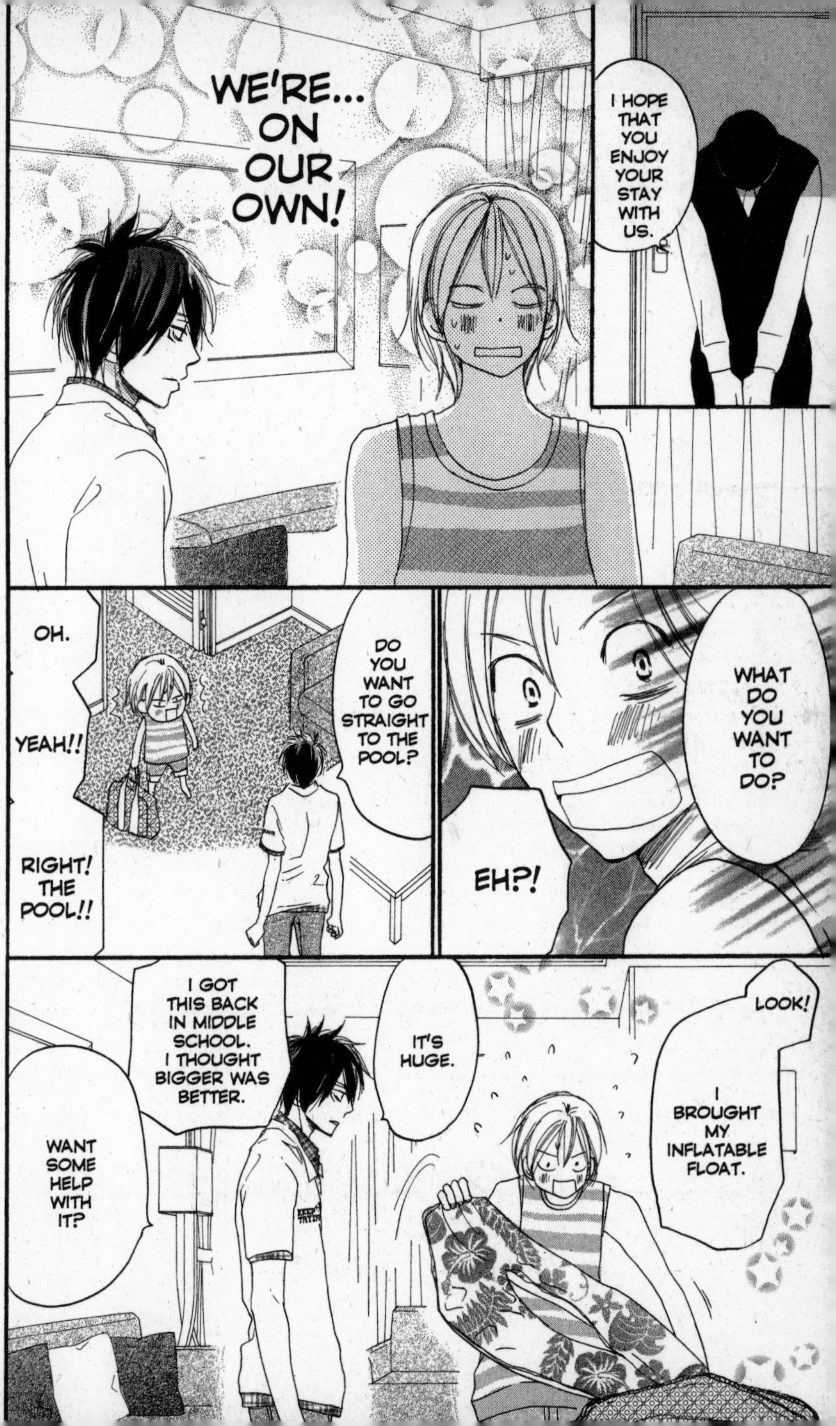
I HOPE THAT YOU ENJOY YOUR STAY WITH US.
WE'RE... ON OUR OWN!
WHAT DO YOU WANT TO DO?
EH?!
DO YOU WANT TO GO STRAIGHT TO THE POOL?
OH.
YEAH!!
RIGHT! THE POOL!!
LOOK!
I BROUGHT MY INFLATABLE FLOAT.
IT'S HUGE.
I GOT THIS BACK IN MIDDLE SCHOOL. I THOUGHT BIGGER WAS BETTER.
WANT SOME HELP WITH IT?

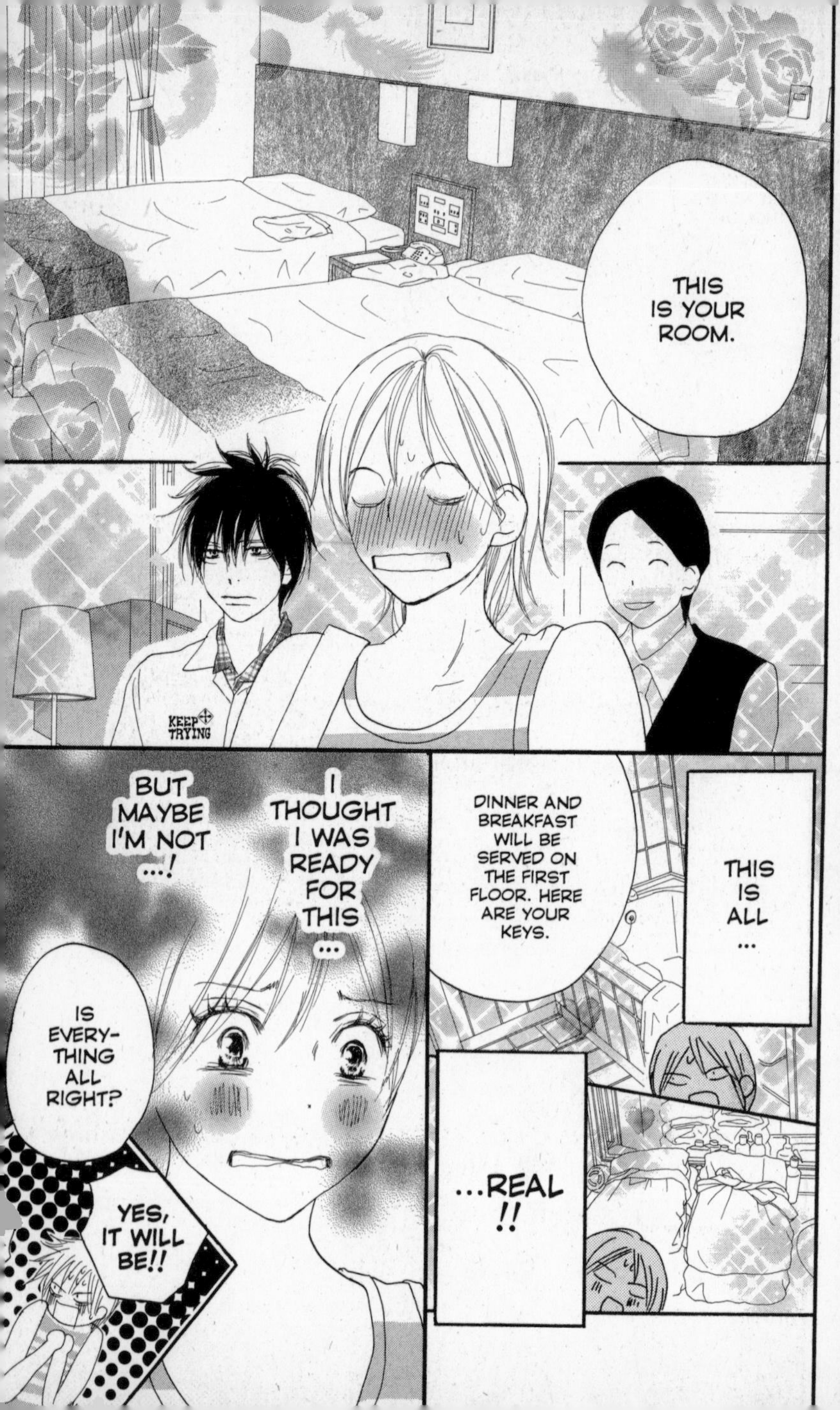
THIS IS YOUR ROOM.
KEEP TRYING
THIS IS ALL ...
DINNER AND BREAKFAST WILL BE SERVED ON THE FIRST FLOOR. HERE ARE YOUR KEYS.
...REAL !!
I THOUGHT I WAS READY FOR THIS ...
BUT MAYBE I'M NOT ...!
IS EVERY-THING ALL RIGHT?
YES, IT WILL BE!!

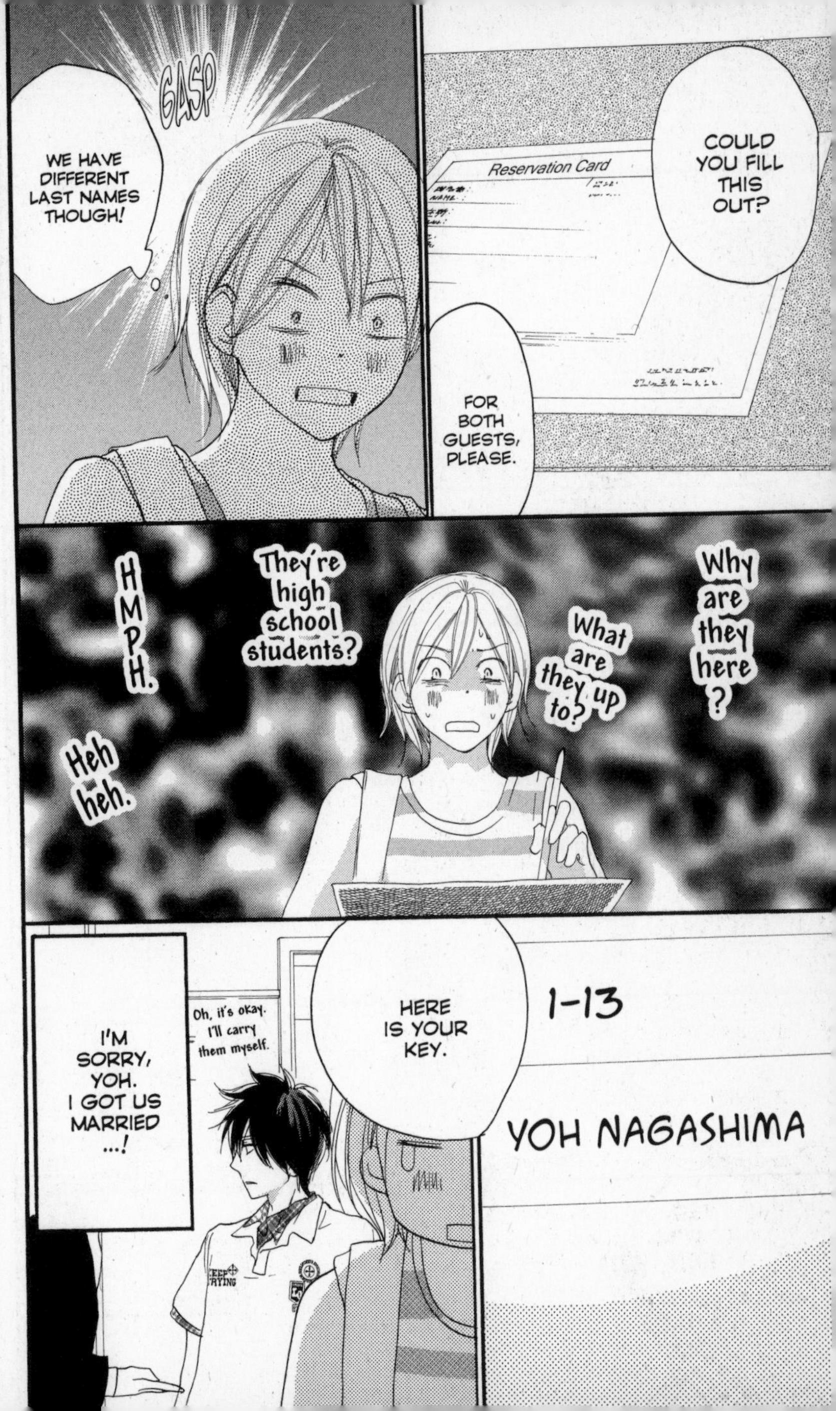
Reservation Card
COULD YOU FILL THIS OUT?
FOR BOTH GUESTS, PLEASE.
GASP
WE HAVE DIFFERENT LAST NAMES THOUGH!
Why are they here?
What are they up to?
They're high school students?
HMPH.
Heh heh.
HERE IS YOUR KEY.
1-13
YOH NAGASHIMA
Oh, it's okay. I'll carry them myself.
I'M SORRY, YOH. I GOT US MARRIED ...!

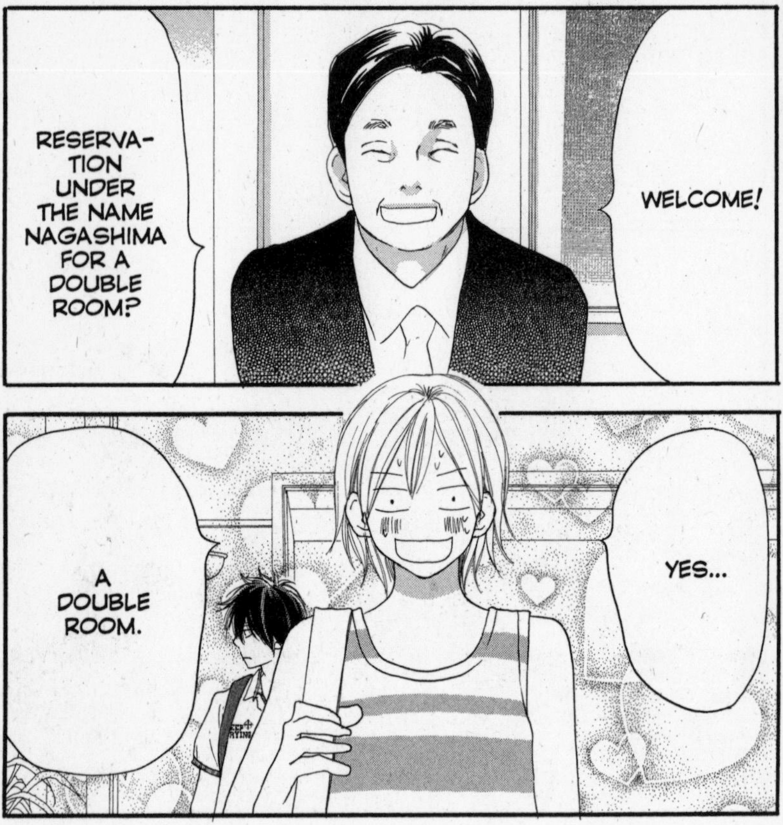
WELCOME!
RESERVA-TION UNDER THE NAME NAGASHIMA FOR A DOUBLE ROOM?
YES...
A DOUBLE ROOM.

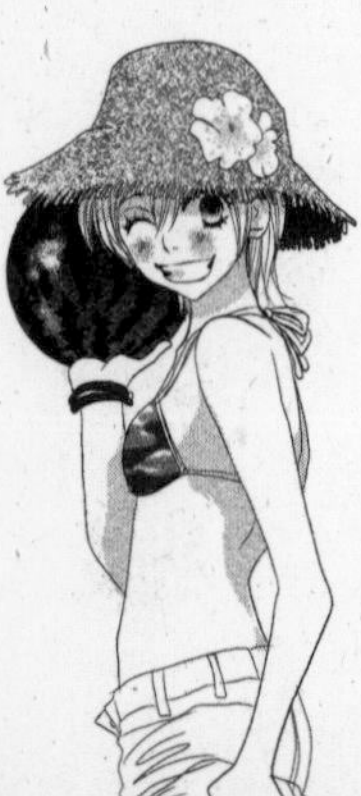